God and Global Order

God and Global Order

The Power of Religion in American Foreign Policy

Jonathan Chaplin
with Robert Joustra
editors

BAYLOR UNIVERSITY PRESS

Cover Design by Michael Silverander

Library of Congress Cataloging-in-Publication Data

Chaplin, Jonathan.
  God and global order : the power of religion in American foreign policy / Jonathan Chaplin.
      p. cm.
  Includes bibliographical references and index.
  ISBN 978-1-60258-250-7 (pbk. : alk. paper)
  1. United States--Foreign relations--1989- 2. Religion and international affairs. I. Title.
  JZ1480.C455 2010
  327.73--dc22
                                    · 2010000796

Printed in the United States of America on acid-free paper with a minimum of 30% pcw content.

Contents

Preface and Acknowledgments

This volume emerged initially from a consultation in 2006 organized by the "USA with the World" project of the Center for Christian Studies (Gordon College, Mass.), under the direction of Harold Heie and sponsored by the Lilly Endowment. Several chapters of this book began their life as workshop presentations at that consultation, while others were subsequently commissioned by the editors. The editors wish to acknowledge the valuable institutional support of Gordon College and the generous financial support of the Lilly Endowment toward the completion of this book. We also gratefully acknowledge the generous support of Cardus, a Canadian think tank. Cardus staff member Robert Joustra served as research assistant to Jonathan Chaplin, a Cardus Senior Fellow, in the early stages of the preparation of the manuscript, under an arrangement whereby senior fellows can avail themselves of an amount of staff time toward research or other projects. As it turned out, Robert Joustra's contribution went well beyond that normally expected of the role of research assistant, and he has in effect served as assistant editor. We are much indebted to the staff of Baylor University Press, with whom it has been a pleasure to work, and we thank them for their professionalism and patience. An earlier version of Andrew Preston's chapter was published as "Bridging the Gap between the Sacred and the Secular in the History of American Foreign Relations," *Diplomatic History* 30 (November 2006). An earlier version of Thomas F. Farr's chapter appeared in *World of Faith and Freedom: Why International Religious Liberty Is Vital to American National Security* (Oxford University Press, 2008). Thomas Albert Howard's chapter draws on material appearing in *God and the Atlantic: America, Europe, and the Religious Divide* (Oxford University Press, forthcoming), and an earlier version appeared in the journal *Hedgehog Review* (vol. 8, Spring/ Summer 2006, 116–26). We gratefully acknowledge permission from the publishers and editors to include them here.

Introduction

Naming Religion Truthfully

Jonathan Chaplin with Robert Joustra

The rejection of religion . . . seems to be inscribed in the genetic
code of the discipline of IR.

Over the past generation international relations scholars have
devoted great time and effort and have achieved impressive
successes in explaining how and whether states attain various
goods for their citizens, including security, sometimes conquest,
economic growth, sometimes great wealth, human rights, sometimes high levels of justice, environmental purity, and a world in
which they can freely express themselves. . . . But people across
the globe seek other ends, too: to worship and submit to their
God, to protect and defend their mosques, temples, shrines,
synagogues, and churches, to convert others to their faith, to
reside in a realm governed by *sharia*, to live under a government
that promotes morality in many spheres of society, to draw on
their faith to extend civil rights to minorities and women, and to
practice forgiveness and reconciliation. . . . Is it any surprise that
such ends spill into the realm of international politics?

This book argues that American foreign policy must more fully acknowledge the power of religious faith in international relations if it is to be credible and effective in the turbulent century that lies ahead. The book shows how a proper reckoning with the presence and power of faith can not only illuminate U.S. foreign policy and enhance its contribution to the promotion of global peace and justice, but perhaps even help it avoid mistakes arising from indifference to religion which have marked U.S. interventions in contexts as varied as Iraq, Afghanistan, Iran, Israel and Palestine, the U.S.S.R. and Russia, the Balkans and Vietnam. Given the unchallenged global preeminence of the United States and the widespread, if overblown, foreign perception that under the leadership of President George W. Bush the United States once again saw itself as heading a religiously charged mission,[1] such a reckoning is now of truly critical significance for the future of global order. Ignorance about the power of faith in global affairs could carry (further) disastrous consequences both for the United States and the entire world. Such ignorance will foreclose intelligent discussion of whether the United States in the century ahead opts to be "with or against the world," as James W. Skillen has put it,[2] and will leave the United States more rather than less exposed to threats to its security. It remains to be seen whether the new direction in foreign policy announced by President Obama will be guided by deeper insight on the role of faith than has been evident in previous administrations. The presence of motifs during his inaugural speech suggesting what might be termed a liberal progressivist version of American civil religion—as potentially hazardous in its own way as a conservative nationalist version— makes this a question of even greater interest and import.[3]

RETURNING RELIGION FROM EXILE

Written from a Christian perspective—a term to be explained shortly— this book presents a range of insights on the far-reaching role that faiths, both religious and secular, have played and might play in shaping U.S. responses to crucial contemporary global developments.[4] It is intended to serve at least three distinct audiences: first, the many actors in U.S. foreign policy at home and abroad who see themselves as guided in some way by Christian faith; second, scholars in International Relations[5] curious about what a religion-sensitive—indeed, "Christian"—perspective in the field might look like; third, practitioners and scholars from other faith perspectives, and those who think they have none, on the role of faith in international affairs. While its claims will likely provoke disagreement from some representatives of all these categories, its editors hope that it will enable any reader to reflect more critically and self-consciously on the global influence of faith. If so, it thereby will have contributed to the overcoming of what Edward Luttwak has bluntly called "a learned repugnance to contend intellectually with all that is religion";[6] or, as Thomas F. Farr more graphically puts it, "the extreme reluctance to get too deeply into a religion's guts."[7]

Recognizing the factual reality of religion does not, of course, amount to an acceptance of its legitimacy as a guiding orientation either in the polity or the academy. There is no lack of analysis today of the role of religious faith as an *empirical* phenomenon, and the contents of this book reinforce the call for governments and other international and national actors to attend to this role if they are to pursue coherent and successful strategies. However, the book also argues that greater attention must now be given to *normative* perspectives (and the explanatory approaches flowing from them), notably those of the leading public religions themselves. "Outsider" evaluations of the role of religion need to be complemented by "the view from inside" if the complex phenomenon of faith is to be properly grasped and responded to.

The book joins the conversation about America's role in the world at two related levels. First, it adds a distinctive voice to the swelling chorus of commentators in the discipline of International Relations who are urging us to take stock of the global resurgence of public religion.[8] When Samuel P. Huntington's "clash of civilizations" thesis made its arresting intervention into the debate over the future of post–Cold War global order in 1993, it was one of the first attempts to argue that religion and culture should be taken seriously as formative elements of U.S. foreign policy.[9] Huntington's account has since been subjected to searching critical scrutiny, yet there is no doubt that it helped stimulate an upsurge of scholarly interest in the role of religion in International Relations.[10] A recent volume published by Palgrave Macmillan announced that religion has now "returned from exile."[11] That a leading publisher should judge it worthwhile to launch an entire series on "Culture and Religion in International Relations"—in which the aforementioned volume appears—indicates the beginnings of a sea change in scholarly perceptions of religion. Another contributor to this series (and to this book), Scott Thomas, observes a "global resurgence of religion" triggering nothing less than a "transformation of international relations."[12]

A particularly thoughtful contribution—no doubt partly since its preparation straddled the events of September 11, 2001—is *The Sacred and the Sovereign: Religion and International Politics.*[13] In 2000, when the contributors met to consult on what was already emerging as a pressing topic, they could never have imagined that within months they would have to revisit and rethink key elements of their theses. What had begun as a project to bring much-needed attention to the issue of religion in global politics quickly became an important contribution for policymakers in crisis.

A strikingly ambitious attempt at a comprehensive treatment of the theme is Eric O. Hanson's *Religion and Politics in the International System Today.*[14] Utilizing theories of globalization and drawing examples from every region of the world, Hanson proposes a "new paradigm" for understanding how religion is, on the one hand, a causative factor in its own right in international relations (and not a mere dependent variable), and, on the other, always deeply and closely interwoven with "material" factors familiar to International Relations scholars. Hanson argues that the explanatory power of studies of global economic, military, and communications systems is seriously incomplete unless it integrates the specific religious factors at work at many levels. The methodological implications of his work are noted below.

Religion is not only being analyzed in macro-studies like those of Huntington, Thomas, and Hanson. It is also being explored as a decisive factor in field-specific investigations. For example, scholars are recognizing the need to take cognizance of the religious factor in the "hard" field of security studies. In *Religion and Security: The New Nexus in International Relations,*[15] Robert Seiple and Dennis Hoover show that—as Hoover puts it in the introduction—when talking about security, "religion gets real" (underlining Farr's observation that religion can no longer be dismissed as "mere sociology"[16]). In addition to fresh political, economic, and sociological perspectives, Hoover argues, we also need fresh religious—even *theological*—perspectives, on which to build new paradigms of peace, stability, and security.[17]

The religious factor is also returning to the agenda of the history of foreign relations after protracted neglect (analyzed in Andrew Preston's chapter). Malcolm Magee, for example, has traced faith-based influences on American foreign policy back through Woodrow Wilson's religiously inspired diplomacy. In *What the World Should Be*, Magee probes beneath generations of secularist diplomatic history to interrogate where, why, and how Wilson's Presbyterianism shaped his presidency. William Inboden's outstanding study of the powerful religious motivations behind the Cold War policies of Truman, Dulles, Eisenhower, and others—*Religion and*

American Foreign Policy, 1945–1960—argues a parallel point about the postwar period.[18]

The cumulative argument of these and other recent works is compelling: as a third title in Palgrave's "Culture and Religion in International Relations" series puts it, it is time to "bring religion back into international relations."[19]

One of the most exciting additions to this new genre, Elizabeth Shakman Hurd's remarkable *The Politics of Secularism in International Relations*,[20] develops the radical proposal that the very discipline is itself sustained by a parochial and contestable faith perspective—"secularism."[21] "Secularism," she asserts, "is located on the spectrum of theological politics."[22] If this is so, she argues, then it is not a matter of bringing some extraneous factor into what would otherwise be a faith-free zone of neutral, rational scholarship, but of discerning the powerful yet unrecognized faith orientations already internally shaping the foundations of the discipline and then confronting the implications of those orientations for the conduct of international relations. We return to her argument below.

The second level at which this book enters the conversation about America's global role is the debate about the practice of diplomacy. The book seeks to supply additional ammunition for the arguments of those foreign policy theorists and practitioners who are urging diplomats to reckon with the potential power of faith—for good and ill—in international affairs. In her book *The Mighty and the Almighty: Reflections on Power, God, and World Affairs*,[23] Madeleine Albright confesses her regret at having adopted, while ambassador to the United Nations and secretary of state, the resolutely secularist approach to foreign policy she had imbibed from former doyens of the foreign policy discipline such as Morgenthau, Kennan, and Acheson. Having absorbed their modernist disdain toward the seventeenth-century wars of religion, a possibility from which the modern liberal state was thought to have liberated us once and for all, she now admitted that "since the terror attacks of 9/11, I have come to realize that it may have been I who was stuck in an earlier time."[24]

Ironically, the year Albright first assumed a foreign policy office, 1993, was the year in which the first path-breaking study of the unavoidable role of religion in foreign policy appeared: *Religion, the Missing Dimension of Statecraft*, edited by Douglas Johnson and Cynthia Sampson.[25] That book argued that religion was not only a powerful fuel for hostility and conflict but could also be a potential force for good: it could be harnessed by suitably alert and creative diplomats for purposes of international (and intra-national) peacemaking and reconciliation.[26] A decade later,

Douglas Johnson produced a sequel demonstrating in further detail how this could work concretely in specific conflict situations across the globe and laying out theoretical foundations for the practice of what he called "faith-based diplomacy."[27]

These innovative studies show that official U.S. anxiety at the resurgence of global religion is misplaced. As Thomas F. Farr puts it: "The United States should not see global desecularization in strictly defensive terms; it is as much an opportunity as a threat. Rather than being inimical to the advance of freedom, as many secularists assume, religious ideas and actors can buttress and expand ordered liberty."[28]

Importantly, Johnson argues that while faith-based diplomacy should "trump realpolitik," it cannot serve as a complete alternative to more conventional diplomacy.[29] Yet both his volumes make clear that even the standard fare of diplomatic initiatives proceeding from Foggy Bottom could benefit substantially from greater attention to the role of faith in many conflict situations. The injunction has been taken up most recently in several studies of specific aspects of U.S. foreign policy, ranging well beyond the category of conflict-zones addressed by Johnson. Some have sought to analyze the empirical influence of faith-based pressure groups on the formation of U.S. foreign policy. For example, Elliot Abrams' edited volume *The Influence of Faith* focuses on how religion and faith groups have shaped the foreign policy process and how those same policies have in turn exercised a feedback effect on the character of American religion itself.[30]

Useful though such studies are, they often remain within the standard conceptual frameworks for analyzing the domestic policy process. Others take in a wider panorama. Walter Russell Mead, for example, notes the resurgence of Evangelical influence on foreign policy but places it in broader historical perspective and argues that Evangelical goals are in any case badly misunderstood by the secular media and academia.[31] Another example is *God and Caesar in China: Policy Implications of Church-State Tensions,*[32] edited by Jason Kindopp and Carol Hamrin, which makes clear how a constructive and effective U.S. engagement with a globally ascendant nation such as China cannot afford to remain ignorant about internal religious developments in the country.

Other works, such as Andrew Bacevich and Elizabeth Prodromou's "God is Not Neutral: Religion and U.S. Foreign Policy after 9/11,"[33] seek to uncover the relationship between the personal piety of a powerful chief executive—George W. Bush—and neoconservative policy alignments.[34] They show that the explicitly religious tone of executive language has sometimes served to obfuscate as much as it has clarified the role of religion in foreign policy. The president's personal faith orientation is important, but an analysis of even very strong personal piety in holders of high office does not at all exhaust the manner in which religion is enlisted in American foreign policy. The structural impact of an administration's (mis)understanding of religion is more important than the personal beliefs of its chief executive. Thomas F. Farr's *World of Faith and Freedom* (which elaborates the thesis of his chapter in our volume) explores the role of religion in relation to a policy where one might have been forgiven for thinking it would already be well understood: U.S. international religious freedom policy.[35]

The proposal that American diplomacy draw on religious resources has not, of course, gone without challenge. The exchanges recorded in *Liberty and Power*, one of the Pew Forum Dialogues on Religion and Public Life, include both powerful defenses of the legitimacy and efficacy of utilizing such resources and continuing anxiety about and opposition to doing so.[36] For example, Michael Walzer, worried that faith can so easily turn dogmatic and so override necessary moral imperatives in foreign policy, asserts straightforwardly, "A faith-based foreign policy would be a bad idea."[37] Other participants, while acutely aware of the perils of appealing to religion to justify particular policy stances, demonstrate that such anxieties are less well founded when the complex relationships between religious faith, morality, and foreign policy outputs are appropriately spelled out.

CHALLENGING SECULARIST ASSUMPTIONS

Responding to such debates, this book poses questions to four common secularist assumptions currently obstructing a proper acknowledgment of the role of religion in U.S. foreign policy: first, that public life in modernizing societies will undergo inevitable secularization; second, that only premodern, traditional cultures have "faith," while modernized cultures have emancipated themselves from it; third, that religion is but a dependent variable requiring explanation in other terms; and fourth—and most provocatively—that "people of faith," whether scholars or practitioners, should keep their faith perspectives out of sight, indeed even out of mind, when analyzing or engaging with global politics.[38]

The first assumption is the prediction of the inevitable secularization of public life wherever "modernization" leaves its footprint.[39] This assumption has been convincingly challenged by leading sociologists of religion such as José Casanova and Peter Berger.[40] The thesis holds that the influence of religious faith will progressively retreat from public life as modernization relentlessly erodes public confidence—both in religious faith as a reliable source of knowledge for managing public life and in the standing of religious organizations to provide normative guidance for the public realm. But it is now clear that, while there is abundant evidence of advanced secularization in Western societies, the causal connection with modernization or with religious decline is no longer so clear. This is not only the case in the United States, which has been recognized by secularization theorists as "exceptional" in being the most modernized Western society while also being the most religious and the most prone to allow religious influence in the public realm. Even in Europe, now acknowledged as the true "exception" to the persistence of religion in the modern world, social scientists have disclosed both hitherto unnoticed religious influences on public life alongside advanced secularization and the return of public religion, especially in the form of a more assertive Islam and a resurgent (mainly conservative) Christianity.[41] Beyond the West, perhaps the most telling and momentous instance of the resurgence of public religion was the Iranian Revolution of 1979, occurring in the most modernized society of the Middle East apart from Israel.[42] But no less important than the rise of political Islam is the astonishing growth of new forms of politically active conservative Protestant Christianity in Africa, Asia, and Latin America.[43] The most recent in-depth studies of this development—the four volumes in the series "Evangelical Christianity and Democracy in the Global South"—lend additional weight to Philip Jenkins' suggestion that we may be about to witness the emergence of "the next Christendom."[44]

The critique of secularization theory is also reinforced by the argument for the existence of "multiple modernities."[45] This idea suggests that modernity and Westernization are not identical and that there are a variety of cultural modes through which "modernity" might be expressed. Citing the effect such a concept might have on foreign policy, Scott Thomas asserts that we can no longer "make the same assumptions about culture and religion for all societies, communities, or states in international relations."[46]

The second secularist assumption that this book questions is that only premodern, traditional cultures are infused with "faith," while the public cultures of modernity are not. Challenging this is more controversial since it problematizes the deep cultural conviction that modernized public realms have cast off what was thought to be the historical obscurantism and oppressiveness of religious faith and are now governed principally by a liberating, universal critical rationality. While the critique of secularization theory has emerged from sociologists working within mainstream modernist empirical methodologies, the critique of modernist rationalism tends to draw more on postmodern thought. Elizabeth Shakman Hurd is one of the most original contributors within the field of International Relations to this line of critique. Drawing on the work of Talal Asad, William Connolly, and others, she argues that the default secularist mindset underlying the discipline is itself a form of "theological politics." But the academic discipline is only a reflection of a much deeper, though hidden, assumption lodged deep in the political culture of modernity, namely that modernization has replaced the "theological politics" typical of premodern traditional cultures in the West and beyond and embraced a secular political order premised exclusively on universal reason and science. On the contrary, Hurd shows, the secularism of modernity is itself a contingent historical construction disclosing a contestable epistemological and ontological stance. Putting the point more explicitly than Hurd, it could even be ventured that secular modernism displays the characteristic features of a particular religious faith.[47]

This claim finds ample support in Charles Taylor's *A Secular Age*. Taylor shows that how we define religion becomes all-important for how we evaluate the emergence of secularism, and specifically the secularist Westphalian consensus shaping Western politics. Taylor distinguishes three forms of secularism. The first two are familiar: the secularization of public space, and the decline of religious belief or practice. The third refers to the cultural presuppositions which make secular modernism plausible: "new conditions of belief," creating "a new shape to the experience which prompts to and is defined by belief" and "a new context in which all search and questioning about the moral and spiritual must proceed."[48] The appearance of such an all-encompassing cosmological matrix leads Taylor to conclude that the commingling of secularity and modernism is a distinct phenomenon of the developed West, one which establishes particular preconditions for what constitutes belief, religion, and secularism.

It is worth noting here that the claim that secular modernity itself is founded on faith-like commitments does not imply that the modern jurisdictional separation of church and state must be put fundamentally into question. José Casanova argues that modernity does indeed necessarily presuppose such an institutional differentiation, but he holds that this is entirely compatible with religious influences operating vigorously within public life: differentiation does not imply either the privatization of faith or the secularization of politics.[49] But this raises the question of what exactly the desecularization of politics means. It is helpful to refer here to Hurd's distinction between two variants of modern secularism: a French- or Turkish-style "laicism" that not only defends the differentiation of church and state but also seeks the complete extirpation of religious influences from public life, and a "Judeo-Christian secularism" which, while also upholding church-state differentiation, insists that this very differentiation is a unique achievement of Judeo-Christian civilization, one which cannot be replicated elsewhere.[50] The latter—represented by Samuel Huntington and Bernard Lewis—is "expressed in international relations in the idea that the secular West has a monopoly over the proper relationship between religion and politics."[51]

Huntington's famous clash of civilizations thesis predicates religion as the most formative civilizational influence. Religion is the central integrating force that holds a civilization's identity together. On this view multiculturalism carries an inherent danger: as Huntington puts it, "multiculturalism at home threatens the United States and the West" just as "universalism abroad threatens the West and the World. Both deny the uniqueness of Western culture."[52] Bernard Lewis is equally explicit about the Judeo-Christian foundations of church-state separation:

> Separation of church and state was derided in the past by Muslims when they said it was a Christian remedy for a Christian disease. It doesn't apply to us or to our world. Lately, I think some of them are beginning to reconsider that, and to concede that perhaps they may have caught a Christian disease and would therefore be well advised to try a Christian remedy.[53]

At this point, the question naturally arises whether a book like this, which entertains the thought of a "Christian perspective" on international relations, is necessarily committed to "Judeo-Christian secularism." We are confident that all contributors would reject what Hurd calls "laicism." But no assumption is made that all of them support what she terms "Judeo-Christian secularism," even though some chapters contain evidence and argumentation that lend support to some version of it. Certainly all contributors accept the broad principles of a clear distinction between jurisdictions of church and state, and extensive religious freedom.[54] But it is worth noting that this is compatible with a wide range of views on precisely what the positive public role of religion should be in a context of institutional differentiation. Apart from a position of strong general support for such a role, the book adopts no party line on that question.

The third secularist assumption challenged by this book is that religion is but a dependent variable requiring explanation in terms of explanatory factors currently accepted in mainstream International Relations. It is being increasingly acknowledged that to proceed as if "religion" were just one more empirical phenomenon readily susceptible to analysis within existing "modernist" theoretical constructs and research methodologies is wrong-headed. Hatzopoulos and Petito claim that "the global resurgence of religion confronts IR theory with a theoretical challenge comparable to that raised by the end of the Cold War, or the emergence of globalization." The need is "to emancipate IR from its own theoretical captivities."[55] Such captivities have produced a blindness to religion as an independent variable and thereby have generated reductionist or otherwise lopsided or shortsighted explanations of international processes or events.

An initial step in this necessary cognitive emancipation is the recognition that the "Westphalian" privatized conception of religion is itself an "invention" of secular modernist social science rather than an objective description of the way things are.[56] As Thomas shows, the way is then open to contemplate religion as a profoundly formative, diverse, and constantly evolving factor within human societies and in relations between them; to explore the multiple ways in which it interacts, at many levels and via many actors, with factors such as economic and technological conditions, social and cultural identity formation or state power maintenance; and to embrace new methodologies for interpreting it correctly.[57] Recognizing religion—naming it truthfully—will make International Relations more productive (perhaps even more predictive) as a richer conceptual apparatus alerts practitioners to a much wider range of relevant empirical data. Hanson's "new paradigm"—an integrated framework relating a sophisticated grasp of religion's diverse contents and contexts to four autonomous global systems (political, economic, military, and communication)—is probably the most advanced articulation of the fertile possibilities lying ahead, when (as Farr puts it) religion's "guts" are examined up close.[58]

The final secularist assumption under critical scrutiny in this book is that "people of faith," whether scholars or practitioners, should keep their faith perspectives out of sight—indeed even out of mind—when analyzing or engaging with global politics. The book entertains the possibility of a different account of "religious faith" than that prevalent in diplomatic discourse or International Relations. The dominant view conceives of religious faith as an individually held set of private, subjective, nonverifiable or subrational beliefs in some sort of supernatural deity, beliefs which may properly guide personal conduct but which lack any standing in the public realm and so cannot inform or direct either the conduct or the analysis of international relations. The dominant view is not necessarily hostile to religious faith but it does regard it as irrelevant to political affairs. Max Stackhouse suggests an obvious explanation:

> Some social scientists . . . reject the very idea that religion could be an important actor in social history, because it is not important in their lives or disciplines, and they cannot imagine how deeply it influences others or the presuppositions of the historic disciplines and society as a whole, even if they acknowledge how it is influenced by other factors. But it is an intellectual fault of major proportions.[59]

This book proceeds from a very different conception of religious faith (though not every contributor explicitly endorses the following account). Over against the dominant view just described, it envisages an account (a "naming") of "faith" as a more or less comprehensive, communally held and dynamic belief set and action-orientation consciously or unconsciously influencing many areas of human life, including political action at any level.[60] So understood, faith would be recognized as powerfully operative (for good or ill) in the thought and action of individuals and communities—both academic and political—even when it goes unrecognized or is suppressed by its adherents.[61]

From within the Christian tradition, such a view might be grounded in an Augustinian understanding of religion as an encompassing spiritual orientation—a highest love—at work not only in every human being but also in every political community. Indeed, Augustine proposed to classify political communities not according to the nature of their regimes but according to the content of their love. But other theoretical foundations for a wider, nonprivatized view of religion—Christian, non-Christian, or postmodern—might also be available (though not all might be equally illuminating for International Relations).[62] Acknowledging this diversity is not to cede the debate about religion in international relations to radical deconstructionists who view any striving for universal explanations as little more than an epistemological land-grab. On the contrary, as Hatzopolous and Petito put it, "genuine universality requires a thick conception of the presence of religion in world affairs."[63]

On such a basis, it becomes more plausible to regard "secularism" as itself operating functionally as a "faith" in parallel ways to what are traditionally understood as "religions"—though this will continue to be resisted by many. Both religion as traditionally understood and "secularism" must be acknowledged as species of comprehensive "faith" perspectives. Religion must be "named truthfully" in both senses.

The acknowledgment that perspectives in International Relations might presuppose some contested faith commitments is not to imply that scholars will be importing some alien, extraneous factor into academic practice. On the view being envisaged, such commitments are already active whether we recognize them or not. Scholarship is not a faith-free zone of neutral, rational understanding; it is shaped by contestable standpoints depending on commitments that cannot be conclusively validated by appealing to some supposed universally available and agreed upon canons of objective rationality. This does not mean such commitments are irrational or subrational.[64] It means that they inhabit the territory of prerational, fiduciary conviction. Faith commitments of some sort are necessary presuppositions of reasoned scholarship rather than an alternative to it. If so, then a necessary and neglected task in International Relations is to discern the powerful yet currently unrecognized faith orientation(s) already internally shaping the foundations of the discipline. Hurd demonstrates how an inability to acknowledge the contested character of the discipline's secularist commitments actually leads to bad social science: it generates defective empirical analyses of contemporary global developments and so hampers the discipline's predictive capacities.

Hanson notes that ignorance about the nature, persistence, and power of faith can also lead to bad policy: "Ignoring religion or reducing it to politics, economics, military action, or media influence leads to grievous errors in world affairs."[65] It is worth remarking here that such errors have been committed by a wide range of regimes, most drastically by Communist or Fascist governments, themselves driven by militantly ideological atheist faiths, bent on driving traditional religious communities out of existence, but just as pervasively by European colonial governments in the nineteenth and twentieth centuries. But various chapters in this book demonstrate that far-reaching misjudgments about the persistence and power of religious faith have also been evident in postwar U.S. policy toward radical Islamism, Israel, Iran, Iraq, Afghanistan, and Russia.

Acknowledging the formative power of faith commitments in International Relations would certainly imply a significant reevaluation of the discipline's capacity to generate universally valid social-scientific findings, but would not suggest any kind of retreat into intellectual tribalism. The academic anxieties about "faith-based scholarship" that Andrew Preston quite correctly identifies in his chapter on diplomatic history are not groundless. Observing that many leading historians of American religion happen to be religious themselves, he records the consequent professional worry that studying religious history will lapse into "partisanship and advocacy." "Religion is thus mistakenly seen not as a topic or a theory, but as an agenda."

It is important to emphasize, therefore, that what this book envisages as a "Christian perspective" in the field implies committed, but not tribal or self-serving, scholarship. It does not imply, for example, that Christian scholars will study religion to the exclusion of other causal factors (thereby reproducing just another reductionism), or that the faith commitments of the scholar, or the scholarly theories or interpretations shaped by them, are purely subjective assertions beyond rational critical scrutiny in the public forum and immune to widely available and verifiable documentary and quantitative evidence. What this book is calling a "Christian perspective" in International Relations is subject to no less demanding procedures of scholarly validation than the dominant "secularist perspective" identified by Hurd as the founding assumption of the modern discipline. Whether, like Hurd, we characterize all such worldviews as placed on a spectrum of *theological* politics or echo Kubálková's call for a new international political *theology* is not the main point.[66] The point is simply to encourage honest intellectual self-disclosure: if all theorists are conditioned at some level and to some degree by underlying worldviews which they must take on faith, it can only assist mutual understanding to make these worldviews explicit.[67] Hanson quite legitimately insists that the project he is engaged in "remains political science, not theology or spirituality."[68] Most readers of this book will certainly recognize the bulk of its contents as "political science," even in chapters containing explicit theological references. Yet the conceptual structure of Hanson's book evidently reflects (to the editors, at least) not only his outsider understanding of religion as an explanatory factor but also his insider appreciation of religion as an existential reality. His book suggests that a religiously informed approach to International Relations is not only a matter of bringing normative principles derived from faith to bear on the empirical reality of international relations but also a matter of reframing the apparatus of explanatory concepts by which sense is made of that empirical reality.

In the light of the foregoing, rather than pretending to a standpoint of illusory religious neutrality, this book proposes that insights guided by the tradition of Christian political thought can both be epistemologically permissible within International Relations and highly relevant for the practice of diplomacy today. It holds out the prospect of not only "faith-based diplomacy" but also "faith-based International Relations."[69]

The faith perspective of the book may at times appear to some readers rather "thin," to use the term by which Paul Marshall describes the Christian perspective of his own chapter. Skeptical readers may find themselves asking whether a "Christian" perspective makes any discernible difference at all to the treatment of the topic at hand. As noted, it is not assumed that every contributor fully embraces the notion of faith-based scholarship as sketched above, and not all of them refer to it. The book's Christian perspective comes out somewhat more "thickly" in the chapters by James Skillen, Daniel Philpott, John Bernbaum, and Daryl Charles, each of which allude to specifically Christian ("theological") political themes. But the same perspective is often tacitly at work in helping set the priorities and frame the approaches of several other chapters.

The project of developing a "Christian perspective on International Relations" is an ambitious enterprise, and this book's claims regarding its own contribution to the advancement of such a project are appropriately modest. Scott Thomas in chapter 9 and the editors in the conclusion reflect on what this and other attempts at such a project might tell us about the feasibility, design of, and prospects for "faith-based International Relations."[70]

GUIDE TO THE CHAPTERS

From different angles, the chapters in this book pose a variety of explicit or implicit questions to the four default secularist assumptions discussed above. They aim to help correct such assumptions by disclosing the causative roles and the explanatory and normative potentials of faith in a series of specific historical processes or contemporary contexts which are generating particular challenges to the concrete practice and academic study of U.S. foreign policy. While making no pretence at comprehensiveness, the book presents eight complementary studies, each shedding a much-needed beam of light on one or another dimension of these challenges.

The following provisional classification of the multiple distinct ways in which faith might potentially relate to U.S. foreign policy may help the reader locate the detailed work of the following chapters against a larger canvas. The chapters where each theme is more fully engaged are noted in parentheses.

- Faith shapes American perceptions of its own history and its role in the world ("manifest destiny") (1, 4).
- Faith shapes American perceptions of the contemporary world ("all nations desire freedom"; "communism must be contained"; "a balance of power must be maintained") (2, 3, 5).
- Faith shapes the phenomena to which American foreign policy relates (e.g., Zionism as a key influence on Israeli strategic objectives) (3, 4).
- Faith shapes American perceptions of how foreign policy should be conducted ("diplomacy is a secular practice"; "we need to get more believers running the Pentagon") (1).
- U.S. foreign policy practitioners take account of the role of faith in their diplomatic efforts (i.e., they recognize the phenomenon of "faith-based diplomacy" and support it where appropriate) (2, 7, 8).
- U.S. foreign policy practitioners draw on their own particular faith perspectives in their conduct of diplomacy (i.e., they practice "faith-based diplomacy" from personal religious conviction) (6, 7, 8).
- Faith shapes foreign perceptions of the United States ("vanguard of freedom"; "Great Satan"; "uncivilized") (3, 5).
- Faith shapes foreign perceptions of how foreign policy/international relations should be conducted ("diplomacy is a secular practice"; "Islamic nations must win back territory lost to the infidel") (5).
- Faith shapes scholarly perceptions of international relations and foreign policy (i.e., through the medium of dominant paradigms such as realism, liberalism, globalism, which themselves rest upon unarticulated faith positions) (1, 2).
- International relations/foreign policy scholars acknowledge the phenomenon of faith in the objects of their study (e.g., by analyzing the phenomena of "public religion," "political Islam," "faith-based diplomacy," etc.) (all).
- International relations/foreign policy scholars consciously work out of a particular faith perspective (i.e., they practice "faith-based International Relations") (4, 6, 7, 8).

The contents of the book address or reflect one or more of these specific types of influence. Part 1, "Taking Religion Seriously," lays out the central argument for reckoning seriously with religion in the understanding and practice of U.S. foreign policy. Its four chapters do so from complementary angles. The first chapter explores the persisting neglect of religion in the writing of the history of American foreign relations. Andrew Preston documents the way in which diplomatic historians have "utilized religion much as a diner would use a menu, selecting specific items that bring immediate but passing fulfillment," thereby failing to reckon with religion as a causative force deserving of historical explanation in its own terms. He expresses skepticism toward the methodological nervousness of many historians about attempting to identify causal connections between tangible historical outcomes and something as "diffuse, unwieldy and imprecise" as religion. Since diplomatic historians already increasingly employ "supposedly amorphous" explanatory categories such as gender and culture, there is no reason to single religion out as uniquely resistant to causal explanation. Indeed, religious notions have in fact already been tacitly at work within the new social and cultural history of American foreign relations. The field is now open to employ such notions more extensively and self-consciously. Using the techniques of the social historian, Preston suggests, "It will not be difficult for diplomatic historians to dust for the theological fingerprints on many episodes of U.S. foreign relations."

The focus of the next two chapters is on American myopia regarding the irreducibly religious nature of the forces the United States finds itself contending with abroad. In chapter 2, Thomas F. Farr explores U.S. policy on the international promotion of religious freedom as a particularly telling case study of how, even in this supposedly religion-sensitive policy track, American diplomacy has failed to grapple adequately with the full reality of religion as a context for, constraint on, and objective of foreign policy. Even here, religion has not been recognized as having any independent causative force on the political contexts in which religious freedom is being fought for around the world. The result has been the development of damaging blind spots,[71] contributing to unexpected policy failures or missed opportunities, even in settings where, as in Afghanistan, defending religious freedom has been a declared priority of the administration. The chapter proposes a comprehensive rethinking of international religious freedom (IRF) policy as if religion really counted. American IRF policy, Farr argues, must move beyond mere "humanitarianism," and also beyond regarding religion merely as a matter of "culture." A fully integrated approach is required, calling for change at multiple points: to the operative understandings of religion and freedom, to strategic decision making and Congressional action, to the conduct of policy, and to diplomatic training and staffing.[72]

In chapter 3, Paul Marshall addresses the greatest current global religious challenge to the United States: expansionist radical Islam. He argues that unless the essentially religious motivation behind radical global Islam is correctly identified, rather than explained away as caused by social, economic, or political factors, U.S. foreign policy will be misinformed, and thereby disabled, in its efforts to combat the threat it poses. The chapter aims to clarify the nature and goals of expansionist radical Islam, especially its terrorist wing. It explores the worldview, especially the understanding of history, held by expansionist Islamic radicals. Their central grievance, continually expressed, is the collapse of the Islamic world in the face of Christendom, a collapse explained by Muslims' apostasy from Islam and which can be reversed only by returning to their version of Islam. Many members of the U.S. foreign policy community, however, persist in reading radical Islamic movements through a dated Enlightenment lens that produces a narrative largely shaped by misleading categories of first world/third world, globalization, ethnicity, U.S. foreign policy, and Middle Eastern nationalism. To the degree that U.S. views of the nature and goals of radical Islam are shaped by these categories, American actors are consistently misinformed about the nature of the conflicts they face.[73] The chapter operates on the assumption that people's religious beliefs motivate at least in part what they do, that such beliefs are part of the explanation for their actions, and that if present conflicts are to be properly understood, these beliefs must be taken seriously. It does not assume that one needs to be a Christian to believe these things, but it does presume that Christians think their own beliefs have some causative force in their lives and so are more open to thinking the same about others than is the average secularist.

In chapter 4, James W. Skillen offers a further case study of how religion shapes the objects of U.S. foreign policy, but adds a new dimension by disclosing the religious beliefs that shape America's own perceptions of these objects. It casts new light on how American Middle East policy actually reflects divergent faith-driven attitudes toward Israel, all of them explicable as variants of "Zionism."[74] The thesis of the chapter is that three different but related Zionisms function as religiously deep ideologies regarding the relation of the United States to the modern state of Israel and that these Zionisms are both biblically and politically problematic. The first of the three modern forms of Zionism appears in America's identification of itself as God's new Israel, destined to lead the way to democracy, freedom, prosperity, and peace for the whole world. A second form of modern Zionism arose among European Jews in the nineteenth century and had an enormous influence in defining and directing the modern state of Israel. The third mode of Zionism is Christian Zionism, which interprets the Bible as prophesying a return of Jews to Israel as one of the last developments in history before Christ returns to earth to bring history to a close. All three Zionisms reach back to the earliest biblical texts that tell of God's electing of Israel as his chosen people and their inheriting of the promised land. Then, depending on their interpretations of the Bible, the three Zionisms morph into forms of new-Israelitism, presenting broad historical, political-religious metanarratives. The chapter also reveals, and critiques against a biblical theology, the roots of one of these forms of Zionism in America's own perception of itself as a "chosen nation" with a religious mission. It shows that, from a different Christian point of view, the three Zionisms misinterpret the Bible and lead to the advocacy of foreign and defense policies that can be highly unjust.

Part 2, "Enlisting Religion Diplomatically," presents four diverse case studies illustrating how a fuller grasp of the way faith perspectives shape the context and motivations of U.S. foreign policy will enable more effective and more responsible policymaking. The theme of this part is already anticipated in the discussion of religious freedom policy in chapter 2 but is articulated here in more detail. The case studies in this part engage with four of the major global reference points of U.S foreign policy: Europe, Russia, humanitarian intervention, and post-conflict situations.

In chapter 5, Thomas Albert Howard approaches U.S.-Europe relations from a novel historical perspective. He brings to light influential but typically unrecognized religious dynamics informing and sustaining negative contemporary European perceptions of the United States. More specifically, the chapter examines historical reasons that might predispose Europeans, at least Western Europeans, to look at American religious life with great skepticism and condescension. It argues that students of European anti-Americanism often concentrate on political, economic, and social differences that divide the two continents, when in fact a substrate of prior cultural and religious factors should also be taken into consideration. It also argues that the accretion of perceptions of difference in the cultural-religious sphere creates a prism of interpretation that informs judgments about numerous contemporary issues. The essay draws material from a number of influential nineteenth- and early twentieth-century

European thinkers (including Jacob Burckhardt, Alexis de Tocqueville, Philip Schaff, Frances Trollope, August Comte, Hegel, Marx, and Heidegger) who sought to "explain" the United States to European audiences. The essay concludes with the observation that policy shifts alone will not necessarily ameliorate long-standing currents of anti-Americanism abroad; much deeper factors of cultural perception and divergence also must be understood and addressed if such an attitude is to be moderated. American policy toward Europe should take more account of these submerged, religiously informed European (mis)perceptions, and work to correct them where it can.

In chapter 6, John Bernbaum addresses one of the multiple entry points for U.S. policy toward Russia, one where religious factors will turn out to play a formative role. He considers a momentous strategic mistake in U.S. policy toward Russia: its failure to recognize the far-reaching role of moral, cultural, and religious factors in the collapse of the Soviet Union and in subsequent efforts toward post-Soviet reconstruction. The chapter charts the studied indifference to religion that marked standard foreign policy analyses of the U.S.S.R. prior to 1989—analyses contributing to a serious misdiagnosis of the U.S.S.R.'s future prospects. It then reports on how this misdiagnosis continued to shape U.S. policy after 1989, issuing in a narrow preoccupation with political and economic factors to the neglect of the crucial role of cultural factors and institutions in laying necessary foundations for post-Soviet reconstruction. The chapter proposes that religious institutions and faith-based NGOs are uniquely well placed to perform a vital role in helping nurture the moral and cultural preconditions for successful democratization and economic development. The argument is that if the United States wants to contribute effectively to sustainable reform in Russia, it should fundamentally review how its diplomatic efforts engage with religion and religious organizations. Core religious principles of humility, mercy, and justice are invoked as guides for future U.S. policy. If the United States wants to assist sustainable reform in Russia, it should review carefully how it might lend support to faith-based NGOs.

In chapter 7, J. Daryl Charles explores a critical challenge that, absent a lurch back into isolationism,[75] will increasingly confront U.S. foreign policy in the immediate future: the ethics of humanitarian intervention in a post–Cold War era. Undergirding this discussion are two assumptions in the contemporary context. First, the geopolitical challenges since 1990 increase rather than diminish the necessity of morally qualifying coercive force, insofar as intervention that falls short of formal war may well require the assistance of military force to safeguard, accompany, or monitor the requirements of justice in unjust or oppressive international contexts. Second, the fact that the United States and Western societies are characterized by a "post-consensus" cultural climate makes it inordinately difficult to make moral judgments of any kind, much less to identify and counter social-political evil in the sphere of international relations. The discussion of humanitarian intervention in this chapter is anchored in classic just-war moral reasoning, which, while principally nurtured in the Christian moral tradition, represents a consensual, time-tested tradition of moral reflection on the qualification of coercive force that transcends both the cultural moment and diversity of cultures. Following a discussion of contemporary geopolitical as well as moral challenges that confront us, the essay surveys more recent developments in both the long-standing political debate regarding intervention over against sovereignty and the humanitarian debate concerning requisite strategies of intervention before drawing conclusions pertinent to responsible statecraft. To intervene or not to intervene? This should always be a difficult question, given (a) the need to morally qualify the use of intervening force, (b) the bewildering variety of contemporary geopolitical crises, and (c) the fact that domestic brutality, civil war, genocide, political tyranny, enslavement, and religious/ethnic persecution are part of the world in which we live. The chapter argues that the task before us, in crafting wise policy, is neither to be "interventionist" nor "noninterventionist"; rather, it is to discriminate morally so that we might engage in *ius ad interventionem* when and where human need and our shared humanity call for it. The moral rationale of intervention, as Grotius observed, is that if the wrong being inflicted on a population is obvious, wholly unwarranted, and patently unjust, then the right to redress cannot be precluded.

In chapter 8, Daniel Philpott presents an explicitly Christian ethic of peacebuilding inspired by the notion of reconciliation as a possible model for a post–Cold War U.S. foreign policy capable of contributing more effectively to situations of post-conflict transition.[76] Since the end of the Cold War, U.S. foreign policy has encountered its thorniest troubles in its efforts to build peace in societies sundered by conflict—a dilemma far more difficult than military victory itself. Yet Christian ethicists, including just-war theorists, have offered no systematic ethic for how to address past political evils in order to establish a more just future regime. Holding promise for such an ethic is a concept that comes from the crux of the Christian tradition and now resurfaces in political transitions and their surrounding conversations all over the globe: reconciliation. The chapter seeks to outline the central features of an ethic of reconciliation and offers some insights for its application to U.S. foreign policy. Theologically, though it echoes the just-war tradition in drawing from natural law, its central source is the Christian notion of God's own atoning action, from which it derives a restorative ethic whose key virtue is mercy, classically understood as the will to assist one in grief or distress. It is then translated into six practices for political orders: acknowledgment, reparations, restorative punishment, apology, forgiveness, and building just institutions. What results is a conception of justice that includes but exceeds traditional concerns of justice like accountability and the restoration of human rights. Were it incorporated into American foreign policy, reconciliation would result in a far more restorative approach toward countries whose political future America tries to influence and would encourage greater cooperation between the U.S. government and other organizations who themselves proffer a restorative approach.

In his response, "Reading Religion Rightly" (chapter 9), Scott Thomas seeks to situate the contributions of the preceding chapters within two broader contexts. The first is that of the notable changes underway in International Relations as a result of the "return of religion" within the discipline. Thomas itemizes five significant achievements resulting from this return, but also sounds an epistemologically skeptical note regarding the continuing limitations of the supposed new "knowledge" of religion now available. The second context is explicitly theological. Thomas revisits the neglected radical Christian critique of contemporary Western civilization propounded half a century ago by the leading figure in the English School of International Relations, Martin Wight. Thomas reviews Wight's disturbing, countercultural analysis of the secularized modern West as the "apostasy of Christendom" and asks whether it has any lessons to teach scholars and practitioners today. If modern Western nation-states are the outcome of religious "apostasy," can Christians in these fields simply pursue business as usual?

In the conclusion, we identify two distinctive contributions emerging from the preceding chapters: first, their summons to scholars and practitioners in international relations and foreign policy to come to grips with what we call the "pastness," the "thickness," and the "potency" of religion; and second, the pointers in these chapters toward what a "Christian perspective" in these fields might look like.

Part I

Taking Religion Seriously

Chapter 1

Reviving Religion in the History of American Foreign Relations

Andrew Preston

With the eruption of global hostilities between two universalistic, mutually exclusive ideologies, the president of the United States sought to rally Americans, and people around the world, to the cause of spreading freedom and democracy. What was most striking about his rhetoric was its explicit grounding in religious dogma and imagery. "The defense of mankind against these attacks," the president told an audience at the onset of the crisis, "lies in the faith we profess—the brotherhood of man and the Fatherhood of God." "Democracy," he proclaimed two years later in the midst of an increasingly unpopular, stalemated war, "is first and foremost a spiritual force." At a subsequent occasion, he warned against complacency because "we are under tremendous attacks" and stressed that Americans must remain vigilant and "establish the fervor, the strength of our convictions, because fundamentally Democracy is nothing in the world but a spiritual conviction, a conviction that each of us is enormously valuable because of a certain standing before our own God." Finally, later still, when it was clear that the global struggle would last years, if not decades, the president informed the American people that although he had "sworn before you and Almighty God the same oath our forebears prescribed" in the eighteenth century, "the same revolutionary beliefs for which our forebears fought are still at issue around the globe—the belief that the rights of man come not from the generosity of the state but from the hand of God."

These are familiar words to the collective post-9/11 sensibility. Yet they come not from the speeches of George W. Bush on terrorism and Iraq, but from the Cold War rhetoric of Presidents Harry S. Truman, Dwight D. Eisenhower, and John F. Kennedy.[1] Indeed, it is the use of gendered language—"brotherhood of man," "Fatherhood of God," and "rights of man"—rather than religious rhetoric that makes these declarations sound anachronistic. That the words of Truman, Eisenhower, and Kennedy could have been uttered today—or, indeed, at almost any other moment of national crisis in American history—demonstrates their continuing resonance and relevance. Particularly striking is the continuing integral role of religion in the formation, execution, and justification of American foreign policy. The importance of religion to American public life, including U.S. foreign policy, is further illustrated by the fact that although they espoused the same message, Truman (a devout Baptist who rarely attended church), Eisenhower (a nominal Presbyterian but in reality a nondenominational mainline Protestant), Kennedy (a moderate Catholic), and Bush (an evangelical Southern Methodist) all adhered to different denominations and held different religious beliefs. Yet while diplomatic historians have been quick to point out the essential continuities between Bush's post-9/11 foreign policy and the traditions of American war and diplomacy, the influence of religion in this process has been relatively neglected and generally unrecognized.[2]

In making the case for religion, terminology is important—both for methodological and historiographical purposes—and so a working definition of religion is in order. What do I mean when I say that diplomatic historians need to pay more attention to religion? What exactly is "religion" anyway? Unlike "ideology," which is infamously difficult to define with any precision and means different things to scholars from different disciplines, religion can be described in a fairly straightforward, comprehensive fashion despite its incredible diffusion and diversity.[3]

The comprehensive, dynamic definition of religion (or "faith") proposed by the editors in the introduction is quite compatible with the thesis of this chapter, but it presents a particular challenge for historians. Due to the many applications of the term religion, the problem is not so much determining what it is, but rather determining how to *limit* what it is, in order to keep the field of investigation within confines narrow enough to identify cause and effect. For example, should a study of religion focus on concepts of "morality," even if those concepts are no longer explicitly religious? Should it include "civil religion"—a societal phenomenon in the United States that Gunnar Myrdal referred to as "the American Creed" and Will Herberg described as a quasi-official "American Way of Life" that "provides the framework in terms of which the crucial values of American existence are couched"—which is sometimes purely religious, sometimes purely secular, and sometimes an impure mixture of both?[4] Should it include "lived religion," a category which does not necessarily entail the institutional apparatus normally associated with definitions of religion?[5] All of these approaches would seem to be implied in the editors' definition and, ideally, diplomatic historians would embrace them all. But in the interests of clarity, by "religion" I will be referring in this chapter simply to the readily identifiable religious affiliations and values that people hold. In what follows, then, "religious" describes those Americans who profess faith in a higher, spiritual reality and belong to a recognized denomination or faith, be it Christianity, Judaism, Islam, Buddhism, and so forth. Such an examination includes civil religion only when it specifically appropriates the values and rituals of an actual, faith-based religion.[6] And such an approach includes lived religion only when it has obvious causal utility in explaining the history of American foreign relations.

Independently, religion and foreign relations are two of the most important and exhaustively studied aspects of American history. Religion has consistently been one of the dominant forces in shaping American culture, politics, economics, and national identity. Indeed, the United States is the only major industrialized democracy where religion is as salient today as it was three centuries ago. America's engagement with the world has had a similarly profound effect on virtually all facets of national life. Moreover, since at least the Seven Years' War, and certainly since the Revolution, American foreign relations have shaped people and events within and beyond North America. Religion and foreign relations, then, are two subjects that have not only been instrumental to the study of American history, but they also have played an instrumental role in making both the United States and the world what they are today.

And yet, despite some specific exceptions that prove the general rule, these two great disciplines are rarely, if ever, comprehensively or effectively bridged.[7] When they have actually bothered to do so, historians of American foreign relations have utilized religion much as a diner would use a menu, selecting specific items that bring immediate but passing fulfillment. In other words, diplomatic historians will often briefly, idio-syncratically, and opportunistically highlight the role of certain individu-als or incidents—say, foreign missionaries or the religious faith of certain American leaders—but specific, singular case studies apart, they have not, in general, deployed religion as an overall theory or method to examine America's role in the world. "Political and diplomatic historians," Leo P. Ribuffo, one of the few historians successfully to bridge matters of church and state, points out, "almost never know the work of such important [religious] scholars as George M. Marsden and Mark Noll."[8]

There is no simple, single explanation as to why this is so, although three possibilities come to mind: partisanship and advocacy, seculariza-tion, and empirical and methodological difficulty. First, partisanship and advocacy. With the demise of liberal religion and its replacement by evan-gelical Protestantism and conservative Catholicism in the United States, and with the dramatic growth of fundamentalist religions elsewhere in the world, the very subject of religion might simply seem too partisan or controversial. Moreover, the admission requirements to the study of reli-gion often appear dauntingly high to the irreligious. For example, many scholars who study the history of American religion—such as Mark Noll, Joel A. Carpenter, and Paul Boyer—are themselves religious or have a religious background, creating an impression that faith is a prerequisite for scholarship.[9] Because of this tightly knit community of scholars, and because religion is so personal, people often assume that someone writ-ing on religion must have a religious view to advance. Religion is thus mistakenly seen not as a topic or a theory, but as an agenda.

This absence is not without precedent in the writing of U.S. diplo-matic history. Consider the discipline's absence, until recently, of ideol-ogy. Most Americans do not think of themselves as ideological because ideology, as Anders Stephanson puts it, is always "something the other guy does."[10] Or, as Sacvan Bercovitch says about the writing of consensus history during the Cold War, Americanists "denied that America had any ideology at all, since ideology meant dogma, bigotry, and repression; whereas Americans," in contrast to the Communists of the Soviet Union, China, and elsewhere, "were open-minded, inclusive, and eclectic."[11] Thus labeling someone as "ideological"—or "religious"—is akin to calling them "radical" because the term often implies a certain lack of reason-ableness, detachment, objectivity, or rationality. Perhaps because of the long dominance of the theories of realism and rational choice in interna-tional relations and diplomatic history, it is this irrationality that political and diplomatic historians often resist.

Second, and related, is secularization. As humanists who strive for objectivity through empiricism, diplomatic historians often instinctually separate matters of church and state. The processes of diversification and secularization—which began in the nineteenth century and supposedly transformed the United States into a "post-Protestant," "post-Puritan," and "post-Christian" nation[12]—have been partly responsible for the lack of religion in the political and diplomatic history of modern America, mostly because modern historians believe in secularization as much as they believe that secularization has actually occurred.[13] As Nathan O. Hatch, a historian of early American religion, argues, "The modern distinction between sacred and secular has allowed the studies of religion and politics to go their separate ways in virtual isolation."[14] Andrew J. Rotter, a diplomatic historian who himself uses religion, concurs. "American scholars have usually resisted interpreting U.S. foreign policy as a product of religious thinking," he notes. "The idea makes many Americans uncomfortable, for we are supposed to live in a country where politics and religion do not mix."[15] And because of the general correlation between higher levels of education and lower levels of religiosity, it probably makes academics especially uncomfortable.[16] For many historians, then, injecting religion into their work might seem to be a rejection of secularization, and perhaps even too close an embrace of proselytizing.[17]

But in strikingly ahistorical fashion, this deliberate neglect refuses to engage historical figures on their own terms. It explicitly addresses historians' concerns and rejects what was important to people of the past. It refuses, in other words, to take religion seriously.[18] Interestingly, the same phenomenon has affected other historical fields. For most of the twentieth century, for example, historians of the Crusades eschewed religion and emphasized plunder, politics, and conquest as the Crusaders' primary motivations. Now, however, perhaps under the influence of religion's dramatic return to world politics since 9/11, historians of the Crusades are once again stressing that it was the sacred rather than the secular that primarily drove the Crusaders eastward.[19] As the example of Crusades history demonstrates, much has changed since Hatch was writing in 1977. But while International Relations theorists and historians working in other fields, from the Crusades to transatlantic slavery to postwar American politics, have in recent years begun to stress the religious influence, diplomatic historians have been slow to accept this change and adopt religion as a method of historical inquiry.

Third is empirical and methodological difficulty. Religion may perhaps appear to be too diffuse, unwieldy, and imprecise for methodologically traditional diplomatic historians to integrate it usefully into their work. Perhaps more than other fields, diplomatic history seeks to identify an explicit relationship between cause and effect to explain how and why Americans interact with the world in the manner they do. And linking such causality with ideas, culture, and values is no easy feat. As Gordon A. Craig notes in an oft-quoted observation on ideology that applies equally to values and religion, "To establish the relationship between ideas and foreign policy is always a difficult task, and it is no accident that it has attracted so few historians."[20] Similarly, in his attempt to trace the relationship among religious, intellectual, and social history, Bruce Kuklick states simply, "Sometimes ideas fit the social order, sometimes they do not; at no time is the connection simple, and occasionally it cannot be fathomed."[21]

With an amorphous and often undocumented phenomenon such as religion, then, causation becomes a key problem for the diplomatic historian, as two renowned scholars have noted in pointing out shortcomings in the field's increasingly popular cultural and social models.[22] After all, while religion has obviously shaped the national agenda in certain eras—the 1740s, 1810s, 1850s, 1890s, and 1950s spring immediately to mind—the United States has never waged a holy war or launched a religious crusade. Since winning independence from the British, U.S. officials may sometimes have been influenced by religion, but were they actually driven by a sense of divine calling? While one could reasonably argue that, say, war with Spain in 1898 was motivated by the search for overseas markets, or that the CIA's role in the 1953 overthrow of Iranian leader Mohammed Mossadeq was motivated by a desire to secure access to oil, or that military intervention in Vietnam a decade later was driven by a fear of Communism, Americans have never gone to war to spread the gospel. How, then, does one even begin to unravel the exceedingly complicated and frequently untraceable relationship between religion and diplomacy? How does one pinpoint causation? Such concerns, however, should be viewed skeptically: the emergence of many innovative studies in diplomatic history that use other supposedly amorphous modes of analysis, such as gender and culture, illustrates that otherwise valid concerns over causation can be misplaced and exaggerated.

Whatever the actual reasons, the interplay between religious faith and public life is, as Paul T. McCartney points out, "an aspect of American identity that is mistakenly ignored in most foreign policy analyses."[23]

While important exceptions to the general rule are noted below, overall the result among diplomatic historians is an odd agnosticism about the place of religion in the history of American foreign relations. Traditionally, secular concerns have dominated the discipline. Diplomatic historians have long argued that the United States wages its wars and conducts its foreign policy in pursuit of rational, tangible, or political goals—to attain or promote power, security, democracy, or trade and economic profit.[24] As useful as they remain, however, these traditional explanations do not always illuminate the values that inform and shape these policies. Over the last decade American diplomatic historians have begun to apply innovative theories borrowed from other disciplines and fields in their examinations of the history of American foreign relations. Among the most influential and popular of these new theories, rubrics, and methodologies are gender and sexuality, cultural hegemony, values and norms, cultural and educational exchange, the role of nongovernmental organizations, the arts, race, and postcolonialism. These theories face the same methodological obstacles of linking cause and effect that challenge the utility of religion, yet through their ingenuity and sophistication they have nonetheless been able to transform our understanding of American diplomatic history.

Yet despite this vibrant and exciting new theoretical and methodological mosaic, there seems to be no space left for religion. As a systematic rubric under which various moments in the history of American foreign relations, or the whole history itself, can be analyzed and explained, religion has been sorely neglected and is rarely a lens through which historians examine America's role in the world. For example, four of the standard historiographical guides to the field of U.S. diplomatic history explore a wide variety of methodological and theoretical schools to explain what drives American foreign policy—including, among several others, realism, bureaucratic politics, corporatism, world systems theory, gender, ideology, and race—but not religion. Indeed, "religion" does not even appear in any of their indexes.[25] Similarly, most of the major broad, thematic syntheses of American foreign relations do not address the role of religion, even when they purport to discuss explicitly religious themes (which have, to be sure, become secularized through popular acceptance and usage) such as "providence" and "mission" or values that in large part have explicitly religious origins, such as "human rights."[26] Military historians have been similarly remiss.[27] Such neglect becomes stranger still when one considers that many diplomatic historians, even those who built their careers understating the importance of ideas and ideology—such as John Lewis Gaddis and Melvyn P. Leffler—now recognize that intangible, cultural, and value-laden factors were essential to the unfolding of the Cold War.[28] But while historians bemoan the absence of other theories and models, none has been as systematically overlooked as religion.[29]

For their part, historians of American religion have been little better in bridging this gap.[30] Granted, it is perhaps easier to trace religion's influence on foreign policy than it is foreign policy's influence on religion. In this sense, one can probably more readily identify the impact of a general and diffuse phenomenon (religion) on a relatively specific subject (foreign affairs) than the other way around. The sheer number of variables decreases as one's focus narrows and, as a result, cause and effect stand in sharper relief. When historians and political scientists link religion to American public life, therefore, they usually do so on particular matters, such as governance (especially the separation of church and state), political issues (such as faith-based initiatives, electoral dynamics, and social behavior), and popular culture—while completely ignoring foreign relations. Clearly this approach should also provide fruitful results for the history of American foreign relations, yet the field generally stands beyond the range of religious historians. Tellingly, historiographical guides to the study of American religious history do not mention the connections to American war and diplomacy.[31]

The contrast with domestic political, social, and cultural U.S. history could not be starker. Religion plays a central role in the study of American history from the earliest years of the colonial era to the Civil War; and although it is, as Paul Boyer and Jon Butler have noted, more peripheral to the study of American history since 1865, especially in the twentieth century, scholars have not exactly ignored the influence of religion on domestic history.[32] Americanists have generally recognized, to take but a few examples, the important role religion has played in the evolution of slavery, urban life, reform movements, the development of mass media, and the rise of conservatism to national political dominance in the last forty years. While it still might be superseded by other historical fields, the integration of religious history into larger social, cultural, and political narratives of modern American history has proceeded much further along than it has in the field of U.S. diplomatic history.

Admittedly, it would be overstating the case to argue that religion has been totally neglected by diplomatic historians and foreign relations specialists. The attacks of September 11, 2001, of course, brought religious motives into explanations of American foreign policy.[33] This had much to do with the views of two religious conservatives: a Sunni Muslim, Osama bin Laden, and a Protestant Christian, George W. Bush.[34] As a consequence, the literature on current American foreign policy is littered with books on U.S. engagement with the Islamic world. Much of the debate centers on the plaintive question Americans found themselves asking in the immediate aftermath of the attacks: "Why do they hate us?"[35] Answers to this larger question have, in turn, focused on whether the United States (and, by extension for Americans if not necessarily for Europeans and Canadians, "the West") finds itself in a "clash of civilizations" with the Islamic world or whether Islamic militancy has political, rather than religious, roots.[36] More generally, as the introduction notes, the 9/11 attacks and the Bush administration's response has also triggered a wave of literature on how religion affects international relations.[37] Yet aside from examinations of Bush's personal faith, there has been remarkably little sustained analysis, even since 9/11, on putting these religious motivations in U.S. foreign policy in broader historical perspective.

Not all is lost, however. As a brief survey of the literature from both religious and diplomatic history will reveal below, scholars have often blended religion with foreign relations without even realizing it. If diplomatic historians are to organize these works within one coherent school of thought, they should look for guidance to the new social and cultural history of American foreign relations. In fact, despite its revolutionary impact, this "new" social and cultural diplomatic history was not exactly new when it emerged a little over a decade ago. It was a popular, if undisciplined, feature in the literature before the 1990s but had never been codified as a separate school of thought within the historiography. The formally theoretical and empirical use of gender, for example, emerged from the work of Emily Rosenberg, among others, and has since been expanded on and enhanced in ambitious, innovative works such as Frank Costigliola's linkage of concerns with American masculinity to the origins of containment and Robert Dean's analysis of masculinity and the escalation of the Vietnam War.[38] While their scholarly rigor is recent, the links they make between, on the one hand, the distorted importance policymakers gave to protecting and preserving their own masculinity and, on the other, the formation of U.S. foreign policy are not so novel.

What is new, then, is not the actual use of "gender" (or other rubrics, such as culture or race), but the explicit categorization of the taxonomy of gender. In other words, gender has not been recently introduced, but recently formalized and theorized. This brief discussion is not meant to detract from the striking originality, ingenuity, and ultimately persuasive causal force of the new cultural diplomatic history. What it is meant to demonstrate is the enormous potential for religion within the new cultural diplomatic history. Thus, while historians have long recognized that American men in the 1890s and 1940s harbored deep insecurities about their own masculinity and about the increasingly assertive role of women in public life, none could appreciate the depth of the policy, political, and cultural implications until Hoganson (the Spanish-American War) and Costigliola (the early Cold War) had published their works. In order to be professionally and intellectually successful, then, historians using religion must emulate their counterparts who have already used gender, race, and culture.

In a situation that resembles the disorganized and unmethodical use of gender before Rosenberg, Costigliola, Dean, Hoganson, and others provided formal systematization and methodological rigor, diplomatic and religious historians have used religion to explain the history of American foreign relations sporadically, haphazardly, and largely in isolation from one another. The result is a wide but formless literature that does not cohere very well into an overarching theory, methodology, or school. These many but isolated specific instances have what Jon Butler, a historian of early America who specializes in religion, has termed the jack-in-the-box effect. "Religion pops up colorfully on occasion," Butler notes in a recent discussion of the paucity of religion in historical surveys of modern America. "But as with a child's jack-in-the-box, the surprise offered by the color or peculiarity of the figure is seldom followed by an extended performance, much less substance."[39] Rather than having a substantive impact on the study of American foreign relations, religion and religious topics have had an occasional, limited, and even ephemeral influence.

To be sure, thematic overviews of the religious influence on American diplomacy do exist—though they usually tend to be short essays designed to influence contemporary foreign policy debates rather than analyze the past. In this vein, political scientist James Kurth argues that one cannot understand the unfolding of America's relationship with the world without also recognizing the guiding, if weakening, hand of American Protestantism.[40] Computer scientist David Gelernter agrees that American Protestantism is central to American foreign policy and has been since the colonial era, but concludes that America has not at all lost its Judeo-Christian religious guidance.[41] With their polemical stridency and advocacy, Kurth and Gelernter help illustrate why academic historians of American foreign relations overlook religion: it is often a subject that eschews neutrality and objectivity and thus requires one to take a partisan position. On a more scholarly level, religious sociologist William Marin contends that to be successful, American diplomats must take into account both the religious views of foreign nations and their own nation's long religious tradition, and that a purely secular foreign policy is as unattainable as it is undesirable.[42] Paul T. McCartney, a political scientist, argues that religion is central to the formation of an American universalistic identity that has shaped Americans' approach to the world since the Revolution.[43] Only Leo Ribuffo, a historian who emphasizes the complexity and diversity of America's religious heritage and the correspondingly complex, and diffuse, influence it has had on American foreign policy, has offered a historical, scholarly treatment of the subject.[44]

The role of religion most often receives detailed scrutiny in overviews of American nationalism, ideology, and sense of mission, which all have obvious applicability to foreign relations. Whether or not they agree that it actually exists, historians of American identity and thought have argued that exceptionalism has religious roots, specifically in the founding of colonial, Puritan New England.[45] And while the Puritans generally are presumed to be culpable in the creation of exceptionalism, historians have found their theological imprint on the extended origins of everything from the American Revolution to the Vietnam War.[46] In his overview of American expansionism, Anders Stephanson stresses that the Puritan legacy of providence, sacred errand, and millennial progress, from seventeenth-century Massachusetts Bay through to the eighteenth-century theologian Jonathan Edwards and eventually to the nineteenth-century concept of Manifest Destiny, did more than anything else to motivate American expansion across the North American continent and, after 1898, across the globe. The Puritans, Stephanson argues, believed themselves to be on a divinely sanctioned, millennial errand from God to settle the New World, build a new Jerusalem, and expand their holy dominion. It is this belief, that Americans are God's chosen people— Calvinist rather than strictly Puritan—that permeates the history of U.S. foreign policy.[47] Conversely, in his provocative survey of American foreign relations since the Revolution, Walter A. McDougall argues for the importance of religion in framing how Americans, from the Puritan leader John Winthrop to George Washington, originally perceived their global role as one of leading by example rather than involvement.[48] Those diplomatic historians who address the Puritans usually perfunctorily concur with Stephanson's version and habitually invoke John Winthrop, the first governor of Massachusetts and the author of the famous "city on a hill" speech, as the founder of American exceptionalism and messianism and, by extension, interventionism and imperialism.[49]

While overarching theories that look beyond the Puritan ethic are sorely lacking and comprehensive surveys are noticeably absent, specific episodes and individuals in American diplomatic history, along the lines of Butler's jack-in-the-box metaphor, have had their religious aspects seriously and systematically examined. Reflecting its prevalence in the everyday life of the colonies, religion remains paramount to the study of colonial America. It is in this period that the religious influence on the American worldview began. The establishment of the very first "American" military units in seventeenth-century Massachusetts, for example, had as much to do with notions of Christian piety, politics, and order as it did with fear of Indians and European desires to expand territorially.[50]

This is as true for colonial wars as it is for other topics in colonial American history. Thus the colonists' major conflicts with various Indian nations have been examined in at least a partly religious light. In addition to Alfred A. Cave's singular monograph, the Puritans' experience in the ethno-religious Pequot War of 1636–1638 has provoked controversy over whether the colonists' destruction of their Indian enemies constituted faith-based genocide.[51] Jill Lepore has brilliantly probed the causes, course, and consequences of another Puritan-Indian conflict, King Philip's War of 1675–1676, to trace the roots of American identity. The war was, proportionately, one of the deadliest in American history, and in its bloody wake, the victorious but disillusioned colonists, in contrast to the savage Spanish Catholics and even more savage Indian heathens, fashioned themselves an exceptionalist history that served to justify the war. "Later on," Lepore writes, "after nearly a century of repetition on successive American frontiers, this triangulated conception of identity would form the basis of American nationalism" in succeeding centuries, a Calvinistic concept of nationality that is still religiously infused today much as it was during its seventeenth-century formation.[52] Religion also played an important role in the outbreak of other colonial wars, such as King William's War (1689–1697, known also by its European name, the War of the League of Augsburg), Queen Anne's War (1702–1713, known also as the War of Spanish Succession), and King George's War (1744–1748).[53]

The colonists' foreign relations, necessarily defined and determined to a great extent by England (Great Britain after 1707), also often erupted in war. While English and British conflict with the Spanish and Dutch would rage, intermittently and briefly, throughout the sixteenth and early seventeenth centuries, it was the French who would pose the gravest danger to the American colonies and, not coincidentally, later contribute most to the formation of an independent American polity. The Seven Years' War marked the zenith of the campaign against the French; its outcome saw France all but wiped out as a colonial power in North America. The fighting in North America was but one theater in what could be called, in the strictest sense, the first world war. Although the disillusioned aftermath of the war would provide the spark for the revolutionary movement a decade later, the American colonists were initially delighted at the defeat of the French. Anti-Catholicism combined with Protestant providentialism and exceptionalism to provide the Anglo-American cause with a good deal of religious support and motivation. Indeed, as Fred Anderson notes in his magisterial history of the conflict, *Crucible of War*, "when the smoke finally cleared, sermons had probably outnumbered bonfires" in victorious New England. It is a thesis that Anderson first argued in *A People's Army*, his history of how the war unfolded in and affected Massachusetts.[54] The dual effect of colonial religion on the Seven Years' War—providing both positive (for Protestantism) and negative (against Catholicism) motivation—is also a central thesis of Alan Heimert's landmark work, *Religion and the American Mind*.[55] Nonetheless, like the religious aspect of almost every other episode in American diplomatic and military history, there is much room for future research: Anderson touches on religion only briefly, while Heimert examines it exclusively without really considering the diplomatic and military contexts.

The Seven Years' War, of course, unleashed the forces that would culminate in the American Revolution. By waging war against the British and allying themselves formally with the French and Spanish, the revolutionaries committed the first acts of U.S. foreign policy (even if the actual American state did not come into being until 1783). The Revolution was a multifaceted conflict—simultaneously a revolutionary war, a civil war, an international war, and an anti-colonial war—and for this reason it remains central to understanding the American worldview and diplomatic tradition. While diplomatic historians recognize this, usually in passing, they have not examined the era in any great depth. Religious historians, on the other hand, have fought tremendously productive historiographical battles over the origins of the American Revolution. The Great Awakening of the 1740s—the first of several widespread religious revivals to engulf and transform America—marked the rise of individual, personal piety and the concomitant erosion of the authority of the established churches. This process, thirty years before the actual outbreak of revolution, was crucial to the very concept of independence. Frank Lambert, for example, notes that George Whitefield, one of the revival's central figures, chronologically and conceptually "provides a direct link between the Great Awakening and the American Revolution."[56] Building upon these religious foundations, several religious historians have argued that the Patriot movement for independence itself was religiously infused and ecclesiastically driven, excepting, of course, the naturally loyalist Anglican church.[57] Mark Noll, perhaps the most prominent and prolific exponent of this view, argues that "American Christians were present, involved, and even in the forefront of promoting an independent United States of America."[58] Moreover, the Patriot movement was not simply carried along by messianic Protestantism. As Lambert has recently shown elsewhere, the patriots were agitating at least as much for religious freedom as they were for political liberty. "Americans," he writes, "also sought a revolution in religion."[59] While some religious historians, most notably Jon Butler, argue that the religious influence has been exaggerated, the general consensus is that religion and politics enjoyed a symbiotic relationship that was crucial to the Revolution's formation and success.[60]

The relationship between religion and American war and diplomacy did not end in 1783. If anything, it deepened irrevocably in the following decades and went on to influence virtually all of America's foreign conflicts. Although most diplomatic historians generally overlook it, the era of the early republic is essential to the study of American foreign relations.[61] The Second Great Awakening, which convulsed and utterly transformed the American religious landscape in the early nineteenth century, did much also to shape early American foreign relations. Fusing antiformalist styles of faith that relied on emotion and devotion—rather than detailed theological debates or close readings of scripture—with already powerful notions of nationalism and expansionism, religion following the Second Great Awakening played a major part in bringing about the War of 1812, Manifest Destiny, and the Mexican-American War. Religion also played an integral role in shaping the antiwar movements that emerged in reaction to each of these campaigns.[62]

If any topic in the history of American foreign relations has had its religious aspects examined thoroughly, it is the role played by Christian missionaries in the turn to formal imperialism in the late nineteenth and early twentieth centuries. Participating particularly heavily in East and Southeast Asia, American missionaries not only sought to bring the religious "blessings" of Christian civilization to the benighted Orient, they also facilitated the imposition of U.S. economic, political, strategic, and cultural imperialism. Indeed, because American missionaries in China were on the ground interacting with the Chinese people and Western agents alike, they have received the kind of sustained academic scrutiny, from both diplomatic and religious historians, normally reserved for diplomats, politicians, intellectuals, industrialists, and theologians.[63] However, although both religious and diplomatic historians have delved thoroughly into the role of missionaries, diplomatic historians have not been as attentive to the wider religious context that was shaping not only America's domestic politics and society but also its foreign relations. Other influences, notably race and Anglo-Saxonism but also gender, have received their due, while religious subjects other than missionaries have not.

While the two world wars have provided fertile ground for religious historians[64] and for diplomatic historians concerned with the politics, strategy, diplomacy, and economics of the wars and the interwar period of "isolationism," the religious influence on U.S. foreign relations from 1914 to 1945 has been noticeably absent in the existing literature. The two most notable exceptions—the religious strain of the isolationists in the 1930s and religious reactions to the dropping of the atomic bomb on Japan in 1945—are usually treated in isolation.[65] As a predominantly political, ideological, and thus conceptual struggle, the same certainly cannot be said of the Cold War. Indeed, the centrality of the intangible, imaginative aspects that propelled the Cold War—credibility, deterrence, propaganda, domino theories, psychological warfare, and the competing ideological constructs of Communism and capitalism—quickly facilitated the rise of International Relations theory, a highly conceptual discipline, as a separate branch of intellectual and academic inquiry. In this sense, it is virtually inconceivable that IR theory and its historical offspring, such as the preoccupation with realism, credibility, and national security, would have attained such academic predominance without the Cold War. Many diplomatic historians, in turn, have viewed the Cold War as predominantly a struggle over concepts and ideas.

Given this general political, academic, and intellectual milieu, it is perhaps natural that the religious aspects of the Cold War have been explored broadly and deeply.[66] Along with the imperial role of Christian missionaries, episodes from the Cold War provide the specific exceptions that prove the general rule about diplomatic historians' agnosticism. Examples from the Cold War abound. British diplomats skillfully played on Truman's religious predilections to draw the United States deeper into a commitment to Western Europe.[67] Towering religious leaders breached the boundaries between theology and politics to promote their own solutions to the Cold War stalemate; Reinhold Niebuhr's Christian realism and Billy Graham's crusading anti-Communism are probably the two most prominent examples.[68] William Inboden deftly navigates the important role religion played in the foreign policies of the Truman and Eisenhower administrations.[69] Andrew Rotter illustrates how American policymakers' perceptions of Christianity, Islam, and Hinduism affected their policy toward South Asia in the early and middle Cold War eras.[70] The creation of the state of Israel in 1948 and the enduring strength of the Jewish presence in America has also had a profound, if contentiously debated, effect on American foreign policy.[71] Likewise, U.S. intervention in Vietnam has had its religious aspects covered extensively. Springing inexorably from the equally pious and anti-Communist 1950s, American religion, as Seth Jacobs has recently illustrated, was a key element in the selection and support of the Catholic Ngo Dinh Diem as leader of South Vietnam.[72] Conversely, a decade later the war unleashed civil trauma, not least of which was the largest antiwar movement in American history. Central to the antiwar movement's stance was a widespread perception that the war was immoral and unjust, and central to this perception was the activism of many of the nation's religious leaders, such as Martin Luther King Jr., William Sloane Coffin Jr., and the radical Jesuit priests Philip and Daniel Berrigan.[73] Nonetheless, outside the Truman, Eisenhower, and Vietnam War eras, there remains an enormous amount of research and analysis to do to link American religion with U.S. foreign policy.

As a genre, biography has also been a fruitful source for religious attitudes and influences on foreign policy, although those whose religious beliefs are examined are usually obvious candidates for such examination because of their famous faith. Due to his father's occupation as a minister and his own avowed Presbyterianism, Woodrow Wilson has been perhaps the easiest target. His idealism is seen mainly as a product of his religious views. However, while some biographers treat Wilson's faith as the primary influence on his approach to foreign policy, others, such as John A. Thompson, conclude that Wilson was essentially politically pragmatic and that religion was Wilson's vague guide to general behavior rather than a blueprint for specific action.[74] Other religious icons of U.S. diplomatic history are equally obvious targets. Although Arthur M. Schlesinger Jr. famously referred to John Foster Dulles as "the high priest of the Cold War," academic historians have been divided, just as they were with Wilson, over just how much Dulles' faith guided his foreign policy.[75] Jimmy Carter, an evangelical Southern Baptist, based his foreign policy on the promotion of human rights, a stance that, according to his national security advisor, Zbigniew Brzezinski, "reflected Carter's own religious beliefs."[76] Ronald Reagan, who proclaimed a devout if amorphous Protestant faith, was even more explicit about religion acting as his guide on foreign policy. Old Testament certainties about good and evil informed his view of the Soviet Union as an "evil empire," while the apocalyptic visions in the book of Revelation had a profound effect on him and provided the source for his efforts to limit nuclear weapons and reduce the threat of nuclear war.[77] And of course, few doubt the importance of religion to the worldview of George W. Bush.[78] Although further research into the religious views of these obvious figures is important, we need to know much more about how religion affected the foreign policies of other major figures of the twentieth century, such as John Hay, Herbert Hoover, Henry Stimson, Franklin Roosevelt, Cordell Hull, Dean Acheson, George Kennan, John Kennedy, Lyndon Johnson, Richard Nixon, Henry Kissinger, George H. W. Bush, and Bill Clinton.

In the end, however, a rubric or theory or methodology that is used to examine history must be able to answer the ultimate historical question: "So what?" Or as Anders Stephanson asks of studies of travel and tourism and their role in diplomatic history, "What precisely does the 'contribution' . . . amount to?"[79] If studies of religion and foreign relations are to have any impact on the field, they must have causal force; they must be able to illustrate, to some degree, a relationship of cause and effect between religious matters and diplomatic events. Otherwise, religion will have little utility and thus little, if any, influence on the ways in which historians perceive the history of American foreign relations. Again, those who wish to utilize religion should look to the historians of gender and race as exemplars. Even the most hardened skeptic could not dismiss gender as a major factor in the origins of the Spanish-American and Philippine-American wars after reading Hoganson's *Fighting for American Manhood*. And few would now doubt the crucial relationship between African Americans and U.S. diplomacy after reading books by Brenda Gayle Plummer, Mary Dudziak, or Thomas Borstelman on the subject.[80]

"Religion," of course, is innately different than "gender" or "race," both as a subject of historical inquiry and as a causal explanation of historical developments. Depending on one's perspective, religion is neither a biological feature of human existence nor a hegemonic, ideological construct imposed from the outside. To be sure, in many important ways religion is as much a cultural construct as are race and gender, including many of the attendant socio-political applications and consequences. But however omnipresent—and, in some societies, perhaps oppressive—it may appear, religion differs fundamentally in that it is both essentially voluntary and escapable. There is an element of choice in the construction of religion that is absent from both gender and race. Patricia R. Hill, a historian of gender who doubts the applicability of religion as a "master variable" in diplomatic history, argues that religion, unlike gender, race, and class, "cannot easily be abstracted as a structural component of social order" because "it has formal, institutional manifestations and authoritative, sacred revelations as well as informal, popular beliefs and practices."[81]

That religion is a different phenomenon is true enough. But is it so easy to dismiss on this basis? If a historical theory is different according to certain and precise criteria but is generally similar in broader, conceptual ways, can it not have a similar causal effect on the historiography? Arguing for the utility of race, Plummer observes that diplomatic historians "have come to realize that U.S. foreign relations are embedded in complex social, economic, cultural, and political factors of domestic as well as foreign origin."[82] Race, Plummer persuasively demonstrates, is one of these factors, but there is no reason why such a description cannot fit religion as well. Arguing for the utility of gender, Costigliola notes "that causes of historical events and situations . . . tend to be complex and diffuse; that not all aspects of such causes are attributable to single agents or conscious intention; and that the connotations of figurative language have real, although never absolute, causal effect."[83] Similarly, Rosenberg argues that "sensitivity to gender ideology can provide avenues for historians of United States foreign relations to investigate the systems of thought that underlie constructions of power and knowledge."[84] Again, it is difficult to see how these descriptions cannot also apply to religion.

Often a strong link between religious cause and diplomatic effect is apparent—Rotter's examination of American attitudes toward South Asia during the Cold War and Jacobs' examination of U.S. policy toward Vietnam in the 1950s are good examples. The biographical approach, in which a pious policymaker's diplomacy is examined in light of his or her religious attitudes, is also a straightforward method. The example of missionaries—as evidenced by their enormous secondary literature, reflecting a field within a field—is probably the best example of the direct link between religious activity and foreign policy.

But religion can also be useful in more indirect ways. Like race and gender, religion is a powerful force in both the domestic and foreign spheres that informs values, norms, and ideas. It is both the producer and recipient, the shaper and the shaped, of culture. Indeed, few human imperatives are as fundamental as the religious. Religion is, and always has been, one of the preeminent forces in American life. On important matters of public policy—especially ones involving decisions of war and peace—there are few who can command as broad, attentive, and responsive an audience as the clergy. Religion can thus help illuminate the intellectual and political origins of any number of diplomatic phenomena, including human rights, collective security, isolationism, morality, preventive and preemptive war, nuclear strategy, foreign aid, imperialism, and inter-ventionism. This is true—one could even argue peculiarly true—of the United States, including its politics, its culture, and its diplomacy. Irreligious, atheistic, or secular elites have not prospered in America. By the more secularized standards of other Western countries, even the figurative descendants of the deist Thomas Jefferson are quite religious and spiritual individuals. In this context, it is the decreasingly religious European continent which is out of step in an increasingly religious world.[85] Rather than the more straightforward political or biographical approaches, uncovering these more indirect influences—what Rotter calls "networks of meaning," in which religion is one of several "filaments that make up webs of significance"—will often require the techniques of the social historian.[86] But it will not be difficult for diplomatic historians to dust for the theological fingerprints on many episodes of U.S. foreign relations. The only trick in doing so will be to decide whether to use a political, biographical, social, or cultural brush.

But no matter how feasible the use of religion is, or how successful it may eventually become, it will certainly not be conclusive.[87] No historiographical interpretation is ever definitive, however powerful or salient or consensual it might seem at the time. There will always exist multiple valid explanations for the same historical development, be it the origins of the Spanish-American War or the Vietnam War. Few scholars know more about the origins of the Cold War than John Gaddis and Melvyn Leffler, yet on the most important questions of causation Gaddis and Leffler do not agree.[88] This is the very nature of historical inquiry. While deploying religion will not settle outstanding, unsettled historiographical debates, it will complicate, and thus significantly add to, our understanding of U.S. foreign relations. And because of the paucity of religion even within the direct approaches to the study of

U.S. foreign relations—case studies, biography, and nongovernmental religious organizations such as foreign missions—it is an understanding that continues to elude diplomatic history. But this means there is also tremendous room for growth.

Yet despite recent encouraging signs and the lack of insurmountable barriers, the histories of American religion and American foreign relations have evolved separately and still remain apart. This need not be the case. Filling such an enormous (but enormously promising) gap will not be too difficult. Diplomatic historians should take advantage of the different and enlightening perspective of religious history. My three theories explaining the existing reluctance need not pose insurmountable barriers. Exploring the religious dimension of diplomatic history need not become partisan because inquiry into and explanation of religion do not equal a rejection of the secularist standpoint assumed by many to be necessary to historical study.[89] Just as historians of slavery are not compelled to adopt the moral or political viewpoint of either the slave or the slaveholder, or just as historians of Britain do not feel obliged to accept the agenda of the British government, historians who embrace religion as a subject do not need to argue on behalf of a particular denomination, faith, or belief system. In this regard, secularist diplomatic historians have a worthy predecessor to emulate: as Jon Butler and Edmund S. Morgan have recently pointed out, it was Perry Miller, an avowed atheist, who rescued the Puritans from historical derision and relative obscurity and remains their most influential historian.[90] Finally, while religion is potentially diffuse, imprecise, and unwieldy, the same could easily be said for gender, race, and culture, and few would doubt their causal utility. In short, there are few justifiable defenses for diplomatic historians' agnosticism. Religion's potential is clear. It is now simply a matter of spreading the faith.

Chapter 2

Bringing Religion into International Religious Freedom Policy

Thomas F. Farr

The Duty which we owe our Creator, and the manner of our discharging it, can be governed only by Reason and Conviction, not by Compulsion or Violence; and therefore all men are equally entitled to the full and free exercise of it according to the dictates of conscience, unpunished and unrestrained by the Magistrate.

INTRODUCTION
The Strategic Salience of Religious Freedom

This chapter proposes a comprehensive rethinking of U.S. policy on international religious freedom (IRF). It argues that American policymakers should, as Scott Thomas puts it, "promote religious freedom as if the truthfulness of people's religious convictions mattered."[1] The argument proceeds from two propositions which are belatedly gaining currency among International Relations scholars and within the foreign policy community. First, for the foreseeable future religion will have a significant and increasing impact on public matters in virtually every region of the world.[2] As one group of scholars has recently concluded, religion has "returned from exile."[3] The vast majority of the world's population will not only be committed to a particular religious tradition but their beliefs will influence social norms and political behaviors, government policies, regional trends, and transnational movements. A world of public faith will continue to have serious implications for the interests of the United States abroad and the security and prosperity of the American people at home. While I cannot demonstrate this proposition here, I consider it sufficiently well established in the burgeoning literature on religion and international relations to serve as a reliable point of departure.[4]

For this reason, the religious teachings and actions of other peoples and other nations should be integrated into the official American understanding of the world and our strategy for engaging it. This does not mean that diplomats must be theologians, any more than they must be lawyers, economists, or political philosophers. It means that they must rediscover the first principle of true realism, which is to understand things as they are and to call them by their right names. Diplomats must therefore attain the capacity to know and to address human behavior in all its forms, including beliefs and practices formed by an increasing global diversity of religious convictions.

Second, the American foreign policy establishment is at present ill-prepared, both philosophically and bureaucratically, to address a world of public faith.[5] A whole variety of principles and habits from across the ideological spectrum of American society feeds a secularist diplomatic culture. The distinction between secular and secularist is important. The United States is a secular society in that it seeks to maintain a proper differentiation between the overlapping spheres of government and religion. Vigorous debates continue about whether the balance has tipped too far in one direction or the other in domestic politics and in the influencing of American foreign policy.[6]

But among many of the professionals and scholars in the American foreign policy community itself, there has long been a *secularist* approach to religion—an official, if sometimes implicit, reticence about addressing the religious factors in other cultures and indeed in seeing culture as an expression of religion at all. The explanations are varied and cut across the red-blue, political-cultural divide in America. Our diplomatic tendencies in such matters clearly flow in some respects from what is commonly referred to as modern liberal secularism. Elizabeth Shakman Hurd even speaks of "the political authority of secularism" in international relations.[7] But such tendencies are also nourished by habits of thought, including theological habits of thought, present in the American right. More importantly, the various schools of American diplomacy struggle mightily either to avoid the subject of religion or to assume it away, albeit for very different reasons. The fact is that no matter which political party has been in charge, and which version of foreign affairs has been in the ascendant, American diplomacy has been largely passive and ineffective in its engagement with an international order influenced by faith.

A 2007 study by the Center for Strategic and International Affairs has confirmed this problem. After surveying the treatment of religion across the spectrum of American foreign policy agencies, it found that U.S. government officials are often reluctant to address the issue of religion, whether in response to a secular U.S. legal and political tradition, in the context of America's Judeo-Christian image overseas, or simply because religion is perceived as too complicated or sensitive. Current U.S. government frameworks for approaching religion are narrow, often approaching religions as problematic or monolithic forces, overemphasizing a terrorism-focused analysis of Islam, and sometimes marginalizing religion as a peripheral humanitarian or cultural issue. Institutional capacity to understand and approach religion is limited due to legal limitations, lack of religious expertise or training, minimal influence for religion-related initiatives, and a government primarily structured to engage with other official state actors.[8]

Ironically, this policy deficiency persists amid a significant increase in the number of scholarly books and articles concerning religion and foreign policy. One of the unanticipated results of 9/11 was an added momentum to something already underway—the abandonment of the so-called secularization theory, according to which religion was inevitably withering with the advance of modernity. A few scholars have questioned the theory for decades, but its assertions were for the most part too comforting to be challenged by mere facts. The attacks of September 11 proved to be, at least for some, the fact that would not be ignored.

Since 2001 we have seen a proliferation of publications and programs dealing with religion and international affairs, especially among policy-oriented think tanks such as the Pew Forum on Religion and Public Life, the Ethics and Public Policy Center, the Rand Corporation, and the Center for Strategic and International Studies (all of which existed prior to 9/11 but whose interest in religion and foreign policy has increased). And yet, as late as four years after the terrorist attacks on the American homeland, the Henry Luce Foundation found it necessary to invite selected U.S. academic institutions specializing in international affairs to apply for grants on religion and foreign policy. Its purpose was to get them to pay attention to an issue that they had largely ignored.[9] While the relationship between religion and foreign policy is getting greater emphasis among some policy institutions, it is still struggling for attention among academic institutions who seek to educate and train our future diplomats—those who will carry out America's engagement with the world. This chapter hopes to assist in that worthy enterprise.

While correcting this deficiency will not be easy, a potentially effective and even potent vehicle is at hand. America's existing statutory policy of promoting international religious freedom should be recalibrated, broadened, and integrated throughout our foreign policy apparatus to help the United States meet the challenges presented by a world of faith. Such a change will require fresh thinking about religion, about freedom, and about the relationship between the two. It will require new policy mandates from a president, the urging of Congress, a determined secretary of state, strongly supportive political appointees at Foggy Bottom, and new training for America's diplomats.

This project will in part constitute a work of recovery. It will be worthwhile for U.S. policymakers and diplomats to recall the relative success that their own country has had in balancing the competing authorities of religion and state. A case in point: on June 1, 1660, magistrates from the Massachusetts Bay Colony hanged Mary Dyer on Boston Commons for her persistence in believing and proselytizing the Quaker faith.[10] In 1791 the first sixteen words of the Bill of Rights guaranteed the free exercise of religion at the national level. What had happened in the intervening 131 years was not the secularization of American society or politics, nor the triumph of Enlightenment rationalism, but the mutual development of religious doctrine and political culture. Rediscovering this American experience will be important for American diplomacy, not in order to impose the First Amendment model on others, but to overcome the crippling presumption that religion and freedom, or faith and reason, are irreconcilable.

SOURCES OF RESISTANCE

A major obstacle to this project will be the premises and habits of thought present in U.S. diplomacy's various schools, such as realism, liberal internationalism, and neoconservatism.[11] These schools are repositories of what ought to be our best thinking on how America should engage the world, but until very recently they have had little to say about religion as a policy issue. In the past decade their reluctance has been challenged by the 1998 International Religious Freedom (IRF) Act, the emergence of Islamist terrorism, and rising concerns on the American left about the influence of the Christian right on foreign policy, all of which have occasioned a good deal of commentary.

Those factors have in some ways actually increased resistance among foreign affairs thinkers and the general public to considering religion as a policy matter. The IRF Act has focused the State Department on the humanitarian objectives of denouncing persecution and saving victims, not promoting freedom in any long-term political sense.[12] As such, IRF policy has neither had a significant impact on worldwide religious persecution nor overcome the perception that it is designed to make the world safe for American missionaries. Islamist terrorism has elicited a wide spectrum of responses from the U.S. foreign policy community, from a denial that religion has anything to do with the terrorists' actions to the arguments that Islam is too evil or too violent to engage. Fears on the left about the resurgence of religion in America—a social phenomenon that some observers have labeled the Fourth Great Awakening[13]—have deepened suspicions about any official policy that treats religious beliefs as a public matter.

The moral and legal framework for America's hands-off approach to religion in foreign policy is provided by the concept of a "wall of separation" between religion and public life. Many Americans, religious and not, liberal and conservative, have come to understand religious liberty as embodied in that phrase. The wall, thought to be established in the Constitution, was putatively built to protect us from the divisiveness and (a more recent fear) the moral judgmentalism of religious groups in America. So understood, "religious freedom" requires that religion-based belief and practice be protected but privatized.[14] Because religion and religiously informed moral judgments are based on absolute truth claims, and such claims and judgments endanger the compromises necessary for democracy, faith-based "absolutism" must be cordoned outside the public square in order to protect the democratic system.

This idea of religious liberty is both ahistorical and tendentious,[15] but it is highly influential in the foreign affairs establishment. Not long ago I queried a lawyer in a foreign policy agency about why U.S.-funded democracy programs in the Middle East avoided direct engagement with religious communities. By way of explanation, he cited parts of the Supreme Court's "Lemon test." We must determine, he wrote, "whether there has been a violation of the constitutionally required separation of church and state . . . [i.e.,] whether the funded activity has a secular purpose and, even if it does, whether the funded activity has a primary effect of advancing or inhibiting religion."[16] In other words, a court test for determining whether the Constitution has been violated in the United States is cited as a rationale for restraining America's engagement of religion abroad.[17]

That view of religious freedom is, of course, controversial as a domestic matter, and has in some ways been abandoned by the Supreme Court itself. Moreover, it is slowly being challenged in foreign affairs by intermittent U.S. programs that do engage religious belief and practice. But in the twenty-first century an ad hoc policy concerning religion is destined to fail. Unfortunately, the "wall of separation" understanding of religious liberty (also known as "strict separationism") and its parallel insistence on the privatization of faith tends to be accepted by most members of the permanent bureaucracy in Washington D.C., by the professoriate, the media, and Hollywood. In American universities it has become so entrenched in academic orthodoxy that a Harvard curriculum committee implicitly made the extraordinary admission in 2006 that Harvard graduates were not being educated to know "the role of religion in contemporary, historical or future events."[18] More to the point, strict separationism is the view assumed by most senior members of the U.S. Foreign Service, many of whom were educated in elite institutions like Harvard, who are charged with "promoting religious freedom" as part of American foreign policy.

But skepticism about official U.S. involvement with foreign religious communities is not the exclusive preserve of strict separationists. Some who reject the "wall of separation" at home believe that our government, especially the State Department, is simply incompetent to address the issue abroad. This view was embraced by some who led the campaign for a new international religious freedom policy and still has its adherents. Responding to my advocacy for more U.S. engagement with Muslim jurists, a veteran religious freedom activist (and a religious conservative) told me he had "no faith in the U.S. government's ability to do this sort of thing intelligently: Washington will end up subsidizing the Islamic counterparts of Hans Küng [a Roman Catholic dissident]."

The upshot of all these views is that, while most of the world is steeped in religious thought and religiously informed action, the agencies charged with understanding the world and furthering American interests in it are not yet up to the task. And, for the most part, there is little public pressure for them to change. There are, of course, exceptions—international affairs thinkers, policy officials, or active diplomats who for whatever reason, happen to have an interest in the subject.[19] Indeed, there are signs that their numbers are growing, especially in the wake of the debate over radical Islam. But, while religion as a topic of discussion in foreign policy has certainly increased, its emergence is not yet part of an integrated pattern.

In the twenty-first century, this simply will not do. Creedal commitments have too much impact on the public behavior that affects American security for our diplomats to avert their eyes, treating religion as a private matter or addressing it only if they happen to have a personal interest. American diplomacy should treat faith much as it does politics or economics—as factors that drive the world of men, women, and nations in important ways. U.S. foreign policy must begin to engage the various aspects of religion systematically, not as it suits, or does not suit, the fancy of whoever happens to be on the spot. The quality and effectiveness of America's engagement with a world of public faith should not depend on whether a Southern Baptist, a Rawlsian secularist, or a lapsed Catholic is in charge.

That said, my concern in this chapter is not with the religious Right or the religious Left or any other direction of religious persuasion. Much has been written about the impact on American national security policy from lobbying by Christians of one sort or another, or Jews of one sort or another, or, increasingly, Muslims of one sort or another. My purpose is not to lionize or demonize one or another. The starting point from which American foreign policy should encounter the world of religion is not the dogma of any particular religious tradition or any particular secularist philosophy. The starting point should be that of American national interests, of religious realism, and of religious freedom properly understood. The United States should address the public effects of religion, both positive and negative, by promoting religious freedom in the fullest sense of that term, including the advancement of solutions to one of the foremost national security issues of our day—achieving a stable and liberal balance between the overlapping authorities of religion and state. The failure to achieve such a balance has in many states fed religious persecution, led to social and political instability, and encouraged the religion-based terrorism of groups like al Qaeda and Hezbollah.

Religion has also had an important but little-noticed influence on the nation many experts believe is the most consequential for American interests—China. There the Communist government fears religion so vehemently that it admits capitalists into the Communist Party but not religious believers. Chinese attempts to control religious practice have led to grave persecution and injustice and have triggered a significant humanitarian reaction within religious and human rights circles in the

United States. Those policies have also reinforced the American diplomatic habit of addressing cases and seeking prisoner releases.

But U.S. policy has virtually ignored a more strategic problem: an economically and militarily powerful, regionally ambitious, and nuclear armed China also has an exploding population of religious adherents. The movements they represent, especially evangelical forms of Protestant Christianity, but also Catholicism, Islam, and Buddhism, present a growing dilemma for Chinese authorities. There is no empirical evidence that China's surge of religion can successfully be repressed or controlled short of another brutal and destructive Cultural Revolution. The trajectory suggests that either the Chinese will find a way to accommodate religion or turn it into the very thing they (and we) most fear: deep social and political instability. The United States must begin to address this problem.

There are, of course, limits to what U.S. foreign policy can and should do with respect to the religious convictions active in other societies. American officials cannot fruitfully engage directly in the theological and religious debates taking place within various areas of the Muslim world—or for that matter within other influential religious communities, such as Russian Orthodoxy or Indian Hinduism. To do so would invite scorn and suspicion and would undermine the mutual respect which must undergird a successful U.S. policy. Muslims must decide on the authoritative interpretations of the Koran and the hadith; Christians, the Bible and its teachings.

But America is not served by ignorance, indifference, or confusion about the impact of religion on the moral and political norms necessary to protect the nation's security in the twenty-first century. American diplomacy must not only understand the religious traditions of the world and their adherents, but must have a clear policy with which to engage and influence them, and the governments under which they live, in ways that further American interests. We must find ways to demonstrate that public religion and liberal governance are not only compatible but can be mutually supportive. My point can best be conveyed by way of an extended example.

BEYOND "HUMANITARIANISM"

The problem came briefly but sharply into focus during the spring of 2006. The news had been dominated for months by the terrible sectarian violence in Iraq and the fragility of that country's struggling democracy. But this particular week's spotlight shifted to a courtroom in democratic

Afghanistan, where a man named Abdul Rahman was in grave danger of being found guilty of the crime of changing his religion. If convicted, Mr. Rahman would be beheaded.

It had been over four years since U.S.-led forces had invaded Afghanistan and ousted the cruel, theocratic Taliban government, one which had not only harbored Osama bin Laden and al Qaeda, but had sanctioned the stoning of women and the brutal execution of men for the slightest deviation from their version of Islamic purity. After the overthrow of the Taliban, Afghans had elected a parliament and a president and had drafted and ratified a democratic constitution. The 2006 U.S. National Security Strategy proudly observed that the constitution guaranteed for Afghans' "rights and freedoms unprecedented in their history."[20] The implications for America's national security were clear: "Through the freedom agenda, we . . . have promoted the best long term answer to Al Qaeda's agenda: the freedom and dignity that comes when human liberty is protected by effective democratic institutions."[21] The wretched rule of the Taliban, and with it Islamist extremism, seemed to have been banished like the memory of a nightmare.

But now, in democratic Afghanistan, Abdul Rahman was being tried for apostasy—converting from Islam to Christianity—a crime meriting death under the prosecution's interpretation of the constitution. What happened in the days surrounding his trial revealed a great deal about Afghanistan and about the foreign policy of the United States. It suggested something troubling about the way both governments viewed the issue of religion, including its proper role in a democracy, the true meaning of religious freedom, and the relevance of those issues to Islamist extremism.

For one thing, the trial afforded a glimpse into the debate among Muslims over what their religion requires of them and of a democratic government, a debate sometimes referred to as the "war of ideas" within Islam. For another, it demonstrated the confusion that often reigns in U.S. policy precincts when it comes to the subject of religion. For most U.S. officials, the Rahman trial was a high-profile humanitarian case.[22] But it was in reality much more than that. The trial pointed to a flaw in Afghan democracy that directly affected the national security of the American people.

When the apostasy charge became public, the U.S. State Department's initial response was to insist on a fair and "transparent" trial.[23] Calls from outraged Christian and human rights groups soon flooded the White House and Congress. Congressional hearings were held. One influential evangelical Christian, Charles Colson, asserted that the trial called into question "the whole credibility of our foreign policy."[24] Soon the president said publicly that he was deeply troubled by the Rahman affair and the State Department swung into action. After pressure from the United States and other countries, Mr. Rahman was released. He immediately fled Afghanistan in fear of his life and was given asylum in Italy.

In one sense, the freeing of Abdul Rahman was a success for the U.S. policy mandated by the 1998 IRF Act. In the years since the passage of that law, a new religious freedom office at the Department of State had managed cases of religious persecution, incidents of abuse that, prior to the law, had not always been pursued with alacrity. Now, in the wake of Mr. Rahman's escape, the head of that office told a congressional hearing that he had "never been more proud of our government's work than I was with regard to this case." Both the president and the secretary of state, he said, had made it clear to the world how important this issue was to the United States.[25]

But what *was* the issue? The saving of Mr. Rahman was certainly a humanitarian act worthy of our nation. But there was another, far more serious problem. The United States had, in two successive National Security Strategies, declared its intent to implant democracy in Afghanistan and Iraq as a means of fighting Islamist extremism, as a way to "drain the swamps" of the social pathologies that fed radicalism. The Afghan constitution was heralded as a major step in that direction, and it was in some ways a very progressive document. It created a presidential system, an elective parliament by universal adult suffrage, and an independent judiciary. It provided for free expression and equality under the law. In its own words, the constitution sought to create "a civil society free of oppression, atrocity, discrimination, and violence and based on the rule of law, social justice, protection of human rights, and dignity, and ensuring the fundamental rights and freedoms of the people."[26]

These were noble goals. But they did not affect the Afghan court's understanding of Mr. Rahman's crime. Nor did U.S. officials pay much attention to the bizarre inconsistency in the Afghan democracy's official declaration that there was no contradiction between protecting human rights and the judicially required execution of a man for his peaceful religious practices. The justice system had endorsed the use of violence by the democratic state to coerce the religious conscience. Afghanistan was not a Saudi theocracy, where public beheadings for religious crimes were routine. It was a democracy, brokered by the United States and celebrated for its nascent liberality precisely because it would provide an antidote to extremism—the kind of extremism that had produced the Taliban and provided a safe haven for Osama bin Laden and al Qaeda.

The Americans had worked hard to make the drafting of the constitution a success. They had pulled together an impressive international effort almost immediately after the events of September 11, 2001. In October the Taliban had been overthrown, and by early December, U.S., UN, and other officials had helped broker the Bonn Agreement, which provided the legal framework for a transitional government. The Bonn Agreement also mandated a commission to draft a new constitution. That process took almost two years, but by January 2004, it was ratified and became law.

That month the U.S. ambassador to Afghanistan, in an op-ed in the *Washington Post*, hailed the new constitution as a milestone on the path to democracy and stability. It set forth, he wrote, "parallel commitments to Islam and to human rights. While embracing Islam as the state religion, the document provides broad religious freedom—allowing adherents of other faiths to practice their religions and observe religious rites."[27]

Clearly something was missing here; there was an evident disconnect or a misunderstanding. How could an American official so confidently declare religious freedom secure in a document that others read to permit the execution of a man for his peaceful religious beliefs? It was not a slip of the pen. The same assertion—"the constitution provides for religious freedom"—was made almost two years later in the Department of State's *Annual Report on International Religious Freedom*.[28]

Nor was Mr. Rahman's case an anomaly. In 2002, just after the formation of the transitional government, Afghanistan's Chief Justice Fazul Hadi Shinwari had publicly denounced the new women's affairs minister, Sima Samar, for telling a magazine that she did not believe in sharia. She was formally charged with the crime of blasphemy, and ultimately resigned for fear of her life. Under U.S. pressure the charges against Samar were dropped, but the problem did not go away. Muslim journalists were tried and convicted for blasphemy, for the crime of offending Islam.[29]

After the constitution was ratified, the Supreme Court created within its administrative structure a "Fatwa Council" composed of Islamic clerics. It was given the job of reviewing questions of Islamic law and began, on its own initiative, to issue rulings in matters not brought to the Supreme Court.[30] In a 2003 meeting with the U.S. Commission on International Religious Freedom—a watchdog agency created by the IRF Act—the chief justice explained that he rejected religious freedom, freedom of expression, and equality of the sexes.[31]

In the State Department, officials knew that such incidents were not good for Afghanistan's image, or theirs. The IRF Commission held public conferences and publicly implored the president to require the department to pay more attention to the issue of religious freedom.[32] But within Foggy Bottom all these problems were viewed as unfortunate humanitarian discrepancies that the Afghans were going to have to work out. The American embassy complained privately to the new government about Shinwari and the blasphemy charges. But it had sprung both Rahman and Samar, had it not? It had the much larger problems of pulling the country together after decades of war and destruction.

It did not occur to most American officials that these were not mere incidents, nor the actions of a single rogue jurist, but indicators of a much larger problem. In fact, the constitution had not guaranteed religious freedom. For non-Muslims it protected the right "to perform their religious rites within the limits of the provisions of the law. In Afghanistan," the constitution noted pointedly, "no law can be contrary to the sacred religion of Islam."[33] This was a pinched version of religious freedom indeed, a "right to rites," as one observer wryly noted.[34] It wasn't much better than what non-Muslims were permitted to do in Saudi Arabia, which was to worship in private.

For some U.S. officials, this "right to rites" constituted the sole content of religious freedom. If people could pray and worship together, what more did they need? Besides, there were only a handful of non-Muslims in Afghanistan. The "other religious groups," as the State Department put it, consisted of "Sikhs, Hindus, and one Jew." As for Christians, there was "a small, hidden Christian community . . . estimates ranged from 500 to 8 thousand." Together the non-Muslims comprised less than 1 percent of the population.[35] When the IRF office and the IRF Commission complained about the lack of religious freedom, some officials wondered if they were not really trying to pave the way for missionaries. That would hardly be helpful to the new government.

The problem for American national security, however, was not missionaries. The fates of Mr. Rahman, Ms. Samar, and the others were indicators that Afghanistan was not moving toward the kind of democracy that would contain Islamist radicalism. The constitution had created a window through which extremism could lawfully enter, contend with the reformers and the moderates, and stand an excellent chance of defeating them. In fact, no one had true religious freedom in Afghanistan, including the Sunni and Shia Muslims that constituted 99 percent of the population. Like the others, they were generally free to perform rites—and to worship and attend to the private imperatives of Islam. They could attend mosques and follow the five pillars of their religion.

But religious freedom means more than private activity. Among other things, it means the right to talk publicly about religion. It apparently did not occur to U.S. policymakers that "draining the swamps" of extremism would require establishing a public space in Afghanistan for facilitating such talk, and ensuring the constitution encouraged it. As it stood, there were compelling reasons for Muslims (let alone non-Muslims) not to express themselves publicly on Islam, its proper relationship with the state, and its value to democratic stability. The courts had virtually unchecked power to decide what the undefined values of Islam were and to apply them in the Afghan public square. Legislators had their own platform, but the court's undefined power was far greater. It would take courage for a Muslim to suggest publicly, as Ms. Samar had done, that Islam did not require the execution of apostates, or that sharia itself permitted broad religious freedom, including freedom of expression and women's rights. Most Muslims would not take the risk.

In short, the U.S.-brokered Afghan polity was blocking precisely what it was intended to energize—democracy as the agent of moderation. In Washington, however, policymakers simply did not see it that way. In deciding what was important to make democracy work and drain the swamps of extremism, they paid little attention to the religion-state issue. In endless discussions of the "war of ideas" raging within Islam, they saw the issue of religious freedom in Afghanistan as largely irrelevant.

CULTURE MATTERS

In the wake of the American experience in Iraq, it seems clear that some cultural groundwork must be laid before a nation can achieve the kind of durable self-government sought by the Bush administration in the greater Middle East as an antidote to Islamist extremism. History provides ample evidence that lasting constitutional democracies do not emerge from elections and constitutions alone, and they are rarely imposed from without. The United States has long accepted a version of this "culture first" argument. In the early 1980s the Reagan administration and Congress established the National Endowment for Democracy (NED), which was designed to implant the institutions of liberal civil society around the world. The goal, in other words, was to seed democratic cultures. But the programs funded by the NED were by and large secularist. They tended to avoid faith communities, as if religion had nothing to do with culture or had to be separated from society in order to grow democratic institutions.

Until 9/11 most of those democracy dollars were spent outside the Middle East, in large part because Arab and Persian versions of Islam were considered antithetical to democracy and because the United States equated "political Islam" with Islamist extremism. With the adoption of President Bush's "foreign strategy of freedom" in Iraq, Afghanistan, and elsewhere, however, U.S. democracy funding began to pour into the broader Middle East. Programs such as the State Department's Middle East Partnership Initiative focused on women's movements and other important aspects of civil society. But here too it remained largely taboo to engage directly the subject of religion.

The influence of religion on culture and politics, of course, is not limited to Muslim nations. The consolidation of liberal self-government in virtually every society will depend in some measure on the role played by religious communities and religiously informed norms and actions. This is true of non-Muslim nations as diverse as Russia, China, and India. Indeed, it is true of virtually every nation on earth.

A handful of officials at the State Department, in the White House, and in Congress developed anxieties about this habit of not thinking systematically about religion—the tendency not to take it seriously unless it was pointing a gun at you or flying aircraft into your buildings. These officials understood that culture drives politics and that in many societies, religion drives culture. They believed that the political reform pushed by American foreign policy could influence but was unlikely to transform the cultures of the greater Middle East, at least not in the course of a few years. They supported the president's freedom agenda, including its premise that democratic procedures and economic growth could help destroy the tyrannies that wracked that region and fed Islamist extremism. But they also feared that political and economic liberties alone were insufficient to alter any countervailing values and attitudes shaped by the extremists and their ideas.

Largely because of their concerns over this issue, these officials had helped to generate more than one "engaging Islam" initiative among U.S. foreign policy agencies.[36] But in the end they had not succeeded in focusing the policy process on the religious aspects of culture. Internally they asked but failed to elicit answers to an increasingly critical policy question: how can the United States succeed in promoting stable, liberal self-government in Muslim nations unless it can influence the religious climate of opinion? There were useful experiments to engage religious ideas in a few countries, such as Indonesia and Nigeria. But these were exceptions that proved the rule. In the end, there was no answer to the question. It was just too hard.[37]

In a 2006 book, former secretary of state Madeleine Albright noted that diplomats and policymakers in the 1990s ignored the role of religion in shaping the world. To them, she wrote, the subject of religion "was above and beyond reason; it evoked the deepest passions; and historically, it was the cause of much bloodshed. Diplomats in my era were taught not to invite trouble, and no subject seemed more inherently treacherous than religion."[38] By 2006 Albright was long gone from Foggy Bottom, but the diplomatic mindset she described was well rooted and still dominant.

The tendency to see charges of apostasy and blasphemy as little more than isolated humanitarian problems, unconnected to the freedom agenda, stemmed from a culture as embedded in the State Department as Islam was in Afghanistan. Most American diplomats and foreign policymakers do not think of public human affairs and political structures in religious categories. This does not mean that they are nonreligious or antireligion. To the contrary, many are deeply religious men and women. But for many in the field of foreign affairs, religion is understood as properly a private matter, largely unconnected to the processes of reasoning and therefore unsusceptible to rational analysis. They tend to understand politics and culture in modern "realist" terms, that is, that people and nations are "rational actors," which means less that they apply reason in any classical sense than that they are motivated by power and economic interest.

Developments in the broader Middle East ought to have provided evidence that a hands-off view of religion is a highly unrealistic basis for U.S. attempts to encourage stable democracy. It not only reinforces the tendency to treat an apostasy trial as a humanitarian issue rather than an indicator of deep cultural and political problems, but also reflects an incomplete understanding of how to root liberal norms and institutions in highly religious societies. Afghanistan is a multiethnic and tribal nation that presents many challenges to an aspiring midwife of democracy. Foremost among them is the fact that some version of Islam has a deep and abiding influence on many of the Afghan people, whether or not the Taliban is in charge. Indeed, an Afghan Islamism willing to employ the democratic state to coerce religious consciences suggested a continuing affinity with Taliban-like belief and practice that should not have been ignored.

Unfortunately for the Afghan people and the American freedom agenda, the Taliban in 2004 began making a comeback in certain areas of the country. Reactions by both the Bush administration and its political opponents understandably emphasized the need for more security. The American commander of NATO forces in Afghanistan requested more troops. Leaders of the Democratic Party agreed and called for both a redeployment of American forces and more funding for infrastructure. As one U.S. commander on the ground put it, "Where the roads end, the Taliban begin."[39]

Clearly the reemergence of the Taliban in Afghanistan is a security issue of the first order. Polls in late 2006 showed that the memory of Taliban terror among Afghanis remained extremely high and that most strongly disapproved of its return.[40] But the problem posed by the Taliban is not merely one of security. If every current Taliban leader were killed along with the leaders of al Qaeda (including Osama bin Laden) living on the border of Afghanistan and Pakistan, an underlying problem would remain. That problem is the set of violent and destructive ideas represented in the trial of Abdul Rahman. The energizing core of those ideas is the conviction of some Muslims that Islam requires violence, by its adherents and by the Muslim state, as a means of fulfilling man's obligation to God.

Among all the strategies adopted by the United States to undermine Islamist terrorism and to encourage stable liberal governments in the Muslim world, we have thus far failed to credit one of the most important objectives: the religious rationale for violence must be turned on its head. Mainstream Muslims who reject violence and coercion not in spite of Islam, but because of it, must move to the fore. Until that happens, U.S. policy in Afghanistan and Iraq and its counter-terrorism efforts around the world are unlikely to succeed.

To put the issue this way raises some sympathy for the religion-avoidance syndrome common among American foreign policy officials. For one thing, the presence of U.S. forces in Afghanistan and Iraq, clearly necessary for security, severely complicates our capacity to influence culture. But even beyond the problems of security and military forces, the obstacles involved in thinking about how to influence the religious aspects of culture are daunting in the theological realm, let alone the policy world. For any policymaker to consider the direct engagement of Islamic and other religious communities—for example, how to facilitate the processes of internal reform—would require serious thought about the role of religion in human affairs. It would also require fresh thinking about a concept that Americans of all political persuasions talk about with great conviction: religious freedom.

Part of the problem is that both religion and religious liberty are often understood as non-public phenomena. This orientation is reflected in the frequent use of phrases such as "freedom of worship" and "religious tolerance," as in the 2002 U.S. *National Security Strategy*.[41] But these formulations for the most part leave unaddressed the issue of *public* manifestations of religion in a democracy. Moreover, American foreign policy officials routinely use terms like "religious liberty," "freedom of conscience," and "freedom of belief" as if everyone agrees on what they mean. But they do not agree.

Most who have had responsibility for U.S. foreign affairs since the end of the Cold War have not attempted to reach a consensus on the meaning of religious freedom any more than they have agreed that they must pay serious attention to the religious beliefs and practices of other societies. They have not internalized the reality—of which the Rahman trial was merely one bit of compelling evidence—that the world in which America is engaged is increasingly affected by public manifestations of religious conviction.

The attitudes that have handicapped American foreign policy in Afghanistan have echoes in the "War on Terror." During the 2006 congressional elections, Democrats and Republicans disputed the question of whether the American military invasion of Iraq had exacerbated Islamist terror—whether the resources and manpower used in Iraq would have been better employed finding Osama bin Laden and fighting al Qaeda and its offshoots elsewhere (including in Afghanistan). Reasonable people might disagree over the answer, but it is the wrong question. At the very least, it is not the only question. What we should be asking ourselves is how to influence the religious war currently taking place *within* Islam over its meaning and its future. And we should be asking similar questions about the religious aspects of other national security issues, such as those presented by China, India, Russia, and even Europe.

TOWARD AN INTEGRATED IRF POLICY

Part of the reason for the relative ineffectiveness of U.S. IRF policy is that even the focus on religious persecution has been compartmentalized and isolated from larger American national security strategies. IRF actions have too often consisted of fruitless rhetorical denunciations of persecuting governments. It is true—and important—that religious prisoners have been freed by State Department efforts. Each removal of a human being from harm's way is a noble achievement worthy of our nation and the American diplomats who have helped to bring it about. But in the world of persecution prisoners are, alas, fungible assets; victims liberated after U.S. pressure are easily replaced by others.

More to the point, opposing persecution and freeing prisoners, however successfully, is not the same as advancing religious freedom. Clearly religious freedom and religious persecution are incompatible, and it is entirely appropriate and commensurate with American values for U.S. human rights policy to oppose this kind of degrading abuse of human dignity, just as it does others (such as torture of people because of their ethnicity or gender). Further, it makes good sense to develop policies that can have a chance of altering or ending persecutory behavior, whether it is by governments or private actors sanctioned or ignored by governments.

But, to repeat, a decade of U.S. IRF policy has for the most part not succeeded in altering, much less ending, persecutory behaviors by governments or private actors. Nor does IRF policy as currently configured seem likely to produce such an outcome. Since the passage of the IRF Act, it is arguable that U.S. intervention has significantly reduced levels of religious persecution in four countries—Serbia-Kosovo, Afghanistan, Iraq, and Vietnam. In the first three cases, the reductions were due to military action, not IRF policy. In each of these countries, human rights abuses on the basis of religion fell dramatically after the respective despotic regimes were overthrown, but in the ensuing years levels of persecution have crept back up. And in none of these cases has the United States sought in any comprehensive way to "advance religious freedom." Its IRF policy has scarcely been involved except in an ad hoc and inconsistent way. In Vietnam, important strides were made by IRF diplomacy and the actions of the IRF ambassador at large, John Hanford. But it remains unclear whether progress in Vietnam will be permanent. In any case, it was the exception that tended to prove the rule.[42]

The fact is that a regime of religious liberty is much more than the absence of religious persecution. Religious freedom anchors a political order in which individuals and religious communities are not only free to worship privately, but also to act *publicly* in significant ways—to worship in community, to manifest religious truth claims, and to influence public policy, bounded by the same democratic norms and laws that limit other individuals and associations in civil society. Where religious liberty truly exists, citizens are certainly free from torture and abuse, but something much more fundamental has occurred in the political order: the religion-state relationship has reconciled by means of a culturally sustainable compact. In such a polity the natural tensions between the claims of religion and the claims of the liberal state are continually reconciled and rebalanced. If U.S. diplomacy were successful in encouraging this aspect of democratic development, it would help ensure that democratic elections and democratic constitutions yielded stable, liberal governments rather than fragile concoctions of sectarian interest groups.

In short, the United States can attack the very structures of persecution by advancing ideas and institutions of religious freedom that support the same goals as liberal governance—the flourishing of citizens in a well-ordered civil society. In order to accomplish this, however, America's international religious freedom policy must recognize the particular role that religion often plays in public lives and the role that it can play in the public life of a liberal democracy, always taking into account variations in culture, ethnicity, nationality, politics, and economic development.

The religion-state covenant in a successful secular liberal democracy entails a proper differentiation between religion and state. As such, it requires religious communities to forswear the use of civil authority to privilege membership in their organizations, advance their forms of worship, or coerce acceptance of revealed truth claims not subject to rational public discourse and assent. Christians in a liberal democracy, for example, may not use the laws to require baptism or belief in the Trinity. Liberal democratic Muslim governments may not mandate legal penalties for apostasy or condition citizenship on being a Muslim. Nor may they employ religious norms to disadvantage women, non-Muslims, or disfavored Muslims in civil society by denying them the vote or equality under the laws.

But liberal democracy does not require the banishment of religion from the moral judgments that inform public policy and shape the laws and norms designed to promote the common good. Indeed, the history of successful democratic societies with powerful religious communities, not least the United States but also some nations of Western Europe and India, provides evidence for the value of religious involvement in the public square. There is even some evidence of this kind of development in a few Islamic democracies, such as Turkey and Indonesia. Lasting, stable democracies—what scholars call "consolidated" democracies—are possible only when culture supports them, and culture in the twenty-first century is increasingly influenced by religion. A properly differentiated democratic regime can liberate religious individuals and communities to contend within the political order on the basis of the rationality and persuasiveness of their views (whether theologically derived or not).

HOW CAN WE TALK TO THE NEIGHBORS ABOUT THEIR RELIGION?

A fruitful way to discuss religious freedom in a democratic political context is to focus on who we are rather than who God is.[43] First, I must enter two caveats. This approach need not require anyone to deny their own theological principles. Indeed, the American democratic system is steeped in a powerful theistic truth claim—that, in the words of Supreme Court Justice William Douglas, American democracy "presupposes a Supreme Being."[44] Moreover, even though Sunni Islam is less doctrinal than Christianity, it is difficult to speak to Muslims (Sunni or Shiite) about politics without taking into account their understanding of God and what God requires of them.[45] In my travels to the Middle East, I often employed to good effect my understanding of the theistic underpinnings of American democracy in discussions with political and religious officials about the relationship between religion and democracy. My experience supplied ample confirmation of Douglas Johnson's thesis that something called "faith-based diplomacy" exists and can make a difference.[46]

Secondly, the focus on the person and his religious nature, rather than on theology itself, does not require us to ignore what Harvard political theorist Michael Sandel has usefully labeled the "encumbered self." Sandel has critiqued both modern American jurisprudence and liberal political thought as deficient in their definition of religious freedom as merely one measure of human autonomy. Religious beliefs are in the modern liberal understanding merely one category of choices in the supermarket of possibilities. Sandel points out that the American founders did not see religion as a choice, but as a duty, and defined religious liberty as the right to fulfill that duty. He also notes that many Americans still see religion not as a "choice," but as a response to something beyond themselves, something that beckons with a force that binds the conscience.[47]

In Sandel's words, the modern liberal understanding of religion as mere choice "fails to capture those loyalties and responsibilities whose moral force consists partly in the fact that living by them is inseparable from understanding ourselves as the particular persons we are."[48] The modern liberal understanding of religious freedom has handicapped America's international religious freedom policy, in particular in those parts of the world where religious individuals see themselves as "encumbered," in

Sandel's phrase, or as responding to something metaphysical rather than choosing among lifestyles. This is a particularly important caveat in our approach to religious freedom in Muslim-majority nations.

But there are also distinct advantages to focusing on the nature of human beings rather than the nature of God. It admits into the conversation those whose religious beliefs are not monotheistic, such as Hindus, or not theistic at all (some versions of Buddhism and Taoism). Within the United States, this approach also accommodates those who deny that theistic principles underpin American democracy, or those who argue that such principles once existed but are no longer relevant under conditions of contemporary religious pluralism. It includes those who, like former secretary of state Madeleine Albright, may accept the role of God in the American story and are calling for more attention to religion in American foreign policy, but still fear that public religion in America has resulted in our leaders confusing their own will with God's.[49] Our anthropological approach relieves us of the necessity of agreeing on the precise content of God's will while focusing us on the human quest to understand it. Among those who do believe in God or gods, however, it does not preclude a reasoned discussion of divine nature, such as the Catholic-Muslim dialogue that developed out of Pope Benedict XVI's 2006 remarks on Islam during a speech in Regensburg, Germany.[50]

To assert a right of religious freedom in this fashion is to affirm a truth claim about human nature and to do so on behalf of all human beings. This claim, of course, may be challenged by secularists or others, but many will acknowledge its rationality and potential for American foreign policy. The claim presupposes that people naturally seek to know ultimate, transcendent truths. Following James Madison and most of the American founders, it assumes a duty and therefore a "natural" right to seek those truths. Unlike civil rights (such as the right to vote), natural rights are not created by governments. Madison believed those rights came from God. But he would also agree that they are rooted in justice and intrinsic to the well-being of every person because of human nature, because each of us is "hard wired," as it were, to seek ultimate truth. Natural rights must therefore be recognized and protected by any government constituted to serve the interests of its citizens.

It is also true that the significance of religion in the modern world (and to American national interests) goes beyond its status as a set of beliefs. Religion sometimes constitutes a source of social identity into which people are born and remain for reasons that cut across the search for transcendence—reasons such as ethnicity, nationality, language, or status. As Vendulka Kubálková writes, "All religions are organized on the basis of beliefs that are fundamental not only to reality, but even more importantly, to human identity."[51] Within religious groupings that themselves are defined by belief, there are inevitably differences over politics, theology, law, and piety. Moreover, the most apparent differences between religious communities are often over power and wealth, not simply views of God and salvation. Although American foreign policy has not dealt effectively with religious communities on either level, the "rational actor" model of human behavior encourages diplomats to address religion as little more than a quest for power and wealth. It is far more difficult, and far more important, to understand and engage the religious ideas within which those quests operate and which lend them meaning and potency.

Virtually all human beings share a thirst for transcendence. Wherever we live, however we are situated socially or economically, most of us are naturally impelled to ask the questions that lie at the heart of personhood: What is the origin, meaning, and destiny of my life? Is there something or someone beyond my personal existence, a transcendent reality that accounts for my being or influences me and the world in which I live? If so, what is its nature and what does it require of me?

The desire to answer such questions is for the most part so natural and so powerful in human nature that addressing them in some fashion is utterly necessary to our private and public well-being. Religious questions have been asked by human beings from ancient Greece and Persia to modern China and contemporary France.[52] They may be asked in different ways, and the answers quite obviously vary widely. A few skeptics, mostly secularists living in the West or educated in the West, despair of discovering answers at all or simply conclude that any certainty about them is unlikely. A smaller minority, also mostly in the West, quite remarkably manage to achieve certainty that there is no God or that there are no answers.[53]

An undersecretary of state once told me that his most powerful existential questions had to do with his tennis swing, not the existence of God. This was a cordial jest, designed to refute my argument that the search for transcendence is universal. But it reflected a point of view that should not be trivialized, much less ignored. Such attitudes, unusual outside the West today, are perhaps disproportionately represented in the U.S. State Department. Whether or not that is true, it is beyond dispute that the world the State Department must engage on behalf of the American people is religious. The vast majority of the world's people appear to believe they have discovered or are in the process of discovering answers to the religious questions.

Properly understood, then, freedom of religion is the right to pursue the religious quest and to embrace or reject the interior and public obligations that ensue. If people are not free in *both* senses, they cannot be said to be living a fully human life. In political terms, religious freedom is the right of every person to immunity from coercion by civil or other human authority in pursuing, or not pursuing, the truths of religion.

So defined, the right is grounded initially in an interior and personal dimension, namely the right of conscience (to believe or not), which cannot be touched by any government or other human agency. The right of conscience, however, also has a public dimension. Moral obligations flow from a conscience that is bound by its apprehension of religious truths, whether apprehended by faith, reason, or both. Those obligations often require a religious believer to take or refrain from taking certain actions. Accordingly, freedom of conscience implies a right to live in accord with the obligations one has derived from the religious enterprise.

It also implies a right peacefully to persuade others that one's beliefs are true. Often labeled "proselytism," this is one of the most controversial aspects of religious freedom, but one that goes to the core of its meaning. The right to convince others of the truthfulness of one's religious beliefs is in one sense a subset of freedom of expression, but it is far more than that. Religious people usually hold their beliefs not simply as "opinion" but as objective truth. The very nature of apprehending religious truth often includes the utter necessity, the duty, of sharing it with others.

Religious truth claims, in other words, are not generally understood as personal possessions, generated by human agents for themselves. Especially in the monotheistic religion of Christianity, and in some interpretations of Islam, those claims are typically seen as universal, belonging to and applying ipso facto to everyone. This is why they are so powerful and so volatile. Proselytism can be mercenary and can exploit ignorance, poverty, and emotional loneliness. It can also interrupt, and even damage, existing social relationships and longstanding communities of faith. As such it deserves condemnation. But if proselytism is understood as peaceful persuasion, necessarily respectful of human dignity as intrinsic to the activity, it can contribute to stable, liberal, and just governance, especially in highly religious societies.

Indeed, the whole enterprise of holding and manifesting religious truth claims can induce charity and winsome persuasiveness, compassion and respect, fidelity and sacrifice—characteristics and virtues that can underwrite social, economic, and political harmony, liberal institutions, and stability. Or it can yield self-righteousness, hatred and intolerance, instability, persecution, and, when combined with modern technologies and weapons, transnational terrorism. It is all the more important, therefore, that any liberal polity address this bivalent potential of religion successfully, and that any U.S. strategy designed to induce liberal governance take it seriously into account.

A final public aspect of religious freedom is of equal and perhaps even greater consequence for the long-term social and political harmony of a nation. Most people do not live their religious lives in isolation. They worship, teach, raise their children, and seek and celebrate religious truths in community with others of like mind and spirit. That is to say, most religious people are members of confessional communities that tend to increase the validity and the power of the truths that bind them in conscience. Accordingly, the right of religious freedom must extend to religious groups just as it does to individuals.[54] Both individuals and religious communities must have access to the interior and exterior rights of religion, including the right to influence the political arrangements under which they live in an attempt to make them consistent with belief.

Politics is the way we order our lives together. Liberal democracy is premised on the equal right of all individuals and groups within civil society, both religious and secular, to influence the constitutions, laws, norms, and regulations that order individual liberty to the common good. If the United States is to continue the quest to undermine religious extremism through the institutions of democracy, it must address this issue forthrightly. The history of religion and democracy, not least in the United States, suggests that the two can flourish together and strengthen each other, provided they arrive at a covenant that regulates their respective, overlapping authorities. A democratic government constituted by citizens with strong religious beliefs cannot bypass this step if their society is to be truly liberal, stable, and free.

This is how American foreign policy should understand its twin goals of advancing religious freedom and, at the same time, engaging a world of public religion by enticing religious communities to the advantages of liberal governance. There are, of course, different ways to achieve these goals. In some cases, it may be necessary or prudent to seek modest, interim objectives, for example in authoritarian societies like Saudi Arabia and Egypt. In other cases it will continue to make sense to convince a dictator like Uzbekistan's Karimov that continuing his persecutory activities will cost more than they are worth. But such punitive approaches should over time occupy a smaller and smaller place in our religious freedom policy. Not only have they proven ineffective in actually reducing persecution over the long run, but they obscure and threaten America's need to adopt a new realism in a world of faith.

Making religious freedom properly understood the centerpiece of U.S. policy does not mean abandoning the humanitarian goal of reducing persecution and the suffering of victims. Indeed the opposite is true. Success in a broadened policy would by definition reduce religious persecution as well as other human rights abuses. Nor would a broadened policy mean placing the entire burden of policy on one office headed by one ambassador—the State Department's office of international religious freedom and the ambassador at large established as its head by the 1998 International Religious Freedom (IRF) Act.

In order to succeed, America's policy of advancing regimes of religious freedom must be mainstreamed within U.S. diplomacy and embraced as a policy that serves the national interest broadly understood, rather than as it is widely seen now—a humanitarian effort that is acceptable, even nice to have, so long as it is absorbed into other human rights efforts and will cede the way when other more strategic interests are involved. That is what happened to U.S. policy in Afghanistan.

For this reason, it will be important to elevate the role and authority of the State Department's office of international religious freedom, even as a broadened IRF policy is integrated into U.S. national security strategy and mainstreamed within American diplomacy. Currently, that office holds the distinction of being the only institution within the foreign policy establishment of the United States whose job it is to engage religious communities and to think about religion systematically. It holds this mandate by law, a considerable advantage in a culture resistant to thinking about religion at all.

Moreover, the fervent (if fragmented) religious rights movement that produced the IRF Act has moved on to other foreign policy issues, such as trafficking in persons and the horrific problem of Sudan, but these groups could quickly be reinvigorated to support the office and its work. They remain a potentially powerful base for support among the American public for a broader religious freedom policy, one that benefits their coreligionists abroad more effectively than at present. And then there are those religious groups who resisted the policy, in particular Muslim Americans, as aimed against their coreligionists overseas. This resistance remains to this day, and has increased with the abandonment of the dialogue begun with Muslims under the first IRF ambassador at large.

Widespread American Muslim support for U.S. policy would be a major step forward, and could have some benefit for U.S. efforts in the greater Middle East.

CONCLUSION

In sum, a policy of actually advancing political regimes of religious freedom as a centerpiece of U.S. foreign policy could have a broad spectrum of benefits. It could strengthen American national security by undermining Islamist transnational terrorism and regional or national extremism. It could help stabilize struggling democracies throughout the Muslim world and beyond, in nations such as Russia and India. In China, it could help encourage a transition to political reform without domestic upheaval. It could reduce the perception abroad that America is imperialist, hedonistic, and peddling a value-free form of democracy that is intrinsically anti-Islam. It could encourage a broadening of U.S. interest group advocacy and encourage cooperation among U.S. religious groups, such as Catholics and Muslims or Muslims and Jews.

One of the most significant obstacles to a more realistic U.S. policy on religion is the "poison hand" problem—the perception that other nations are going to resist what the United States offers simply because it is the United States that is doing the offering. Some of this problem is endemic. It goes with the territory of being the most powerful country in the world. But some of the problem is self-inflicted. It derives from a belief, however inaccurate, that America is dismissive of the cultures of others and intends to remake the world in its image. Promoting true religious freedom can help counter that perception. There are several reasons that this is so, but the primary one is straightforward: if the United States stops peddling strict separation and privatization of religion and begins to address the way religions and religious communities can flourish within liberal states, it will be perceived as grounding its policy in respect rather than in hostility or in arrogance. It will thereby help resolve global doubts over whether it is "with or against the world."[55]

Chapter 3

Understanding Radical Islam

Paul Marshall

INTRODUCTION

After 9/11 it became painfully clear that U.S. intelligence and the Department of State had little religious literacy with which to read these terrible events. There were few senior Muslim officials in American embassies overseas or in the Department of State.[1] The Arabic specializations that did exist tended to focus on nonreligious aspects of Middle Eastern political culture. The higher echelons of foreign policy leadership were trapped in the same secularist worldview that ruled during the Cold War. "Mere sociology" was the dismissive label the CIA posted onto a proposed intelligence analysis of Iran in the 1970s that discerned a religious basis for brewing opposition.[2] Political Islam was conflated with Islamic extremism, and neither was taken seriously as a religious movement; instead both were perceived—at best—as mobilizing forces for underlying material or ethnic cleavages. The sad truth of that day was that the American people and their leadership truly had no idea what had hit them.

In this chapter I am concerned with understanding how to read Islam as a public religion, particularly in its radical and violent forms. By radical Islam I mean that form of Islam with global goals to restore a unified Muslim ummah, ruled by a new caliphate, governed by a reactionary version of Islamic sharia law, and, for the violent wing, organized to wage jihad on the rest of the world.[3] This includes those groups whom the administration has in the past described by the euphemism "terrorists of global reach." This grouping need not include Muslims, including terrorists, who have local political goals, for example in Kashmir, Chechnya, or in the Palestinian areas, and who might be susceptible to local political solutions.

My concern is that many of our policymakers, professors, and pundits continue to view these movements through an Enlightenment lens that results in a narrative still largely shaped by the categories of first world/ third world, globalization, ethnicity, U.S. foreign policy, and Middle Eastern nationalism. This reflects what Elizabeth Shakman Hurd calls "the unquestioned acceptance of the secularist division between religion and politics."[4] To the degree our views of the nature and goals of radical Islam are shaped by these categories, we are consistently misinformed about the nature of this conflict.

One reason for these anachronistic narratives is a neglect of these movements' central religious dimension. Strategic theorist Edward Luttwak remarks that recent currents in international relations "prohibited any sustained intellectual interest in religion itself . . . As for religious motivations in secular affairs, they were disregarded or dismissed as mere pretense, and because this could not be done in the case of the entire history of Byzantium, the quandary was resolved by simply abandoning its study."[5] Sometimes religion is almost dogmatically excluded. As Luttwak further notes, analysts "who are ready to interpret economic causality, who are apt to dissect social differentiations more finely, and who will minutely categorize political affiliations are still in the habit of disregarding the role of religion, religious institutions, and religious motivations in explaining politics and conflict and even in reporting their concrete modalities. Equally, the role of religious leaders, religious institutions, and religiously motivated lay figures in conflict resolution has also been disregarded—or treated as a marginal phenomenon hardly worth noting."[6]

This does not necessarily reflect someone's "personal attitudes toward religion" but rather "a learned repugnance to contend intellectually with all that is religion or belongs to it—a complex inhibition compounded out of the peculiar embarrassment that many feel when faced by explicit manifestations of serious religious sentiment."[7]

Despite the fact that the United States has in recent years been under attack by an enemy that defines itself in religious terms, these attitudes have persisted. As Thomas Farr, the first director of the State Department's Office of Religious Freedom, has pointed out, "principles and habits from across the ideological spectrum of American society tend to nourish a secularistic diplomatic culture, one that encourages an official reticence about religion and in some cases its willful exclusion from any systematic consideration of how to pursue America's vital interests." He concludes, "The fact is that the U.S. foreign policy establishment does not know how to think about religious forces operating in other societies or to develop strategies that might influence them."[8]

Similar attitudes are prevalent in the press. As CNN political analyst William Schneider has opined, "On the national level, the press is one of the most secular institutions in American society. It just doesn't get religion or any idea that flows from religious conviction. The press is not necessarily contemptuous of serious religion. It's just uncomprehending."[9]

In this analysis, my Christian perspective is very thin. I simply maintain that people's religious beliefs motivate, at least in part, what they do, that such beliefs are part of the explanation for their actions, and that if we are to understand our present conflicts, we must take them seriously. One certainly does not need to be a Christian to believe these things, but Christians, presumably, necessarily think their own beliefs have some causative force in their lives, and so are more open to thinking that this is true for others than is the average secularist. In any case, it is my experience that many secular analysts continue to ignore and downplay religious motivations, rationales, and goals.

WRONG EXPLANATIONS OF RADICAL ISLAM

Common explanations of radical movements tell us little about these extreme movements. They are not composed of poor or uneducated people groups know nothing of the world. Hassan al-Turabi of the Sudan has advanced degrees from the University of London and the Sorbonne. Abbasi Madani, a leader of Algeria's Islamic Salvation Front, received a doctorate in education from the University of London. Mousa Abu Marzzok, the head of Hamas' political committee, has a doctorate in engineering from Louisiana Technical University. Sayyid Qutb, the shaper of the Egyptian Muslim Brotherhood, spent several years in the United States, which is precisely where he became a militant. The Ayatollah Khomeini lived in Paris for many years. Khalid Sheikh Mohammed studied in a Baptist college in North Carolina.

Nor does poverty explain much. No doubt, extremist leaders can get foot soldiers from among people who rot in refugee camps and who can get no education other than the radical training in madrassas subsidized by extremists. But most poor people, including Muslim poor people, have never fought as terrorists. The people from the poorest countries in the world, such as Haiti or Mozambique, are not attacking the United States or anyone else. The terrorists themselves are usually wealthy and privileged. They are common among second- and third-generation immigrants in Europe, who are more militant than their much poorer first-generation parents or grandparents.

Nor is this simply a response to repression or injustice. Tibetan or Vietnamese Buddhists have at least as good a claim of persecution and repression as any Islamist cohort, but we do not find the followers of the Dalai Lama or the patriarch of the Unified Buddhist Church of Vietnam resorting to terrorism.

Nor are the attacks caused chiefly by globalization—the spread of a capitalist economic order dominated by large corporations and suffused with goods and cultural products from television to blue jeans. Certainly the threat posed by globalization to traditional social orders produces an alienation in which extremism can flourish. But terrorists have also killed Christians in Sudan, Indonesia, the Philippines, and Nigeria, attacked Hindus in Bangladesh and India, killed Buddhists in Thailand, and slaughtered Muslims in Sudan and Algeria. The Taliban made Hindus and Buddhists in Afghanistan wear distinctive clothing and demolished the two largest Buddhist statues in the world (which other Muslims had let stand for 1,000 years). None of these victims were westerners, and most had little to do with the West.

While Hamas and Hezbollah react to events surrounding Israel and the Palestinians, the al Qaeda networks have usually seemed much less interested. The attacks on the World Trade Center and the Pentagon in September 2001 were planned and carried on right through the period of extensive peace talks between the Israelis and the Palestinians from 1992 to 2000, when hopes were highest for a peace settlement. As Egyptian president Hosni Mubarak has pointed out, bin Laden never mentioned the Palestinians or the Iraqis much in the years before his attacks on the United States: "He never talked about them before."[10] In the lists of grievances mentioned in his fatwas and TV interviews, he referred to the

Al-Aqsa Mosque in Jerusalem (Islam's third holiest shrine) but not to the Palestinians per se.

While poverty, ignorance, globalization, and U.S. policy may play some background part, this wave of radicalism and terrorism cannot be understood apart from its religious outlook. Certainly bin Laden's views are not those of the majority of Muslims around the world. But there is no hiding the fact that bin Laden, his lieutenants, and his foot soldiers have repeatedly stated their aim to impose their version of Islam, first on the Muslim world and then on the rest of the world. They want each country to accept or be forced into submission to their version of Islamic sharia law. As the Ayatollah Khomeini put it, "We did not create a revolution to lower the price of melon."[11]

THE WORLD ISLAMIC FRONT'S IDEOLOGY

On August 23, 1996, bin Laden issued a "Declaration of War Against the Americans Occupying the Land of the Two Holy Places." Its focus was, as its title implies, the Arabian Peninsula, where it indicted the Saudis for the religious offense of "suspension of the Islamic Shari'ah law and exchanging it with man made civil law." However, the declaration surveyed the world and also described Muslims whose "blood has been spilled in Palestine and Iraq. The horrifying pictures of the massacre of Qana, in Lebanon, are still fresh in our memory. Massacres in Tajikistan, Burma, Kashmir, Assam, Philippine, Patani, Somalia, Erithria, Chechnya and in Bosnia-Herzegovina took place, massacres that send shivers through the body and shake the conscience." It also expounded on what it claims is worldwide war against Islam waged by Indian Hindus, Burmese Buddhists, Russian, Ethiopian, and Eritrean Orthodox, and, above all, Zionist Jews and the leader of the whole *kuffar* cabal, the Crusader Americans. The declaration's grievances culminated with what it described as "the latest and greatest of these aggressions, the greatest incurred by the Muslims since the death of the Prophet," the presence of the "American Crusaders and their allies" in Islam's holiest places.[12] In response to these alleged crimes, remembering that Muslims had fought against "the Russians in Afghanistan, the Serbs in Bosnia-Herzegovina, and today they are fighting in Chechnya . . . they are also fighting in Tajikistan," bin Laden called for "fighting [*jihad*] against the disbelievers in every part of the world."[13]

Bin Laden did mention the Palestinians, but, since he believes that nationalism is anti-Islamic and is even a form of apostasy from Islam, his concern was not with a people fighting for a homeland but rather with the fact that infidels were in control of the Al-Aqsa Mosque, often thought by Muslims to be the site of the Furthest Mosque, the destination of the Prophet's Night Journey and as such Islam's third holiest place.[14] He also described Israel and the Palestinian areas as really part of the Arabian Peninsula, and hence accused the Israelis of "annexing" the "northerly part" of the land of the two Holy Places, so that all three of Islam's holiest places were lying under the feet of infidels.

While control of the three holiest places remained central to bin Laden's worldview, he also insisted that all lands that have ever been ruled by Muslims must now be returned to their control. In the year following his "Declaration of War," he reiterated that "Jihad will remain an individual obligation until all other lands that were Muslim are returned to us so that Islam will reign again: before us lie Palestine, Bokhara, Lebanon, Chad, Eritrea, Somalia, the Philippines, Burma, Southern Yemen, Tashkent, and Andalusia [Spain]."[15]

On February 23, 1998, he and Ayman al Zawahiri, along with "Abu-Yasir Rifa'i Ahmad Taha, Egyptian Islamic Group, Shaykh Mir Hamzah, secretary of the Jamiat-ul-Ulema-e-Pakistan, and Fazlul Rahman, amir of the Jihad Movement in Bangladesh," released the manifesto of their "World Islamic Front for Holy War Against Jews and Crusaders." It echoed previous statements and called for attacks on Americans based on charges that "for over seven years America has occupied the holiest parts of the Islamic lands, the Arabian peninsula, plundering its wealth, dictating to its leaders, humiliating its people, terrorizing its neighbors and turning its bases there into a spearhead with which to fight the neighboring Muslim peoples."[16] Later that year, in December, the "World Front for Jihad against Jews and Crusaders" announced, "There are two parties to the conflict: World Christianity, which is allied with Jews and Zionism, led by the United States, Britain and Israel. The second part is the Islamic world."[17] It also repeated the demand for the return of "Andalusia" to Islam.[18]

Following September 11, 2001, bin Laden reemphasized the religious nature of his side of the war: "This war is fundamentally religious. . . . Those who try to cover this crystal clear fact, which the entire world has admitted, are deceiving the Islamic nation. This war is fundamentally religious. . . . This fact is proven in the book of God Almighty and in the teachings of our messenger, may God's peace and blessings be upon him. This war is fundamentally religious. Under no circumstances should we forget this enmity between us and the infidels. For, the enmity is based on creed. . . . The unequivocal truth is that Bush has carried the cross and raised its banner high."

He went on: "Following World War I, which ended more than 83 years ago, the whole Islamic world fell under the crusader banner— under the British, French, and Italian governments. They divided the whole world, and Palestine was occupied by the British." In response, he called for "revenge for those innocent children in Palestine, Iraq, southern Sudan, Somalia, Kashmir and the Philippines. . . . Take for example the Chechens. They are a Muslim people who have been attacked by the Russian bear which embraces the Christian Orthodox faith. . . . A year ago, Putin demanded that the cross and the Jews should stand by him."

He then castigated the United Nations for its purported attempt "to divide the largest country in the Islamic world. . . . This criminal, Kofi Annan, was . . . putting pressure on the Indonesian government, telling it: You have 24 hours to divide and separate East Timor from Indonesia by force. The crusader Australian forces were on Indonesian shores, and in fact they landed to separate East Timor, which is part of the Islamic world."[19]

The consistent themes of these lengthy statements, declarations, and manifestos are the occupation of the three Muslim Holy Places and the purported worldwide war waged by infidels against Muslims, both of which are part of a cosmic battle of belief that will continue until judgment day. The language use is explicitly religious and embedded in a version of Islam and of religious history without which it would make no sense. He castigates regimes throughout the world and describes Russia in addition to the United States as a Christian power attacking Islam, with Vladimir Putin purportedly demanding "that the cross and the Jews should stand by him."

This language and pattern of argument have continued in bin Laden's and Zawahiri's utterances, as well as those of their confreres. However, there are some exceptions, in which in addresses aimed at English speakers, though not in those targeting Arabic speakers, both bin Laden and Zawahiri have tried to submerge their basic and explicitly religious agenda and instead harp on some peculiarly Western grievances such as environmentalism or campaign finance reform. These pronouncements usually show a marked change in tone, as if he had taken public relations advice that his previous statements had played well in Peshawar but not in Peoria or Paris. His October 6, 2002, "Letter to America" mentioned the Kyoto accord on global warming, environmental problems, election campaign finances, and the use of nuclear weapons on Japan—matters he had consistently ignored in the previous decade. He also added mention of President Clinton's "immoral acts" in the Oval Office, homosexuality, intoxicants, gambling, charging interest, and using women in advertising. Even in this somewhat crude attempt to play to American prejudices, he returned to his basic religious message and, above all, condemned the American constitution for not enshrining Islamic sharia law and instead allowing the American people to make their own laws. He concluded with a fervent appeal to Americans to repent and become Muslim: "The first thing we are calling you to is Islam."[20] Meanwhile, his addresses to his primary Muslim audience focused on his longstanding concerns. His January 2004 message "to the Muslim nation" emphasized that, since the West "invaded our countries more than 2,500 years ago [sic] . . . It is a religious-economic war. . . . Therefore, religious terms should be used when describing the ruler who does not follow God's revelations and path and champions the infidels by extending military facilities to them or implementing the UN resolutions against Islam and Muslims. Those should be called infidels and renegades. . . . the confrontation and conflict between us and them started centuries ago. The confrontation and conflict will continue because the conflict between right and falsehood will continue until Judgment Day."[21]

At the end of 2004, bin Laden lamented the "control exerted by the Zionists and the Cross worshippers" and described the world conflict once again as "a struggle between two camps. One camp is headed by America, and it represents the global Kufr [infidelity], accompanied by all apostates. The other camp represents the Islamic Ummah [nation] headed by its Mujahideen Brigades."[22] Similarly, his December 27, 2004, "Letter to the Iraqi People" referred to the war as a conflict "between the army of Mohammed, the army of belief, and the people of the cross." He stressed the primacy of Islamic law and warned Iraqis not to participate in the January 30, 2005, elections since the Iraqi constitution is "a Jahiliyya [pre-Islamic] constitution that is made by man," and Muslims may elect only a leader for whom "Islam is the only source of the rulings and laws." Voting in Afghanistan was likewise forbidden on the grounds that the Karzai government is "apostate." Finally, on similar grounds, he forbade voting in Palestinian Authority elections since "the constitution of the land is a Jahili made by man" and added the novel, but certainly religiously loaded, claim that Fatah candidate Mahmoud Abbas "is a Baha'i."[23] Since Baha'is are regarded by Islamists as apostates who should be killed, this was a grave and dangerous charge.[24]

These religious themes have continued. On April 23, 2006, while castigating the United Nations, bin Laden denounced "pagan Buddhists," presumably the Chinese. He claimed that the "world's crusaders alongside pagan Buddhists hold the five permanent seats" in the UN Security Council. (The following year, Indian police spokesman Prem Lal said Lashkar-e-Toiba, an al Qaeda affiliate in South Asia, had threatened to kill the Dalai Lama "on the directions of a foreign organization," which he declined to name.[25]) Bin Laden also stressed India's role and referred to a "Crusader-Zionist-Hindu war against the Muslims," even seeking to blame Hindus for their role in the alleged conspiracy to separate East Timor from Indonesia. In addition, he complained at length about the 2001 Sudan Peace Act passed by Congress, which facilitated an end to the North/South civil war in that country and may allow the southern part, largely Christian and animist, to separate from the rest and to be exempt from sharia law. Bin Laden tied the fate of Sudan to the earlier destruction of the Ottoman state, the ending of the caliphate, and the subsequent division of the area by the British in 1956. He claimed that the infidels were again using Darfur to divide the Muslim world and called on the Mujahideen to gather landmines, anti-armor grenades, and RPGs and go to Darfur to fight the infidels. He also condemned the Danish cartoonists at the center of the 2005–2006 Muhammad cartoon controversy as well as "free thinkers" and heretics among Muslims, especially Muslim reformers in Kuwait and Saudi Arabia, asserting that all of these supposed offenders should be killed.[26]

Meanwhile, Zawahiri was echoing the same themes. On June 9, 2006, he claimed that the United Nations was preparing to occupy and divide Darfur.[27] On June 23, he interrupted his praise of Abu Musad al Zarqawi to denounce U.S. ambassador to Iraq Zalmay Khalilzad as "the Afghan apostate," and to denounce Turkey for being secular.[28] In September 2006, he stressed Darfur once again and responded to what he regarded as Pope Benedict XVI's criticism of Islam. His response went on at length trying to condemn and refute Christianity, criticizing Christian views of the nature of Christ, the sanctity of the church, the crucifixion, the resurrection, and the Holy Spirit. He concluded that Benedict's comments, as well as Salman Rushdie's books and the cartoons of Muhammad published in the Danish newspaper *Jyllands-Posten*, are part of the "War on Islam."[29]

REMEMBERING HISTORY

It is important to emphasize that this ideology, while incorrect, is not nonsense. It draws on a theology and, in particular, a view of history that is coherent, matches many key historic trends, and has great resonance in the Muslim world, particularly its Arab portion.

Americans, especially, are prone to try to put things historic behind them; indeed, we often believe that we can do so. The rest of the world, especially the Muslim world, is different. There a version of history lies close to the heart and gives rise to ideology, emotion, and ambition. Saddam Hussein could refer to George W. Bush as "Haglulu" knowing that his Iraqi listeners would remember the Mongol sack of Baghdad. Bin Laden knows that his references to al-Andalus will find a receptive audience.

Muhammad was successful as a religious teacher, as a political leader, and as a military leader. He promised his followers similar success. They expected to be victorious and to keep on being victorious. For centuries, the promise and expectation of victory turned out to be correct. After Muhammad's death, Muslim armies attacked and invaded the then majority Christian areas that are now Jordan, Israel, Syria, Iraq, Egypt, Turkey, Libya, Tunisia, Algeria, and Morocco. They were blocked by the Byzantine Empire centered in Constantinople, but went around it in the east by attacking Persia, then Afghanistan and Pakistan, and in the west by invading Spain and France. One hundred years after the death of the prophet, Muslim armies were simultaneously two hundred miles from Paris and in western China, and they controlled most areas in between. The expansion continued with the invasion of India and Russia, repeated attacks on Italy, and the gradual encroachment on the Byzantines, who held out against the Arabs but succumbed to the Turks.

On this scale, the Crusades were irrelevant: they were a short-lived, failed counterattack that briefly pushed the invading Muslims back a few hundred miles before their advance resumed, eventually into Bulgaria, Romania, Hungary, Serbia, and Austria.

Islam stretched across Europe, Asia, and Africa, from the Atlantic to the western shores of the Pacific, from Nigeria to China, from Tanzania to the rivers flowing into the Baltic Sea. It stood at the crossroads of the continents and controlled world trade. In comparison, the Christian world was poor and barbaric. The Hindu world of India was under Islamic control. China remained powerful but was content to maintain its civilization within its borders. The rest of the world was considered marginal. In this sense, Islam ruled the world. For over a thousand years it was the dominant power. For Muslims, their success confirmed the rightness of their beliefs and the finality of their revelation.

Then everything changed. The changes happened gradually, of course, with increasing defeat interspersed with victory. But if we want to put one symbolic date on the turning point, the best candidate might be September 11, 1683. This was the high-water mark of Islamic expansion. The following day, combined European forces defeated the Ottoman Turks at the second siege of Vienna. It was the beginning of an ongoing, grinding, disheartening process of defeat, surrender, and subjugation that lasted for centuries, spread throughout the world, and reached into the heart of Islam itself. After the Ottoman armies were driven out of Austria, then Hungary, Romania, Bulgaria, Serbia, Croatia, Bosnia, and Albania were freed from Ottoman rule. The Greeks revolted against their overlords and slowly drove the Ottomans back to Istanbul. The Russians drove east and south, conquering Muslims as they went.

This was bad enough, but the European advance did not stop at recovering European lands. Through their naval power and newly discovered sea routes to the east (largely developed as a way to get around the Islamic realms), the Europeans challenged Islam throughout Asia and Africa. The British took over India from Muslim rulers, and did the same with what is now Pakistan and Bangladesh. They then conquered Muslim Malaysia and Singapore. Only the Afghans resisted them successfully. The Dutch took over Indonesia, the world's largest Muslim country. The Spanish conquered the Philippines, including its southern Muslim areas.

The advance continued through East and West Africa, as the French, Spanish, Belgians, Portuguese, Germans, and British took over areas formerly controlled by Muslim rulers. Meanwhile, the Russians continued their expansion and took over Muslim areas in the Caucasus, such as Chechnya, Dagestan, and Azerbaijan. They also invaded east, taking over the ancient Muslim civilizations of Central Asia, which are now Kazakhstan, Uzbekistan, Turkmenistan, Tajikistan, and Kyrgyzstan. They were stopped only when they, like the British, tried to take over the vast mountains and fiercely independent tribes of Afghanistan.

Worst of all, the unbelievers of Europe inexorably invaded and overcame Arab lands seen as the center of the Islamic universe. In 1798 Napoleon invaded Egypt, easily conquering it. The French stayed several years and were only driven out by a British force under Admiral Nelson. In the nineteenth century, French forces took over what is now Algeria and the Muslim areas of the Sahara desert. The Spanish took over the Atlantic coast. Now, infidels were overcoming even those who spoke the language of the Qur'an itself.

The final debacle came at the beginning of the twentieth century. In the First World War, the Ottomans allied themselves with Germany, and they shared in its defeat. When their empire, which had been fragile for years, finally collapsed, its remnants were picked up by the victorious Europeans. The Greeks annexed more of the land that they desired. Under a mandate from the League of Nations, the French took over the governance of Lebanon and Syria; the British took over Palestine, Jordan, Iraq, and portions of the Arabian Peninsula. Unbelieving powers now ruled in the Middle East itself.

By the first decades of the twentieth century, more than 90 percent of Muslims lived under Christian European—and, to them, infidel— rule. Only five areas remained independent—Turkey, Iran, Afghanistan, Yemen, and Saudi Arabia. As Osama bin Laden put it in his November 3, 2001, videotape broadcast, "Following World War I, which ended more than 83 years ago, the whole Islamic world fell under the Crusader banner—under the British, French, and Italian governments. They divided the whole world."[30]

For strict Muslims, Turkey and Iran were as good as lost anyway. Ataturk had grabbed Turkey by the scruff of its neck, separated religion from the state, written a secular constitution, liberated women, adopted Western dress, and mandated that Islam be denied political power. Since he had established a secular state and decreed that Islam would never again rule there, for Muslim extremists he was an apostate, deserving of death, and Turkey was an apostate country. For many, Iran was little better.

This left Afghanistan and Saudi Arabia/Yemen as the only remnants from the dominant Muslim world empires of scarcely two centuries before. The former was populated by warring tribes and was remote, poverty stricken, and isolated. But Saudi Arabia was, and is, the heartland of Islam, the land of the Two Shrines, and the only significant Islamic territory not to fall under the sway of the infidel. It is where Muhammad lived, taught, fought, ruled, and died. It is the destination of the *hajj*, the pilgrimage enjoined on all pious Muslims. It is the focal point of prayer. For extremist Muslims, Saudi Arabia's independence and submission to Allah alone has now been lost. They believe that, with the initial arrival of American troops to protect the Saudis from Saddam Hussein, the land fell to the infidel. Osama bin Laden has called this "the latest and greatest" example of infidel aggression: "Now infidels walk everywhere on the land where Muhammad was born and where the Qur'an was revealed to him."[31]

In a sweeping generalization, we can say that Islam has experienced a thousand years of stunning success followed by three hundred years of crushing failure, and, of course, the burning question is, "Why has this happened?"[32]

There are several suggested answers, and one of the most influential is the assertion that the core problem is that most Muslims, especially Muslim leaders, have forsaken true Islam. Muslims have become corrupt and impious, refused to follow the teachings of the Prophet, and copied the ways of unbelievers. The failure of the Muslim world is rooted in the unfaithfulness of Muslims themselves. Hence, the only solution to their problems is that they return to the purity of the faith as some think it existed during the life of Muhammad and his immediate followers in the seventh century. This argument has great resonance within the Muslim world, especially among its radical members.

While one does not have to be a radical to believe this, it is certainly the common belief of the Sunni radicals, including the Wahhabi movement, springing from Saudi Arabia, the Muslim Brotherhood, springing largely from Egypt, and the Deobandis, influenced by Mawdudi in India and Pakistan. Consonant with this, these groups' primary targets are regimes in the Islamic world that they think have compromised with the Christian West. First, Saudi Arabia, for allowing infidels near the holy shrines of Mecca and Medina. Second are apostate regimes such as Egypt, Algeria, Turkey, Jordan, and Malaysia, who are accused of adopting Christian views of secularity. Third are those who are believed to oppress Muslims, such as, first, Israel, then Christians in Indonesia, the Philippines, Serbia, and the "crusader" world of the West, represented especially by America. America must be attacked because it is *the* world power, *the* barrier to all these other goals. It must be immobilized so it will not interfere with attacks on Islam's immediate traitors and oppressors.

MISSING RELIGIOUS REFERENCES

Faced with a narrative centered on the fall and anticipated rise of the caliphate, the restoration of sharia law, and the inevitable conflict between true Muslim believers and infidels destined to last until the day of judgment, the media have tended to ignore this fundamental religious dimension and instead concentrate on those terrorist statements that might fit into a Western view of oppression, freedom, and progress. A *New York Times* article from 2004 described a speech given by an Iraqi insurgent, saying that "the man's long speech is addressed to President Bush, who is called a dog at one point." In fact, the man called Bush a "Christian dog," a much more illuminating phrase, since "dog" is merely a qualifier of the more fundamental fact that Bush is portrayed as Christian.[33]

Similarly, when Al Jazeera broadcast bin Laden applauding an attack on a tanker off the coast of Yemen, the Associated Press quoted his praise for the heroism "of the faithful holy warriors in Yemen against a crusader oil tanker. . . . [that] hit the umbilical cord and lifeline of the crusader community," but then offered its own guidance by suggesting that Islamist terrorists "often referred to the United States as 'crusaders.'" This attempt to equate crusaders not with Christians but with the United States was especially confusing since the tanker in question was French.[34]

When the Afghan government made public its draft constitution enshrining an undefined Islam as the source of law, a document the U.S. Commission on International Religious Freedom described as "Taliban lite," the *Washington Post* headlined its story "Proposed Afghan Constitution Fits U.S. Model." But—to reiterate Thomas Farr's analysis in the previous chapter—while Afghanistan would indeed have a president, a bicameral legislature, and no prime minister, you do not need to be an expert in the Federalist Papers to realize that there is rather more to the U.S. Constitution than these structures. It is not quite the American model to declare, "no law can be contrary to the sacred religion of Islam" (Article 3) or that "provisions of adherence to the fundamentals of the sacred religion of Islam . . . cannot be amended" (Article 149). The *New York Times* wrongly stated that the draft had "no mention of Shari'ah, a legal code based on the Koran," a sentiment echoed by Reuters and the Associated Press. In fact, Article 130 says that, in the absence of an explicit statute or constitutional limit, the Supreme Court should make its decisions "in accord with Hanafi jurisprudence," one of the four main Sunni schools of sharia. Supreme Court justices, like the president and cabinet members, must take an oath to "support justice and righteousness in accord with the provisions of the sacred religion of Islam."[35]

On October 13, 2006, *Newsweek* published an article entitled "Caliwho? Why Is President Bush Talking about an Islamic Caliphate? And What Does the Word Mean?" that criticized George W. Bush's increasing use of the term "caliphate" when he described the goals of al Qaeda and like-minded groups. The article's authors, Lisa Miller and Mathew Philips, called it a "fifty-cent word" and pointed out that most Americans had no idea what it meant. They appear to have missed the fact that al Qaeda, and other groups, have consistently and repeatedly asserted that their long term goal is the restoration of the caliphate, and therefore if we want to understand al Qaeda's goals we must understand its vision of the caliphate. The authors compound this oversight by claiming that the caliphate ended in Baghdad in 1258, something that would no doubt be a great surprise to the Ottoman caliphs who ruled from Istanbul for centuries until Ataturk abolished the institution. The fact that most Americans do not know this is surely a good reason not to ignore it; rather it is essential that the president, or any other government official, or any journalist, inform them of its importance.[36] In an address to the French ambassadors in Paris on August 27, 2007, newly installed French president Nicolas Sarkozy said of the challenges facing France, "The first challenge, and no doubt one of the most important: how to prevent a confrontation between Islam and the West. There's no point in waffling: this confrontation is being called for by extremist groups such as al-Qaeda that dream of establishing a caliphate from Indonesia to Nigeria, rejecting all openness, all modernity, every hint of diversity."[37]

CONCLUSION

Islamist extremists are not shy about stating their goals and justifying them. Indeed, they are the most garrulous of enemies: repeatedly and at length they explain their actions in a plethora of videotapes, audiotapes, declarations, books, letters, fatwas, magazines, and Web sites. Each bombing or other atrocity is accompanied invariably by all but a press kit attempting to justify their actions in terms of Islamic teaching and history. Consistently, they outline their program to restore a unified Muslim ummah, ruled by a new caliphate, governed by reactionary Islamic sharia law, and organized to wage jihad on the rest of the world.

Bin Laden and his confreres are indeed concerned about America, Israel, the Palestinians, Iraq, and Afghanistan. But they are especially concerned about Saudi Arabia and the Al-Aqsa mosque, and continually point to attacks by infidels in Lebanon, Tajikistan, Burma, Kashmir, Assam, the Philippines, Fatani, Ogadin, Somalia, Eritrea, Chechnya, Bosnia, Bokhara, Bangladesh, Turkey, Chad, Mauritania, southern Sudan, Darfur, Algeria, Yemen, Tashkent, Indonesia, and East Timor. They are in a global war until judgment day. If we are to understand them, we must take their religious beliefs, including their view of history, seriously. Intelligently *reading* radical Islam—both religiously and historically—is the first step to understanding and acting in constructive, just ways in global affairs.

Chapter 4

Three Zionisms in the Shaping of American Foreign Policy

James W. Skillen

INTRODUCTION

A materialist disdain toward religion has been unconsciously at work in the minds of many of the theorists and practitioners of American foreign policy and international relations. The precipitous collapse of the Soviet Union abruptly called attention, and not for the last time, to the abiding power of religion in political developments around the globe. Yet despite mounting evidence of the profound influence of religion and religious identity on global affairs, American foreign policy analysis of religion has for too long remained content mainly with sporadic analyses of the *empirical clout* of conservative religious organizations on national foreign policymaking.[1] Why have the *normative religious* domestic sources of U.S. foreign policy been so poorly understood? Part of the answer to this question lies in what Scott Thomas calls the modern invention of "religion" as a private affair, a myth that is alive and well in the field of foreign policy in the United States.[2] The myth of private religion, he notes, is closely linked to the modern understanding of the "separation of church and state," often thought to mandate a hermetic seal between religion and politics in American civil identity. A privatized religion would never have the capacity to affect America's interaction with other nations. Such conceptions were hardly likely to encourage an investigation of American domestic religious beliefs as a formative factor in the shaping of foreign policy. Moreover, the gatekeepers of the discipline of International Relations have long made careers out of keeping not only religion, but ideational and ideological factors altogether, away from the investigative lens of the discipline. Jonathan Fox and Shmuel Sandler write in *Bringing Religion into International Relations* that the disciplinary bias against such investigations is rooted in its character as perhaps one of the "most Western of the social sciences."[3]

These conceptual and professional barriers are now under severe strain in light of the irruption of religious factors in international crises across the globe in recent decades. Serious questions about ideology, religion, faith, and foreign policy are being asked once again. One of the most important, and unsettling, is whether America's own religious identity might itself be a significant influence on its foreign policy orientations. If, as Fox and Sandler argue, religion is a primary source of identity and legitimacy, the implications on the foreign policy of a democracy, or indeed any state, may be profound indeed.[4] This chapter presents a case study of such influence: the role of "three Zionisms" in the shaping of U.S. Middle East policy. It proposes that these three strands of religious thinking must be properly distinguished, and their interrelationships then grasped, if we are to make sense of the recent direction of U.S. policy in the region. It concludes by calling for a critical assessment of the three strands in order to clear the way for a more successful Middle East policy. Let us begin with a more recent signpost, and work our way back.

On December 22, 2007, the United Nations General Assembly voted 142 to 1 to approve a two-year budget of $4.17 billion. The lone vote against the budget was cast by the United States. Why? Because some of the funds were designated for a conference that the United States thought might prove to be "prejudicial to Israel."[5] The United States cast that vote one month after it had hosted a multinational conference in Annapolis, Maryland, to promote renewed peace talks between Israel and the Palestinians. But just as the UN vote showed the Bush administration's solicitous preoccupation with Israel, so U.S. actions (or non-actions) following the Annapolis conference showed unwavering support of Israel despite the latter's decision to move ahead with construction of a major settlement project on occupied Arab land east of Jerusalem, something the Annapolis agreement was to put on hold.[6]

Those two actions might seem questionable given the need of the United States to win friends in the world at a time when American influence has weakened. But the actions are not surprising; they reflect a strong and fairly consistent position the United States has taken since the founding of the state of Israel in 1948 and especially since September 11, 2001. Nations throughout the world now take for granted America's unwavering and heavily funded support for Israel even when that support appears not to be in the interest of the United States itself.

Why is this the case? Why has American foreign policy come to be so closely tied to the interests of Israel? The aim of this essay is to offer at least part of an answer to these questions by elucidating one of the driving forces of American-Israeli relations. The force to which I am referring is the product of three seemingly incongruous yet intermeshing modes of modern Zionism. The first and the oldest is America's originating vision of itself as God's new Israel—a newly chosen nation entering a new promised land (Zion) to fulfill a climactic, world-historical mission. The second mode is Jewish Zionism, or simply Zionism, which emerged in late nineteenth-century Europe to become the strongest force leading to the birth of the modern state of Israel. The third is Christian Zionism, an immensely influential American prophecy movement with roots reaching back before the American founding that now plays a strong political role in helping to tie America's mission closely to the security and interests of the state of Israel.

These three modes or movements of Zionism, I will argue, function as religiously deep ideologies or civil-religious visions and, even when incompatible with one another, have combined to establish certain enduring aims and defining limits of U.S. foreign policy. We cannot make sense of American foreign policy today, particularly in the Middle East, in other words, without understanding the dynamism of Zionism in its three modern modes.

AMERICA AS NEW ISRAEL

The first and earliest of the three modern Zionisms is America's originating vision of itself as God's new Israel guided into a new promised land. American new-Israelitism has its roots in the self-interpretation of the Puritans who settled New England early in the seventeenth century. By the time of the American Revolution that self-designation, with modifications, had been adopted by the country as a whole so that America, and not only the Puritan colony, saw itself as a new Israel.[7] By our day that self-understanding has lost most of its Puritan distinctiveness, but the derivative idea of American exceptionalism, whether admired or detested by others, continues to mark American identity and to drive U.S. foreign policy. Americans continue to think of themselves as the world's leading nation, the first and greatest of democracies, the nation specially blessed by God through which all other nations will be blessed.[8]

"The brand of Reformed Protestantism the Puritans brought with them from England's Puritan commonwealth," writes George McKenna, "had within it a strain of intense political activism, one rooted in the image of the Puritan community as the collective agent of providence. It did not take long for this to become a basic component of the American 'constitution,' using the word in its broadest sense of *politeia*, or 'way of life.'"[9] Barbara Tuchman adds that the Puritan conviction of being called into covenant with God as "the re-embodied saints of Israel" was not understood to be a mission "for the sake of the Jews, but for the sake of the promise made to them." Israel of old no longer existed, and the Puritans who came to America took to themselves, by an analogical mode of thought, the identity of Israel entering a new promised land.[10]

In one sense, because the American Puritans were vehemently distancing themselves from the corrupt Church of England and the fallen Church of Rome, they saw themselves as restarting Christianity. Their self-understanding was not primarily that of one group of congregations among many Christian communions worldwide but rather that of a single people, like Israel, following God's call as his chosen people. They alone somehow represented God's recovery of true Christianity. Obviously there was a new amalgam taking shape that combined, on the one hand, the view of a self-contained, covenanted people serving as a model for the nations, and on the other hand, an outreach mission that would not be fulfilled until the whole earth had been reached and transformed by the originating nation's mission. The ambivalence contained in this amalgam has shown up throughout American history in the frequently remarked pattern of American foreign policy that moves between isolationism and internationalism, between securing the city on a hill and extending the reach of that city's purpose to the far corners of the world.[11]

How does this understanding of the nation as new Israel comport with the modern Jewish nationalism of Zionism that would emerge at the end of the nineteenth century? And what would happen to the self-understanding of America as God's chosen nation when vast numbers of American Christians began to believe that the return of Jews to ancient Palestine represented the fulfillment of God's promises to his originally chosen people of Israel? The answer to these questions comes later in our story. Yet as early as the American founding and into the early years of the nineteenth century, we find political and missionary-minded con- nections being made between the new American nation and the return of Jews to the older promised land.

In 1810, for example, New England church and professional leaders established the American Board of Commissioners for Foreign Missions. The Middle East figured prominently in their thinking, particularly in the mind and heart of Levi Parsons. As Michael Oren explains, "If 'Zion,' for the Pilgrim leader William Bradford, referred to the new Promised Land of America, then for American evangelist Levi Parsons two cen- turies later it meant the old and original Land of Israel. . . . Only there would the Protestants' longing to reunite with their spiritual forebears, the Jews, converge with their yearning for the Messiah's reappearance."[12] Evangelistic ventures into the Middle East by these American Protestants were not disconnected from their political identity as Americans. Yale's late-eighteenth-century president Ezra Stiles compared Israel's 3 million people gathered around Mount Sinai after their exodus from Egypt with what he judged to be the identical number of Americans at the time of their independence.[13] In an election day sermon in Connecticut in 1783, Stiles "described [George] Washington as a 'man of God, greatly beloved of the Most High,' reasoned that the cooperation of 'Moses and Aaron . . . the magistracy and priesthood' constituted the United States 'the happiest on earth,' and told how God's special and particular blessings were directly the cause of success in the late war."[14] Harvard's Samuel Langdon "suggested that 'instead of the twelve tribes of Israel, we may substitute the thirteen states of the American union.'"[15] The Second Great Awakening, early in the nineteenth century, "called on Americans to revel not only in their spirituality but also in their national pride. . . . 'What could be more suitable, than the glowing fire and burning zeal of politi- cal enthusiasm consecrated to Christ?'" asked evangelist Pliny Fisk, who would lead one of the first missionary expeditions to the Middle East in the early 1820s.[16]

Although by the end of the eighteenth century, as McKenna explains, "there was not much left of Puritanism" in its original New England theology and polity, the popular conviction that America was pursu- ing a "biblical errand survived and worked its way deeply into even the most (seemingly) secular undertakings."[17] All too often, historians and political commentators start with the mistaken notion that the separa- tion of church and state is America's distinctive mark and they presume thereby that the republic became something *nonreligious* as it made room for the religious freedom of different churches and eventually other religious groups in private. But that presumption misses what McKenna recognizes as the all-embracing meaning of the "American way of life," a public way of life that was nothing if not religious, albeit in a profoundly modern, nationalist sense. "The very definition of America," he contends, is "bound up with the biblical paradigm of a people, like the ancient Hebrews, given a holy mission in a new land."[18] In the eighteenth as well as the seventeenth century, McKenna explains, "politics and theology were so thoroughly intertwined that it was often impossible to say where one left off and the other began. . . . By the end of the eighteenth century Americans of all stripes were calling themselves republicans, but their republicanism was, as Joseph Conforti writes, 'imbued with Puritanism.' Religion, far from being sidelined, played a central role in animating and shaping the politics and institutions of the American Enlightenment."[19]

It is not necessary at this point to try to answer the question of whether this self-identification of the American nation as God's new Israel is compatible with the Bible's story of Israel and of those who followed Jesus Christ in the belief that he is the Messiah of Israel and the light to the Gentiles. There certainly exists a considerable incongruity between the American new-Israel myth and the story of Israel conveyed in biblical revelation. Nevertheless, the self-identification of the American nation as a divinely chosen people, however peculiar and unbiblical it may be, represents a deeply religious self-understanding and a compelling political force despite the fact that the earliest Puritan language eventually morphed into a less theologically charged idea of American exceptionalism, the vanguard of history. American civil-religious nationalism is certainly *not* a secular ideology if by the word "secular" one means "nonreligious."

One foreign observer, Geiko Müller-Fahrenholz, who has participated closely in American affairs, describes his reaction to the religious service held at the National Cathedral (Episcopal Church) in Washington, D.C., five days after the 9/11 attacks in New York and Washington. The ritual of that service, he remarks, "was not a worship service or any other kind of church affair; it was more clearly an expression of America's civil religion. One can conclude, I think, that this civil religion has become the religion of the state—in other words, a national faith—with a president officiating as its high priest."[20] One need not agree with Muller-Fahrenholz that the American president functions as the chief priest of America's civil-religious ceremonies. The important thing is to see that the president is expected to act on behalf of the whole country in conducting domestic and foreign policies for the purpose of articulating, guarding, and advancing America's exceptional mission. And insofar as that mission is understood by most Americans to represent a divine appointment, which constitutes the United States as the unique vanguard of history's forward movement toward freedom and prosperity for the whole world, one cannot avoid seeing that the president acts to fulfill a "higher calling" that belongs to his office in this chosen nation.

Yet it is not only the president who is looked to and called upon to articulate America's mission as God's new Israel. A diversity of American prophets and priests carry out that responsibility. Martin Luther King Jr.'s famous "I have a dream" speech in 1963 is perhaps the most eloquent of them all. In that address, during the renewed fight for civil rights for African Americans, King laid stress on equality as an essential element of America's special calling and identity.

> I have a dream deeply rooted in the American dream that one day this nation will rise up and live out the true meaning of its creed—we hold these truths to be self-evident, that all men are created equal. . . .
>
> I have a dream that one day every valley shall be exalted, every hill and mountain shall be made low, the rough places shall be made plain, and the crooked places shall be made straight and the glory of the Lord will be revealed and all flesh shall see it together. . . .
>
> And when we allow freedom to ring, when we let it ring from every village and hamlet, from every state and city, we will be able to speed up that day when all of God's children—black men and white men, Jews and Gentiles, Catholics and Protestants— will be able to join hands and to sing in the words of the old Negro spiritual, "Free at last, free at last; thank God Almighty, we are free at last."[21]

For a modern state to think of itself as God's new Israel, to see its land as the promised land, and to understand its mission as bearing climactic, world-historical importance cannot by itself, of course, produce international consequences. However, with the gradual expansion of American wealth and power over the course of two centuries, with its deepened civil-religious identity as the "redeemer nation" during and after the Civil War, and with its rise to the status of the world's lone superpower in the 1990s, we can easily see how the nation's self-understanding helps to explain much of its impact on world affairs throughout its history and particularly in the last sixty years.[22]

ZIONISM

A second form of modern Zionism, and the one usually identified as such, is the movement that arose among European Jews late in the nineteenth century, organized and led most forcefully by Theodor Herzl (1860–1904), a journalist and playwright in Vienna and Paris who was born in Budapest. Herzl's *Der Judenstaat* ("The Jewish State: An Attempt at a Modern Solution of the Jewish Question") was published in 1896.[23] In this case, the original inspiration and the compelling motivation behind the movement to establish a homeland and then a state for Jews in what had become known as Palestine could not have been more unlike the Puritan quest to enter a new promised land as God's new Israel. The American Puritans were not Jews but were highly religious. The leading Zionists were Jews but were not religious—at least not religious in the traditional sense of that term. Both, however, laid the foundations of modern states.

Zionism, we must emphasize, was not a movement among Jews who longed to restore a Torah-keeping way of life organized around a rebuilt temple in the land of promise. To the contrary, it arose as a secular reaction to, and mirror of, modern European nationalism. Under the influence of the French Revolution and the Enlightenment, a number of European countries had granted civil rights to individuals, including Jews, regardless of their religious identification. The Enlightenment ideal was liberty, equality, and fraternity. Nevertheless, anti-Semitism, leading to the persecution of Jews as outsiders, was not extinguished. Those who established the intellectual groundwork on which Herzl built were driven to conclude that Jews would never find genuine freedom and self-realization unless they established their own independence as a nation like other modern nations.

Despite the fact that over the previous centuries Jews had become a part of French, German, Polish, Russian, and other European societies, even if not with an equal standing in those societies, they had long understood themselves to be exiles from the land of their fathers. And for a variety of social, racial, economic, and theological reasons, Jews had suffered discrimination and persecution at the hands of Roman, Christian, and Muslim political authorities ever since the destruction of the temple in 70 AD.[24] Following the French Revolution, however, and in the course of less than a century, Jews became beneficiaries of the European Enlightenment, political emancipation, and the Industrial Revolution. "Secularization and liberalism," as Shlomo Avineri explains, "opened European society for Jews as equals. For the first time since the destruction of the Temple, schools, universities, the public service, politics, and the professions were opened to Jews as *citizens*."[25]

However, the forces unleashed by the French Revolution "were not only those of liberalism and secularization but of nationalism as well. . . . The religiously oriented self-perception of gentile society was not replaced by an undifferentiated, universalist fraternity," Avineri continues, "but by a new identity distinguished by nationalism, ethnicity, a common language, and past history, either real or imagined."[26] Beneath the surface of liberty, equality, and fraternity, in other words, anti-Semitism, arising with the new nationalisms, remained very much alive. "What ultimately shocked Theodore Herzl during the Dreyfus affair [1894–95]," Avineri explains,

> was the fact that here was a completely emancipated, successfully integrated, and largely secularized Jewish person. One could hardly be more chauvinistically French, more militaristic, and more "un-Jewish," in the stereotyped sense, than Captain Alfred Dreyfus. Yet when a suspicion of treason arose and one of the suspects turned out to be Dreyfus, the public consensus tended to say, "Well, of course, yes, it must be him; after all he is not really French, he is Jewish."[27]

Consequently, what stirred many secularized, emancipated Jews such as Herzl to call for the establishment of a Jewish national homeland was the realization that Jews were not in their deepest root French, or German, or Polish nationals, even if individual, acculturated Jews wanted to think of themselves that way and aspired to nothing more than that status.[28] Thus, to obtain full self-possession, Herzl argued, Jews would have to organize themselves in a self-governing, national way. This had nothing to do with trying to establish Jewish faith and religious practices as the defining characteristic of a nationally organized people. The founders of Zionism "were all products of European education, imbued with the current ideas of the European intelligentsia," as Avineri shows. "Zionism, then, is a post-Emancipation phenomenon. . . . It was a response to the challenges of liberalism and nationalism much more than a response merely to anti-Semitism. . . . Zionism was the most fundamental revolution in Jewish life. It substituted a secular self-identity of the Jews as a nation for the traditional and Orthodox self-identity in religious terms."[29]

Leo Pinsker (1821–1891), a Russian Jewish doctor and author of the influential pamphlet *Autoemancipation* (1882), was critical of Orthodox Judaism because, in his view, it simply helped to sustain a passive attitude among Jews. What was needed was action of a self-emancipatory kind, not more endurance of suffering and waiting for the Messiah.[30] In an important essay, "On Zionism" (1902), Max Nordau (1849–1923), a man of German letters, insisted that "Zionism rejects all mysticism, does not believe in a Return to Zion through miracles and wondrous happenings, but sets out to create it through its own efforts. . . . The idea of nationalism has taught all the nations to acknowledge their own worth, to view their specific qualities and values, and it implanted in them the strong desire for self-rule."[31] Aharon David Gordon (1856–1922), a successful Russian businessman who decided in 1904 to immigrate to Palestine, believed that Jews needed to come together to establish their own economic infrastructure. Political liberalism was not adequate. He joined the Labor Zionism movement and frequently spoke of the need for a new "Religion of Labor" that would lift Jews from passive, merely historical memory to the active shaping of a modern self-supporting nation.[32] Many Zionists turned to socialism, rejecting liberalism as an insufficient and misleading ideology.[33] David Ben-Gurion (1886–1973), who would become Israel's first prime minister, wrote in 1933 that Zionism was a revolutionary movement: "It means taking masses of uprooted, impoverished, sterile Jewish masses, living parasitically off the body of an alien economic body and dependent on others—and introducing them to productive and creative life, implanting them on the land, integrating them into primary production in agriculture, in industry and handicraft." "The very essence of Zionist thinking," he wrote, "is basically revolutionary— it is a revolt against a tradition of many centuries, helplessly longing for redemption. Instead of these sterile and bloodless longings, we substitute a will for realization, an attempt at reconstruction and creativity on the soil of the homeland."[34]

In its early phase, Zionist thinking and dreaming did not focus first of all on establishing a state in Palestine but in fashioning a national idea. This is evident from two directions of Zionist thinking and action. First, the initial hope was simply for a homeland, not necessarily an independent state, and many, like Gordon, immigrated to Palestine to set up small communities of Jews to promote self-sufficiency.[35] The second line of thought, explored by some Zionists, was the possibility of finding a suitable homeland somewhere other than in Palestine. Pinsker, for example, had been chiefly concerned with the Jewish people, not with land in Palestine. "The goal of our present endeavors," he wrote in 1882, "must be not the 'Holy Land' but a land of our own."[36] Insisting on an autonomous state in the land of ancient Israel only gradually became the consensus.[37]

Shlomo Avineri, Walter Laqueur, and others have detailed the rise of Zionism and accounted for its intellectual underpinnings from the early provocations of Nachman Krochmal (1785–1840) and Heinrich Graetz (1817–1891) to the more comprehensive arguments of Moses Hess (1812–1875), Leo Pinsker, and Herzl. It was Herzl who engineered the great political and public relations success at the end of the nineteenth century and into the first years of the twentieth, says Avineri: "Herzl was the first one to achieve a breakthrough for Zionism in Jewish and world public opinion. He turned the quest for a national solution to the plight of the Jewish people from an issue debated at great length and with profound erudition in provincial Hebrew periodicals . . . into a subject for world public opinion. From a marginal phenomenon of Jewish life he painted the Zionist solution on the canvas of world politics—and it has never left it since."[38] After Herzl, those who carried the torch through the First World War to the Balfour Declaration and out from the Holocaust to the founding of Israel in 1948 included, most prominently, Max Nordau, Asher Ginsberg (pen name Ahad Ha'am—"one of the people"—1856–1927), Chaim Weizmann (1874–1952), and David Ben-Gurion.

Although it is not our purpose here to try to present the broader historical context in which Zionism developed and worked to reach its goals, it is important to emphasize that Western interests, including Western *Christian* interests, in having constructive relations with the other peoples of the region functioned as both a drag on and a boost for the establishment of a homeland (or state) for the Jews in Palestine. Ambivalence, equivocations, and vaguely worded statements by politicians, lobbyists, and governments continued right up to 1948 (and continue today). The reasons for this were (are), for example, that Christians had developed extensive educational, medical, and church contacts with Arabs and other peoples in the region for more than a century,[39] that oil became an increasingly important preoccupation of diplomacy,[40] and that until World War II, French and British imperial concerns remained foremost in the greater Middle East.[41] Consider just one vignette from the Paris Peace Conference of 1919 that followed World War I. Margaret

MacMillan explains that in negotiations that continued for a number of months the fate of Palestine rested chiefly with France and Britain.

> The United States, in contrast to what happened after the Second World War, played a minor role. The American government had quietly approved the Balfour Declaration and [President Woodrow] Wilson himself was sympathetic to Zionism. "To think," he told a leading New York rabbi, "that I the son of the manse should be able to help restore the Holy Land to its people." It would do the Jews good, he thought, to enjoy their own nationality. . . . But then there was [for Wilson] the sacred tenet of self-determination. Why should the wishes of a minority of Jews prevail over those of a much larger number of Arabs?[42]

For the negotiations, Lord Balfour and U.S. Supreme Court Justice Louis Brandeis came up with an "ingenious solution" to that way of weighting numbers. The relative numbers of Jews and Arabs in Palestine, they argued, should be considered in relation to the greater number of Jews who live outside Palestine. The weight then falls in favor of the Jews. "And Zionism," said Balfour, "be it right or wrong, good or bad, is rooted in age-long traditions, in present needs, in future hopes of far profounder import than the desires and prejudices of the 700,000 Arabs who now inhabit that ancient land." In any case, he pointed out, reverting to the language of the old diplomacy, the Great Powers were behind Zionism. Wilson nevertheless insisted that his Commission of Inquiry into the Middle East include Palestine. The two American commissioners, Charles Crane and Henry King, the businessman and the professor, reported back at the end of the summer of 1919 that the Arabs in Palestine were "emphatically against the entire Zionist program" and recommended that the Peace Conference limit Jewish immigration and give up the idea of making Palestine a Jewish homeland. Nobody paid the slightest attention.[43]

For the next three decades the arguments and struggles continued until, following the Holocaust and World War II, the state of Israel was born in 1948. Finally, at that moment, in Laqueur's judgment, Zionism and its institutions came to an end.[44] The Zionist dream had been fulfilled; the goal had been reached. Now the management of a state—one nation-state among others—in which most of the world's Jews did not even live, became the responsibility of the Israeli government. However, the question of whether Zionism has, in fact, reached its end remains open even today—open to the future of the actual endurance and achievements of the state that Zionism helped to create. If, in contrast to Laqueur, one believes, for example, that Zionism has not and cannot come to an end until the Jewish state controls all of the land promised to ancient Israel and/or is finally secure within its borders, then one can recognize in the Settler movement, among other efforts, the continuation of Zionism as it presses on toward goals that have not yet been realized.

This is the juncture at which we must say something about the ongoing debate within Israel and among Jews throughout the world about the legitimacy of the state of Israel and of the Zionist movement that brought it into existence. Laqueur does not doubt for a minute that "the establishment of the Jewish state has been the greatest turning point in two thousand years of Jewish history and has had a profound effect on Jewish life all over the world."[45] However, writing in 1972, Laqueur says, "the main source of Zionist weakness has been the fact that conditions for the realisation of the Zionist dream were never favourable. [The state of Israel] has served as a national home for less than one-fifth of world Jewry. Even of those in sympathy with Zionism only a few went to Palestine. Only an infinitesimal portion of American, British, French or German (before 1933) Jewry has settled in the Jewish national home."[46] One question that remains open, then, is whether the state of Israel is even necessary to assure the common identity of world Jewry. To what degree do Jews, whether inside or outside Israel, see it as central to their identity as Jews? Another question is whether Israel is serving to unite Jews or is contributing to a division between those who accept Israel and think in terms of Jewish-ethnic nationalism, and those, particularly in the Orthodox camp, who reject the state of Israel (or at least its mode of operation) as a violation of some or all of the principles of Judaism.

The greatest opposition to Zionism and Israel among Jews comes from the most Orthodox (though not from all of them) who believe that the recovery of Zion and the fulfillment of God's promises are not something that Jews in exile can choose to make happen on their own terms. And a modern, secular state, even if organized by ethnic Jews, certainly does not represent the fulfillment of the prophetic hope of celebrating the great ingathering "next year in Jerusalem." Even if exile entails suffering and persecution, true Judaism calls for obedience to God's will as expressed in the Torah and in the patient waiting for God to restore his people to Zion.[47]

One of the first rabbis to try to develop a comprehensive politico-religious philosophy to reconcile religious Judaism with Zionism was Abraham Isaac Kook (1865–1935).[48] "The People of Israel, the Torah, and the Land of Israel are One," according to Kook. "The hope for the Redemption is the force that sustains Judaism in the Diaspora; the Judaism of Eretz Israel is the very Redemption." Many Jews returning to the promised land may be hostile to religion, Kook recognized, but that is only the subjective side of the matter. "In the divine cosmic order, where every detail has its own place and *telos*, the true meaning of a person's action may be unknown to himself." The objective achievement of Zionism may represent divine providence even if secular Jews do not recognize it. Kook acknowledged that once a state is formed and "Judaism re-enters the practical, historical arena, it might become entangled in the game of power politics and be tainted by it." He even believed that the Jews should not engage in political life if "statehood requires bloody ruthlessness and demands a talent for evil." Nevertheless, he thought that the rebirth of Israel and the ingathering of exiles could be part of the "universal restoration (*Tikun olam*)" that Jews had always anticipated. "God did indeed choose Israel as his people, but the whole world is his Creation, and every human being, Jew and non-Jew alike, was created in his image."

Here one can see the primary lines of internal Jewish disagreements that continue up to the present: tension between the use of political power and doing justice, between recovery of the land and obedience to God, between earthly redemption and eternal fulfillment, between national politics as practiced by any state and the practices that are incumbent on Jews as God's chosen people. For our purposes here, we need not try to sort out the many camps of agreement and disagreement on Zionism and the legitimacy of Israel. Now that Israel exists, no Jew can remain neutral.

Among contemporary Jews who, for moral or religious reasons, call into question the legitimacy of the state of Israel or its present conduct is Marc Ellis, a professor at Baylor University. Ellis discusses a number of older and contemporary witnesses who have maintained a critical distance from Israel. Roberta Strauss Feuerlicht, for example, argued (in the 1980s) that the "essential heritage" of the Jews is ethics, not power. What binds together ancient and contemporary Jews "is not statehood but the burden they placed upon themselves and posterity when they internalized morality and gave the world the ethical imperative."[49] If achieving and maintaining state power undermines the ethical imperative, then Jews have lost rather than gained their security and identity.

While a number of critics of Zionism and of the state of Israel appeal to the Torah, others draw on the prophetic tradition, as Ellis shows. One such spokesman is the American activist and *Tikun* editor, Michael Lerner. Now that Israel exists, it must be evaluated, says Lerner, according to Jewish prophetic terms and not simply in terms of the secular national interests of other states. Thus, for example, for Israel to forcibly occupy Palestinian territory and to treat Palestinians unjustly threatens the survival of Judaism worldwide. "A Judaism that has lost its moral teeth and becomes an apologist for every Israeli policy, no matter what its moral context, is a Judaism that not only betrays the prophetic tradition, but also risks the adherence of the Jewish people."[50] From Lerner's point of view, "There is no right to the Land of Israel if Jews oppress the ger (stranger), the widow, the orphan, or any other group that is powerless."[51]

Having surveyed the recent history of Israel and called up the voices of a host of Jewish dissenters who are seldom heard in American media, Ellis concludes his book with these words: "In the twenty-first century the synagogues are plush and inviting; the Holocaust memorials are part of the landscape of America; Israel flourishes in economy and technology. But, whither the prophetic voice in Jewish life and beyond? Can we, as Jews, speak for others in the name of justice, when the people we can free [now under Israeli occupation] have been denied their freedom in its fullness?"[52]

What does Zionism have in common with American new-Israelitism? Or are the two nationalisms incompatible with, and unrelated to, one another? The United States only haltingly came to support the formation of the state of Israel, but it was the first state in the world to grant Israel formal recognition.[53] Today, the United States recognizes Israel as a democratic ally, showing that democracy can exist outside Europe and the Americas. But democratic camaraderie has little to do with the deeper driving motives of Zionism and the American civil religion. It is true that many Americans, not only American Jews, feel strong sympathy with the Jews because of the Holocaust and want to support Israel for that reason.[54] Perhaps we must simply recognize that there is a very close bond between the two states and leave it at that. But the nature of that bond requires further investigation because of an additional factor, namely, the contemporary alliance between the very strong Israel lobby in the United States and millions of American Christian Zionists.[55]

CHRISTIAN ZIONISM

Christian Zionism is today overwhelmingly an American phenomenon,[56] though its roots reach far back into British history. In its earliest phases, vivified by the Reformation, Christian anticipation of a return of Jews to the promised land was connected with the expectation that they would be converted to Christianity; their conversion and return would then precipitate the return of Christ and the end of history. In the nineteenth century, however, as Stephen Sizer explains, premillennial movements emerged in Britain and the United States that diverged in their interpretation of the timing of the conversion and return of the Jews. "Covenantal premillennialism," which remained strongest among British Christian Zionists, held that the Jews would first convert to Christianity and return to Palestine with other Christian believers before the return of Christ. By contrast, "dispensational premillennialism," which became dominant in the United States, held that the Jewish people might return to the land either before or after their conversion, but they "would remain distinctly separate from the church."[57] Charles Haddon Spurgeon (1834–1892), England's most famous nineteenth-century preacher, objected to the dispensational argument "that God had separate purposes for the Jews apart from the church."[58] At the opposite end of the spectrum from Spurgeon are today's *political* premillennialists—mostly American—who disavow any need for an evangelistic outreach to the Jews and who support unquestioned U.S. support of Israel on the grounds that "Jews are accepted by God on the basis of their own covenant and will recognize their Messiah when he returns."[59] The chief responsibility of Christians now in relation to the Jews, therefore, is simply to encourage American support of Israel until Christ returns so that America itself will be blessed.

Each of these Christian premillennial reasons for supporting the return of Jews to the promised land has a basis quite different than the one supported by Zionism. Nevertheless, insofar as many Christians have come to believe that the founding and continued existence of the state of Israel represents a fulfillment of biblical prophecy, Christian Zionism meshes closely with almost any argument that calls for unwavering American support of Israel. Christian Zionism, therefore, inventively draws together the first two Zionisms in arguing that God's most important mission for new-Israelite America is to fulfill its responsibility to help shepherd Jews back to the promised land and, since 1948, to support the state of Israel at all costs.

Christian Zionist Michael Evans, for example, in his *The American Prophecies*,[60] writes of the divinely ordained action of American presidents who prepared the way for the founding of the state of Israel. And once Israel came into existence, America's own new-Israelite calling gained a sharpened focus, namely, to serve as the protector of the new Jewish state. God's admonition to the United States is this, writes Evans: "If you abandon Israel, God will never forgive you." The United States is thus specially implicated in God's promise to Abraham: "I will bless those who bless you, and whoever curses you I will curse."[61]

How are we to make sense of Christian Zionism and the powerful influence it exerts on America's foreign policy toward Israel and the wider Middle East? Let's probe further into the historical background and development of the movement.

One can find the source of both American new-Israelitism and Christian Zionism in early British history. Long before Britain was an empire or even a maritime power, writes Barbara Tuchman, "an attachment to Palestine had been developing for spiritual or sentimental or moral or religious reasons or what might be called collectively cultural reasons. Among these the English Bible and its prophecies was the most important single factor. For the Bible, which was a history of the Hebrews and of the prophet they rejected, came to be adopted, in Thomas Huxley's phrase, as 'the national epic of Britain.'"[62] In 1649 Tuchman recounts, at the peak of Puritan rule in England, Joanna and Ebenezer Cartwright petitioned the government to become the first, along with the Dutch, to "transport Izraell's sons and daughters in their ships to the Land promised to their forefathers, Abraham, Isaac and Jacob for an everlasting Inheritance."[63] The Cartwrights' petition was not a "single eccentricity" in the mid-1660s, says Tuchman. It arose from a widespread Puritan adoption of the biblical narrative as their own as "re-embodied saints of Israel," responsible in some way to carry forward the biblical promises to Israel. "According to Scripture," these English Puritans believed, "the kingdom of Israel for all mankind would come when the people of Israel were restored to Zion. Only then would the world see the advent of the Messiah or, in Christian terms, the Second Advent."[64]

Two hundred years after the Puritan era in Britain, the seventh Earl of Shaftesbury (1801–1885), an ardent Bible believer, expressed an attitude that would increasingly come to characterize British and American Christian Zionists, namely, a preoccupation with the prerequisites of Christ's return. To Lord Shaftesbury, writes Tuchman, "as to all the Israel-for-prophecy's-sake school, the Jews were simply the instrument through which biblical prophecy could be fulfilled. They were not a people, but a mass Error that must be brought to a belief in Christ in order that the whole chain reaction leading to the Second Coming and the redemption of mankind might be set in motion."[65] Sizer emphasizes that Shaftesbury's motives were not narrowly religious but also political since he and other British leaders wanted a greater British presence in Palestine. But the two aims might be combined in a complementary fashion.[66] Shaftesbury's influence was immense in promoting what came to be called Zionism. "Indeed," writes Sizer, "it was probably Shaftesbury who inspired Israel Zangwell and Theodore Herzl to coin the phrase: 'A land of no people for a people with no land.' Shaftesbury, a generation earlier, imagining Palestine to be empty, had come up with the slogan, 'A country without a nation for a nation without a country.'"[67]

Among the British Christian political leaders who helped realize the Zionist dream were William Hechler (1845–1931) and Arthur James Balfour (1848–1930), author of the all-important Balfour Declaration. Hechler, who became chaplain to the British Embassy in Vienna in 1885, "became Herzl's chief Christian ally in helping to realize his vision of a Zionist State, [and was] one of only three Christians invited to attend the [first] World Congress of Zionists" in 1897.[68] Hechler's booklet, *The Restoration of the Jews to Palestine* (1894) came out two years before Herzl's *Der Judenstaat*. And Hechler's diplomatic efforts eventually led him, like a number of later American political dispensationalists, away from the belief that evangelism was a priority and that restoration to the land would only come about as a consequence of the Jewish people turning to faith in Jesus Christ. After 1897, "Hechler was insisting instead that it was the destiny of Christians simply to help restore the Jews to Palestine,"[69] not to convert them.

Church of Ireland pastor John Nelson Darby (1800–1882), considered the father of dispensational theology, laid the basis for American Christian Zionism. He had a great influence on those who developed and preached dispensationalism, including James H. Brookes (1830–1897), Dwight L. Moody (1837–1899), and C. I. Scofield (1843–1921), to name only three. Scofield, like Hechler, believed "that restoration to the land would occur before Israel's conversion and only after the Lord had returned."[70] The preaching and teaching of these leaders inspired millions of Americans to believe that the United States bore a special responsibility to support the return of Jews to Palestine. And after Israel's establishment in 1948, that same faith led to the conviction that the United States should support the state of Israel at all costs without regard to whether

Jews had become or were becoming Christians. "Since Christian Zionists believe the Jews remain God's 'chosen people' and that their final restoration is prophesied, it follows that the promises made to Abraham concerning their original inheritance in the land of Canaan must also still apply."[71] Although ancient Israel's prophets delivered God's word of judgment on them for their idolatry and injustice, leading to the destruction of the northern kingdom by Assyria and of the southern kingdom by Babylon, dispensationalists have long held that God's promise of the land to Abraham is unconditional and perpetual and thus that the land from the Nile to the Euphrates, including all of Jerusalem, belongs to today's Jews and not to any other people. God's promise to bring the exiles back to Jerusalem and to restore Israel, these interpreters of the Bible believe, means precisely that the modern state of Israel is the fulfillment of God's promises and that all of the land promised by God to Israel should come back under the sovereignty of modern Israel. Therefore, most Christian Zionists are strongly committed to Israel's territorial expansion until the state is coincident with, or controls all of, that land.[72]

Lest one imagine that these theological convictions and arguments remain confined to church sermons and Sunday School classes, it is important to emphasize that they are among the few ideas that compel millions of American Christians to engage in political action. The action for some includes phoning the White House or members of Congress when Christian Zionist leaders alert them that a government decision might be made that could endanger Israel or limit American support of Israel.[73] For others the action may include marching and displaying placards at events such as the Annapolis conference in November 2007. And for others the action may be taking friends on regularly sponsored trips to Israel, often including meeting with Israeli officials, to see for themselves what God is doing to build and expand the territory promised to the Jews.[74] Among the groups pursuing one or more of these action agendas today (in addition to other activities) are Bridges for Peace, the International Christian Embassy Jerusalem, Christians for Israel, Christian Friends of Israel, Christian Israel Public Action Campaign, Christian Witness to Israel, Churches Ministry Among Jewish People, Christians United for Israel, and the Unity Coalition for Israel (UCFI). The UCFI was founded in 1994 and is now the largest and most powerful Christian Zionist network in the United States. According to Sizer, it is "a broad coalition of 200 different and autonomous Jewish and Christian organizations representing 40 million members who are 'dedicated to a secure Israel.'"[75]

According to Evans, "Prophecy declares that Jerusalem will be united and in Jewish hands when the Messiah comes. Satan's goal: to divide Jerusalem and stop the prophet clock that will seal his doom. . . . The battle being fought over Jerusalem is not politics—it's prophecy. It's not a foreign policy battle, but a heavenly battle! When our president says that East Jerusalem and Judea and Samaria are illegal, he is shaking his fist in the face of God Almighty, like ancient Nebuchadnezzar, and challenging him." Consequently, Evans argues, "The restoration of Israel is not an American gift to God Almighty—it was prophesied to happen!"[76] Although Evans' statement that control of Jerusalem and the West Bank is a prophetic, not a political matter, his purpose in writing and speaking is certainly to promote a political action agenda for American Christians.

Elements of Evans' agenda for American foreign policy include the following:[77] (1) "Allow Israel to finish her security fence in order to save both Palestinian and Israeli lives"; (2) "Recognize Jerusalem as Israel's capital and ratify the Jerusalem Embassy Act," which includes the mandate to move the American embassy from Tel Aviv to Jerusalem; (3) "Ratify the 1987 Anti-Terrorism Act," which includes naming the Palestine Liberation Organization a terrorist group; (4) "Require the Arabs to end the Palestinian Refugee problem by taking the refugees into their nations just as Israel, Germany, the United States, Jordan, and other nations have done with other refugee groups." In other words, help cleanse the land of Palestinians; and (5) "fight the racism of anti-Semitism as fervently as we fight other racism in our nation."[78] And anti-Semitism here means almost any condemnation of Israel and its actions. In other words, Christian Zionists should be demanding that the U.S. government support Israel in every way, giving no consideration to the Palestinians and other neighbors of Israel except to make sure that they do nothing to interfere with Israel's expansion and security.

However strange the theology behind this movement may sound to people unacquainted with it, the political power of American Christian Zionism is immense. Sizer provides the following excellent summary of the movement.[79]

1. Christian Zionism, through its active and public support for Jewish restoration to Palestine, predated the rise of Jewish Zionism by at least sixty years.
2. Its origins lie within nineteenth-century British premillennial sectarianism. . . .
3. While the strategic value of a Jewish homeland in Palestine was a factor in British foreign policy during the nineteenth century,

it became a feature of American foreign policy by the end of the twentieth century.

4. Without the initiative and commitment of British Christians . . . during the nineteenth century, it is questionable whether the Jewish Zionist dream of a national homeland in Palestine would have been realized.

5. Without the sustained political support of Christian Zionists in America, and significant government funding, it is doubtful whether the State of Israel would have remained in existence since 1948, let alone continued to occupy and settle the West Bank since 1967.

6. Conservative estimates would suggest that the Christian Zionist movement is *at least ten times larger* than the Jewish Zionist movement and has become a dominant lobby within contemporary American politics [emphasis added].

CRITICAL INTERPRETATION

It has long been remarked that many different modern ideologies—religiously deep, overarching narratives about the meaning of life and history—manifest a dependence on, or derivation from, the grand biblical narrative of history even when those ideologies, knowingly or unknowingly, secularize and deform the biblical story.[80] In the biblical narrative, God is the creator of all things and in response to human disobedience not only delivers judgment on fallen humanity but chooses Israel to be a restorative light and blessing to the nations, to show the way to a properly reordered human life in the service of God. Because of Israel's disobedience, God drives them out of the land but promises a return for a remnant who will be connected with God's reconciling redemption of the whole world through the establishment of his kingdom forever. For Christians, that narrative comes to its culminating focus in Jesus Christ, the Messiah of Israel, God incarnate, who has inaugurated God's kingdom through his death, resurrection, and ascension. Through Christ, God has broken down the wall separating Jew and Gentile, and when he comes again in glory to complete the establishment of God's kingdom, the faithful from all nations and all generations will be gathered into the new Jerusalem to live in peace with God and one another forever.

Whether one considers Enlightenment rationalism, or revolutionary Marxism, or different forms of nationalism, a biblically derived and deformed story can be found within. The modernist narrative will begin with a world that has been deformed by human ignorance, or priestly manipulation, or oppression of the poor by the rich. That "sinful," "fallen" condition can be overcome only by a new "messiah" of scientifically enlightened educators, or of democratic liberators, or of proletarian revolutionaries, or of anti-colonial nationalists. And the resulting redemption will bring into existence the "new man" and a "new society" of freedom and democracy for every nation, or of a world Communist society, or of peace and security grounded in a scientifically enlightened consensus.

Against that backdrop, the best way to understand the broad sweep and the close intertwinement of the movements we have examined in this chapter—American new-Israelitism, Zionism, and Christian Zionism—is, I believe, to see them as peculiar among modern ideologies because of their indebtedness to selected themes in the original biblical narrative. In my judgment, however, none of these Zionisms interprets its favored themes in a way consistent with the larger biblical narrative.

Jewish Zionism is the most direct in affirming its revolutionary character in turning away from religious Judaism. Nevertheless, its insistence on restoring Jews to the supposed territory of ancient Israel draws on familiar, fundamental elements of the biblical story (covenant, promised land, chosen people) and thereby even draws support from many religious Jews.

The American civil-religious narrative, derived from the Puritans' application of a part of the biblical narrative to themselves, is for most American Christians, I believe, thought to be consistent, in a this-worldly sense, with a providential extension of the Christian biblical narrative. Such an understanding is made possible, however, only by a separation of the story about God's providential appointment of America as a this-worldly new Israel, on the one hand, from the story of the salvation of souls in Christ for eternity, on the other. Both parts can seem to fit together because they make use of selected elements in the biblical narrative, even though the dualistic, synthetic result represents a deformation of the biblical story.

Christian Zionists will, I believe, be the most ardent critics of my judgment that theirs is a modern ideological construct that is neither biblical nor consistent with the biblical narrative. They will contend, to the contrary, that they are, in fact, purely and simply telling or prophesying the last chapters of the one and only biblical story.

No other modern ideology of which I am aware tries so deliberately to draw on or connect with explicit themes in the biblical narrative to galvanize adherents into a way of life that can move history toward its intended destiny.[81] This is not the place to engage in the extensive biblical interpretation and ideological analyses that are needed to support a judgment that none of the three modern Zionisms are consistent with the larger biblical narrative. But by drawing attention to the fact that all three draw more fully on elements of the biblical story and on Jewish and Christian history than do any other religiously deep modern ideologies, we can begin to understand why each of them, and all three combined, have had so much influence in the contemporary world of politics and government. Anyone who wants to understand America's role in the world, and particularly its role in the Middle East, must, therefore, seek to understand the powerful, enduring influence of these visions—these commitments, these ways of life—as narratives about the meaning and movement of history toward its true destiny.

This conclusion also invites us to consider the possibility that a Christian reading of the biblical narrative along the lines suggested might point toward not only a different set of foreign policy priorities for the United States but also a different scholarly analysis of the dynamics of the region. That is, it might point toward an example of a Christian form of "faith-based International Relations."

Part II

ENLISTING RELIGION
DIPLOMATICALLY

Chapter 5

American Religion and
European Anti-Americanism

Thomas Albert Howard

The previous two chapters have illustrated from different vantage points
the extent to which American foreign policymaking has historically
been conditioned by the religiously formed perspectives, held tacitly or
explicitly, of its leading practitioners and of the diverse but pervasively
religious citizenry to which such leaders responded. The larger purpose
of Part 1 has been to exhibit the importance to informed foreign policymaking of "taking religion seriously." This chapter opens an examination
of how religion might be "enlisted diplomatically" by calling attention to
neglected religious factors at work in America's oldest, and in some ways
its most complex, foreign relationship: that with Europe. The suggestion that there are formative religious undercurrents in that relationship
is likely to be greeted from the European side with the rejoinder that
religion is America's problem and European secularism the solution. The
argument of this chapter, however, is that European anti-Americanism
is itself a legacy of deeply rooted cultural perceptions upon which religious orientations have exercised a substantial impact. Placing relations
between the United States and Europe on a more constructive footing
than they have been in the recent past will require more patient attention

to these religiously formed historical currents than both International Relations theorists and foreign policy practitioners on either side of the Atlantic have so far been willing to devote to them.

As has been widely observed, the American invasion of Iraq in 2003 roiled transatlantic relations, offering a jarring impetus for intellectuals and policymakers to consider afresh various social and cultural differences between Western Europe and the United States, many of which had been wholly or partially obscured during the Cold War and its immediate aftermath. "The war in Iraq has made the Atlantic seem wider," the German journalist Peter Schneider noted in a 2004 *New York Times* op-ed, "but in reality it has had the effect of a magnifying glass, bringing older and more fundamental differences between Europe and the United States into focus."[1] Topping Schneider's list was what we might call the religion factor. The United States is a deeply religious nation, he noted, "while in Europe the process of secularization continues unabated."[2] In a recent book, Andrei S. Markovits seconds this sentiment, observing that "the divergent paths [of] religion . . . differentiate the United States from Europe perhaps more than any other single social, political, or cultural factor."[3]

Many European intellectuals, in fact, have expressed similar, if less dispassionate, sentiments, agitated in the extreme that the high moral pitch of President Bush's post-9/11 foreign policy—underwritten by a cabal of "neoconservative" intellectuals and "evangelical" electoral shock troops—constituted no episodic phenomenon, but expressed something entrenched, and irredeemable, in American history and culture. This worry helped give rise to a spectacularly staged series of essays in Europe's newspapers of record on May 31, 2003, spearheaded by Jürgen Habermas, with the late Jacques Derrida riding shotgun. In the *Frankfurter Allgemeine Zeitung*, Habermas and Derrida called for a "core Europe"—principally France, Italy, Germany, and the Benelux countries—to serve as a "locomotive" of European integration "to counterbalance the hegemonic unilateralism of the United States."[4] Besides offering policy suggestions, their essay engaged in transatlantic cultural analysis, touching upon religious differences: "In European societies, secularization is relatively developed. . . . [This] has had desirable consequences for our political culture. For us, a president who opens his daily business with public prayer . . . is hard to imagine."[5]

The Italian philosopher and member of the European Parliament Gianni Vattimo lent a supporting voice in Italy's *La Stampa*. Claiming knowledge of "something felt in the consciousness of all Europeans," he made clear that "our spirit differs from the currently prevailing spirit in American society," opining further that "our hope is that this difference will become the inspiring principle for a political system able to bestow on Europe the dignity and significance it deserves in world politics."[6] When detailing the differences, religion, once again, came to the fore: "We [Europeans] are certainly familiar with the religious roots of North American society. . . . But . . . [the] religiosity that characterizes the American spirit has ended up manifesting itself as what we fear it really is: the notion that 'God is with us,' and the proof of it is in our economic and military superiority."[7]

For sociologists preoccupied with the so-called secularization thesis, the transatlantic religious divide has emerged as a truism in recent scholarship. While once sociologists held that modernity led almost inexorably to secularization in society, most now concede that this is not necessarily the case: the United States is at once a thoroughly modernized nation, indeed the paradigmatic example of modernity in many respects, and is simultaneously awash in a sea of faith, especially when compared to most Western European societies.[8]

However, for scholars of international relations and those interested in the genealogy of European anti-Americanism, religion has received far too little attention, despite being frequently invoked, almost offhandedly, as a leading dividing factor and source of misunderstanding across the Atlantic.[9] Behind these invocatory references lies the assumption that disparaging assessments of religiosity in the United States—not unlike those of Habermas, Derrida, and Vattimo—emanate from a secular historical consciousness, inclined leftward politically, passing skeptical judgment on overly credulous "Yankees" slow to accept that enlightenment and the disenchantment of the world stand or fall together.

Religion generally, and transatlantic religious differences in particular, need to be taken more seriously by students of international relations. Skillen's arguments have already intimated that anti-American sentiments vis-à-vis religion are not simply a byproduct of Europe's exceptional secularism and leftist political traditions. I want to develop the more specific argument that, to understand the genealogy of European anti-Americanism in its full historical complexity, one must actually fix one's gaze at the opposite end of the political spectrum, to misgivings about the United States emanating from voices on Europe's historical Right—or, borrowing from British political parlance, what I'll call "the Tory imagination." To be sure, European anti-Americanism has a recognizable "Whiggish" aspect too, a secularist-leftist mien, but this is of more recent provenance, nourished largely by socialist political currents in the twentieth century and the juggernaut of "critical theory" in the postwar transatlantic academy. However, if we cast our glance farther back, to the nineteenth century, it becomes apparent that most European liberals and social democrats, even those inclined to radicalism, regularly lionized the United States—praising its religious voluntarism in particular—as an example of what European nation-states should aspire to, if only they could shake off the backlash against the French Revolution and Napoleonic upheaval inaugurated by the political Restoration of 1815, the resurgent ecclesiastical establishmentarianism of this era, and the climate of Romantic nostalgia in literature and the arts.

But it was also during the post-1815 era of Restoration and Romanticism that lasting anti-American images and metaphors first gained wide currency in European thought; they have since migrated to various points on the political landscape, perhaps particularly to the far Left today, although repositories of an older Tory anti-Americanism have by no means been extinguished.[10] *Les extrêmes se touchent*, as the French say, and this is perhaps especially true when considering anti-Americanism and the European political spectrum.[11]

After the collapse of the democratic experiment in France in the early nineteenth century, the fledgling American republic was the only state of any size in the world to still practice what many considered the invalidated ideas of democracy, equality, and religious voluntarism. At this time, numerous European visitors, immigrants, and intellectuals (many who never went abroad) sought to "explain" America to an Old World audience seemingly insatiable in its curiosity to make sense of the upstart nation. "America was the China of the nineteenth century," as one scholar has put it, "described, analyzed, promoted, and attacked in virtually every nation struggling to come to terms with new social and political voices."[12] What had been regarded as a remote backwater of colonial exploitation in the eighteenth century became for Europeans, virtually overnight, truly a *novus ordo seclorum*, a phenomenon to be examined, a moral and political experiment to be judged, and a possible laboratory of the future, as Alexis de Tocqueville believed.

Tocqueville's own assessment of the fate of religion in the United States is fairly nuanced, but quite positive in many respects. "Upon my arrival in the United States," run often quoted lines from his *Democracy in America*, the religious aspect of the country was the first thing that struck my attention. . . . In France I had almost always seen the spirit of religion and the spirit of freedom marching in opposite directions. But in America I found they were intimately united and that they reigned in common over the same country.[13]

When coupled with tales of persecuted religious minorities finding safe haven in America, Tocqueville's interpretation suggests a fairly sanguine view of religious conditions in the new nation.

But we should resist equating Tocqueville's views on America with those of Europe's intelligentsia *tout court*. To the conservative imagination of the nineteenth century, the American religious experiment in "voluntary" belief and the political institutions enabling it represented a perilous plunge into cultural confusion and social anarchy. The French archconservative Joseph de Maistre might well serve as the archetype of this mindset; he saw the American and French revolutions, if not identical, as signs of profound impiety, political hubris against divinely sanctioned traditions. Austria's Count Metternich, the diplomatic architect of the post-1815 order, once opined that the new American state set "altar against altar" and represented an abiding insult to time-tested Old World institutions.[14] The United States' want of an established church, as the Austrian jurist and diplomat Johann Georg Hülsemann put it in 1823, represented a "strange" aspect of the new transatlantic polity and "a sharp point of opposition to everything that our [European] civilization rests upon."[15]

The Catholic Church, a pillar of the Restoration era, viewed the American experiment through the lenses of the French Revolution and the Italian *Risorgimento*, both judged to loose anarchy upon the world and drown the ceremony of innocence. When Félicité de Lamennais, an early Catholic champion of religious liberty, made his famous appeal to Rome in 1832, he brought to the pope's attention the example of the constitutional freedoms of the United States, suggesting that modern freedoms and true religion need not be sworn enemies. The pope, Gregory XVI, was not impressed. In *Mirari vos* (1832), the encyclical rebutting Lamennais, the pope condemned religious liberty, defining it as the error of "indifferentism." From "this most foul font of indifferentism," the pope wrote, "flows that absurd and erroneous teaching, or rather that folly [*deliramentum*] that it is necessary to assure and guarantee to whomever it may be the liberty of conscience."[16] The point was echoed later by Pius IX in his more famous "Syllabus of Errors" (1864).

The Catholic Church not only regarded the American experiment as deficient in its assertion of religious freedom. As a nation founded by Calvinist separatists, and harboring numerous Protestant emigrants from Europe, the United States represented for some the land where the principles of the Reformation would be reduced to absurdity. Not surprisingly, ultramontane Catholics were keen to call attention to the proliferation of Protestant sects in the United States, depicting the new nation as a grand bedlam of religious schism and theological charlatanism. For example, the entry on America in a Catholic encyclopedia (1854) depicts the United States as a land of bizarre religious enthusiasms; the authors even list one nonexistent sect alleged to require its members to pluck out their right eye in literal interpretation of the biblical passage in Matthew 5:29![17] In his *History of Modern Protestantism* (1858), the Catholic scholar Joseph Edmund Jörg portrayed American society as floundering in "chaos," resulting from the "religious individualism" and "sectarian spirit" of Protestantism.[18]

La Civiltà Cattolica, a Jesuit publication founded in Naples in 1850, emerged as a leading organ of ultramontane opinion, often exhibiting a pointedly anti-American slant. An article from 1860, "Mormonism in its Connections with Modern Protestantism," penned by the cardinal archbishop Karl August von Reisach (1800–1869), is an apt case in point. The success of Mormonism in the United States had long been a source of bewilderment to Europe's traditionalist imagination. In Reisach's interpretation, Mormonism's rise amounted to an indictment of Protestant "religious individualism," to which the American republic had given free reign. He traced the malady of American Protestantism back to colonial New England. Trying to govern society theocratically "in a state of total reliance on the Bible," Puritans were ultimately unable to limit individuals from interpreting the Bible for themselves and "thus the same foundational principle of the Reformation naturally and necessarily caused the collapse of such a theocratic system and caused new sects and religious societies to emerge."[19] The proliferation of sects in the nineteenth century gave rise to conditions of religious confusion, allowing Mormonism fertile ground to take root and, at least for many, to pass itself off as the one true way, a safe passage from sectarianism and individualism to a secure collective and religious certainty. But in Reisach's view, Mormonism itself represented simply a sect writ large, a symptom of American Protestantism, not its cure, and thereby a powerful, inadvertent witness for the Catholic Church as the authentic bulwark of religious truth and social cohesion.

European Catholic misgivings about the American polity continued apace during the pontificates of Pius IX (r.1846–1878) and Leo XIII (r.1878–1903), arguably reaching a high-water mark in the latter's encyclical *Testem benevolentiae nostrae* (1899), which condemned the so-called heresy of Americanism (to my knowledge, the only time a national identity has ever been associated with a heresy).[20] The complex background to this papal condemnation need not be belabored here, but it found its center of gravity in debates about American freedom and ecclesiastical order. Many European clergy, particularly those in France, worried that their counterparts in the United States had succumbed to the American environment of "indifferentism," in that some had advocated a church remodeled along liberal democratic lines. Other clergy even equated "Americanism" with the degenerate spirit of modern times itself.[21] In Leo XIII's encyclical, European clergy got what they wanted, even if in a much less alarmist voice: a warning against the "Americanist" heresy. The events surrounding this controversy negatively colored Catholic attitudes toward America until a time when Catholic thinkers such as Jacques Maritain and John Courtney Murray—not to mention Vatican II's epochal *Declaration on Religious Freedom* (1965)—allowed for a more positive estimation of the United States.[22]

The Catholic Church, of course, had no monopoly on anti-American sentiment in the nineteenth century. For anyone—Catholic, Anglican, Lutheran, or Reformed—who took Europe's state-church system to be the proper state of things, the hurly-burly pluralistic ethos of American religious life, with its revivals, camp meetings, and itinerant preachers, elicited a skeptical, condescending attitude, if not one of bemusement and ridicule.

The Anglicans Frances Trollope, Anthony Trollope, and Bishop Samuel Wilberforce exhibited such attitudes. After traveling throughout the United States and residing for several years in Ohio, Frances Trollope published (in London) her widely read *The Domestic Manners of the Americans* (1832). Her portrait of America as a nation of tobacco-spitting, revivalist zealots and as a people lacking in social refinement became a top seller in British literary circles. One cannot remain long in the United States, she observed, "without being struck with the strange anomalies produced by its religious system. . . . The whole people appear to be divided into an almost endless variety of religious factions."[23] The lack of an established church was the taproot of the problem, she believed, and this point was driven home by her son, the novelist Anthony Trollope. He felt the term "rowdiness" best described the American religious scene, and its manifestations were both a sign and cause of deeper pathologies in American politics and society:

> For myself, I love the name of State and Church, and believe that much of our English well being has depended on it. I have made up my mind to think that union good, and not to be turned away from that conviction. . . . I feel very strongly that much of that which is evil in the structure of American politics is owing to the absence of any national religion, and that something also of social evil has sprung from the same cause.[24]

Bishop Wilberforce of Oxford reached a comparable conclusion in his history of the Episcopal church in the United States. "Every fantastic opinion that has disturbed the peace of Christendom," he wrote, "has been reproduced in stranger growth on the other side of the Atlantic. Division has grown up in all its rankness, and seeded on every side a new crop of errors."[25] This reality, he feared, threatened to produce a generation of untowardly zealous and schismatic individuals who in turn would "obliterate civilization."[26] He found a modicum of comfort in that this uncivilized anarchy existed in the far reaches of the American frontier, at a safe distance from the gothic tranquility of Oxford.

Concerns about religious anarchy easily passed over into broadsides against American culture and society generally. In his *American Notes* (1842), based on his extensive travels in the United States, Charles Dickens wondered how the lack of an established church might have contributed deleteriously to American society, which he viewed as a cauldron of mob passions in politics, libel in the press, and swindling in business. The American Revolution had produced "a degenerate child," he concluded, driving the point home in *The Life and Adventures of Martin Chuzzlewit* (1843), a 700-page novel-cum-anti-American polemic.[27] Dickens' disparaging musings on America, far from standing alone, fit a larger pattern of derisory commentary on the United States by eminent visitors from Victorian Britain.[28] Another revealing example is Matthew Arnold's *Civilization in the United States* (1888), in which the apostle of high learning portrayed the United States as a country of "uninteresting" Philistines given to venal pursuits, in possession of "a defective type of religion."[29]

In continental Europe, leaders of Lutheran and Reformed communities regularly expressed puzzlement at the religious free-for-all of the upstart nation. While the economic and political opportunities in America were rarely gainsaid, Continental religious leaders were less sanguine about the effects of American society on the Old World religion and culture that were being transplanted across the Atlantic by waves of German immigrants during the middle decades of the nineteenth century. Philip Schaff, a Swiss-German Reformed émigré theologian, worried, for example, that the church in America (his adopted home) lacked a principle of authority and mechanism toward unity and thus appeared destined for a career of fissiparous, obscurantist ignominy:

> Tendencies, which had found no political room to unfold themselves in other lands, wrought here without restraint. . . . Every theological vagabond and peddler may drive here his bungling trade, without passport or license, and sell his false ware at pleasure. What is to come of such confusion is not now to be seen.[30]

Less devout German-speaking intellectuals also expressed their misgivings about the United States. The Austrian Romantic author Ferdinand Kürnberger, for example, in his highly popular *Amerikamüde* (A Man Weary of America) of 1855 contrasted the so-called German religion, rich in history and tradition, with the "arid sectarianism" of the Americans, whom he felt were bereft of any sense of the church as an established, culture-bearing entity. He illustrated this point by having the novel's Old World protagonist, one Dr. Moorfeld, visit the city of Philadelphia and there encounter Quakers and other religious communities. Moorfeld is taken aback at the state of the American clergy, whom the author depicts as divisive, hypocritical, and greedy to a man. In his journal, Dr. Moorfeld records:

> In Europe, where there are *established* churches, the clergy . . . exist with a fixed and distinguished position and with a feeling of corporate identity. This provides comfort, rendering them often amiable members of society. Things are different here, where the church as such simply does not matter, where religious communities form and dissolve like tea parties, where it is easier to protect a pasture from grasshoppers than keep a religious society together. Here importance does not rest on churchly authority, but rather on the authority of individual personality. Consequently, among the clergy [in America] a nest of Pharisees has been established, the repulsiveness [*Ekelhaftigkeit*] of which is hard to understand from a European standpoint.[31]

Castigating Philadelphia as a "Zion of religious hypocrisy," the fictional character concludes that it is only right and good that "our governments [in Europe] do not want to tolerate the formation of . . . sects." Without such measures, he implies, Europe would resemble America by giving free reign to a "narrow spirit of obscurantism."[32]

Among nineteenth-century German intellectuals, arguably none held more influence than G. W. F. Hegel. In his *Lectures on the Philosophy of History*, America occupies a marginal position. Hegel's famous division of the world into "three distinct world-outlooks"—Oriental, Greco-Roman, and Germanic—made no place for the indigenous peoples of the New World, and he dismissed the culture of the United States as derivative from Europe and ultimately of negligible importance. "America," he wrote, "has severed itself from the ground that world's history has taken place until now. What has taken place in America so far is a mere echo of the Old World, and the expression of an alien vitality."[33]

To be sure, Hegel admitted that America might represent "the land of the future," "the land of longing for all those who are weary of the historic arsenal that is old Europe."[34] Even so, this land of longing presented for him a problem, particularly in the religious sphere. While dismissive of traditional, creedal Christianity, Hegel was supportive of the Prussian state church and the Ministry of Culture, which had secured for him his influential post at the University of Berlin. To his mind, America constituted a deficiency insofar as it lacked a strong state and a European-style ministry of culture, which, among other things, served to check popular religious enthusiasm. From the august Prussian capital, society across the Atlantic appeared to him a hatchery of religious misfits, isolated from the truly important currents of world history. The United States is the land of "every sort of capriciousness," he wrote.

> This explains the proliferation of sects to the point of sheer madness. . . . This total arbitrariness is such that the various communities hire and fire ministers as they please: the church is not something that [has] . . . an external establishment; instead, religious matters are handled according to the particular views of the congregation. In North America, the wildest freedom of imagination prevails.[35]

Such derisory preoccupation with religion and culture in the United States enjoyed a long life in modern Continental thought—a minor, if not a major, note in the thought of numerous intellectuals influenced by Hegel. Yet it was arguably in Hegel's own stomping grounds, the "mandarin" guilds of the German university system in the late nineteenth century, that anti-American sentiment in general and contempt of American religious life in particular attained a stage of true virtuosity.[36] Although no haven of religious orthodoxy, fin-de-siècle German academic culture, as Fritz Ringer has persuasively argued, constituted a spiritual aristocracy of sorts, empowered by ideals of cultural organicism, criticism of democracy, and an ethos of daunting academic accomplishment. Scholars felt their collective worldview best preserved the genuine spiritual values necessary for a deep and rich culture (*Kultur*), one capable of producing a Goethe, Schiller, or Kant. By contrast, "Western" countries, and America foremost, represented a utilitarian, shallow, mass civilization (*Zivilization*) that threatened to place all "spiritual" (*geistige*) motivations and actions into the maw of purely individualistic, commercial interests. "The [Anglo-American] trader," wrote Werner Sombart after the outbreak of World War I, "regards the whole existence of man on earth as a sum of commercial transactions which everyone makes as favorably as possible for himself, whether with fate or God," adding that "the trader's spirit molds religions in its own image too."[37] One finds similar sentiments in the writings of a wide spectrum of thinkers, such as Oswald Spengler, Adolf von Harnack, Emil Dubois Reymond, and Eduard Spranger. The "breathless haste" of the American, Friedrich Nietzsche had written, precociously capturing a widespread fear, "is already beginning to infect old Europe with its ferocity and is spreading a lack of spirituality [*Geistlosigkeit*] like a blanket."[38]

Max Weber's well-known writings on American religious life reflect his milieu. While he was less politically illiberal and hostile to America than many of his peers, his writings on the "sect spirit" in American society bear witness to a distinctly pre-democratic, European disquiet toward the United States. In the famous final passages of his *Protestant Ethic and the Spirit of Capitalism*, the only nation Weber mentions by name is the United States, the site of capitalism's "highest development," before wondering who will live in this "iron cage" of the future, this site of "mechanized petrifaction, embellished with a sort of convulsive sense of self-importance."[39] In a shorter essay, "The Protestant Sects and the Spirit of Capitalism," written after visiting the United States in 1904, Weber expressed amazement at the high levels of church affiliation in the United States despite the severance of church-state ties. The transference of religion from the public to the private sphere helped account for the voluntary and "ascetic" character of American churches. But, in his interpretation, this asceticism only helped "put a halo around the economic 'individualist' impulses of the modern capitalist ethos."[40]

The German mandarin depiction of America as a religiously deformed, economically utilitarian, and culturally shallow civilization arguably reached its apogee in the writings of Martin Heidegger and in his highly symbolic conception of America—or "Americanism"—as a site of cultural catastrophe. In many respects, Heidegger is a pivotal and revealing figure in the story of European anti-Americanism. Growing up in provincial Baden in southwestern Germany and once a devoted student of Catholic theology (he sought to become a Jesuit as a young man), Heidegger had deep roots in a rural, pre-democratic conservative religious milieu. The ponderous anti-modern, anti-technological outlook that he developed—in, for instance, *An Introduction to Metaphysics*—has exerted an estimable influence on the European Left: on the existentialist Marxism of Jean-Paul Sartre and Simon de Beauvoir and their successors; on the 1960s "New Left" counterculture generally; and, not least, on leaders within Germany's Green Party, the gold standard of contemporary leftist anti-Americanism. One also thinks of postwar *au courant* thinkers such as Herbert Marcuse (*One-Dimensional Man*) and Jean Baudrillard (*L'Amerique*), whose influence in the modern academy, on both sides of the Atlantic, has been considerable and in whose writings the Heideggerian image of "the American" as a history-less "mass man" or "collective man," holding desperately to a simple and irrational faith, emerges as an article of certainty.[41]

But we should not forget Heidegger himself in considering his influence and appeal. Germany, he wrote in 1935, two years after the Nazis had seized power,

> lies today in a great pincer, squeezed by Russia on one side and America on the other. From a metaphysical point of view, Russia and America are the same, with the same dreary technological frenzy and the same unrestricted organization of the average mind.[42]

But in 1942, as the Holocaust was underway, he would write that Americanism is the purest and most problematic form of modernity. "Bolshevism is only a variant of Americanism," he wrote, "the most dangerous shape of boundlessness, because it appears in the form of a democratic middle-class way of life mixed with Christianity, and all this in an atmosphere devoid of any sense of history."[43] "Americanism," as he put it in yet another formulation, "is the still unfolding and not yet full or completed metaphysical essence of the emerging monstrousness of modern times."[44]

To be sure, "anti-Americanism" is a diffuse and complicated phenomenon, polygenetic in its origins, protean in its manifestations, and diverse in possible interpretations. Few would deny, however, that it ranks among the most potent and consequential forces afoot in the contemporary world.[45] At a minimum, I hope to have suggested in this essay that in its early European manifestations, anti-Americanism is not simply a product of "the Left," a secularist, progressive mindset passing judgment on a more religious, conservative one. The deepest historical currents of anti-American sentiment vis-à-vis religion derive from the traditionalist political Right, from "the throne and altar" milieu of reactionary, post-1815 Europe. This particular form of anti-modern conservatism—one of established churches, social hierarchy, and cultural organicism, often expressed by aggrieved aristocrats, bishops, clergy, and professors—is quite foreign to American political thought, with the partial exception of southern Agrarianism. And in Europe today this tradition is vestigial at best (and should not be confused with more recent nationalist and anti-immigrant right-wing voices). Even so, passionate moods of being and thought perish reluctantly in history, especially when the truth of religion and the social order is at stake; more often they live on in transmuted, residual, and unexpected ways. A longer treatment would be necessary to establish this point definitively, but one can reasonably conjecture that a rather venerable aristocratic condescension and contempt of New World religious enthusiasm prowls about today ghost-like in the general (secular) European body politic and historical consciousness, an embedded element of cultural memory.

This point bears underscoring because too frequently discussions of anti-Americanism have been narrowly presentist, revolving around questions of whether the phenomenon is simply a product of "policy" disagreements. Policy plays a crucial role, no doubt (and one can only hope that the Obama administration will help usher in a new chapter in this respect), but to focus on policy preponderantly or exclusively ignores the immense historical tableau informing it. Put more fully, the high levels of anti-Americanism in Europe in recent years—worrisome often to Europeans as much as to Americans[46]—cannot be explained strictly in terms of contemporary developments, divergences on social questions, or recent foreign affairs disagreements, although, again, these admittedly are not negligible issues. One gains deeper and more penetrating insight, I believe, by evaluating contemporary anti-Americanism as an example of a convergence of causes, in this case where two sets of factors—one more diachronic (with a cultural-historical base), the other more synchronic (with an emphasis on policy disagreements)—together produce an effect that is significantly greater than the sum of the parts.

With the respect to the diachronic, European anti-Americanism includes a significant, if often obscured, religious dimension, one that historians of the modern Atlantic world and scholars of international relations would do well to retrieve and understand. One cannot properly understand its deep-seated hold on the imagination if the scope of inquiry is limited to recent developments and the domains of politics, economics, and diplomacy. What is more, intellectuals such as Habermas, (the late) Derrida, and Vattimo certainly might have important and quite valid grievances with recent directions of American foreign policy; and these deserve honest and candid discussion in the media and political arena. Still, their efforts—and those of many others—to insinuate a straightforward link between contemporary policy and America's general religious identity might, finally, tell us as much about elite-European attitudes toward America as about America itself. These attitudes and the long history of concerns, perceptions, and anxieties informing them deserve greater attention from students of International Relations, even as these same students recognize that religion itself can no longer be ignored when evaluating relations among the powers and principalities of the world.[47] Equally, foreign policy practitioners who wish to escape the debilitating mutual misapprehensions of the past should be far more attentive to the underlying religious dynamics that still today shape relations between the United States and Europe.

Chapter 6

Getting Russia Right

John A. Bernbaum

Ten years. Ten months. Ten weeks. Ten days. The years 1989, 1990, and 1991 witnessed the culmination of an incredible acceleration of revolutionary events in Eastern Europe and the Soviet Union. What took ten years in Poland, ten months in Czechoslovakia, and ten weeks in East Germany took only ten days in Romania. The Marxist regimes in these satellite states of the USSR collapsed in an amazing sequence that no one anticipated.[1]

Then, in December 1991, the Soviet Union itself, the imperial power that previously controlled these Eastern European states, dissolved into fifteen republics with barely any bloodshed. These years, these events, will go down in history as seminal years, hinge years in the course of world developments.[2]

The catastrophic nature of those events in the former Soviet Union is hard to comprehend, and as time passes, the full scale of these dramatic changes is often forgotten. A cartoon by Mike Peters of the *Dayton Daily News*, later reprinted in the *Washington Post*, captured the character of the revolutionary changes in the former Soviet Union. The cartoon portrayed a conversation between a Soviet astronaut and an old babushka (grandmother). The exchange went as follows: The astronaut says, "Comrade, I've been in space for a year. It's good to be back in Leningrad." The babushka corrects him: "Sorry, Leningrad is out. This is now St. Petersburg." The shocked astronaut replies, "Leningrad out? But Lenin is the father of Communism." The babushka again corrects him: "Sorry, Communism is out. We are now capitalists." The astronaut can't believe it and says, "Capitalists! But how could Gorbachev allow this to happen?" The babushka explains, "Sorry, Gorbachev is out. He was overthrown by the hard-liners." The astronaut asks confusedly, "You mean the hard-liners are in charge?" The babushka responds, "No, the hard-liners are out. And Yeltsin took over." The astronaut says, "You mean Yeltsin is the head of the Soviet Union?" The babushka corrects him a last time saying, "No, the Soviet Union is out too." The astronaut yells, "No Soviet Union! Quick, alert the Warsaw Pact!" The babushka shakes her head and says, "We need to talk."

In this chapter I argue that a deep religious illiteracy on the part of American diplomatic and academic observers, and Western observers generally, not only prevented them from foreseeing the collapse of the USSR but also from rightly diagnosing its causes and prescribing the remedies called for in its aftermath. It is beyond the scope of the chapter to speculate on how U.S. foreign policy might have followed a different path had its leading practitioners acquired any real grasp of the role of culture and religion in the life and death of the Soviet Union. But if my account of that role is anywhere near the mark, this chapter will lend additional support to the claim that both practical diplomacy and academic International Relations omit religion from their field of vision at their peril. The chapter also attempts a second goal: not only to call for a greater reckoning with the empirical reality of religion on the part of diplomats and scholars but also—in the same vein as the chapters by Daryl Charles and Daniel Philpot—to point toward substantive Christian principles of statecraft which might suitably inform American policy toward Russia in the future.

A FAULTY DIAGNOSIS

The radical changes that took place in Russia were unique phenomena in modern history and they were completely unanticipated by Western scholars. The massive Soviet Empire unraveled and the Union of Soviet Socialist States imploded—not as the result of a war or even of revolution in the streets.

Conventional wisdom did not prepare us for these events. In 1983, the Center for Strategic and International Studies, one of Washington's leading think tanks, published a book entitled *After Brezhnev*. The volume contained the results of an intense eighteen-month research effort by thirty-five scholars. Their task was to sum up all the available knowledge on the Soviet Union and the central issues that Soviet society faced. Here was their conclusion: "All of us agree that there is no likelihood whatsoever that the Soviet Union will become a political democracy or that it will collapse in the foreseeable future."[3]

Hedrick Smith's popular book, *The Russians*, also got it wrong. When he followed this book issued in 1976 with its companion, *The New Russians*, published in 1990, he admitted his mistake: "I left Russia sixteen years ago thinking that fundamental change was impossible. And I wrote that in my book *The Russians*. The decline and stagnation that sank into place for the next decade, into the mid-eighties, seemed to confirm this judgment. Soviet politics appeared as frozen as the Siberian tundra. As it turned out, of course, I was wrong."[4]

It is hard to fault Western scholars for not seeing these dramatic events coming, since almost no one did; but what is troubling is that once they occurred, they were consistently misdiagnosed.

Why did Communism fail and what caused the complete collapse of the former Soviet Union? Western scholars have answered the question in several different ways. One group basically believes that Mikhail Gorbachev should get most of the credit. Robert G. Kaiser, the *Washington Post* correspondent stationed in Moscow during these critical years of *perestroika*, put it this way: "In just over five years, Mikhail Gorbachev transformed the world. He turned his own country upside down. He woke a sleeping giant, the people of the Soviet Union, and gave them freedoms they had never dreamed of. He tossed away the Soviet Empire; he ended the Cold War. These are the most astounding historical developments that any of us are likely to experience."[5]

Other Western scholars, mostly conservatives, give President Ronald Reagan the credit. Although Reagan was not the catalyst for the revolutions of 1989, they would argue that he created conditions which proved indispensable for these events to occur. Advocates of this perspective argue that his rhetoric about "the evil empire" was powerful and laid bare the cruelty of the Soviet regime. Reagan's policies of exporting democracy, supporting anti-Communist resistance movements around the world, and the Strategic Defense Initiative (SDI) were all critical factors that undermined the Marxist regime in Moscow.[6]

A third group of Western scholars argues that the reasons for Communism's failure are primarily economic. The technological and managerial sluggishness of the Soviet economy brought the entire system to a grinding halt by the mid-1980s, and Gorbachev could read the handwriting on the wall. The pressing need to overhaul the Soviet economy and to dismantle the centralized planning functions controlled by the Communist Party is credited by many observers as the source of the revolution. No one, not even Gorbachev, expected the whole system to unravel. It was the reform of socialism, not its demise, that the Communist Party leadership was after.[7]

The vast majority of Western analysts have focused their attention on political and economic causes for the collapse of Communism. In the aftermath of Communism, what Vaclav Havel calls "the post-Communism nightmare," this same preoccupation with the political and economic spheres dominates the writings of foreign policy elites in the West.

Unfortunately, analysis that ignores the moral and spiritual dimensions of Communism's failure is scholarship done with one eye closed. Political and economic factors are important in understanding Communism's collapse, but they do not tell the whole story. There are missing dimensions in their critiques which most foreign policy analysts fail to see.

To illustrate this point, essays by two of the best-known scholars of modern Russia are worth exploring. Zbigniew Brzezinski's book, *The Grand Failure: The Birth and Death of Communism in the Twentieth Century*, is one of the few studies published before 1989 that discussed the explicit overthrow of the Communist regime as one of four possible options. Few scholars were brave enough to even imagine this.

It is interesting to note that in Brzezinski's entire book, there are only four references to religion and only a few passing references to the "moral roots" of Soviet society. His list of the ten dynamics of disunion highlights economic factors, political pressures, ethnic forces, and foreign policy concerns.[8] Clearly these are all of significance, but there is much more to the story.

The same limited perspective is evident in Richard Pipes' essay, "The Soviet Union Adrift," which appeared in the *Foreign Affairs* journal in early 1991. The distinguished Harvard professor described the Soviet Union as a "thoroughly decrepit structure" and then analyzed the Soviet crisis. Although he noted that the most visible manifestation of this crisis was economic, in his judgment the "root problem" was political. He then discussed the "vertical conflicts" between conservatives and democrats and the "horizontal conflicts" between the center in Moscow and the republics.[9] While his essay offered many helpful insights, his analysis was essentially confined to the political and economic spheres, including the issue of ethnic conflict.

The failure of Marxism-Leninism actually resulted in five revolutions which were unfolded simultaneously, a phenomenon unique in modern history. First, there was the political revolution, which resulted from the people's rejection of the Communist Party as the sole ruler of their state and the related emergence of new political factions. This led to a dismantling of the one-party political regime and the creation of free elections for the presidency and the parliament (Duma). Second, there was an economic revolution, which resulted from Gorbachev's decision to restructure the economy and remove the restrictive controls of the centralized planning bureaucracy. Socialism gave way to free market initiatives and radical changes followed quickly. Third, there was an imperial-military revolution in which Russia voluntarily gave up its empire in Eastern Europe and dissolved into fifteen independent republics. This decision to release satellite states and move back Russia's borders to their eighteenth-century position without being forced to do so by military defeat was truly remarkable. In addition, Gorbachev agreed to reduce the size of Russia's impressive nuclear arsenal and dramatically shrinking its standing army.

Foreign policy analysts have focused all of their attention on these three spheres where revolutionary changes were taking place in Russian society. But they missed two other revolutionary spheres. The fourth was a social revolution, a dramatic domestic upheaval, in which all of the supporting mechanisms for families and communities collapsed, such as Young Pioneers and their summer camps. "Houses of culture," often owned and operated by industrial plants, were abandoned when these plants lost their state-supported subsidies. Many families who relied on these camps and cultural centers to assist them in the child-raising years were now without any external support. The fifth and final revolution was a moral and spiritual one that was intimately related to the other four revolutions. It is this revolution that foreign policy elites have largely missed. After all, it is hard to see everything with one eye closed.

Because analyses in the West are mostly done by secular-minded scholars for whom religion is unimportant and transcendent values of little interest,[10] it is not surprising that this moral and spiritual crisis has been overlooked. Within the U.S. government, especially among Foreign Service officers, where a "genteel secularity" is the default position, American diplomacy and intelligence are at an immense disadvantage.

There is a "tone deafness" in the foreign policy establishment that fails to recognize the fact that, for the overwhelming majority of humanity, religious conviction provides the story line through which life's meaning is read.[11]

What is surprising, however, is that these moral and spiritual factors were overlooked even when Russian leaders involved in the drama made references to them. In Mikhail Gorbachev's bestseller, *Perestroika*, he discusses the reasons for his and his colleagues' "new thinking" related to the restructuring of the Soviet Union. He describes how Communist Party leaders in the late 1970s "began to realize that the country began to lose momentum"; a kind of "braking mechanism" had formed affecting social and economic development. In addition to economic stagnation and deadlock, Gorbachev identifies the "gradual erosion of the ideological and moral values of our people." He notes how a "breach had formed between word and deed" which caused a "decay" in public morals.[12]

To the author of *Perestroika*, the challenge was clear: to restructure Soviet society, including its moral life. In his own words, Gorbachev made this point: "Today our main job is to lift the individual spiritually, respecting his inner world and giving him moral strength and help. . . . Perestroika means the elimination from society of the distortions of socialist ethics, the consistent implementation of the principles of social justice. It means the unity of words and deeds, rights and duties."[13] Gorbachev was describing a moral and spiritual revolution.

During his visit to the Vatican in 1989, Gorbachev again made his views explicit: He said, "We need spiritual values, we need a revolution of the mind. This is the only way toward a new culture and new politics that can meet the challenge of our time. We have changed our attitude toward some matters—such as religion—that, admittedly, we used to treat in a simplistic manner. Now we not only proceed from the assumption that no one should interfere in matters of the individual's conscience; we also say that the moral values that religion generated and embodied for centuries can help us in the work of renewal in our country."[14]

Gorbachev obviously was not blind to the moral and ethical crisis of Marxism-Leninism. Neither were his colleagues. From the many examples that I could choose, I will pick only one. Fyodor Burlatsky, one of the leading democratic reformers in the Soviet Union, a man chosen by Gorbachev in 1987 to head the new Soviet Public Commission for International Cooperation on Humanitarian Problems and Human Rights, put it this way: "The Soviet Union has to be a free country where everyone can pray to his or her own god. In fact, religion has to play a role in our return to elementary moral values. There have been so many crimes and so much corruption in our history, nobody knows what the foundation of morality is anymore."[15]

Most Western scholars fail to see that a moral and spiritual revolution preceded and, in fact, made possible the political and economic revolutions of 1989–1991. The prestigious *Foreign Affairs* journal published twenty-one articles concerning these events in the first two years after the fall of the Iron Curtain; only three articles even mentioned the role of the church or the moral and cultural revolutions that had occurred, while focusing largely on political, economic, and ethnic factors. The same blindness is evident in other leading journals such as *Foreign Policy*, *World Politics*, and *National Interest*.

Throughout Eastern Europe and the former Soviet Union, clerical and lay leaders prepared the way for the dramatic, nonviolent changes that occurred. Pope John Paul II was a great inspiration to many people, and countless Christians active in human rights groups and humanitarian organizations helped to build the groundswell of support that eventually led to democratic change. George Weigel has eloquently captured this insight with these words: "The Revolution of 1989 was, at its heart, a triumphant revolution of the human spirit; an expression of the final revolution, and of the transcendent nature of human aspiration."[16]

Scholars should have seen the moral and spiritual dimensions of the anti-Communist revolutions not only because of explicit comments and writings of Eastern European and Russian leaders active in these movements, but also because the evidence was readily available in published literature and the popular media. A moral and spiritual revolution had been underway for years, stimulating the consciences of many and giving them a basis for hope that their repressive regimes would be overthrown. Despite one of the most systematic persecutions that religious communities have experienced in modern times, religious faith in the USSR was not destroyed, but instead showed signs of vibrancy and renewal during the 1970s and 1980s.[17]

In my many trips to Russia in the early 1990s, I often asked Russian university students what their favorite books were. One book stood out with no challenger in sight—Mikhail Bulgakov's *The Master and Margarita*. I know a number of Russian students who have read this book 20–25 times. This brilliant novel, written in 1940 but not published until 1967 because of the opposition of Soviet censors, creatively weaves together three stories.

The first is a love story about an author, named "The Master," and his girlfriend, Margarita. The second is a delightful satire on life in Moscow in the 1930s, in which a professor of black magic (who is Satan portrayed as Professor Woland) causes havoc through his supernatural powers; the third story deals with the encounter between Jesus and Pilate leading up to and including Jesus' brutal crucifixion. This book was read by thousands of Russian students and intelligentsia during the 1970s, 1980s, and 1990s.

A brief summary of the principal message in *The Master and Margarita* would be this: only a fool believes there is no God. The brilliance of Bulgakov, writing under the repressive censorship of the Stalinist period, is that he used Satan's testimony to prove the existence of God. The book demonstrates the power of moral and spiritual ideas, often ignored by Western scholars, which prepared the ground for the political and economic changes that followed.

There are many other examples in the creative arts and in mass media that illustrate the basic crisis that Marxist-Leninist ideology was going through. Films were one of the major influences at work during the 1980s in this moral and spiritual revolution. For example, the film *Repentance* is a powerful surrealist allegory of the Stalinist terror and the cult of Stalin. The film was written in the early 1980s and produced by Tengiz Abuladze in 1984, but was not released until 1986, two years after Gorbachev came to power. Its appearance caused a political earthquake.

The essential moral lesson of the film is graphically depicted in its final scene when an old woman appears at the window of a cake-maker's home and asks, "Is this the road to the church? Does this road lead to the church?" The cake-maker replies, "This is Varlam Street [the street named after the movie's dictator, who is clearly Stalin]. It will not take you to a church." As the old woman walks away, she says, "Then what's the use of it? What good is a road if it does not lead to a church?"

MISDIAGNOSIS LEADS TO THE WRONG CURE

It should not be a surprise that a misdiagnosis leads to a faulty or insufficient cure. Western foreign policy elites clearly understood the dramatic changes in the political and economic institutions of the former Soviet Union—the collapse of the one-party state and its centralized economic planning bureaucracy—but they failed to understand how these revolutionary changes were caused in large part by the corrosive deterioration in the moral and ethical values of Soviet society.

Foreign aid programs from the West, especially from the United States, were superficial responses that failed to address deeper cultural issues. Seminars on the mechanics of the free market or how to organize political parties did not prove helpful in these traumatic days of the late 1980s and early 1990s. Helping Russians replace Soviet-style economic and political institutions with structures that were more Western was shortsighted. Seventy years of Communism did serious damage to the moral and cultural foundations of Russian society, and the depth of this damage was not fully understood in the West.

Michael Novak argues that the practice of democratic capitalism has been informed by presuppositions and values that are essential to the development of its political and economic structures. There are core values that are needed to form the foundation of a liberal, pluralistic culture upon which democratic political and economic institutions can be built. Without these core values, such as trust, integrity, and accountability, democratic capitalism cannot be developed. The success of democratic capitalism is based on the inherently greater moral and spiritual foundation of its underlying social system that is grounded in respect for the rights of the individual as a human being created in God's image.[18]

The euphoria that followed the collapse of the Soviet Union in December 1991 blinded many Western elites, as well as Russian officials, to the difficult realities that lay ahead. The collapse of the Soviet economy and the support network for families that it subsidized left the vast majority of Russians in desperate straits. The ruble collapsed twice in the 1990s and the entire savings of most families evaporated. The breakdown of political authority that accompanied Boris Yeltsin's second term as president opened up the door for widespread corruption and massive theft of the country's natural resources by unscrupulous oligarchs. The average Russian soon correlated the words "democracy" and "capitalism" with anarchy, exploitation, and lack of concern for the vulnerable.

Rebuilding Russian society from the rubble of the Soviet regime was no easy task, and this task was made even more complex by failure to understand the need to address the deep cultural and moral issues that were at stake. Atomized Soviet society, in which structures were formed to prevent individuals from working together, required a massive change of mindset. People needed to be encouraged that the days of fear and terror were over and that rebuilding society required their full participation. Trust needed to be restored in a society where it had been destroyed. Speaking the truth needed to be practiced in a society where "double-talk" was a way of life, a way to survive the grasp of the KGB.

Restoring integrity and developing truthfulness—critical moral values that underlie democratic capitalism—require cultural change in the post-Communist world, since these values were lost under Soviet leadership, as Gorbachev and his advisors realized. Western foreign policy elites failed to see how cultural institutions, including the churches, could play a much more important role in this process were they given the opportunity and the support needed.

Richard Pipes has highlighted the fact that Russians long for stability, especially after the upheavals of the 1990s, and that part of the legacy of the Soviet experience involves no sense of community and no trust of government. Because there has not been a clean break with its totalitarian past, Pipes also argues that this creates additional obstacles in the path of the rebuilding of a healthy society.[19]

What has emerged in Russia in the last decade is a vibrant free market economy, one of the fastest growing economies in the world, but the moral values that should form the foundation for this economy are not yet in place. As a result, corruption is rampant and serves as a "brake" on what would be an even more dynamic economy. Russians have become consumers, but not yet citizens.[20]

In recent years a group of scholars have emerged who are studying the issue of how culture shapes society. The Culture Matters Research Project at the Fletcher School at Tufts University has brought together large groups of development experts who agree that culture, not politics, determines the success of a society, but that politics can change a culture when it addresses deeper moral and ethical issues.[21] Unfortunately, these analysts were not engaged in the post-Communist transition in Russia.

These scholars have studied how "progress-prone" worldviews are different than "progress-resistant" worldviews, and their analyses have involved societies in every part of the world, not just among the least developed nations. Their studies concluded that a "progress-resistant" worldview involves the following characteristics: a sense of irrationality that is prone to fatalism or utopianism; a belief that wealth is a gift of fate or chance; a conviction that personal advancement only comes through the "right connections"; an assumption that group identity is more important than the individual; a negative view of punctuality and saving; and a high degree of mistrust beyond one's family or clan.[22] In my experience working in Russia since 1980, most, if not all, of these characteristics are evident in Russian society. In fact, it could be argued that these characteristics are connected to a related discussion about Russians' "DNA."[23] These are important cultural and moral issues that need to be addressed, since they are clearly a part of the legacy of the Soviet experience. People do not quickly shed cultural patterns that are deeply ingrained in a society, especially over three generations.

Democracy, as we have experienced it in the West, involves both individual freedom and popular sovereignty—rule by the people, as Michael Mandelbaum has noted. Freedom has a long pedigree, dating back to the days of ancient Greece and Rome. Religious liberty grew out of the Reformation in the sixteenth century and later political freedom followed, which included free speech, free assembly, and the right to political participation. Political sovereignty emerged later and became a universal value in the second half of the twentieth century.[24]

What we are learning today is that putting the principle of liberty into practice is very difficult because it requires institutions, such as functioning legislatures, legal systems with independent judges, honest police, and truthful lawyers and prosecutors. Operating these kinds of institutions requires some highly specialized skills and—more importantly—a firm grounding in moral values. In addition to the basic belief in the value of each individual and that individual's human dignity, there is also the belief that social life and civic life need to be protected from state interference.

Mandelbaum has argued that the skills and values required to create conditions of liberty and freedom "can not be called into existence by fiat any more than it is possible for an individual to master the techniques of basketball or ballet without extensive training." It is his judgment that the relevant unit of time "for creating the social conditions conducive to liberty is, at a minimum, a generation."[25]

A CONSTRUCTIVE ROLE FOR RELIGION
IN POST-COMMUNIST RUSSIA

Although religion is often viewed by foreign policy elites as a source of conflict or as a marginal phenomenon that does not deserve serious analysis, it should play a constructive role in helping us understand the complex transitions underway in the post-Communist world. It can also offer positive responses. We have already discussed how secularist foreign policy elites misdiagnosed the radical changes in Russia by not seeing the deeper moral and cultural changes at work, so it should be evident that understanding the role of religion in Russian society helps to provide a fuller, more accurate analysis of the five simultaneous revolutions that traumatized the former Soviet Union.

Seeing the full picture instead of focusing narrowly on developments in the economic and political spheres is the first contribution that religion can make to foreign policy issues. As the events of the last few decades have demonstrated—most notably the Iranian revolution, the rise of the Solidarity movement in Poland, and the September 11, 2001 attacks, ignoring the role that religion plays in the global context is shortsighted and can be dangerous.[26]

But a religious perspective also offers helpful insights and guidelines that can positively inform and shape policies relevant to the rebuilding of a society that has experienced the collapse of Communism. For all faith traditions grounded in Judeo-Christian values, there are key religious principles that are applicable and constructive. Two key biblical verses come to mind. The first is Micah 6:8—"To act justly and to love mercy and to walk humbly with your God," which is a response to the question, "What does the Lord require of you?" The second is the Golden Rule— "So in everything, do to others what you would have them do to you" (Matthew 7:12).

EXERCISING HUMILITY

The principle of exercising humility would be a good place to begin. Too many times we have witnessed Western analysts telling Russians how they should rebuild their society with an arrogance that offends their listeners. We do not have all the answers; we have not lived through the trauma that Russians have personally experienced; yet too often the advice from the West has been given in a condescending spirit. A faith perspective begins with the conviction that offers to assist others in distress must be made humbly and sensitively. Here is where the Golden Rule can help: how would we like to be treated by another nation's leaders whose success we would like to match? Being treated with respect is an important first principle.

Rather than telling Russians that they need to become like us, a wiser, humbler approach would be to help them rediscover positive attributes in their country's past and then adapt modernization to these traditional cultural attributes. Nicolai Petro has tracked the post-1989 development of the Novgorod region, situated near St. Petersburg, which has been atypically successful both in consolidating democratic institutions and promoting economic development. Leaders in the Novgorod region redefined reform by calling for people to return to the values of the region's more prosperous past, when it was a center of trade in medieval times, rather than trying to impose reforms "from the outside."[27]

Another practical way of exercising humility in international relations is for Western diplomats to openly acknowledge that the influences their countries have on Russia are both good and bad. For example, rather than always emphasizing the virtues and strengths of the "American system," it would be wise also to acknowledge that the pornography, sexual mores, and violence that are so much a part of our popular culture can be destructive. For these abuses of freedom, we can at least apologize.

DEMONSTRATING MERCY

A commitment to demonstrate mercy, especially toward the vulnerable, is another constructive principle that a faith perspective contributes. The call for "shock therapy" that Western advisors encouraged Russian reformers to implement without adequate concern for a "social net" illustrates how a misguided policy can cause unintended consequences that are harmful in the long run. The decisions to implement "shock therapy" caused pain and trauma for millions of Russians and subsequently alienated them from what they understood to be democracy and freedom.[28] Many Russians asked themselves: Is this what democracy and liberty means? People lose everything—all of their life savings, their jobs, their support networks—while others steal the nation's resources and become extremely wealthy because of their former Communist Party connections and corrupt practices? Where is mercy and compassion in this situation? Who cares about those who are especially vulnerable, like the elderly, the sick, and the developmentally challenged?

Prioritizing mercy would mean dramatically changing how the West relates to the rebuilding process in Russia. Instead of focusing almost exclusively on preventing the spread of nuclear weapons and combating terrorism, which are important goals, a faith perspective would also highlight the critical need to provide protection for those who are most vulnerable when radical reforms are needed. By restoring the moral and ethical foundation of Russian society, as well as instituting major economic and political reforms, the security and protection of common people would receive greater attention.

After the damage inflicted by three generations of Communist leadership, encouraging the development of nongovernmental organizations (NGOs)—especially churches, mosques, and synagogues—is a wise policy that is often not a priority for Western foreign policy advisors. Places of worship have extensive grassroots networks which can reach people in ways that governmental agencies cannot. In post-Communist Russia, the church is the most trusted institution in society. Its credibility is far greater than that of any government agency, the media, the police, or the army.[29] In the Russian context, where Christianity has over 1,000 years of history, forming partnerships with Russian Orthodox, Catholic, and Protestant churches is a wise move. The same is true with Islamic mosques. These institutions, with their extensive networks across the eleven time zones in the Russian Federation, are worthy allies in the effort to restore the moral and ethical values so badly needed in the rebuilding process. The reality is that NGOs, working with the full range of churches and religious groups, are already active in numerous humanitarian programs, including work with orphans, the developmentally challenged, and HIV/AIDS patients. They are doing works of mercy that never get reported in the Western press and they are often doing their work without any federal support, either Western or Russian. Policymakers need to realize that much creative activity in places like Russia is underway and hundreds, if not thousands, of volunteers are actively engaged in these humanitarian programs. If Russia is to develop as a democratic and free market entity, built on an open, pluralistic societal base, NGOs—and especially the churches—have a pivotal role to play as agents of mercy.

DOING JUSTICE

Another constructive role that religion can play in policy formulation is its emphasis on doing justice, a commandment that is repeatedly emphasized in the Judeo-Christian tradition. Doing justice is different from demonstrating mercy; mercy involves helping those who are victims and who are vulnerable, reaching out in compassion to help the truly needy. Doing justice, in the Judeo-Christian tradition, involves changing the structures of society that create injustice and oppression. In the well-known story of the Good Samaritan, the response of the foreigner to the injured victim of highway robbery was an act of mercy. An appropriate act of justice would involve creating safety on the highway from Jerusalem to Jericho so that robbers no longer could take advantage of innocent travelers.

In the Christian and Jewish traditions, doing justice involves creating "right relationships" in society. It also means especially protecting the vulnerable; in biblical terms these would be "the widow, the orphan, and the foreigner"—those categories of people who are defenseless, who lack an advocate. A religious perspective puts the focus of public policy on justice issues since these faith traditions understand that "the political community exists to uphold public justice for all."[30]

This focus on the poor, on those at the bottom of the social ladder, is an important way in which religion can encourage a shift in priorities. "Without justice there can be no peace"—this biblical theme, which is often advanced by Old Testament prophets (Jeremiah 8:8-12 and Isaiah 59:8), needs to be emphasized to policymakers who often are inclined to partner with the wealthy at the expense of all others. In Russia, the plight of the poor has been given a low priority since the collapse of Communism. Only in the last few years has attention been paid to their situation, and the churches in Russia have played an important role in emphasizing the needs of the poor.

According to government statistics, 13.5 percent of the Russian population currently lives in poverty. While this is an improvement over the beginning of 2005, when this number was 24.5 percent, it still represents a large number of Russians—20 million—who are suffering when the country's economy is booming and its federal reserve is one of the largest in the world. In Russia as a whole, the richest 10 percent of the population earned, on average, 16.8 times as much as the poorest 10 percent in 2007.[31] Again, religion has a helpful role to play in shaping public policy and in building a healthy, vibrant domestic society where no one is left out.

SUPPORTING RELIGIOUS FREEDOM

As Thomas Farr's chapter has convincingly demonstrated, in a world that is profoundly religious, analysts and policymakers need to understand the critical importance of faith worldwide. Religion is not just important because it can sometimes lead to violence; religion can also support and expand liberty. If democracy is to endure, we must protect religious freedom and harness its resources for the common good.[32] In America's experience, religious freedom has often been referred to as the "first freedom." Freedom of conscience, freedom of religion, is viewed in our society as a basic human right. It is important for policymakers to understand that social science research has demonstrated that nations that promote and protect religious freedom also have a significantly higher level of socioeconomic well-being.[33] This is not an accidental correlation.

Research has shown that religious freedom generates competition among different faiths and this leads to increased religious participation, which in turn results in larger numbers of religious groups who produce tangible benefits for society, such as programs in literacy, vocational training, marital and bereavement counseling, and poverty relief.[34]

It was this realization, among others, that drove Mikhail Gorbachev to sever the link between Marxism-Leninism and atheism and support the new "Law on Freedom of Conscience," issued in 1990. Soviet religious policy dramatically shifted from conflictual to cooperative; religion was no longer viewed as an enemy to be combated, but rather as a potential ally in the struggle for reform. Gorbachev and his leadership team came to the conclusion that religious institutions were encouraging their members to be loyal, hardworking, and peaceful, and he could win their support for his reforms by expanding their freedom to worship as they pleased.[35]

Recently, Russian political leaders have expressed similar sentiments, after years in which there was a reversion back to governmental support primarily for the Russian Orthodox Church as the "first among equals." An official from President Dmitry Medvedev's office recently visited the headquarters of the Russian Baptist Church in Moscow and commented that, in his twenty years of working with Baptists, he found them always willing to help, and he discussed a possible "social partnership" with them to combat substance abuse. The vice chairman of the Federation Council also called on Russian Baptists to help deal with "psychological problems" evident in Russian society and noted that "nothing will be accomplished without hard work—and Baptists know how to work."[36]

Support for religious freedom and its ancillary benefits is another practical way in which a faith perspective can constructively inform and shape foreign policy. Making this a priority, rather than just a marginal activity, would positively nurture the rebuilding process in the post-Communist world. The 2007 Pew Global Attitudes Survey highlighted the fact that 84 to 98 percent of the people surveyed in thirty-four countries said they wanted to be able to exercise their religion freely; less than 2 percent disagreed.[37] Religious freedom is much more than the right not to be persecuted for one's faith or the right to worship as one pleases in private. Religious liberty protects human dignity and helps to build civil society.[38] Knowing that religious freedom—and therefore religious competition within a country—is a sign of a nation's health, support for it deserves much greater attention by diplomats and policymakers.

SEEING RELIGION AS SOCIAL CAPITAL

Scholars have recently paid more attention to another aspect related to the building of civil society that involves religion. In studying social capital formation, which can be viewed as a set of moral resources that lead to increased cooperation among individuals, scholars have noted that religious institutions are often the principal shapers of cultural values and practices that affect how politics operates in a society. In America's development, civic associations, especially churches, not only protected individual liberty from the coercive powers of the state; they also mitigated against the dangers of excessive individualism. These private associations contributed substantially to the "common good."[39]

Religious social capital, as opposed to other forms of social capital derived from secular associations, is distinctive in the West. For example, "nearly half of all associational memberships in America are church-related, half of all philanthropy is religious in character, and half of all volunteering occurs in a religious context."[40] Religion can also contribute to the foundation of democratic society by shaping the character and virtue of its citizens. In addition, religious organizations have a history of giving "a voice to the voiceless."[41]

CONCLUDING THOUGHTS

Because foreign policy scholars and practitioners have not taken religion seriously, the results have handicapped the ability of the West to understand what is occurring in different regions of the world, to best support positive change, and to anticipate possible scenarios that could relate to global security. The case of post-Communist Russia illustrates this. A faulty diagnosis of why Communism collapsed led to a series of foreign policy decisions that did not adequately help the Russians to rebuild their society. The ethical and moral foundations of Russian society had given way, as Gorbachev and his leadership team observed, but Western consultants and advisors never understood this and therefore paid little attention to it.

How do you rebuild political and economic systems when the moral base of society has disintegrated and there is no trust in any institution or in anyone except close family members? After seventy years of Marxism-Leninism, with its faulty anthropology which viewed men and women as solely economic beings and its years of terror and oppression, cultural change is needed. However, trying to impose political and economic systems "from the outside" has never worked, as the Culture Matters Research Project has made clear. It is only when the leaders within a society conclude that some traditional values and attitudes are obstacles to creating democratic governance and social justice that substantial reform can occur.[42] When progress-resistant values are prevalent in a society like Russia, they can be changed, and religion is one of the key factors in making these deep cultural changes. We can no longer afford an American foreign policy that is characterized by a "genteel secularity," a foreign policy that ignores religion or minimizes its constructive role in international affairs, as this case study of Russia demonstrates.

Chapter 7

The Ethics of Humanitarian Intervention
Rethinking the Implications of Neighbor Love

J. Daryl Charles

INTRODUCTORY THOUGHTS ON THE STATE OF THE QUESTION

In an important essay that appeared in the aftermath of the Rwandan tragedy, James Turner Johnson rightly noted that the end of the Cold War found policymakers poorly prepared to deal with geopolitical crises that have since arisen, not to mention that it exposed an utter lack of moral discourse related to these developments.[1] Moreover, for those who viewed the Cold War as the result of defects in the international order, the post–Cold War period was thought, however briefly, to usher in an era of increased power and prestige for the United Nations. The tragic reality is that geopolitical catastrophe after geopolitical disaster has visited the international community, leaving the UN to scramble for any sort of coherent and effective approach and showing most nations to be relatively nonresponsive. As one Burmese human rights activist recently lamented, "There are no countries in the world which have gained liberation through the help of the United Nations."[2]

How, then, might those who are responsible for policy propose to deal with the scale of humanitarian need that in our day is massive and frequently the result of unstable regimes?[3] And what moral and political resources might inform our response to such situations—situations that fall short of formal war per se but which require some measure of interventionary force for humanitarian purposes?[4] As it affects American foreign policy, few questions will be more pressing in the years to come.

Here difficult issues confront us. When, if ever, should a nation engage in coercive intervention for the primary purpose of saving lives or protecting the relatively innocent where vital national interests are not at stake? Should governments respond and intervene to prevent—or to retard the effects of—genocide, mass murder, enslavement of peoples or people groups, and egregious human rights violations? Why or why not? If so, then when, by what rationale, and by what criteria?

This chapter seeks to address these questions by harnessing the neglected resources of the Christian tradition of just-war thinking. To proceed thus may seem to skeptics to offer little to the (supposedly) morally and religiously neutral business of contemporary International Relations or the hard-nosed practice of American foreign policymaking. In this chapter I will not rebut that skepticism head-on, but I venture to suggest that my discussion of what is a core challenge to contemporary global order today helps show why claims to the moral and religious neutrality of both IR and foreign policy cannot stand. Most mainstream debates about humanitarian intervention (HI) proceed from contestable modernist assumptions regarding state sovereignty, human rights, or moral relativism that are anything but neutral. If so, then reviving an approach to both IR and foreign policy rooted in a particular tradition of religious thought cannot be dismissed as inherently illicit.

Writing on the ethics of intervention four decades ago, Princeton ethicist Paul Ramsey set forth the argument that military intervention for the sake of justice remains both a right and a duty of states.[5] According to Ramsey, the failure of free nations such as the United States to intervene, based on a stewardship of responsibilities in the world, would be "tragically to fail to undertake responsibilities that . . . are not likely to be accomplished by other political actors."[6] Responding to the common objection that intervention can be unjust, Ramsey acknowledged both possibilities—unjust as well as just causes. But the mere possibility that intervention can be unjust, in Ramsey's thinking, did not release political actors from their moral responsibility. Furthermore, he insisted, "Anyone who is impressed only by the immorality and probable ineffectiveness of interventionary action should sensitize his conscience to the immorality and probable ineffectiveness of nonintervention."[7] Nor, in Ramsey's view, did the presence of the UN (or conventional construals of international law) change this moral equation, since the UN does not supplant individual states' sovereignty or reorder their respective societies. Rather, the moral obligations that issue from justice must remain our constraining justification, and these obligations are the fruit of charity toward one's neighbor.[8]

Ramsey's views, of course, were not popular then, just as they would be unpopular today. Nevertheless, Ramsey's wrestling with the obligations that attend "neighbor love" placed him squarely within the mainstream of classical just-war thinking and the Christian moral tradition.[9] We readily grant, of course, that extending charity toward the "neighbor" or the stranger is counterintuitive to human inclinations. Indeed, it is arguably a unique contribution of Christian moral reflection to social ethics and political theology. Christian theology affirms that all people, based on their shared humanity (which derives from being created in the *imago Dei*), have an intrinsic dignity and hence are to be sheltered from arbitrary and inhumane acts of oppression.[10] We do this not merely out of the sense of duty (though such, at minimum, surely *is* our duty); rather, it is based on an awareness of human solidarity. At the same time, this sense of solidarity or neighbor love accords with natural-law moral reasoning and the "Golden Rule": based on our shared humanity and as moral agents we treat others as we ourselves would wish to be treated. Apart from these rudimentary and universal moral intuitions, justice is impossible to realize. To be sure, one does not need Christian faith to intuit moral obligation toward others based on the universal and transcendent character of justice. However, Christian theology should sharpen our awareness of (a) the fact that justice and charity are owed to all fellow human beings and (b) the manner in which justice and charity cohere. This realization applies every bit as much to the community of nations of which we are a part as it does to the local neighborhoods in which we live.

Understandably, during the last decade the issue of humanitarian intervention has generated one of the most heated debates in the field of International Relations—among both political philosophers and policy analysts, among theorists as well as practitioners. At the heart of the debate, in narrower political terms, is the reputed tension between the principle of state sovereignty and international law on the one hand and human rights and the use of interventionary force on the other. Surely, the observation made by Johnson appears to be accurate: at both the theoretical and the practical level, IR has shied away from moral discourse—indeed, from using any sort of moral vocabulary whatsoever. As in most spheres of life in Western culture, it is assumed that moralizing is the equivalent of the embarrassing cousin who from time to time stops by the house, a veritable pain in the side and always unwelcome. IR, it is thought, just like any policy domain, must proceed calmly and rationally, without the bothersome intrusion of the religious or moral viewpoint. After all, the well-being of nations is at stake.[11]

Not helping matters is the fact that, in the realm of religious ethics, HI has been largely ignored. Part of the reason for this aversion, sadly, is that theologians and ethicists by and large have not concerned themselves with the implications of justice in the Aristotelian and Thomistic sense. That is, they have not discerned the political and moral predicates that are foundational to "civil society"—predicates which properly order human community and underpin "the common good." Rather, they have tended to "spiritualize" politics, arguing for a particular brand of "social ethics" on the basis of a vague (and mostly benign, albeit trendy) platform of "social justice"[12] which tends to be removed from the grueling political realities of the world in which we live.[13] Among other things this anemic form of "social justice" fails to give a morally responsible account of statecraft in a world characterized by human depravity and thus in need of reasonably just ordering (what Augustine referred to as the *tranquillitas ordinis*). Hence, while this essay does not presume any cleavage or division between politics and ethics, its focus will be the latter. Most importantly, it proceeds on the assumption that policy is the meeting place of politics and morality and that our duty toward justice depends on our recognition of this symbiosis.[14]

CONTEMPORARY GEOPOLITICAL AND MORAL CHALLENGES

To wrestle today with the implications of egregious and widespread human rights violations around the world is to be caught between two reputed claims—that of "imperialism," or Western cultural bias, over against an oft-cited "particularity" of culture. A graphic example of this, as helpfully pointed out by Paul Marshall, is the 1993 Bangkok Declaration, in which China, Vietnam, Indonesia, Iran, Syria, and Singapore—all being regimes that have been among leaders in human rights violations—demanded that human rights be addressed "in the context of national and regional particularities and various historical, cultural and religious backgrounds."[15] While the question of cultural particularity (at least in the current climate of pluralism and cultural diversity in the West) seems eminently reasonable, it tends to turn a blind eye toward nations in which egregious and widespread human rights violations in fact are occurring. But a nagging question keeps reemerging in inconvenient ways: On the secularist (i.e., Western) account, cannot Rwanda, Bosnia/ Kosovo, the killing fields of Cambodia, and, in the end, the policies of pre-WWII Germany be protected on the basis of "cultural particularity" and "diversity"? And on what moral basis might they be condemned?

Political responses to this sort of question in relatively free nations tend to be generally predictable and weak. While activist groups on occasion may make inroads—e.g., in helping to foment resistance to oppressive tendencies in Sudan (and more recently Darfur)—there exists in the West a conspicuous lack of any epistemological, and hence moral-philosophical, basis upon which to construct responsible policy as it applies to humanitarian disaster. And while U.S. policies may vacillate as administrations change (and I write from the North American perspective), this lack of moral-philosophical grounding remains broadly true of U.S. policy regardless of who inhabits the Oval Office or which party presides over Congress. To appreciate the lack of grounding of human rights in any enduring notion of political theory, and hence to understand the moral malaise of contemporary political theory, one need only consider those who are considered the doyens of modern rights talk.

And if we are to look for wisdom from Christian thinkers and moral philosophers, alas we find a paucity of substantive contributions to public debates that might bear on responsible policy. Even the highly esteemed moral philosopher Alasdair MacIntyre, whose *After Virtue* has recently gone through a third edition and whose follow-up volume *Whose Justice? Whose Rationality?* was intended to extend MacIntyre's thinking about justice (an eminently public virtue),[16] ultimately has difficulty positing the universality of human rights, even in the Christian moral tradition. "Natural or human rights . . . are fictions," MacIntyre concedes as he reflects on the "failures" of the Enlightenment project.[17] While there is much to commend in MacIntyre's critique of modernist thinking, in the end the engaged reader never learns from MacIntyre about what human rights might mean in the Christian scheme of things, why they might be important as an expression of "justice," and how they might be safeguarded because of human beings' shared commitment to justice.[18]

While the business of constructing a philosophical basis for the universality of human rights is decidedly out of fashion in a post-consensus cultural climate, it is nevertheless urgently needed. Part of the necessary framework by which to properly construe human rights, and thus to understand humanitarian intervention in some cases as a moral obligation, is to disassociate them from a legal, contractual, and highly individualistic conception of law that has so characterized Western thinking[19] and to anchor them in the permanence of the natural-law tradition. This is especially necessary given the inability of political and moral philosophers to posit any foundation for universal human rights that transcends either the individual or cultural particularism.[20] From the standpoint of Christian faith, given the primacy of neighbor love as the expression of one's faith, one might argue that our concern for our neighbor's essential well-being, in light of our shared humanity, leads us intrinsically to value our neighbor's life and thus to safeguard human rights. This valuing, it needs emphasizing, will entail both negative and positive responsibilities. Positively, it will entail our willingness to work for his or her greater well-being; negatively, it may entail our willingness to defend our neighbor when and where his well-being and right to exist are threatened.[21]

Despite the hegemony of a positivist, legal, contractual, and highly individualistic conception of law and human rights that has come to characterize Western culture, this lock-step way of thinking is open to serious challenge as we navigate the twenty-first century. Alas, the end of the Cold War did not bring an end to human suffering, cruelty, and catastrophe, nor did it usher in the new peaceful order that some had projected and for which many had longed. If anything, it heralded new contexts in which human depravity might show itself—from Kuwait, Iraq, and Afghanistan to Bosnia-Kosovo-Herzegovina and Rwanda; from Burundi, Sierra Leone, and Liberia to Somalia and Sudan. And these are wholly aside from the production of chemical, biological, and nuclear weapons by sundry unruly nations, drug trafficking on most (if not all) continents, human trafficking on most (if not all) continents, and the breathtaking rise of a maturing international terrorism which is typically religiously motivated and increasingly global. These crises, at the very least, herald the need for reinvigorated debates about the merits and moral substructure of humanitarian intervention.

But the political or geopolitical challenge is perhaps not the greatest; rather, more pressing may be the West's inability to make moral judgments that, in the end, would reflect serious statecraft and translate into responsible policy. In the aftermath of the Second World War, Hannah

Arendt, whose postwar reflections on the "banality of evil" are well known, ventured to predict in an essay titled "Nightmare and Flight" that the problem of evil would be the fundamental question of postwar intellectual life in Europe.[22] Yet strangely, already in the 1950s, even when atrocities associated with the Holocaust remained a permanent scar on the European psyche, concern with moral evil and the political problems that it causes had begun to disappear from Western political thought.[23] Thus, for an American president to speak of "evil" in the geopolitical context, as two of our last four presidents have, is to invite scorn of the greatest magnitude, both at home and abroad. For the moment, however, let us agree to put aside our own political sympathies; what was unforgivable to most people was the fact that someone in public office would name evil and then contextualize it in the field of IR. The point is not whether making moral judgments can be done in a more nuanced or diplomatic fashion; the point is, rather, that IR generally is ill-prepared to deal with moral categories.[24] This reality invites thoughtful responses; at the very least, it invites thoughtful moral discourse that is not *severed* from geopolitical realities.

The fact that we in the West live in a post-consensus cultural climate does not prepare us very well to understand, let alone deal with, many of the pressing geopolitical and international crises of our time, fully aside from the need morally to reinvigorate "civil" society here at home, where we have been living off borrowed capital for multiple generations.[25] This present moral state of affairs, it seems, is reminiscent of the scenario depicted by Albert Camus in *The Plague*. Despite the fact that rats and vermin are everywhere in the city of Oran, its citizens are in absolute, blissful denial thereof. There are no rats. Why? Because rats *cannot be permitted* to exist in Oran. But, as veteran human rights advocate Nina Shea has written, "genocide doesn't just happen."[26] Something in the culture has been afoot, and that "something" consists of an incremental social transformation which in some cases has been tolerated (as in Oran), but more than likely has been nurtured.

HUMANITARIAN DEBATE AND THE ETHICS OF INTERVENTION

At the outset of this essay, ongoing humanitarian debate was noted to be concentrated in two primary arenas. One is the political debate occurring in IR regarding sovereignty versus human rights and the use of interventionary force.[27] This particular debate, it needs emphasizing, would greatly benefit from a shift in argumentation—a shift from "sovereignty as authority" to "sovereignty as responsibility."[28] The policy implications of such a shift would be monumental. At any rate, HI remains controversial in IR for obvious reasons. Many members of the international community oppose it because it undermines their autonomy. As a result of this international opposition, it has great potential for dividing the United Nations, rendering the organization ineffective.[29]

The second debate, which has grown quite intense in the last decade and which is the focus of the discussion that follows, is "intramural" in nature. There is considerable disagreement among international humanitarians themselves as to what strategies are to be adopted. The reasons for this are not hard to find as we look around the world today. At the philosophical level, we do well to remember that, historically, the International Red Cross (IRC) has remained doggedly and conspicuously apolitical. Traditionally, groups such as the IRC have operated on the basis of three nonnegotiable principles—consent, neutrality, and impartiality. As veteran humanitarian scholar Thomas G. Weiss notes, many of the crises since 1990 have shaken humanitarians to the core because of the total disregard for international law by war criminals, terrorists, and despots who use tactics such as targeting civilians, women and children, even relief personnel. The result has been a collective identity crisis among aid workers themselves.[30] One central question that will continue to be debated is whether humanitarian action can and should be entirely insulated from "politics"—the "classicist" position—or whether the two cannot and should not be disassociated.[31]

The position taken in this essay is the latter. Humanitarian action, it needs emphasizing, must be comprehensive rather than insulated in its character. If not, then greater crises are invited—indeed, guaranteed—in the future, since to deny the foremost political nature of "humanitarian" work is to deny the political causes of suffering that are inflicted on the victims. Moreover, all human activity can be said to be "political," in the Aristotelian sense. In the πολις (polis), humanitarianism and politics are intimately and ineluctably intertwined. So, for example, we simply cannot deliver food and medical supplies to a nation in which famine caused (or exacerbated) by oppressive policies has contributed to such dire conditions and not attempt, in good conscience and in consultation with "neighbor" states, to deal with the problem at the root. Where political stability is absent, any attempt to prop up impoverished nations is bound to fail, and where there exists no structure for political sovereignty, law, and human rights, the frequency of what we call "humanitarian catastrophes" is guaranteed to escalate.[32] Ultimately, the traditional humanitarian principle of "neutrality," by which HI and aid are supposed to be insulted from politics, would appear naïve. Humanitarian activities have inevitable political consequences and thus are inextricably "political" in nature. More to the point: one cannot remain "neutral" toward war criminals, ethnic cleansing and genocidal practices, or outrageous human suffering that has been perpetrated by other human beings. Dictators and their accomplices do not possess defensive rights against interventions aimed at removing them.[33] State "sovereignty," therefore, cannot be viewed as an absolute good.[34]

As a general rule of thumb, intervention must always be proportionate to the degree of human suffering where it is found and oriented toward a greater good in a reasonably comprehensive manner. This logic issues from the repository lodged in the "Golden Rule," as advocated by Plato and Jesus, and natural-law thinking, which proceeds on the assumption of self-evident moral truths accessible to all. Wisdom calls us to be measured, to qualify our action or inaction morally, and to reflect on the what, where, why, and how of implementing justice—precisely those parameters that are lodged at the core of classical just-war thinking. That is, in continuity with classical just-war moral reasoning,[35] we agonize over conditions such as the justness of a cause, the rightness of intention, the proportionality of means, the safeguarding of the relatively innocent, and the reconciling of ends and means. But just-war moral reasoning is more than mere redress, although it entails that. Rather, its logic might be depicted, in the words of one astute social critic, as a "citizenship model" for international justice. The reason for such a depiction is this:

> Just war argument insists that no unbridgeable conceptual and political divide be opened up between domestic and international politics, [which is] precisely the cleavage central to the ancient Greek world, and, as well, to realpolitik with its insistence that the rules that govern domestic moral conduct and obligation apply to the body politic internally and are inapplicable to relations between states.[36]

The moral wisdom that undergirds just-war reasoning calls us to both positive and negative moral obligations. Not only does it require that we be measured, qualify our action or inaction morally, and reflect on the what, where, why, and how of implementing justice, it also calls us to protect, preclude, and prevent. Regardless of how we might differ about the specifics of interventionary force, moral wisdom does not call us to be indifferent toward the suffering of others. Hence, it is impossible for actors to remain "neutral" or "impartial" in the face of atrocity or geopolitical catastrophe.[37]

It hardly needs stressing that "consent" to intervention is rarely granted by the host nation; such are the realities of the world in which we live and the nature of regimes that systematically abuse their people or foster widespread human rights violations. For this reason, as Hadley Arkes suggests, justification for coercive humanitarian intervention compels us to recognize that the evil we seek to prevent is "literally beyond calculation," which is to say, "it has nothing to do with matters of locale or scale or with the absolute numbers of the victims."[38] On the same basis, Michael Walzer insists that humanitarian intervention is justified when it is a response—with reasonable expectations of success—to acts that "shock the moral conscience of mankind."[39] The wrongness of genocide, thus, is indifferent to matters of calibration.[40] Genocide is only one reflection among many, albeit the most extreme, of a political order founded on premises that are incompatible both with the logic of morals and the principles of constitutional government. Therefore,

> once it becomes clear to us that the justification for war turns on the nature of the regime we seek to resist; once we understand that the nature of the evil is indifferent in principle to the size of the country and the race of the victims—once we are clear on these points, we can truly ask: Why indeed *was* the Second World War "different"?[41]

Arkes' moral reflections lead naturally to the question of preemptive action, and the lack of ambiguity with which Arkes addresses the preemptive question may strike many of us as remarkable:

> We need not wait, then, for the regime to show a genocidal bent before we may find fault with it: the regime would be offensive on the most fundamental points of principle, and we would be warranted in resisting it even before it acts out its character in policies of wholesale killing. The possibilities for genocide are likely to be strongest in those places where the rejection of the principles of lawfulness and constitutional government have been most radical and thoroughgoing, and it should not be surprising that we have called governments of this kind "totalitarian."[42]

Both Arkes and Walzer stand in vigorous opposition to the sort of deficient utilitarian calculus that has come to thrive in academic—and in some political—circles and which is indicative of the contemporary zeitgeist. Their moral seriousness stands in bold contrast, for example, to the questionable moral foundation upon which Todd Gitlin's recent analysis of moral atrocity, in the Summer 2008 issue of the journal *World Affairs*, struggles to stand:

> History does not repeat itself, either as tragedy or farce or anything else. Saddam Hussein was neither Slobodan Milosevic nor Ho Chi Minh, neither of whom in turn was Stalin or Hitler, any more than Yalta was Munich, Kyto was Yalta, or September 11, 2001 was December 7, 1941. Nor should we regard al-Qaeda as the equivalent of the Nazis, the Communists, the Baathists, or of anyone but themselves. All challenges qualify as unique challenges, as do all enemies and the dangers they present. Wars will always be atrocious, but sometimes the absence of war will be atrocious, too . . . Metaphorical overstretch bids to be the thought disorder of time . . . A quick survey of the historical ledger reveals that U.S. foreign policy since World War II has done far more damage through an excess of interventionary zeal than through a lack of it.[43]

Over against the moral vacuity of Gitlin's analysis, Arkes and Walzer argue that a proper understanding of basic human rights must force us to put aside utilitarian calculations and to acknowledge, apolitically, that "the destruction of the innocent, whatever it purposes, is a kind of blasphemy against our deepest moral commitments."[44] Both thinkers are convinced that there exist non-fluid canons of justice—canons that issue out of classical just-war moral reasoning—which assist us in discerning whether, why, when, and how intervention might proceed.

JUSTIFYING INTERVENTION OR NONINTERVENTION
The Debt to Just-War Moral Reasoning

In his important work *Just Wars: From Cicero to Iraq*,[45] Alex J. Bellamy views the evolution of humanitarian intervention in three general stages: (1) Augustine to the Middle Ages; (2) late medieval period to 1945; and (3) 1945 to the present. On this account, a broad consensus existed in the first period that rulers possess a duty to uphold law and protect the innocent. In the second era, wherein individual political communities replace Christendom, rights and duties are viewed as having been decoupled; while a right to intervene exists, there is not a duty. Positive law and national sovereignty chiefly characterize the third era, while a natural-law consensus, which had held sway for virtually two millennia, begins to evaporate. While we might quibble over the organizational particulars here, this basic schema helps frame the questions that need addressing in a post-consensus era.

Philosophically, the realm of "humanitarian" concern confronts us with universal aspirations and basic rights that inhere in our being human. Humanitarian values, because they mirror the natural moral law, transcend human religious, ethnic, and ideological differences. What all human beings share in common invariably is brought into bold relief by cases of great injustice, suffering, and egregious human rights violations. For this reason, humanitarian action, if it is truly "humanitarian," will be proportionate to the degree of human suffering wherever it may occur.[46]

HI may take different forms, apply to diverse situations, and seem justifiable for a number of reasons. At the same time, intervention by definition is *extraordinary*, which is to say that it constitutes a departure from the normal pattern insofar as it is imposed from the outside.[47] And because it is extraordinary in the sense of defying territorial sovereignty, it raises the important question of authority and thus requires moral justification.

According to James Carafano and Dana Dillon, the U.S. military has conducted an operation related to peacekeeping, peacemaking, or post-conflict occupation roughly every two years since the end of the Cold War.[48] By peacemaking, Carafano and Dillon refer to operations undertaken with the consent of all warring parties for the purpose of implementing a peace agreement, whereas peacekeeping entails the use or threat of coercive force to compel compliance with resolutions or sanctions designed to end a conflict.[49] Andrew Natsios, who served as director of Foreign Disaster Assistance with the U.S. Agency for International Aid during the early 1990s, paints a similarly disturbing picture, calling attention to the rising tide of ethnic and tribal conflict that parallels the failure (or unwillingness) of states to prevent egregious human rights violations.[50] And Stanley Hoffmann identifies three categories of unstable statehood that plague the post–Cold War era, distinguishing between "failed" states, "troubled" states, and "murderous" states.[51]

Those working in the sphere of HI speak in terms of "complex humanitarian emergencies" (CHEs). CHEs, according to Natsios, may be distinguished according to five general categories: (1) ethnic, religious, or tribal conflict that includes widespread atrocities against the civilian population; (2) the deterioration of governmental authority; (3) macroeconomic collapse; (4) widespread health and nutrition problems, coupled with food shortages; and (5) massive population movement of displaced people.[52] Natsios was able to identify in the year 1996 alone no fewer than twenty-three CHEs that involved nearly 40 million people who were at risk of death from violence, epidemics, or starvation.[53] These types of statistics are both staggering and deeply compelling. Neither laypersons nor policymakers can ignore these dimensions of sociopolitical evil in the post–Cold War era. Tragically, the assessment of one student of humanitarian aid remains unchallenged: the vast majority of interventions in the 1990s might be described as "too little too late."[54] That is, they were "too little" in the sense that intervention was performed by military forces that were insufficiently configured in numbers, equipment, supplies, strategy, and oversight. And they were "too late" to the extent that their delay, which was produced by a lack of political will on the part of potentially intervening states, resulted in far greater suffering or evil than should have been tolerated by relatively free nations.[55]

The idea of HI, it goes without saying, challenges the conventional paradigm of international law. At the very least, it raises the question of what constitutes "sovereignty" and whether this value can be considered absolute. What remains, then, is the task of morally qualifying intervening force for humanitarian purposes. The case both against and for intervention, in the end, is best understood against the background of just-war moral reasoning. This mode of reasoning represents a deep, consensual tradition of reflecting on the ethics of war and peace and coercive force, and it does so in its commitment to *qualify* justice and to *restore* a human community to its normative peaceful functioning.

To understand the moral criteria that constitute the mainstream of the classical just-war tradition is to appreciate the moral-philosophical assumptions that lie behind and undergird the tradition. Misconstrued by many as a means to endorse any war a nation pursues by throwing a mantle of "just" or "justice" over intrusion, just-war thinking is best thought of as an approach to *comparative justice* applied to the considerations of war or intervention.[56] Philosophically, it understands itself as a mediating position between the ideological poles of realpolitik or militarism on the one hand and pacifism on the other. In the wise words of Hugo Grotius, it neither says that everything is always permissible nor that nothing ever is.

Just-war thinking best facilitates the task of weighing HI because it subjects the relevant conditions that must justify intervention or nonintervention to intense scrutiny. And while it is true that HI remains hotly contested (even from within the just-war tradition), the criteria are still able to provide moral guidelines. But at the macro level, just-war moral reasoning refuses to do what is fashionable in our day, namely, to separate ethics from politics. Moreover, it insists that there is no gulf between domestic justice and international justice. It might be useful in this regard to consider analogous thinking in the realm of domestic policy.

Consider, for example, how conventional law enforcement weighs various threats, deliberating over whether, what, why, when, and how. As responsible policy, we neither tolerate police brutality on the one hand in order to deal with deviant behavior, nor do we acquiesce passively to violent crime around us on the other. Justice, rather, is mediate, measured, qualified, proportionate, and intended for a greater good. We look neither to proponents of realpolitik in the Machiavellian mold nor to pacifist withdrawers, both of whom refuse to wrestle with the complexities of maintaining justice in an imperfect world. For the just-war thinker, "might" never makes "right," but on occasion it may *serve* what *is* right. Thus, it can be argued, just-war moral reasoning is rooted in an "Augustinian realism" about human nature.[57] At the level of policy and responsible statecraft, of course, this "realism" will express itself in important ways. It will promote a healthy skepticism about the use (and abuse) of power, at the same time refusing to opt out of political reality altogether in favor of utopian fantasies. It will also require moral judgment and subsequent action in a world of limitations, ambiguities, complexities, and partial justice. As a result, it will rightly presume the provisional nature of all political schemes, systems, and arrangements. At bottom, just-war thinkers insist that the linkage between politics and morality must not be severed, for an important part of politics is how we respond to a world of conflict, disagreement, and opposition.

Historically, two sets of moral criteria or conditions, familiar to most, have served to define what is permissible and impermissible. The traditional *ius ad bellum* criteria—just cause, proper authority, and right intention—provide terms under which coercive intervention may be undertaken, while the *ius in bello* conditions—proportionality and noncombatant immunity—govern the means by which to proceed.[58] For our present purposes, the central questions relating to the morality of intervention are defined by the three primary *ius ad bellum* criteria—just cause, proper authority, and right intention—which constitute the core of the classical just-war tradition. These three criteria set the context for a moral examination of whether or not intervention can be justified.

To establish the justness of a cause is to make fundamental moral distinctions—for example, between innocence and guilt, between the criminal and the punitive act, between retribution and revenge, between egregious human rights violations ("crimes against humanity") and the need for "humanitarian" intervention to restore basic human rights. In principle, just cause is motivated by two chief concerns: to rectify injustice or to prevent injustice.[59] While there is a sense in which all violence is tragic, even more tragic is the permitting of human oppression, gross injustice, and crimes against humanity.[60] Admittedly, in the context of HI there is a problem with the criterion of just cause to the extent that it is difficult to define with any sort of precision the scope of the evil that would justify intervention. Should it be confined solely to genocide? I am inclined to extend the qualification, with Stanley Hoffmann, to "massive violations of human rights, which would encompass genocide, ethnic cleansing, brutal and large-scale repression to force a population into submission . . . as well as the kinds of famines, massive breakdowns of law and order, epidemics and flights of refugees that occur when a 'failed state' collapses."[61] Coercive intervention, then, seeks to defend the basic order of justice that has been violated.[62] And unpopular as it might seem in our own day, given the temper of the times, it needs emphasis that even where intervention might create dependencies that last well into the future, it can nevertheless not be regarded *in principle* as morally wrong or unjust.[63]

But there may well arise an objection to just cause in the case of HI. What shall we make of the problem of nations' disagreement over just cause, or even the lack of universal assent to just cause, in a particular case? Surely, this lack of accord would seem to present an insuperable moral obstacle, since intervention might be condoned in one region of the world while it is condemned and rejected in another. But the problem is really not so problematic; rather, it may be an issue of moral consistency, or, as is often the case, it may reflect a failure to distinguish between a *right* and a *duty* to intervene. Most debates over intervention, after all, focus on the permissibility of intervention.[64] And it is also true that many nations, based on issues of sovereignty and internal politics, will reject and resist outside intervention regardless of how compelling a "catastrophe" might be to onlooking nations.

Right intention presupposes that morally guided force will have a humanitarian design, seeking to advance a greater good and secure a greater peace. Aquinas insists that actors must have a right intention "so that they intend the advancement of good, or the avoidance of evil." "It may happen," he notes, that coercive force is declared by the legitimate authority, and for a just cause, but it could be rendered unlawful by a "wicked intention."[65] Unjust intervention is perhaps best illustrated by what does *not* constitute right intention. Such scenarios include a sovereign's pride or reputation, vengeance, national aggrandizement, bloodthirst or lust for power, and territorial expansion.[66] For war to be just, its aim must be a greater good, and that greater good is a justly ordered peace, what Augustine called the *tranquillitas ordinis*.

Thirdly, to address matters of sovereignty and to announce intervention or wage war, there must exist a public authority that has responsibility for the people. Aquinas writes that it is not the business of individual citizens to do such, for private acts of justice—acts of *duellum* over against *bellum*—are rooted in vengeance; only public acts of justice are legitimate. And as the care of the common weal is committed to those who are in authority, it is their business to adjudicate matters of injustice.[67] What might classical just-war theory mean today, especially in light of the sovereignty debate? It is dubious whether the responsibilities of the magistrate can be passed on to a coalition of states, who by their anatomy and by definition do not—indeed, cannot—represent a particular sovereign state or community. Can in fact the relative sovereignty of a particular state be transmitted to an international body or coalition? While a coalition of nations can help to confirm the relative justness of a cause, it cannot constitute or replace the political sovereignty of a nation.[68] Moreover, what if, for example, there exists in this international coalition a majoritarian or consensus rule and this consensus is made up of predominantly unjust states? What if, subsequently, the consensus rules in a manner that is unjust?[69] The position represented in this essay is that where and when intervention is undertaken for humanitarian purposes, in principle it is clearly preferable to have broad-based support of the community of nations (as, e.g., represented by the UN). At the same time, a lack of wider support, although regrettable, does not render the intervention illegitimate or unjust per se, as the tragedies of Rwanda and Kosovo illustrate.[70]

Typically, additional secondary or "prudential" *ad bellum* criteria—for example, last resort, chances of success, declaration of intent—are cited as belonging to the qualification of interventionary force. These, however, are "secondary" to just cause, right intention, and sovereign authority—secondary not because they are insignificant but rather because they subsist in and derive their importance from the three core *ad bellum* criteria. This derivative nature may be illustrated by the criterion of last resort, which is often misconstrued in both its essential character and its application. Not infrequently, contemporary discussions of "just war" *begin* with last resort rather than understanding it as a byproduct, and thus a derivative, of just cause. Properly conceived, last resort forces us to ask whether all reasonable efforts to utilize nonmilitary (i.e., diplomatic, economic, political) alternatives have been exhausted. Last result is a factor only *after* other principle conditions have been weighed.

A second (and related) misunderstanding invites our attention. If we insist on viewing "last resort" as the mathematical *last* in a serial line of possibilities, there will always be something that might be tried as an alternative to force. Hence, it is necessary to qualify "last resort," as I have done above, with the descriptor "reasonable." This qualification is important for two reasons. First, all who oppose war in principle will never acknowledge that diplomatic possibilities have been exhausted. This is simply the bottom line for the ideological pacifist, whose philosophical precommitment is to view coercive force, and not injustice, as evil. Second, last resort is immoral—and counterproductive—when it stalls or impedes a just response to the extent that it becomes too late to defend the innocent and those who are suffering. For this reason, Michael Walzer writes,

> Taken literally . . . "last resort" would make war [indeed, any forceful intervention] morally impossible. For we can never reach lastness, or we can never know that we have reached it. There is always something else to do: another diplomatic note, another United Nations resolution, another meeting . . . it is always possible to wait a little longer and hope for the success of (what looks like but isn't quite) nonviolence.[71]

This, however, is not the intent of last resort in classical just-war thinking. For if there is some great evil that must be prevented, we are not morally permitted to wait on every possibility. Delay at some point becomes immoral, inhumane, and complicit with the crime that needs interdiction. Such illustrates why last resort must be rooted in just cause and not vice versa. Hereby I only wish to demonstrate a priority of moral criteria and not to suggest that last resort is unimportant.[72]

Earlier in this essay I advanced the claim that just-war thinking best facilitates the task of weighing HI because it subjects the relevant conditions that must justify intervention or nonintervention to intense scrutiny. One of the reasons for this intense "weighing" is that, in its classical expression, just-war thinking locates itself within a framework of what political ethicist Jean Elshtain calls an "Augustinian realism."[73] Given the fact that "estrangement, conflict and tragedy," to use Elshtain's terms, are the constant features of the human condition, this sort of moral realism is requisite for any civilized culture. Why?

> Augustinian realism . . . embeds deep skepticism about the exer-
> cise of power, beginning with the aims and claims of sovereignty
> and of any concentration of power. At the same time, this realism
> recognizes the inescapability of politics and calls on citizens to
> engage the world of politics faithfully . . . Politics requires that
> we respond in some concrete way to a world of conflicts and
> oppositions.[74]

In addition to promoting a healthy skepticism and uneasiness about the use (and abuse) of power, and without "opting out of political reality altogether in favor of utopian fantasies and projects," just-war thinking "requires action and judgment in a world of limits, estrangements, and partial justice," insofar as it "fosters recognition of the provisional nature of all political arrangements." Moreover, it "recognizes self-defense against unjust aggression but refuses to legitimate imperialistic crusades and the building of empires in the name of peace."[75]

Political historian John Hittinger has well summarized the mediating character of just-war moral reasoning as a nation contemplates intervention. He writes that

> there are [certain moral] goods worth the risk . . . [of interven-
> tion] and . . . "peace at any price" is unacceptable . . . The pacifist
> misses this complex reality of the possibility and political condi-
> tions for human flourishing ... The realist approach, by which
> the conduct of war is bound by no moral limit, undermines the
> very moral and political legitimacy of the regime.[76]

Hittinger's assertion that certain human goods need protecting and that force can be morally guided finds confirmation not only in foreign affairs but in the domestic context as well. Recall the observation made earlier: there are not only two options in dealing with criminal behavior; we must neither tolerate police brutality on the one hand nor acquiesce to violent crime on the other. The answer lies somewhere in the middle: justice on occasion requires that coercive force be applied for the good of the criminal, the good of the victim, the good of potential victims, and the good of society as a whole.[77]

The Christian moral tradition adds yet another ingredient to the moral equation by which HI in some cases is justified. Because of its view that human beings—all human beings—are a representation of the *imago Dei*, one important ramification is that human beings *qua* human beings possess an intrinsic dignity and thus deserve equal regard. This dignity cannot be revoked by governments or other political actors. It follows, then, that

> the spectacle of people being harried, deported, slaughtered, tortured, or starved en masse constitutes a prima facie justice claim. Depending on the circumstances on the ground as well as the relative scales of power—who can bring force effectively to bear—an equal regard claim may trigger a movement toward armed intervention on behalf of the hounded, tortured, murdered, and aggrieved.[78]

On theological as well as ethical grounds, the "universalist" character of neighbor love is extended to the "stranger," and this moral obligation forms the heart of just-war reasoning as it wrestles with the duties of tending approximate justice in an imperfect world.

CONCLUDING THOUGHTS ON HUMANITARIAN INTERVENTION
Present Realities and Future Prospects

Following World War II, Article 6 of the Charter of the International Tribunal at Nuremberg declared that sovereign legislative power belonged to the nations to which the German Reich had surrendered. This charter was viewed as binding by the civilized world. The United Nations, created in 1945, from the beginning resolved itself "to reaffirm faith in fundamental human rights, in the dignity and worth of the human persons, in the equal rights of men and women and of nations large and small" (this from the UN Charter Preamble). From its very inception, the UN's General Assembly passed numerous resolutions to prevent human rights violations by its own member nations. Among the most significant was the passage in 1948 of the Universal Declaration of Human Rights,[79] which contained provisions for the right of every person from birth onward to life, liberty, fundamental human rights, and security of person. Article 5 of the declaration specifies: "No one shall be subject to torture or to cruel, inhuman or degrading treatment or punishment."

Also passed by the General Assembly in 1948 was the Convention on the Prevention and Punishment of the Crime of Genocide,[80] which defined genocide as "acts committed with intent to destroy, in whole or in part, a national, ethnic, racial or religious group." The convention codified, in a universal and comprehensive manner, the moral obligation of nations to prevent genocide and to protect basic human rights, representing a post-Holocaust commitment on the part of the human community collectively to prohibit—and intervene to prohibit—the deliberate systematic murder of a people group.

Remarkably, humanitarian scholars Thomas G. Weiss and Cindy Collins identify no less than twenty-one international humanitarian and human rights accords or conventions between 1946 and 1990 to illustrate the extent of codification and institutionalization of the ideal humanitarian concern. These conventions cover an extraordinarily wide range of scenarios in which basic human rights are denied, including

- Political asylum
- International refugee status
- Transfer of refugees
- Prevention and punishment of genocide
- Political rights of women and children
- The status of stateless persons
- War crimes
- Civil and political rights
- Hostage taking
- Torture and inhuman or degrading treatment of human beings
- Children's rights.[81]

It is impossible to ignore the supreme irony here. Precisely in the very era when an international commitment toward human rights has been codified and institutionalized, the most widespread and tragic cases of gross human rights have occurred. Why? Clearly, the community of nations (inclusive of the West) lacks the political and moral will to prevent what, at least in theory, should be noncontroversial. For this reason, then, the twofold failure of the world to prevent genocide in Rwanda in the mid-1990s[82] as well as genocide, enslavement, and displacement of people in Sudan since 1990 constitutes one of the greatest moral indictments of our time.[83]

To intervene or not to intervene? This should always be a difficult question.[84] As Michael Walzer has persuasively argued in his essay "The Politics of Rescue," the use of force in other people's countries should always induce hesitation and anxiety. At the same time, the mood of Western nations currently is decidedly noninterventionist. The aim of much humanitarian intervention, where it *is* found, is only to ameliorate symptoms of the catastrophe—for example, bringing food and medical supplies to populations under siege or oppression—rather than to interfere with the siege and oppression at the causal level, that is, at the level of power structures. Stated differently, would a nation reach the moral limits of intervention once food and medical supplies were delivered—or in more extreme scenarios, once the killing had subsided? Would that nation be morally obliged to withdraw from the region or country in which it had intervened and once more leave those people in the hands of the regime that helped create (whether locally or nationally) the problem in the first place? To suggest that withdrawal would be obligatory after the symptoms were addressed is morally unsustainable. If we can be obliged to intervene in a nation or among a people group, whether to provide basic "aid" or even to save lives, then it seems that the same moral reasoning impels us to help secure a form of *lawful* government that human beings, regardless of where they are found, deserve.[85] Nevertheless, it is a fact that today Western nations tend to focus less on the costs to men, women, and children who are suffering egregiously than on the costs to their own political standing at home.[86]

Perhaps part of the West's rationale for nonintervention is that few of the crises today technically qualify as external aggression; rather, more often than not they are internal collapses and catastrophes, characterized by rape, murder, ethnic cleansing, state terrorism, political tyranny, and domestic brutality. If we assume that HI, wherever possible, should be a multinational concern and effort, a position that this essay takes, then we must ask: when should the world's agents and powers—for example, the UN, the EU, NATO, the Pan American Alliance, the Organization of African Unity, and the United States—not merely protest but intervene? At the same time, the sad truth must be acknowledged that where a humanitarian commitment to save lives and relieve suffering *has* been demonstrated and well intended, not infrequently we have learned that offering aid only served to strengthen the regime in power, with minimal (if any) redeeming effects reaching those who in fact were suffering. As it turns out, most catastrophes are not politically neutral.

Without question, the presumption against intervention is strong and should not be easily overridden. Nevertheless, nonintervention is not an absolute moral principle. It is well possible—indeed, it would seem increasingly commonplace in the post–Cold War era—that a government can do things to people within its own borders that are so evil and corrupt, so thoroughly wrong, that another nation would be justified in intervening and even in displacing that government. The point at which that threshold has been reached is the point at which the moral absurdity of a "doctrine" of nonintervention must be acknowledged.[87] Put differently, the right of a people or people group to escape evil being inflicted upon them cannot necessarily hinge on whether they themselves possess the strength and resources to defend their own interests. Might there exist, or come into being in the future, geopolitical catastrophes that oblige relatively free societies both (a) to deliver, where possible, a particular people from oppressive regimes and (b) to help establish the sort of government that might be more conducive to being "human"?

There indeed are situations of local or internal catastrophe in a nation that simply should not be tolerated, any more than you and I should tolerate rampant domestic abuse or crime in our neighborhoods or among our neighbors. Where we possess both the knowledge and the wherewithal to stop or prevent evil, we must do so; to tolerate it is neither charitable nor just. Where, for example, we have the capacity to swim, we are morally obliged to plunge into deep water and rescue someone who is drowning; where, on the other hand, we do not have the ability, there is no "ought" that constrains us. The "can," thus, is a precondition for the "ought."[88] Therefore, "humanitarian intervention"—which is clearly susceptible to abuse—may be a moral necessity where cruelty and suffering are extreme. Or, in classical just-war terms, the issue might be framed as follows: the very principle of proportionality, which enjoins us to inflict as little harm as possible for the purposes of acting justly and establishing a better end, must also morally oblige us to do good where and however possible. Thus, says Hadley Arkes:

> If it is within our power to relieve the suffering of the innocent, this principle would at least oblige us to offer reasons as to why we did not act. If we could not have acted without creating comparable dangers for other innocent people (including ourselves) the act of holding back becomes comprehensible and justified. But if one held back from a good act for reasons merely of convenience or self-interest or even of indifference, then one would neglect to do a good for reasons which cite no countervailing

interest or harm, and which may therefore claim no comparable moral weight.[89]

In an important address in 1997 at the U.S. Holocaust Museum, South African Justice Richard Goldstone, who had previously been chief prosecutor of the International Criminal Tribunals for the former Yugoslavia and Rwanda, had this to say:

> The one thing I have learned in my travels to the former Yugoslavia and in Rwanda and in my own country is that where there have been egregious human rights violations that have been unaccounted for, where there has been no justice, where the victims have not received any acknowledgement, where they have been forgotten, where there's been a national amnesia, the effect is a cancer in the society. It is the reason that explains, in my respectful opinion, spirals of violence that the world has seen in the former Yugoslavia for centuries and in Rwanda for decades, to use two obvious examples . . . So justice can make a contribution to bringing enduring peace.[90]

In the end, Goldstone recommends doing four things practically in the name of justice: (1) exposing the truth of specific guilt and avoiding general guilt; (2) recording the truth of moral atrocity for the historical record in order to counter attempts by the guilty to avoid guilt; (3) publicly acknowledging the victims' loss, who, as terrified people, need justice; and (4) applying the deterrent of criminal justice, since human nature is deterred from criminal behavior by the fear of punishment.

Goldstone's remarks, fresh on the heels of unprecedented genocidal violence, serve to remind us that no authority on earth can remove from social charity and social justice (so-called) the moral obligation to rescue from dereliction and oppression all whom it is possible to rescue. That justification can never be withdrawn, only "limited, supplanted, or put in abeyance."[91] As Paul Ramsey insisted, it is simply an "illusion" to believe in an "absolute principle of nonintervention" by which nation-states ultimately are impenetrable.[92] After all, "peace" must be highly qualified, for it is not a social-political good unless it is *justly ordered*, as the Mafia or any cartel of organized crime well illustrates.

But what might not qualify as justification? Two examples might be cited: intervening for the sake of territorial expansion or imperial design, and, less obviously perhaps, intervening for the sake of democracy, free enterprise, or economic justice. As Michael Walzer insists, the reasons for intervention, by necessity, are profoundly negative in character; they aim to stop human behavior and policies that constitute "crimes against humanity." Common sense and our shared humanity together would seem to suggest that the agent of intervention is a "neighbor." But in the present world, the reality is that neighbor nations probably will not intervene, or be able to intervene. Thus, absent a willing "neighbor," the next potential actor is any nation, or cluster of nations, near enough and strong enough to stop what needs stopping.

A final thought on HI. Most politicians, many military personnel, and most of the public are of the view that there must be an exit strategy before there can be an intervention. While wisdom calls us to think through the implications of our actions, having in place way out before we intervene or requiring a relatively short in-and-out strategy of intervention may not be realistic. In fact, it may in effect serve as an argument against intervening at all. Should we in the West have intervened to stop the genocide in Rwanda? Yes. Had we had the backbone to do so, would we have had a sufficient plan in place for reconstructing Rwandan society? Probably not. Which in no way releases us from our moral culpability.[93]

Despite the cultural climate in the West and the unpopularity of this argument, one student of humanitarian politics suggests two forms of longer-lasting intervention that warrant reconsideration. These would be vastly unpopular today at all levels—among politicians, among policy analysts, and among the general public—unpopular because they would hearken back to an era of imperial politics. One form is a kind of trusteeship, by which the intervening power assists in "ruling" the country it has just "rescued," acting in trust for the inhabitants and attempting to establish a stable mode of self-government. This, of course, is a long-term project. The second form is a kind of protectorate, through which those intervening attempt to bring local groups or a coalition of groups to power and then serve a defensive role in making sure that the overthrown regime does not return to power.[94]

But such arrangements are extremely unfashionable. Who would support them in today's political climate? Lest the reader be too critical of these proposals, however, the alternative is to do nothing. Bosnia and Rwanda are only two of several tragic examples of the West's failure.

But I can surely hear the objections, and they are shrill. *No one really wants the United States to be the world's policeman.* Nor should it be. But what we can do, short of assuming the role of sheriff, is to make wise and strategic use of the power and influence we possess and to do so in many venues. So we must press other nations, diplomatically, to do their share of the work. At the same time, because of the status of the United States in the world, it *will* be more involved in international affairs than any other nation, for better or worse. This, however, in and of itself is not imperialism; rather, it is stewardship and, it should be added, a large part of responsible statecraft.[95] We do well to be reminded that to possess much and be privileged is not wrong per se; but it does mean that we have much to give, and many in the world need our help. Recall the truth in the adage that to whom much has been given, much will be required.

It has been said that people will not cherish their own freedom if they are unwilling to intervene on behalf of others. Ancient proverbial wisdom beckons people of principle, irrespective of their location in life, to act on behalf of the traumatized. Such a call bears repeating, especially in a post-consensus cultural climate:

> If you faint in the day of adversity,
>   How small is your strength.
> Rescue those who are being led away toward death,
>   Hold back those stumbling toward the slaughter.
> If you say, "But we knew nothing about this,"
>   Does not He who weighs the heart consider it?
> Does not He who guards your life
>   Not know it?
> And will not He repay each person
> According to what that person has done?[96]

The controversial claim of this chapter is that the contemporary practice of both IR scholarship and U.S. foreign policymaking can be meaningfully guided and beneficially informed by theoretical and strategic approaches inspired by ancient religious texts such as these.

Chapter 8

Why U.S. Foreign Policy in Iraq Needs an Ethic of Political Reconciliation and How Religion Can Supply It

Daniel Philpott

Since the end of the Cold War, U.S. foreign policy has encountered its thorniest troubles in its efforts to build peace in societies sundered by conflict. The problem has proved far more difficult than military victory itself. The Clinton administration's worst foreign policy disaster—in Somalia—came not in securing the delivery of relief supplies but in seeking to build state institutions afterwards. The knottiest dilemmas of President George W. Bush arose in trying to secure order after formal military victories in Iraq and Afghanistan. It is fitting, then, that in late 2005 the Department of Defense raised post-conflict reconstruction operations to a "core mission," and that the State Department, the Agency for International Development, the World Bank, and the United Nations have performed similar elevations. The global struggle against terrorism lends peacebuilding still more urgency as policymakers conclude that riven societies are terror's most fertile incubators.

Are the problems of peacebuilding ones for which religious ethics can provide guidance? In the United States, Christian and Jewish ethicists had far more to say about the justice of the war in Iraq that defeated Saddam Hussein—as they did about interventions in Bosnia and Kosovo—than they have had to say about the far more difficult aftermath of these conflicts—unsurprisingly. After all, when it comes to going to war, ethicists have at their disposal the centuries-old just-war tradition. But this tradition has much less to say about the dilemmas faced when the formal part of a war is over but a just and stable peace is still distant. What obligations do outside intervening states have to build stable and just institutions? May perpetrators of war crimes receive amnesty? What about mere combatants? Or does justice require trials and punishment? If so, again, for whom? Should members of an unjust regime be debarred from holding office? Which ones? Can apologies and forgiveness be appropriate political practices? If so, who should practice them, and under what circumstances? What is the most just way to acknowledge and remember victims and their wounds? Should victims receive reparations? If so, which ones? What about living representatives of the dead? These questions beg for a development of the tradition for moral reasoning about a new set of dilemmas. Such a development could advance the project of generating what in this book is called a "Christian perspective on International Relations." That question will not be explicitly addressed here, but what is clear is that the development will certainly contribute to making "faith-based diplomacy" an effective reality.

Here I propose and outline the broad contours of an ethic of peacebuilding. Its unifying concept is reconciliation. The ethic shares the just-war tradition's foundations: the Bible and philosophical sources. It incorporates, too, a core proposition of St. Augustine and St. Thomas Aquinas, two of the just-war tradition's pioneers: that the purpose of a just war is a just peace. But it addresses a problem that presidents have faced since the end of the Cold War: that a just peace requires more than going to war and fighting it well. It requires also an effort to build peace after the war is over. I will then deploy the ethic of reconciliation to Iraq, the site where peacebuilding dilemmas are now at their most difficult. Reconciliation has indeed risen to prominence in the parlance of policymakers and other influential voices in the United States as well as in Iraq. It is a buzzword, a focal point, an organizing concept, proffered as a solution yet debated in its meaning. Most commonly, it means some combination of political measures meant to heal communal rifts in the Iraqi political order: amnesties, a reversal of de-Ba'athification measures, changes in the constitution, the sharing of oil revenue, and the like. But the ethic that I propose calls for more. Stability and a modicum of justice—Augustine's *tranquillitas ordinis*—themselves require a broader range of activities conducted by a broader range of actors in a wider range of social spheres, all aimed at healing the munificent wounds bequeathed by Iraq's past.

AN ETHIC OF RECONCILIATION

It is not only the United States that has faced the problem of peacebuilding. Confronting the dilemmas of past injustices in order to construct a stable liberal democracy has been the central challenge of at least forty societies that have emerged from dictatorship amidst the "third wave of democratization" over the past generation and of a concentration of societies that have settled their civil wars since the end of the Cold War.[1] These efforts have involved international peacekeeping and peacebuilding forces, economic aid from the World Bank, the European Union, the U.S. Agency for International Development, and other international institutions, as well as truth commissions, election monitoring, trials, reparations schemes, official apologies, dramatic statements of forgiveness, and many other measures.

These efforts, and broadly the U.S. effort to reconstruct Iraq, generally follow the moral logic of the "liberal peace," the paradigm that predominates in the world's most powerful institutions.[2] It can be described through seven tenets. First, armed conflict must come to a halt through a ceasefire or a more enduring settlement. Second, human rights, democracy, the rule of law, and free market economic institutions are to be established. Third, prominent among the actors who build peace in societies that have suffered massive violence and other injustices are international organizations like the United Nations and the World Bank as well as powerful liberal democracies like the United States and Germany. The next three tenets, though not always included in descriptions of the liberal peace, prescribe responses to past injustices that resonate with liberalism's philosophical commitments. The fourth tenet is punishment for violators of human rights—trials, imprisonment, sometimes (though controversially among liberals) execution, and often "vetting" procedures that debar past perpetrators from holding certain jobs—measures justified either through Kantian retributivist arguments, consequentialist appeals for the importance of accountability in establishing new regimes based on the rule of law, or a combination of the two. The fifth tenet is reparations for victims. The sixth is a wariness toward the political promotion of personal and spiritual healing, the transformation of emotions, and interpersonal reconciliation—phenomena properly relegated to the private realm, liberals say.[3] Seventh, included in the liberal peace is a commitment to expressing rationales through secular language.[4] It is because of their promotion of values like rights, democracy, constitutionalism, and certain rationales for punishment that are found in the thought of Locke, Kant, and their philosophical descendants, most notably John Rawls, that these tenets can be called collectively "the liberal peace."

At least one other paradigm for peacebuilding has sprung up across the globe in recent years, though, one that is rooted in religious traditions, that sets forth a vision of peacebuilding that differs distinctly from (though it also overlaps with) the liberal peace, and that can be best called reconciliation. It is found in the leadership of Anglican Archbishop Desmond Tutu, Chair of South Africa's Truth and Reconciliation Commission (TRC), and of Guatemalan Catholic Archbishop Juan Gerardi, who formed and oversaw an independent truth commission; it is found in the theological writings of Popes John Paul II and Benedict XVI, of Yale theologian Miroslav Volf, of the Jewish scholar Marc Gopin, of the Muslim scholar Mohammed Abu-Nimer, and several others.[5] But if these figures have succeeded in bringing reconciliation into global policy discourse, none has developed it into an ethic to be practiced in political orders, an ethic that addresses the moral and policy dilemmas that are involved with peacebuilding. How might such an ethic be conceived?

Reconciliation is a concept of justice: this is the ethic's central claim. It will seem a strange claim to citizens steeped in the modern liberal tradition, for whom justice is a matter of rights, fairness, economic equality, and punishment rightly meted out. It is indeed the Bible that grounds the claim. The case for it begins with the linguistic observation that in both the Hebrew of the Old Testament and the Greek of the New Testament, the terms that are translated into the English word *justice* also frequently translate into the English word *righteousness* (*sedeq* and *mishpat* in Hebrew and the family of words beginning with *dik-* in Greek). This righteousness is comprehensive, involving right relationship between all the members of a community, as prescribed by God's covenant, in their political, social, economic, legal, familial, cultic, and professional affairs.[6]

Reconciliation itself appears fifteen times in the New Testament (rendered as *katallage* and *katallosso*), though hardly at all in the Old Testament, and means either the process of restoration of right relationship or the condition of right relationship that results from this restoration.[7] If right relationship, or comprehensive righteousness, is the biblical meaning of justice, then it follows that reconciliation can equally connote the restoration of justice or a resulting state of justice. It is in this sense that reconciliation is a concept of justice. Second Isaiah speaks of justice in just this way—as a "saving justice" in which God comprehensively restores the people of Israel to righteousness, ultimately through a messianic suffering servant. In his Second Letter to the Corinthians, Paul explicitly connects reconciliation with the Greek word that translates to both righteousness and justice, *dikaiosunê*: "God made him who had no sin to be sin for us, so that in him we might become the [*dikaiosunê*] of God" (5:21).[8]

The biblical concept of reconciliation not only describes justice but is also a vision of peace, just as the ethic of reconciliation developed here aims to build peace in political orders. Isaiah 32:16-17 is only one of the many passages in scripture that closely links justice, righteousness, and peace: "Justice [*sedeqah*] will dwell in the desert and righteousness [*mishpat*] live in the fertile field. The fruit of righteousness [*sedeqah*] will be peace [*shalom*]; the effect of righteousness [*sedeqah*] will be quietness and confidence forever." *Shalom,* the Hebrew word for peace, in fact means something much like comprehensive righteousness, prescribing a vision for the life of the entire Jewish community that involves health and prosperity, economic and political justice, and honesty and moral integrity in relations between persons.[9] *Eirene*, the New Testament word for peace, is the direct translation of *shalom* into Greek, and connotes similarly "a condition reaching into almost any aspect of human life, communally or individually considered," involving material welfare, justice, and good order.[10] Peace is that aspect of reconciliation which entails a state of right relationship.

That virtue which animates the process of restoring right relationship is mercy. Mercy, here, is biblical mercy, a far wider, far more restorative virtue than mercy in the Enlightenment tradition, which is primarily a release from justly deserved punishment. As Pope John Paul II explained in his second encyclical, *Dives in misericordia*, mercy in the scriptures is "manifested in its true and proper aspect when it restores to value, promotes and draws good from all the forms of evil existing in the world and in man."[11] Such a concept of mercy complements and indeed quite resembles the biblical concept of saving justice. Only thus could Micah 6:8 consistently declare: "He has showed you, O man, what is good. And what does the Lord require of you? To act justly [*mishpat*] and to love mercy [*hesed*] and to walk humbly with your God."[12]

Reconciliation as a concept of justice—and of peace, and of mercy— is manifested not only in the Bible's language but also in its accounts of God's response to evil. It is a response that differs quite distinctly from the intellectual "solutions" to the problem of evil that Enlightenment philosophers proposed. God's response to evil is rather one of action, action that restores the nation of Israel through forgiveness, reinstatement of the rights of the poor, the renewal of creation, and even punishment.[13] In the Jewish scriptures of the Old Testament, these actions make up *tikkun olam*, the repair of the universe through which God renews his covenant. The Gospels later identify Jesus as the one who fulfills Isaiah's prophecy of the suffering servant who "leads justice to victory."[14] This justice of victory, which, here again, involves forgiveness, a judgment upon evil, hope for the poor, and the renewal of creation, climaxes in his death on the cross and his resurrection.

The meaning of this death and resurrection—the atonement—theologians have interpreted in quite different ways over the course of church history. For early church fathers, most vividly perhaps St. Irenaeus and St. Athanasius, Christ's death and resurrection were both a victory in a battle with sin, evil, and death as well as a restoration of humanity and creation—a "recapitulation," as Irenaeus put it. Far less supportive of an ethic of reconciliation is an interpretation that St. Anselm adumbrated in the Middle Ages but that reached its climax in some strands of the Protestant Reformation, one holding that Christ paid to God the penalty that humanity deserves for its sin and in so doing procured a not-guilty verdict for humanity and appeased the wrath of God the Father, but did not at the same time restore persons, relationships, and creation.[15] Far more hopeful for an ethic of reconciliation was the revival in the twentieth century of thinking much along the lines of the early church's victory interpretation but with an additional stress upon the implications of Christ's death and resurrection for the restoration of the social and political realm. Unsurprisingly, much of this revival came in response to war and carnage on a level unseen for centuries. It can be discerned in the writings of nineteenth-century Protestants like Albrecht Ritschl and twentieth-century Protestants like P. T. Forsyth, Karl Barth, Dietrich Bonhoeffer, Jan Milic Lochman, and Miroslav Volf, who have argued that Christ's justification begets the transformation and reconciliation of political orders.[16] Among popes, it can be seen in the arguments for forgiveness, apology, and mercy in politics proposed by Pope Benedict XV, who commended forgiveness to European states at the end of World War I, by Pope John Paul II, who advocated forgiveness and reconciliation in the political realm in the closing sections of *Dives in misericordia* and in subsequent addresses for the World Day of Peace, and more recently by Pope Benedict XVI. Catholic theologian Gustavo Gutiérrez has made the case that salvation involves the transformation of unjust social structures and the liberation of the poor from their confinement.[17] Protestant theologian Jürgen Moltmann has developed a theology holding that on the cross, Jesus acted in solidarity with the poor, the tortured, the murdered, and the marginalized, but also with perpetrators.[18] This thinking resonates strongly with the restorative justice movement, one that first arose in juvenile criminal law in the West, has been championed by the Mennonite tradition but also endorsed by the U.S. Catholic bishops, and was famously applied to national political orders by Archbishop Tutu in his leadership of South Africa's Truth and Reconciliation Commission. From all of these sources and strands, the building blocks of a biblically based ethic of reconciliation have emerged.

Importantly for building a consensus around principles of reconciliation in a context like Iraq, many of these same building blocks can be found in Islam. As they appear in Islamic scriptures and tradition, Arabic words for justice, reconciliation, peace, and mercy are far closer to Jewish and Christian understandings than to those of the Enlightenment. With some interpretive effort, the Qur'an's words for justice, 'adl and qist, can be understood to mean comprehensive right relationship. The Arabic sulh means settlement of differences through a restoration of relationship, while musalaha translates directly to reconciliation and carries a connotation of comprehensiveness. Further, salaam, the Arabic world for peace, refers to a general state of harmony, not just a cessation of hostility, much like the Jewish shalom. Likewise, the words for mercy, rahma, rahim, and rahamin, connote a broadly construed compassion, a general will to restore.[19] Whereas the Qur'an contains no notion of divine atonement—it does not teach that humanity collectively fell through Adam's sin in the Garden of Eden, nor that Jesus is the Son of God who rescues humanity from this plight—it does portray God as restoring relationship with sinful humans through their repentance and his forgiveness.[20] At least some portions of Islamic criminal law arguably contain a notion of restorative justice.[21] Most powerfully, traditional Arab Muslim rituals of sulh and musalaha, employed to restore relationships within villages and communities in the wake of serious crimes, entail richer notions of restoration than virtually any comparable communal rituals that I have found in the Christian or Jewish traditions.[22] My claim is not that Islamic notions of justice, peace, mercy, and reconciliation are univocal with Christian conceptions, but rather that meaningful dialogue and achievement of consensus around the principles of reconciliation that I set forth here can occur both in Muslim contexts and in contexts where Muslims and Christians mingle.

If reconciliation as a conception of justice is rooted in ancient theological texts, what form might it take in modern politics? Modern political orders, at least ones characterized by human rights, democracy, and limited constitutional government, will promote less than the whole range of relationships involved in *sedeq* and *shalom*—they attend primarily to those relationships embodied in public law. (Human rights, for instance, are a legal guarantee but also a complex form of relationship among persons, involving specific claims and duties among citizens and between citizens and states.) But if political reconciliation promotes less than *sedeq* and *shalom*, it involves much more than the mere restoration of rights and institutions. It also involves a wide range of measures aimed at healing the wide range of wounds that political injustices inflict.

Just what are these wounds? The definition of political injustice arises from contemporary transitions themselves: political injustices are violations of the human rights and the laws of war that are spelled out in international conventions. But if these norms define political injustices, they do not describe the multiform and textured ways in which they wound their victims. There are at least six:

1. *The violation of the victim's basic human rights.* This first form of woundedness indeed resembles the very definition of a political injustice. But since the legal guarantee of a person's human rights is a key aspect of what he or she is entitled to vis-à-vis the community of citizens in the state, this violation is one of the forms of woundedness that arises from a political injustice.

2. *The many forms of harm to the victim's person.* Among these are death, the death of loved ones, permanent bodily injury, grief, humiliation, trauma, the loss of wealth and livelihood, the defilement of one's race, ethnicity, religion, nationality, or gender, sexual violation, and many other harms.

3. *Victims' ignorance of the source and circumstances* of the political injustices that harmed them.

4. *The failure of community members to acknowledge victims' suffering,* either through ignorance or indifference.

5. *The "standing victory" of the perpetrator's political injustice.* It is not only harms to the victim's person that political injustices leave behind, but also an unchallenged, undefeated message of disregard for the victim's dignity—a message that constitutes an additional harm to the victim and to the shared values of the community.

6. *The wounded soul of the perpetrator.* Deep in several religious and philosophical traditions is the idea that evil injures the soul of the perpetrator. Often, this injury will redound in severe psychological damage.

Because these six forms of wounds are inflicted directly by political injustices, they may be called "primary wounds." But they also result in "secondary wounds"—acts of further injustice and withdrawals of assent from new regimes that arise from the emotions of fear, hatred, resentment, and revenge that emanate from memories of the original injustices themselves. As the experiences of countries like Bosnia, Ireland, and Rwanda attest, these secondary wounds further stunt the project of building just and stable political orders—sometimes for generations.

Correspondingly, an ethic of political reconciliation aspires to heal the range of primary and secondary wounds that political injustices inflict. Reflecting the sense in which the religious traditions view reconciliation as action every bit as much as they view it as principle, it is through practices that the ethic is realized: indeed, it is through six multiple and interdependent practices that the ethic is realized—building institutions for social justice, acknowledgment, reparations, punishment, apology, and forgiveness—each of which manifests reconciliation's core logic of restoration of right relationship and heals a distinct dimension of woundedness.[23] Inasmuch as they heal primary wounds, these practices effect what can be called "primary restorations." These restorations, though, can then effect "secondary restorations": certain forms of "social capital," including an increase in popular trust in the political order, democratic participation, and identification with the nation. It is important to remember that in the political realm, as the experience of the past generation has shown, these restorative practices will always be achieved only in part, always hampered by power and unresolved differences over the meaning of justice, and limited by their sheer size and complexity. But as the past generation has also shown, the practices are not merely the brainchild of theorists. Each of the six that I describe below has in fact taken place in numerous settings over the past generation, however messily, and might now contribute to the building of peace in Iraq. It is just this predicament that calls for an ethic, one that would be irrelevant if the practices never occurred and that would be unnecessary if they occurred without difficulty.

RECONCILIATION IN IRAQ

Is not all talk of reconciliation in Iraq naïve and utopian, especially a concept of reconciliation whose endpoint is *shalom* or *salaam*? Admittedly, it is rather a Hobbesian peace that U.S. policymakers have overridingly prioritized in recent years—an end to levels of political violence that they neither anticipated nor planned for when they first went to war and a securing of a degree of order that will allow them to begin to withdraw U.S. troops. Yet, is it not also true that the very sources of violence are just the sort that reconciliation addresses?

A 2003 *New York Times* story tells of a Shiite Iraqi, Sadri Adab Diwan, whose younger sister, Hamaa, was abducted and killed by Saddam Hussein's regime in 1980 for giving a Qur'an to a classmate. "If I catch Saddam," Diwan promised, "I won't kill him. That won't be enough. I'll suck his blood. And if he escapes, I'll follow him to the ends of the earth."[24] Such pursuits of revenge on the part of Shiites as well as Kurds, both of whom were subordinated by Sunnis since the beginning of the Ba'athist regime and brutally suppressed by Saddam, have been common since Saddam's fall and have redoubled with subsequent attacks and killings. Sunnis have responded in kind. After the February 2006 destruction of the Shiite Golden Mosque of Samarra and the wave of retaliation that it sparked, observers began to speak of a full-fledged civil war. It is a conflict between partisans with religious, national, and ethnic identities driven by communal loyalties, fear of the other's domination, and the emotions of revenge and hatred that memories of past injustices have generated—loyalties, fears, and emotions whose moderation and assuagement are indispensable to any achievement of stability in Iraq.[25]

Far from being confined to academics and church leaders, reconciliation has indeed risen to become arguably the most frequent and most salient principle to which policymakers—U.S. and European, but also Iraqi—make reference in their proposals for Iraq. The *Iraq Study Group Report* of November 2006, a landmark set of recommendations by a bipartisan commission appointed by the U.S. government, mentions reconciliation sixty-three times and devotes a major section to it. The term has shown up frequently in the benchmarks that Congress has set for U.S. policy and that the U.S. government has set for the Iraqis, and has been proffered vigorously in the speeches of former secretary of state Condoleeza Rice, U.S. ambassador Zalmay Khalilzad and his successor, Ryan Crocker, and other voices in the U.S. government like Congressman Chris Smith. Former UN secretary general Kofi Annan, Special Envoy

Lakhdar Brahimi, and heads of state like Tony Blair and Sylvio Berlusconi have also urged it. Iraqis themselves have taken up the concept as well. Not least is Prime Minister Nouri Al-Maliki, who, in June 2006, unveiled a twenty-eight-point comprehensive plan for reconciliation, one said to be inspired by South Africa's Truth and Reconciliation Commission, that received wide support from several parties in the Iraqi government as well as Turkey.[26] Conferences of Iraqi civil society, including religious leaders, have advocated reconciliation, too.[27]

None of these initiatives, nor reconciliation's establishment in political discourse, means that reconciliation has been successful or even effectual. At the present writing, U.S. policymakers and other analysts widely believe that violence in Iraq has waned and that prospects for settlement have improved, but also that stability is unlikely without reconciliation.[28] When they speak of reconciliation, what political officials both inside and outside of Iraq mean is usually some combination of the following: a greater incorporation of Sunnis into the constitution and the national government; a reversal of the de-Ba'athification policies through which the Bush administration widely purged the Iraqi government of Ba'athist party members shortly after the end of the formal war in 2003; a sharing of oil revenue among Sunnis, Shiites, and Kurds; provincial elections to boost local autonomy; a wider amnesty for both members of Saddam's security forces and more recent insurgents; a pension plan for former officials; and great autonomy for Kurds.[29] Recently, U.S. political and military officials have come to place the adverb "political" before reconciliation, perhaps to distinguish their approach from a more ambitious and realistic one involving religion, civil society, and hearts and minds.

But is "political reconciliation" enough to bring peace and stability to Iraq and allow the United States to pull its troops out—America's central foreign policy goal? Can the goals of political reconciliation themselves be achieved apart from a broader array of measures conducted by a broader array of actors with a broader array of goals, including a significant transformation of the memories, emotions, and desire for revenge that brought about the current violence in the first place? The top negotiator of the 1993 Oslo Accords between Israel and Palestine, Dennis Ross, made much the same point in a speech six years later when he attributed the subsequent breakdown of the settlement to its failure to take hold in the attitudes of the population. The same insight also lies behind the truth commissions that over thirty countries have undertaken in the wake of dictatorship and civil war in the past generation. The argument is one of simple realism: an Iraq that the United States can plausibly exit requires stable institutions, which in turn require legitimacy in the eyes of the population, which turn requires dealing with the wounds that give rise to the desire to withhold such legitimacy and to take up arms.

Providing the moral framework for the job that is required is an ethic of reconciliation grounded in biblical (and Qur'anic) conceptions of justice, mercy, and peace and enacted through a set of six practices that transform the wounds of injustice. The first practice, building socially just institutions, is the one that corresponds most with current U.S. policy in Iraq and with the ideals of global institutions: the liberal peace. It includes the rule of law based on a constitution that promotes democracy and human rights and a commitment to economic growth and a just distribution of goods. The wounds that it heals are the lack of recognition of the rights and dignity of the person that existed under the regime of Saddam. Today, basic human rights are guaranteed in law but not in practice. It is to secure these goals that U.S. forces ought to remain in Iraq.

But far more is required. Acknowledgment is the practice of conferring recognition upon the suffering of victims of human rights violations. It seeks to overcome the community's ignorance of this suffering and some-times even the victim's own ignorance of the circumstances in which the violations took place. Accounts of transitional justice from around the world show that victims are often willing to forego revenge and give their assent to a new political regime—a "secondary restoration"—once they have received recognition for their suffering. Discovering and exposing the injustices of the past creates legitimacy for the regime of the future.

In recent transitions away from war and dictatorship, states have practiced acknowledgment through a novel form of institution: the truth commission, an official body charged with investigating and producing a public record of past injustices. Truth commissions practice acknowledg-ment best when the recognition they confer is most personal, occurring through public hearings or other opportunities for witnessed testimony. Respected voices in the international community have indeed put forth proposals for an Iraqi truth commission.[30] At present, Iraq is not stable enough to conduct a national truth commission. But global practice has shown that acknowledgment can also be practiced effectively—and all the more personally—through community-level forums, which are now thinkable in many Iraqi cities and villages.[31] A remarkable survey of Iraqis conducted by the International Center for Transitional Justice and the Human Rights Center of the University of California, Berkeley, shows broad popular support for truth-seeking processes, especially local forums and ones conducted by nongovernmental organizations. "That the Iraqi people need to learn from the lessons of the past to be able to create the future—not merely say that we remember the past," is a typical sentiment voiced by a Sunni man from Baghdad.[32] Acknowledgment might also take place through documentation centers, the unearthing of mass graves, museums, and memorials, for which the same report shows strong support and which leaders like the prominent Iraqi exile Kanan Makiya have vigorously promoted.[33]

The logic behind the third practice, reparations, is much like the argument for acknowledgment: it is a form of recognition that the state or even the perpetrator himself confers on victims. The difference is that reparations are material, taking the form of money, mental and health services, access to education and employment, and the like. The wound that they address is in part lack of recognition for the victim but also the victim's material loss—economic, physical, and psychological. Understood, no amount of reparations could reverse the loss of a loved one or a permanent injury. But often, reparations can both compensate in part for the material dimension of the loss and symbolically communicate recognition to the victim. Like acknowledgment, reparations might help to reduce victims' resentment and elicit their assent for the new regime.

Among the respondents in *Iraqi Voices*, support was widespread for material and symbolic compensation.[34] Former deputy secretary of state Stuart E. Eizenstat has proposed that a compensation fund, overseen by both Iraqi and international representatives, be established for victims of torture, assassination, or other human rights abuses. European foundations for victims of Nazi injustices can serve as a model. Eizenstat also proposes a property commission to resolve the claims—often complex and conflicting—of the tens of thousands of Iraqis who were displaced from their homes under Saddam's rule.[35]

The fourth practice, punishment, might at first seem like a strange one in an ethic of reconciliation. In settings of transitional justice all over the world, reconciliation is pitted against punishment, restorative justice against retributive justice, and forgiveness against imprisonment and accountability. Punishment, though, need not be at odds with reconciliation—but only if it is justified differently than through the logics of retributivism and consequentialism between which Western arguments about criminal justice have oscillated for the last couple of centuries. It is rather what theologian Christopher B. Marshall calls "restorative punishment," grounded in biblical texts, that can contribute to reconciliation.[36] Addressing the wounds of the "standing victory" of the human rights violator's message of injustices and the disorder in the soul of the wrong-doer himself, restorative punishment seeks to repair persons, relationships, and political orders in the wake· of massive political injustices.

Restorative justice may involve long-term imprisonment for the top masterminds of human rights violations and jail for politically motivated acts of murder, rape, torture, and assault. In Iraq, this means Saddam's top leaders and those who have committed terrorist acts since his fall. Lower-level perpetrators might receive amnesty, but amnesty that is conditional on participation in public forums like truth commissions and other public rituals that perform other dimensions of the repair of wounds. Even those who have committed the most serious crimes might face such a public forum in addition to trials and imprisonment. It is hard to imagine a less restorative form of punishment than the public hanging of Saddam Hussein, which inflamed tensions between Sunnis and Shiites not only in Iraq, but throughout the Arab world.[37] Restorative punishment also implies a version of vetting that involves far more careful scrutiny of past complicity with Saddam's crimes than the Bush administration's sweeping de-Ba'athification.

The fifth practice, apology, and especially the sixth practice, forgiveness, are the most distinctively theological of the six—and the rarest in global politics today. Through a public apology, an individual perpetrator or head of state or other leader can nullify his or his group's ongoing commitment to its injustices, delegitimize the political injustice of the previous regime or faction in a war, and contribute to the legitimacy of a new regime. Apologies by former Ba'athist leaders, or by today's heads of Sunni and Shiite armies and factions for their members' acts of terrorism, might go a long way toward defusing tensions. Through its own apology for the abuses perpetrated by its armed forces, especially those at Abu Ghraib prison, the United States might also gain legitimacy for the remainder of its stabilizing operation and contribute noticeably to reconciliation in Iraq.

Forgiveness complements apology. In Christianity, forgiveness is an imitation and participation in God's own redemptive act on the cross. Theologians are divided over whether victims ought to initiate it or perform it in response to a prior apology. In Islam, God forgives the repentant sinner and commands the victim to forgive a wrongdoer who apologizes, as the Qur'an stresses over and over. When practiced toward political injustices, forgiveness might strengthen the agency of victims, defeat the wrongdoer's message of injustice by condemning and then overcoming it, defuse cycles of revenge, and greatly facilitate the building of a new political order. In the context of transitional justice, forgiveness has occurred most commonly in the context of truth commissions or other forums where the acknowledgment of victims' suffering and the apology of perpetrators has first occurred. *Iraqi Voices* shows significant support for forgiveness among ordinary Iraqis, though far less when it is seen as an amnesty that would replace the punishment of top perpetrators. Indeed, it need not be. If punishment is justified restoratively, then forgiveness can supplement it as a common restorative practice.

Again, the six practices all manifest the restorative logic of an ethic of political reconciliation. As such, each of them manifests mercy understood as a broad will to restore, peace as a broad state of right relationships, and the justice of reconciliation, a justice that restores right relationships in a political order. In Iraq, this ethic implies a far wider set of activities than what policymakers now mean by political reconciliation, but these activities may well be vital to the success of political reconciliation.

RECONCILIATION AND REALISM

But the skeptic may persist: does not such an ambitious vision strain an already burdened U.S. military mission? Reconciliation's success, in fact, depends on these activities being conducted by a far wider array of actors than the U.S. military. The U.S. armed forces themselves have recognized this conclusion insofar as they have sought to construct "Provincial Reconstruction Teams," "Concerned Local Citizens Programs," and bottom-up reconciliation programs that coordinate U.S. efforts with those of local Iraqi citizens.[38] What is needed, though, and what the United States would do well to recognize and promote, is a much broader incorporation of both international institutions and civil society actors in reconstruction and reconciliation efforts. "Reconciliation must be an Iraqi process, led by Iraqis. But to give the political process the greatest possible chance at success, the United States must remain actively involved in shoring up the security situation," concludes analyst James Phillips.[39]

The UN and the legitimacy that it confers can bolster the work of a truth commission or a reparations board. The International Criminal Court would provide a far better mode for trying and punishing top Iraqi war criminals than Iraqi national courts, helping to alleviate the divisive perception of victor's justice. NGOs, especially ones that focus on transitional justice, could provide both expertise and objectivity. Religous leaders are an asset that has been overlooked, especially by a still-secularized U.S. foreign policy establishment. Prestigious voices in a religious society like Iraq, they are potential carriers and promoters of a faith-based ethic of reconciliation. The Iraq Study Group—hardly outside the policy mainstream—drew just this conclusion in its report.[40] Religious leaders have already gathered in a handful of major conferences designed to bring together divided factions. Dramatic here is the work of Anglican Canon Andrew White, who created an Iraqi Interreligious Initiative that brings together high-level Shiite and Sunni leaders as well as representatives of minority groups, including Iraqi Christians.[41] The support of a united front of religious leaders for the practices of reconciliation that I have outlined could crucially enable their occurrence and their success.

To envision such an array of actors conducting the portfolio of practices that make up an ethic of reconciliation is not to invoke easy optimism but to offer an approach that can improve the prospects of a most difficult operation. Not an alternative to U.S. military efforts, this approach is rather a broader framework for peacebuilding that includes these efforts but situates them in partnership with other players and stratagems. Broadest of all, it is an alternative conception of justice, one whose roots lie in the texts of the Abrahamic religious traditions. But it is a conception with concrete operational implications, ones that might well contribute to stability in Iraq and the opportunity for American troops to exit Iraq having achieved success. Therein lies the realism of reconciliation.

Chapter 9

Response: Reading Religion Rightly
The "Clash of Rival Apostasies" amidst the Global Resurgence of Religion

Scott M. Thomas

All theories of society are founded on dogma—what causes a dogma to go unrecognized is its unquestioned acceptance; it is not recognized, that is, as dogma when it has sunk so deep into the structure of our thought that we take it for granted.

The little things we do must be moral acts and they must be done in the real interest of the peoples whose friendship we need—not just in the interest of propaganda . . . To the extent that our foreign policy is humane and reasonable, it will be successful. To the extent that it is imperialistic and grandiose, it will fail.

Religion has certainly returned to the study of international relations and foreign policy, and this book confirms why, after long neglect, it needed to. The expanding influence of religion in international affairs was already being recognized before September 11, 2001. It is worth noting at the outset the profound significance of the language with which this return has been described. Typically it has conveyed a deeply negative image of the role of religion. Language such as "the revenge of God" (Gilles Kepel), "God fights back" (BBC documentary), or "terror in the mind of God" (Mark Juergensmeyer) suggests that the deity believed in by people of faith is angry, violent, and bent on winning back lost territory across the world.[1] Provocative titles like these do not arise in a social or political vacuum. Religion as violence sells and makes the headlines, but the quiet work of religious peacemaking or faith-based development is not as newsworthy. The public is aware of Hamas, Hezbollah, and al Qaeda, but what percentage of the public has heard of the Community of Sant' Egidio, the Catholic peacemaking organization? The way events are represented and socially constructed by actors, agents, scholars, states, governments, and the news media is itself becoming an increasingly important part of the field.

The recognition that religion shapes international affairs has accelerated appreciably since September 11, 2001—in course offerings and degree programs on religion and politics, in the scholarly literature, in research programs, and in the output of research institutes.[2] The role of faith in foreign policy and faith-based approaches to diplomacy, peacemaking, and development are increasingly an important concern of development NGOs, citizens, governments, faith communities, as well as the Davos World Economic Forum and the Alliance of Civilizations started by the United Nations. This book offers an important commentary on and contribution to these trends.

More distinctively, the book seeks to offer a "Christian perspective" on U.S. foreign policy—or at least some signposts for such a perspective—and why it is important for a credible and effective approach to U.S. foreign policy in the twenty-first century. Undoubtedly this is a laudable objective, although given the fact that for many Americans the last eight years *already* represented a "Christian perspective" in U.S. foreign policy, it is a tall order for any set of contributors to accomplish. In the second part of this chapter, I present some provisional thoughts of my own on the enterprise. In the conclusion, the editors offer a suitably modest and realistic assessment of how far this book has advanced this specific objective.

My task in this response is not to comment in detail on the foregoing chapters but rather to help situate their insights within some wider perspectives. I do so by exploring two proposals. The first is that we need to ask more self-consciously what it is that we—scholars, practitioners, Americans, and Christians—are trying to *do* in seeking to understand the role of religion in international relations. That will involve asking why there has been a "religious turn" in the field and what this turn reveals about what is happening both in international politics and in the disciplines of International Relations and foreign policy.[3] This involves taking stock both of how we have made progress in "reading religion rightly" and of how we may still be in danger of "reading religion wrongly."

The second proposal is addressed principally to Christian scholars and practitioners, though it should certainly be of interest to others. Drawing on the neglected theological writings of International Relations theorist Martin Wight, I pose the question whether, in addition to exploring the many diverse ways in which a recognition of religion assists both understanding and action in many particular policy contexts—as this book's contributors do so illuminatingly—Christian scholars should not also stand back and pose some radical theological questions about the very foundations of the international system and the place of the West within it.

READING RELIGION RIGHTLY

What is it that we are trying to explain in the study of religion and international relations? Will the religious turn prove to be any different from previous intellectual shifts in the field, the insights and achievements of which have now been absorbed, forgotten, marginalized, or perhaps even rediscovered? What has so far been gained by the religious turn and what are its limitations? It may be too soon to answer such questions with any certainty, but posing them now sets out critical, reflexive markers for trying to grasp what might be occurring. Five achievements can be observed.

The first achievement, obviously, is simply to have brought religion "back in" to the field. As indicated by many of this book's contributors, religion is "returning from exile." Its salience for, relevance to, and pervasiveness in global affairs is now being widely recognized, however grudgingly. The case for bringing religion back in has now been effectively made, and scholars and practitioners who resist this are increasingly seeming to be caught in a time warp.[4] The agenda is now shifting to *how* to bring religion back into diplomacy, peacemaking, conflict resolution, and even academic theorizing.

The second achievement is also now widely accepted. The global resurgence of religion since the 1970s—characterized variously as the growth of "public religion," the "deprivatization of religion," or the "desecularization of the world"—is well rehearsed in the book. Indeed,.I think we can now see an emerging consensus in the field on the following ways in which religion matters:

- The recognition that nationalism is often rooted in religious affiliation and can be a powerful source of identity, legitimacy, and social cohesion.
- An acknowledgment of the positive role of religion in constructing civic norms such as tolerance, in encouraging the development of civil society, and in extending and consolidating democracy.
- The realization that religion matters for international security (with some even speaking of religion and security as "the new nexus in international relations"[5]).
- The acceptance that religion matters for foreign policymaking and that faith-based approaches to diplomacy, peacemaking, conflict resolution, and international development make a tangible difference on the ground.
- The recognition that religion can play a role in the formation of international norms such as human rights, international law, the laws of war, poverty alleviation, and protection of the environment.

An additional, and so far less well-recognized, theme is religion's role in the formation of international institutions such as the United Nations and the European Union and in processes of regional integration—in Latin America, for example, where the role of Christian Democratic parties has been significant. Relatedly, the story regarding the ecumenical movement in the interwar years and the way the same band of ecumenical Christians helped to found the United Nations and the World Council of Churches (itself part of the larger story of the religious contribution to the foundations of the postwar international order) has yet to be told adequately.[6] While the role of Christian Democratic parties and Catholic social doctrine is broadly recognized in the history of European integration, it is less well known in theories of European integration. In addition, given religion's role in supporting international norms, another topic that remains to be probed further is the possible relevance of the early English School's insights into the role of the cultural and religious foundations of state-systems in the construction of international norms (a theme to which I return in the second part of the chapter).

The third achievement of the return of religion is a growing consensus on *why* religion has been marginalized in the study of international relations. Several reasons for this neglect are noted in the book, of which four leading ones can be summarized. First, secularization was considered to be an inherent part of modernization, including political modernization.[7] Second, the dominant understanding of modernity was predicated on the model of Western European experience of modernization, capitalism, and industrialization as interpreted by the founding fathers of modern sociology.[8] Implicit in this model were parochial assumptions regarding the place of Christianity in public life and church-state relationships drawn narrowly from "European Christianity" rather than "global Christianity." But troublingly for the secularization thesis, Europe is now being acknowledged as the exception (rather than the United States).[9] Third, on the powerful "Westphalian presumption," it was held that deep religious pluralism could not be successfully accommodated in a global multicultural international society and so must be disciplined by the state through the privatization and nationalization of religion in order to secure a stable international order. Finally, religion was marginalized because of the dominance in the field of a "rationalist" epistemology. "Rationalism" is the name given to the way in which a convergence of positivism, naturalism, and materialism influenced the core paradigms of International Relations (realism, liberalism/neoliberal institutionalism, and globalism/Marxism). Methodologically, rationalism laid the foundations for the social scientific study of international relations which proceeded by means of the deductive-nomological method as an explanatory approach in which law-like regularities were allegedly discovered using the methods of the natural sciences. Rationalist methods and assumptions strongly influenced the determination of what counted as legitimate "knowledge" in the field, what constituted a good "theory," and what knowledge and theory were supposed to achieve. Rationalism established a clear dominance over rival "reflectivist" or interpretive approaches which sought instead to understand phenomena by eliciting the meanings that actors give to their actions.[10] It also curtailed the influence of two countervailing schools of thought influenced by Christianity, namely Reinhold Niebuhr's Christian realism and the scholars of the early English School: Martin Wight, Herbert Butterfield, Adam Watson, and Adda Bozeman.[11]

The fourth achievement secured by bringing religion back into the field of International Relations is the recent attempt to clarify the meanings—or at least identify the contested meanings—of key concepts used in the study of religion. Elsewhere I have tried to make the case that the concept of a "global resurgence of religion" has deeper and broader explanatory power regarding the role of religion than concepts of, for example, religiously motivated "militancy," "extremism," and "fundamentalism."[12] It is noteworthy that the concept of "fundamentalism" used to describe the Islamic Revolution in Iran emerged in the Western media at the same time as the rise of the Moral Majority and the "Christian Right" in the United States. From the outset, the concept of "religious fundamentalism" was not a neutral, objective descriptor but was parasitic on the theory of modernization, according to which secularization was considered to be modernization's inevitable consequence. Any outbursts of religion were then unthinkingly interpreted by the broadly secular and liberal media and academic establishment in terms of the supposedly universal category of "fundamentalism" (and, later, "global religious fundamentalism")—a backward, reactionary, and conservative response by those socially and economically marginalized by American-style modernization.[13]

Another core concept that is now rightly being contested is "secularism." As noted in the introduction, Elizabeth Shakman Hurd has insightfully analyzed the unquestioned acceptance in International Relations of a very specific division between the domains of politics and religion. She argues that secularism needs to be analyzed as a form of political (indeed *theopolitical*) authority in its own right: defining the *boundaries* of the secular, the religious, and the political is itself a *political* decision.[14] When this is not acknowledged, it is inevitable that any "religious resurgence" is interpreted as a form of fundamentalism—that is, a *religious backlash* against secular modernity. Thus, Islam is portrayed as monolithic and unchanging, defined as "political Islam," and seen inevitably as a threat to Western security.[15]

In other words, a set of supposedly objective, value-free concepts—extremism, militancy, fundamentalism, terrorism, secularism, political religion, political Islam, Islamism, etc.—have in fact concealed the operation of a distinctively secular and modernist teleology, an entirely secular *mythos* of salvation history which has shaped the standard representations of international politics and political actors. Many commentators continue to use these concepts uncritically. But they are "essentially contested" concepts in which there is limited possibility of agreement on their meaning, either because of different epistemological premises underlying them or because of quite different worldviews underpinning them.[16] One of the achievements of the religious turn, then, has been the stimulation of a more critical debate on the adequacy of such concepts in describing (what I believe is better characterized as) the global resurgence of religion. Like "fascism," many such terms are simply used as terms of abuse, disclosing more about the commentators than the phenomena being commented on.

It is increasingly acknowledged that "religious," "secular," and "political" are not stable, value-neutral concepts or categories but socially and politically constructed (and contested) concepts reflecting particular settings, cultures, and time periods, including our own.

The fifth achievement in bringing religion back into the field of International Relations is the growing consensus that some existing concepts at the theoretical core of the entire discipline need to be recast: sovereignty, the state, territoriality, nonintervention, the balance of power, and others. Such rethinking, it is being slowly recognized, may challenge the supposedly secular foundations of the modern international system itself.[17] There is even a grudging recognition that some of the core concepts in the field not only have political and philosophical foundations but also "theopolitical" ones or even foundations in theological ethics. The dawning awareness that modern international relations may itself have (hitherto concealed) religious roots is in turn having an impact on the discipline's intellectual history, and so on its self-understanding, in ways that are profoundly unsettling to some of its leading scholars.[18]

Daniel Philpott has led the way here by developing a case for the role of ideas—actually a set of distinctly Protestant ideas, indeed a type of Protestant political theology—in the establishment of the Westphalian settlement. Claims such as these have generated vigorous debate on the role of the Reformation in the origins and character of Westphalia. Clearly, ideational and material factors, social and property rights, technology, and the rise of the dynastic, absolutist state all played a role in the origins of Westphalia.[19] But whatever is thought to have been achieved at Westphalia, the formative role of religion on that epoch-making settlement is now firmly on the scholarly agenda.[20]

Why does this seemingly arcane historical debate about the origins of the international system in the seventeenth century matter now? It matters because what the revisionist reading of Westphalia challenges is an interpretation of the origins of the modern world itself and of the grand narrative which interprets Westphalia as the portal to the modern international system. This narrative has legitimized the political mythology of modern liberalism according to which, as a result of the wars of religion, the modern state had to discipline religion by privatizing and nationalizing it. What is at stake in this debate is, fundamentally, the religious identity of the modern West itself. I will argue later in this chapter that this question merits a more radical theological response than is often forthcoming in debates about religion and international relations.

READING RELIGION WRONGLY

Each of the contributors to this book convincingly shows how, in specific settings, bringing religion back into the study of international relations will help toward what the introduction calls a "more credible and effective approach to U.S. foreign policy." At the same time, the history of attempts to redirect American foreign policy by changing the way we think about it suggests that a degree of skepticism may be in order here to keep our expectations realistic. We have been here before, many times. Each previous intellectual shift in U.S. diplomatic thinking during the Cold War was also supposed to make foreign policy more credible and effective: the idea of managing war scientifically, theories of insurgency and counterinsurgency, theories of modernization and development, and so on.[21]

Already half a century ago the indifference to religion on the part of the American government was brilliantly depicted by William J. Lederer and Eugene Burdick in their best-selling novel *The Ugly American* (1958). This charts the breathtaking scale of ignorance about religion on the part of U.S. officials, their ridicule of local knowledge, their lack of expertise in local culture and languages, their refusal to seek an in-depth understanding of the countries and conditions in which the United States had found itself, and the way in which the attitudes of officials, politicians, and bureaucrats could undermine the country's efforts to spread democracy around the world.[22] Given the criticisms of the lack of human intelligence prior to September 11, 2001, and that (as we now know) Osama bin Laden had nothing to fear from the U.S. intelligence community,[23] and the superficiality of recent attempts to learn "the lessons from Iraq," one has to wonder what has really changed in half a century of U.S. foreign policy.

This underlines the extent to which the key question of epistemology—what constitutes knowledge—is so crucial in the field. In reviewing the past half-century we are confronted with the question of whether knowledge is after all cumulative, as was widely assumed. Is it not the case that each generation simply ends up relearning the lessons the previous generation forgot—or making the same mistakes?[24] How then can we assess appropriately the reliability of what is *now* claimed as "knowledge" about the impact of religion in international relations? How might we evaluate what bringing religion back into the field could actually accomplish for U.S. foreign policy? There may be no complete answer available to those questions, but noting the limitations of the supposed new knowledge may at least instill in us a suitable humility as we seek to put it to work.[25]

The first limitation—and here I anticipate my proposal later in the chapter—is that the return of religion has not yet been accompanied by a critique of the ideological hegemony of the secular and liberal modern state. I want to suggest that one indication of ideological capture on the part of many contemporary commentators is the absence of any sustained reflection on the distinction between two kinds of killing. There is the violence of "religious fundamentalists," routinely denounced by Western observers as "medieval" and "barbaric"—the catch-all phrases for all that Western moderns find unintelligible. And there is our own "good" killing in defense of the secular liberal state, which we consider noble, heroic, and patriotic. But on the basis of *what precise criteria* is killing to defend religion categorically worse than killing to defend the modern state? If, as William Cavanaugh argues, being willing to die for the modern state is a bit like being willing to die for the telephone company,[26] no wonder there are so many martyrs willing to die for Islam. After the horrors of twentieth-century wars, it is difficult to argue that the (allegedy) "religious wars" of early modern Europe were any more violent than the "secular wars" of modern Europe. What if killing to defend the modern secular liberal state needs far stronger justification and defense than we moderns have so far felt it necessary to supply? What if such a justification is unavailable?[27]

The second limitation is the absence of sufficient critical reflection on the real motivations driving the renewal of interest in religion on the part of governments, research funding agencies, and academic specialists. Too often what seems to be of chief concern is the possible threat to international security posed by political Islam or by American "fundamentalism."[28] The question arises whether, if "religion" is not "securitized"—to use the concept of the Copenhagen School—it is of any interest to governments and commentators. For the Copenhagen School, the concept of "security" is analyzed using theories of linguistics. Security is not a fixed, clearly defined concept (as in the realist or liberal paradigms) but a type of *speech act* with distinct consequences in the real world of international relations. By classifying something as a "security threat," an actor is seeking to lift a topic—such as migration, immigration, drug trafficking, terrorism, or religion—out of ordinary political debate and into an area of dire security concern.[29] The act of securitization—deeming something to be a "security threat"—then legitimates extraordinary, emergency measures. Yet "security" and "security threat" turn out to be concepts that are socially constructed—examples of an *inter-subjective* process of meaning construction—rather than neutral descriptors of objective realities. The securitization of a phenomenon depends on an audience accepting the securitization speech act, a process in which the media, politicians, religious leaders, and citizens all play a role.[30]

Religion has been securitized for a number of reasons, but the most basic one has already been stated: the secular modernist, Westphalian assumption that if religion (re)enters the public square it will be inherently threatening to the liberal democratic state and to international order. This assumption is what makes transnational religion seem so exceptionally subversive to both domestic and international peace. The potentially or actually constructive role of religion in working for peace, justice, and reconciliation is then ignored or marginalized, for such activities may indicate the need for significant redistributions of power within existing liberal democratic states and in the management of the international order. One sign of a possible paradigm shift, perhaps, is the invitation issued to leaders of the main world religions to the Copenhagen climate change summit in December 2009, who for the first time will address the assembled delegates in the plenary session. What is systematically excluded when religion is simply "securitized" is any awareness of "the ambivalence of religion"—religion's role both as a possible ferment of violence but also as a contributor to democracy and conflict resolution.[31]

The third limitation is related to the question of ontology. In the study of international relations, ontology examines claims about what the world is made up of, the kind of objects constituting and shaping world politics. Contrary to prevailing opinion in the discipline, ontological claims are central to the study of religion and international relations. When concepts such as militancy, extremism, radicalism, and fundamentalism are used to distinguish between "radical" and "moderate" Islamists, ontological claims are being made about the fundamental categories in which religion and international relations are classified. These kinds of claims reveal that international relations is a *social world* of ideas, beliefs, and values as well as a *material world* of power and wealth, guns, missiles, battleships, trade, foreign investment, and manufacturing. The Copenhagen School draws our attention to the vital role of language in the construction of the social world of international relations. As Kratochwil notes, the point is not whether "the 'world' exists 'independent' from our minds. The question is rather whether we can recognize it in a pure and direct fashion," as positivist social science assumes, or "whether what we recognize is always already organized and formed by certain categorical and theoretical elements."[32]

Further achievements deriving from the return of religion to the field of International Relations, then, will be substantially hampered unless scholars can escape from these (and other) ways of "reading religion wrongly."

RETURNING TO THE CATACOMBS?
Living amidst the Rival Apostasies of Islam and Christendom

The second proposal I want to offer toward locating the contributions of this book on a larger canvas involves posing some serious theological questions about the very foundations of the international system and the conduct of American diplomacy within it. Many critiques of "modernity" and "the West" have been mounted in recent years (and with varying degrees of plausibility) from within the discipline of theology, but I hope readers of this book will find especially interesting one that has been developed from within the discipline of International Relations itself, by the leading figure in the English School, Martin Wight. I suggest that Wight's analysis of half a century ago remains surprisingly fresh and disturbingly pertinent to our own times. It invites the unsettling question whether defending "the national interest" of a modern liberal nation-state is, from a Christian perspective, a legitimate foreign policy objective. What is the aim of a "Christian" approach to U.S. foreign policy? If religion was brought back in, and U.S. foreign policy was more credible and more effective, toward what end would it be more credible and effective? To simply manage better the existing international order, or to change it?

Wight raises the deep question of what it is that the West actually represents. If it is conceived to be simply the remnant of Christendom, then it becomes easy to confuse defending the West with defending the church or defending Christianity. Indeed, this has become the position of many Christians, even secular Europeans.[33] However, if from a Christian point of view the West represents something else—what Martin Wight calls the "apostasy of Christendom"—how then should national or international security be conceived? Wight observes that the last time such an apostasy was judged to have occurred, the response of Christians was to return to the catacombs, or later, following St. Benedict, to create new forms of authentic Christian community which converted and transformed the society around them.[34] Could this be a remotely conceivable option today in a global age?

In the early days of the Cold War, Wight, a devout Anglican, made the surprising proposal that "the level on which a Christian political philosophy has to be worked out is ultimately that, not of the White House and Downing Street, but of the catacombs."[35] What did he mean by this? Wight, who had been Arnold Toynbee's research assistant at Chatham House, the Royal Institute of International Affairs,[36] was cautious about what could ultimately be accomplished through the corridors of power.[37] He was aware of the way each generation self-consciously thought it was at the peak of human achievement (recall Fukuyama's "end of history" declaration), unprecedented prosperity (an assumption which even the global financial crisis of 2009 seems not to have overthrown), or unparalleled danger or catastrophe (the Cold War, and now the global "war on terror"). Wight argued, however, that ultimately each generation was faced with similar moral and analytical predicaments in international affairs, with a remarkable degree of repetition and recurrence; he compared, for example, the ideological battles of the Cold War to the wars of religion in early modern Europe.[38] A key part of the wisdom of statecraft—and for him it was an *art*, not a science—was in recognizing this to be the case and so being open to learn from the ideas, judgments, and arguments of our predecessors.[39] Hope, Wight reminded us, was a theological virtue, not a political one.[40] It may be that American optimism, pragmatism, and belief in progress bristles at such a suggestion. But Wight was critical of what he called the "neo-pelagianism" of the West, with its sense of will, agency, and autonomy so characteristic of liberal modernity.[41]

That is precisely the point Wight made in the Britain of the 1950s. He invoked the metaphor of the catacombs because he believed that to live in the secular, modern, Western world was to live amid the "apostasy of Christendom." Wight, unlike Truman, Eisenhower, and many other American leaders, refused to identify Britain, the United States, or even the West with the cause of God in history. He did not equate the spread of the Church of England or the expansion of the British Empire with divine providence (as a young man he vehemently opposed British imperialism in India). Neither did he as a mature scholar identify the cause of God with the West during the Cold War. He certainly did believe that the struggle against Nazism was a just war (even though he was himself a pacifist at the time) and that the West should oppose the Soviet Union. Yet his theological analysis of the West and Russia led him to believe that ultimately God was not straightforwardly on the side of either superpower.

Yet he was not naïve about the prospects for overcoming the antagonism between liberal democracy and Communism. Wight observed that during the Cold War the churches saw one of their main responsibilities to be "contributing to the reconciliation of the opposing blocs, and of showing that the church abolishes the Iron Curtain."[42] But he held that the call for peace and reconciliation, central as they are to the gospel, are not exhaustive of the Christian message. Wight's response to similar ecumenical statements on the eve of the founding meeting of the World Council of Churches in Amsterdam was this:

> There may be truth in this, but since it resembles the kind of thing the Church has been saying for years without appreciable effect, we may wonder *whether it goes deep enough*, or what is the *right* way to interpret it.[43]

"The question," he wrote, "is whether we are speaking politically or theologically." Although the church was in the West, the church was no more identified with the West than it was with Russia, nor was the church "non-aligned" in the sense of being between Russia and the West. "The church is within and without and above Russia and the West: this is a theological fact overriding the political circumstances of which churches may come to at Amsterdam."[44]

"Any statement," Wight claimed, "about the church's position in the present international crisis . . . will be true in proportion to its theological depth." He believed Christians had what he called "the double task" of analyzing the crisis in world politics in historical terms and interpreting it in theological terms.[45] Indeed, the latter was finally more important, because examining world politics in *theological* terms would necessarily include a historical analysis, whereas examining it in purely historical terms would omit the theological dimension. Thus the place to begin to understand the Cold War—and, he judged, *any* global crisis—would be to reconsider the nature of "Christendom."

Accordingly, Wight developed a distinctively theological interpretation of the Cold War. He began with the rival historical phenomena of Russia and the West, doing so in a way that even today many Christians might find uncomfortable. He identified the East-West axis of world division during the Cold War as a conflict between "two blocs or groupings or civilizations" whose antagonism determined world politics. In theological terms, he identified the two blocs as a "clash *within* civilizations," that is, as an antagonism between two parts—Byzantium and Latin Christendom—of what was once a unified Christendom. Wight believed Russia *and* the West "were no longer Christendoms," as he put it, but were what he called "post-Christian" and "neo-pagan" civilizations.

The Cold War was a conflict with an inescapable historical connection to Christianity. It was distinct from the conflict between the West and China, India, or even Islam since these were cultures or civilizations with no historical connection with Christianity. The idea that Islam had no historical connections with Christianity will, to many, seem on its face simply wrong. What did Wight mean?

> For more than a thousand years the conflict which occupied Christian men was of this kind [i.e., one without a historical connection to Christianity], the conflict with Islam. But that conflict was triumphantly *or shamefully* won by Christendom, and Islam is now moribund [*sic*]. Our conflict is *fratricidal*. It is a continuation, in another form, of the ancient conflict between Byzantine and Latin Christianity, with Russia as the inheritor and organizer of the Byzantine East, America as the inheritor and organizer of the Catholic and Protestant West.[46]

Wight identified the conflict between the West and Byzantium as a fratricidal conflict within Christendom. This was the difference with Christendom's conflict with Islam. The East-West conflict reached the frightful dimensions it did during the Cold War because Christendom, of which the two blocs were parts, was now dead.[47] Thus, viewed theologically, the Cold War was a result of the "apostasy of Christendom."

What then did Wight mean by "apostasy" and by "Christendom"? He defined Christendom in the following way:

> A society in which 1. the majority are practicing Christians; 2. the church is therefore the most venerated and influential of all institutions; 3. the church itself is vigorous and uncorrupted— and are we to add, united? 4. social and political organization is therefore saturated with Christian presuppositions.[48]

Wight wrote: "These conditions are no longer found anywhere in the world. Christians are everywhere a dwindling minority with decreasing influence in a society whose presuppositions are non-Christian and increasingly anti-Christian."[49] Wight argued that in Eastern Europe and the Soviet Union, Marxism had become a substitute for Orthodox

Christianity, and in the West, what he called "bourgeois liberalism" had become the secular substitute for Western Christianity.[50]

Why did Wight characterize the liberal, capitalist democracies of the West, now caught in a global competition with the Soviet Union, as evidence of the "apostasy of Christendom"? Apostasy is the abandonment of or defection from religious faith or a set of religious vows or principles. Wight presented his notion of the apostasy of Christendom as a message to both the conservatives and liberals of his day. The conservative concept of the "chosen nation," implying a corresponding call to identify one's country with the will and purpose of God—whether during the era of British imperialism, the Cold War, or indeed any period of history—he considered one form of apostasy. Equally, those liberals who identified Christianity with the comfortable, optimistic values and assumptions of liberal modernity, and who simply called for peace and reconciliation when there was no likelihood of peace with Hitler's Germany or the Soviet Union, were guilty of another. Liberalism was a symptom of a Western society that had displaced the God of the Bible with the gods of "bourgeois liberalism," the worship of mammon, the self, and individualism.

Perhaps even more provocatively, Wight believed that the doctrine of the antichrist was crucial to a theological understanding of the West as the apostasy of Christendom.[51] Ahead of his time, he properly recognized that the main purpose of biblical apocalyptic literature was to unveil for its readers a way to interpret their own societies from a divinely revealed perspective and thus from the standpoint of the ultimate goal of history.[52] What is now called critical theory seeks to criticize, deconstruct, and bring out into the open the underlying or hidden assumptions of existing perspectives and approaches to politics and society.[53] We might say that, from Wight's perspective, the proper study of biblical apocalyptic can be called "God's critical theory," since its purpose is to unveil a theological evaluation of history, human society, and world politics.

No doubt all this will seem bizarre to most contemporary scholars of international relations. Even Hedley Bull and most other scholars of the English School did not know what to do with Wight's lengthy manuscripts on apostasy, the antichrist, progress, history, and Christianity. I suggest, however, that if getting the problem right is half the battle, then recognizing the salience of the doctrine of the antichrist may be a necessary part of a cultural-theological critique of Western modernity insofar as it discloses the deepest pathology of the modern West.

The political theologian Oliver O'Donovan, for example, has emphasized that the doctrine of the antichrist speaks to recurrent periods in
history marked by apostasy, deception, demonic possession, and persecution and may be the earliest description of what we have come to call
"ideology"—that is, the religious absolutizing of political doctrines.[54] The
antichrist is an "anti-spirit," a "false prophet" propagating a false gospel
which challenges the claims of God's kingdom with its own. In other
words, as Wight acknowledged a generation earlier, "antichrist" refers
to *any political or social order that implicitly or explicitly presents itself as a
necessary and sufficient medium of human flourishing.*

This is why Wight was not satisfied simply to identify "cultural
Christianity"—the residue of nineteenth-century Protestant liberalism—
with the economic and political ideas of liberal modernity. He would
likely have agreed with O'Donovan that Western modernity could be
conceived as "antichrist," that is, as a parody, a corruption, of a Christian
social order. When a political order makes a claim to self-sufficiency, it
is often called "totalitarian." But for Wight, the doctrine of the antichrist
offers a more searching description of the apostasy of *any* society or
civilization which claims to have a self-sufficient account of human flourishing—the secular libertarian capitalism of the United States, the statist
welfare capitalism of Europe, and certainly radical expansionist Islam.

If Wight's theological analysis is anywhere near correct, then Samuel
Huntington was only partly right: there *is* a clash of civilizations, but it is
not between Islam and the West. The real clash is between what Alasdair
MacIntyre calls tradition-based modes of rationality and visions of the
common good and those modes and visions based on the Enlightenment
project. If so, then the real clash is between, on the one hand, orthodox
Islam and Christianity, and, on the other, all modern forms of fundamentalism, whether they are faith-based or secularist. Perhaps the difference
between religious fundamentalists (such as those in either Islam or Christianity) and the readers of liberal-leaning newspapers like the *Guardian*
or the *New York Times* is not really as stark as each would like to think.
Perhaps there is only a "sibling rivalry" between them since both religious
fundamentalism and liberal fundamentalism accept the "secular" criteria
of technocratic, instrumental rationality to provide an account of the
good life and human flourishing.

It is, of course, true that radical expansionist Islam is an extreme,
religiously motivated form of identity politics[55]—the purpose of waging
jihad is to reconstitute the global Muslim community. But it freely avails
itself of the fruits of globalization in order to achieve this: via the use of

English, the Internet, satellite phones, and aircraft it demonstrates that it is an authentic product of the modern, globalized world and not at all a return to the Middle Ages, as so many liberals would like to think. And yet it is also in fundamental conflict with this world. In other words, the alleged clash between radical expansionist Islam and the apostate Christianity or modernism of the West is not a fundamental clash, "the West versus the Rest."[56] The clash of civilizations is really a sibling rivalry since the apostate West and radical global Islamism spring from a similar source of apostasy: post-Enlightenment modernity.

If this analysis has any truth to it, it implies that the task for Christians is to struggle to live lives of integrity and faithfulness amidst a world of rival apostasies. This is the sense in which we can begin to interpret Wight's call for a "return to the catacombs." It is not a literal call to withdraw from either the polity or the academy but rather a challenge to discern new forms of integrity and community in the post-secular and postmodern world of the twenty-first century. Perhaps we may interpret the varied recommendations offered by the authors of the foregoing chapters as contributions toward that process of discernment. That, at least, is my proposal.

Conclusion

Jonathan Chaplin with Robert Joustra

To conclude this volume, we first present some interpretive reflections on recurring themes in the foregoing chapters and then ask to what extent this book has clarified the possibilities and limits of the program of developing a "Christian perspective on International Relations."

One way to summarize the conclusions emerging in diverse ways from this book is to observe that they cumulatively call attention to three distinctive but neglected features of religion that bear powerfully upon international politics: its *pastness*, its *thickness*, and its *potency*.

Part 1 explicitly makes a case for "taking religion seriously," but the whole book implicitly makes a parallel case for taking history seriously. Religion and history constitute mutually reinforcing elements of the inescapable social rootedness of all human activity, and religious narratives, grand or otherwise, continue to supply the orienting frameworks in which political action occurs. Religious commitments are more than mere shifting brand loyalties or markers of individual self-expression, as they are typically construed by Western modernists: they often have deep, sometimes ancient, formative histories that must be reckoned with if the religious dynamics shaping global politics are to be rendered intelligible.

As Alasdair MacIntyre reminds us, we are "at best co-authors of our own narratives. Only in fantasy do we live what story we please . . . we enter upon a stage which we did not design and we find ourselves part of an action that was not of our making."[1] MacIntyre also claimed that secularist liberalism has itself become a "tradition," albeit one whose constitutive self-understanding compels it to deny its traditional character.[2] In the introduction we ourselves proposed that secularist liberalism functions in many ways akin to a "religious faith," and Scott Thomas echoes that view in claiming to discern beneath the conceptual apparatus of contemporary IR "the operation of a distinctively secular and modernist teleology, an entirely secular *mythos* of salvation history." The uncovering of the grand historical narratives of a modern secularist faith, then, is just as important as attending to the histories of what are typically thought of as "religions." This is complicated, of course, by the fact that modern liberalism is to a great extent an outcome both of the successes, and of the subsequent secularization, of Christian culture, just as modern Christianity has itself been partly formed by modern liberalism. So discerning the pastness of modern secularism involves a close critical scrutiny of those complex historical intertwinements over five centuries.[3] Most of our authors, however, do focus on the role in IR of religion as traditionally understood.

Andrew Preston illustrates the significance of the pastness of religion by calling attention to the often-overlooked religious influences at work in the history of American foreign relations. He compares, for example, the relatively high level of scholarly awareness of the ideological factors operative in the Cold War with the relative neglect of the impact of the Great Awakening on the Revolution. The undoubted definitional and methodological challenges confronting a study of the causal force of religious factors in diplomatic history are, he ventures, no more serious than those which have been faced, successfully, by those incorporating the study of race and gender into the discipline. Students of religion in diplomatic history can thus usefully proceed by learning the methodological lessons of the new social and cultural history. While, as he acknowledges, the study of religion will never settle particular historiographical debates, it will add to our understanding of U.S. foreign relations precisely by complicating and thereby enriching their history.

James Skillen discloses how three quite distinct and historically rooted variants of "Zionism" continue to drive American Middle East policy, often in unrecognized ways. Skillen even reaches back to antiquity to suggest that events like the conquest of Jerusalem in 586 BC have lasting resonance for foreign policy right up to the present day. The study of the role of religion in American diplomatic history is every bit as relevant to coherent and effective foreign policy today as engaging the specific political aspirations of our current interlocutors. A lasting peace in (and with) the regions of Islam in particular should strike us as unlikely apart from a serious, protracted engagement with the histories of its peoples and beliefs. Dates like 1258 and 1683 are not incidental blips on the inevitable march of all cultures toward Western modernity but deeply formative chapters in the narratives that are still passionately embraced by many of the current inhabitants of these regions. A rediscovery of the historical momentum powering contemporary religion would then serve to question modernity's characteristic indifference (or hostility) to the present weight of pastness, and would challenge its parochial presumption that "progress" will (or should) cleanse us of our traditions.

Paul Marshall's chapter reminds us that Western policymakers remain very much in the dark about Islam's pastness. It also brings to the fore that there is a density, an intensity, and a complexity—a *thickness*—in religion that we overlook at our (literal) peril. Ignorance of the thickness of religion is evident wherever attempts to overcome political conflicts fueled by religious division proceed on the basis of a thin, liberal cosmopolitanism which erases the deepest impulses and identities of those whom we seek to engage (or resist). Thomas Farr's penetrating critique of U.S. foreign policy on international religious freedom underscores the same point by exposing how, in spite of important initiatives, current policy has been stymied by an excessively thin, privatized conception of religion. This explains why even with the best of intentions, diplomats still cannot take the widely expressed desire for religious freedom with full seriousness, assuming that disaffected believers can be palmed off with a merely formal legal guarantee of negative religious freedom— which, in any case, is often systematically ignored or suppressed by the regimes being engaged anyway. If we take Marshall and Farr seriously, we must assert that only a *rooted, tradition-sensitive* internationalism will enable American diplomacy to succeed in the Middle East—or indeed anywhere else. Religious identities are not mere embellishments of "real" material or ethnic interests—not even, as Thomas Farr points out, of loftier "humanitarian" ones—and American foreign policy will fly blind if it fails to grasp religion's thickness both in those it is dealing with and in America's own history and identity.

At this point many secularists will retort that "getting too deeply into a religion's guts" (as Farr put it) will drag us into tribal perspectives and compromise our ability to affirm universal principles. But taking thickness seriously is not incompatible with acquiring a universal vision of global order. It is rather a precondition of so doing. As Hatzopolous and Petito write, "Genuine universality requires a thick conception of the presence of religion in world affairs."[4]

Thomas Albert Howard demonstrates the importance of pastness and thickness in a dimension of U.S. foreign policy where such realities are often thought to have been superseded in a shared embrace of secular modernity—relations with Europe. Howard intriguingly suggests that left-wing European intellectuals like Habermas and Derrida owe their distaste for American foreign policies as much to the lingering impact of the political theologies of the nineteenth-century "Tory imagination" as to contested readings of contemporary world events. The recurrent policy tensions between the United States and Europe might be partially explained as failures of historical self-understanding (on both sides of the Atlantic) and not only as expressions of divergent strategic interests. The implication is that a more searching, historically and religiously informed transatlantic dialogue on the appropriate global responsibilities of the United States is required. The incremental recession of unchallenged American global supremacy in the light of the rise of nations such as China and India—where religious factors will only increase in significance—will make that dialogue no less necessary in the decades ahead. Such a dialogue could unblock entrenched misperceptions between Europe and the United States and even make for more successful diplomatic cooperation between two regions that in fact share far more culturally and strategically than what divides them. We wait to see whether President Obama will be able to take the measure of that challenge.

John Bernbaum's analysis of the collapse of the Soviet Union and of subsequent U.S. policy toward Russia further underlines the costs of ignoring pastness and thickness in foreign affairs. Bernbaum shows how a momentous moral and spiritual revolution—invisible to Western observers reading events through secularist lenses—accompanied the more palpable political and economic revolutions in the former Soviet Union. Western commentators failed to anticipate collapse on the horizon because they lacked the conceptual tools to interpret the moral and spiritual malaise of Soviet culture and politics in the 1980s. Kremlinologists closely monitored things like shifts in military spending but did not bother to track cultural indicators (such as novels and films or religious upsurges) of deeper tectonic movements beneath the surface. And Western diplomacy post-collapse was hampered by a serious misunderstanding of what was actually occurring: the Russian people were not simply yearning for political democracy (if they were) and economic prosperity but recovering from an abusive regime that had robbed them of their religious traditions and cultural identity. Bernbaum shows how recognizing the pastness and thickness of Russian religion would imply significant shifts in Western policy: "Rather than telling Russians they need to become like us, a wiser, humbler approach would be to help them rediscover positive attributes in their country's past and then adapt modernization to these traditional attributes."

Another way to put this is to say that the transformative *potency* of religion for global politics needs to be identified and harnessed. Everyone is aware that, depending on the content and context of particular religious beliefs, this potency can be unleashed in terrifying ways. But Bernbaum's study of Russia shows how core (Christian) theological virtues like humility, mercy, and justice could be constructive guides for U.S. diplomacy. Daryl Charles and Daniel Philpott also engage in critical retrievals of core Christian theological and ethical commitments as a way to demonstrate the potency of religious convictions for better policymaking. Charles argues that classical and Christian just-war thinking can restore much-needed moral clarity and strategic courage to current debates over humanitarian intervention. Responding critically to thin, liberal theories of intervention, Charles draws on the insights of the natural-law tradition—which points to universal principles of practical reasoning accessible in principle to all—as a basis for an explicitly normative foreign policy. The guidelines flowing from this approach may offer little comfort to Western nationalists, realists, or isolationists who would shy away from costly humanitarian interventions, but Charles shows how such interventions need to be inspired, at bottom, by the affirmation—lodged deep in the Christian tradition—of a universal commitment to relieving the suffering of "the stranger." Charles counsels neither "more" nor "fewer" interventions, but wiser and braver ones.

In similar vein, Daniel Philpott proposes that a theologically grounded concept of reconciliation can serve as a source of effective policy guidelines for the United States in addressing post-conflict situations—even for practitioners who do not themselves endorse the theological grounding. Such a concept will affirm and yet go beyond the "liberal peace" typically offered by Western post-conflict policymakers and NGOs: it will seek to operate through multiple actors, will deploy multiple means, and will acknowledge the importance of, and hold out the possibility of, public acknowledgments of justice, truth, and even forgiveness. We might add that it will thereby testify to a richer (Christian) anthropology and sociology than that animating currently dominant liberal post-conflict strategies.

To what extent has this book clarified the possibilities and limits of the program of developing a "Christian perspective on International Relations?" Scott Thomas echoes our own awareness that this is an ambitious enterprise. Appreciating the considerable achievements of the "return to religion" in International Relations, he nevertheless offers some sobering, indeed skeptical, reflections on what this return might actually amount to both in terms of the creation of supposed "new knowledge" in the discipline and in terms of the effective practice of foreign diplomacy informed by it. The first thing to say about a Christian perspective in IR, then, is that the attempt to bring a particular religious perspective overtly to bear on the scholarly study of the field should proceed cautiously, modestly, and self-critically. It hardly need be said that no claim to privileged insight is implied by the idea of a Christian perspective. As we indicated in the introduction, the fruits of such an approach simply take their place alongside those of every other perspective, and each offering will get what it deserves—whether approbation or opprobrium—in the cut and thrust of rigorous scholarly exchange.

Nor is it claimed that a Christian perspective will uncover insights or discover findings unavailable in principle to other scholars. Thus those who consciously operate from, say, secularist assumptions can in principle analyze what we have called the pastness, the thickness, and the potency of religious traditions and beliefs just as thoroughly as those who assume the truth of Christian faith. As Thomas Farr puts it, it is not necessary to be a theologian in order to study religion. And, as Andrew Preston points out, "it was Perry Miller, an avowed atheist, who rescued the Puritans from historical derision and relative obscurity and remains their most influential historian." We might add, of course, that this was apparently because Miller was willing to think outside the reductionist box into which many secularist historians and political scientists have been inducted and which has prevented them from understanding religious movements like Puritanism—or, in our own times, Islam—from the inside.

It is worth noting that the point about privileged access to knowledge would also be true, by analogy, of any two rival basic perspectives in the discipline: a Marxist globalist would not (or should not) assert that they had access to knowledge in *principle* unavailable to a Kantian liberal or a postcolonial deconstructionist. What each could legitimately assert is that their distinctive ontology, anthropology, and epistemology would likely lead them to uncover data, identify causal relationships, formulate research problems, or propose theoretical constructs to which rival perspectives were inattentive or blind. Christian IR scholars should claim no more—but aspire to no less.

The foregoing chapters illustrate this potential perspectival fruitfulness in modest yet, we think, visible ways. Consider, first, the issue of how to define "religion." It seems evident that, while it is obviously not necessary to be a religious believer in order to recognize the reality of religion, those who have had close encounters with religion are often better equipped to appreciate not only the presence of religion but also what we called its density, intensity, and complexity. For example, those who can testify that engaging in the worship of God actually liberates them to think more creatively and act more responsibly than they did before (though not necessarily more than anyone else) could be invaluable sources of information on the dynamics of religion both for scholars and practitioners of diplomacy. While Thomas Farr does not write from an explicitly theological perspective, he shows how a proper grasp of "thick" religious freedom—that is, freedom of public and corporate manifestation as well as private adherence—is likely to be easier for those who recognize, as he ventures, that "virtually all human beings share a thirst for transcendence." While that is a descriptive assertion that could in principle be made by any scholar, it is one that is tacitly, and sometimes explicitly, denied by many secularists and is much more readily embraced by those who can actually imagine what it is to experience such a "thirst for transcendence." The lack of proximity to religious practice among most leading American political scientists, noted by Wald and Wilcox,[5] then appears not as yielding the supposed advantages of "objectivity" but rather as a deficiency in scholarly training.

Bernbaum's analysis of the collapse of the USSR implies a multidimensional explanatory methodology in which as many as "five revolutions" should be investigated. A study of the familiar and extensively researched triad of political, economic, and military upheavals needs to be complemented by greater attention to a radical social upheaval taking place (the collapse of social support networks for families) and the deeper moral and spiritual crisis enveloping the entire society. The broader implication is that Christian scholars will not only seek to avoid the pitfalls of reductionist or "materialist" research methodologies (such as those which would merely "securitize" religion, as Thomas notes) but will also be inclined to gravitate toward, or even design, explicitly multi-causal explanations of empirical phenomena.

Relatedly, scholars operating out of a Christian perspective might also be expected to gravitate toward or generate different explanatory concepts for the functioning of religion in politics. Thus Scott Thomas proposes the concept of a "global resurgence of religion" as containing more explanatory power than the concepts of "fundamentalism" or "religious backlash" utilized by many secularist scholars. This doesn't imply that the two approaches will generate different data sets, but it does suggest that they may yield contrasting theoretical and interpretive frameworks and different research methodologies or policy prescriptions implied by them. Thomas also shows how a difference of basic perspective will lead to differences in epistemological assumptions. We would venture that Christian scholars might well be expected to share his critique of the dominant rationalist epistemology in IR and be more supportive of reflectivist or interpretive approaches.[6]

Another larger conclusion emerging here is that scholars operating from a Christian perspective (or some other religious perspectives) can be expected to gravitate toward or generate different, possibly more complex definitions, not only of religion itself but of any political phenomena under investigation. Indeed, Thomas notes that the "return of religion" to IR is precipitating much-needed critical reflection not only on religion itself but on some of the core conceptual and ontological assumptions that have long organized the field. One of the most important of these is sovereignty. Daryl Charles, for example, subjects the inherited Westphalian conception of sovereignty, and notably its implication of the doctrine of nonintervention, to a searching critique. He shows, first, how an adequate notion of humanitarian intervention cannot cling to the pretense of political neutrality but must be reconceived as flowing out of the richer and longer tradition of just-war thinking and so as part of a larger normative obligation falling on political authorities to promote a "just peace" between nations. Second, he reminds us that just-war thinking itself is only coherent if situated within a wider conception of statecraft as the pursuit of the common good (of which "just peace" is a necessary component). A robust critique of the modern notion of sovereignty, then, calls for the articulation of a comprehensive and normative theory of the nature and purpose of the state, a task from which mainstream IR, under the lingering influences of behavioralism and rationalism, has recoiled for too long. To be sure, a revived normative theory of the state would have to be able to respond to provocative questions like that posed by Thomas: why is killing for a state which has become "the telephone company" ultimately any more defensible than killing for religion? In our view, the resources of classical (including Christian) political thought invoked by Charles are well able to meet that challenge, yet such resources have barely begun to be deployed effectively either in intramural theological debates or in the wider academy and polity. On that there remains much work to do.

These, then, are examples of how some of the contributors in the book operate with different conceptual toolboxes which, while not in any way uniquely deriving from Christian faith, seem to comport well with the characteristic concerns of Christian social and political thought. Some contributors, however, go further and proceed from explicitly Christian convictions to generate normative principles to guide policymaking. Bernbaum, Charles, Philpott, and Thomas all invoke distinctively Christian theological themes as a basis for ethical or political analysis and prescription. Bernbaum suggests that the Christian principles of humility, mercy, and justice are not otherworldly ideals but can yield new and imaginative options for diplomats faced with difficult choices and limited resources in constrained situations. Charles argues that the resources of a long-standing tradition of religiously inspired but eminently public ethical reflection—Christian just-war thinking—can put some theoretical and diplomatic backbone into our currently muddled and hesitant thinking about humanitarian intervention. Similarly Philpott—also calling for a critical development of the just-war tradition—proposes a Christian theology of reconciliation as a source of innovative ideas that can supplement a "liberal peace" in post-conflict situations. One of its distinguishing marks, for example, is attentiveness to the full range of wounds that violent conflicts inflict on human beings. Philpott does not, of course, claim that these can only be identified through the lens of Christian faith, but the complexity of his account of human vulnerability is what one would expect to be suggested by a thick theological anthropology in which full personhood is inseparable from bodily and sexual integrity, community, social belonging, justice, and memory.[7] We might add, too, that Philpott's six-fold classification of wounds suggests not only a distinctive normative prescription for, but also a distinctive empirical analysis of, post-conflict situations: a scholar equipped with such a classification would go in search of particular kinds of empirical data that might be overlooked by a scholar guided by the model of a "liberal peace."

Such explicitly Christian normative theorizing is offered on the same terms as any other normative perspective advanced in diplomatic debates, both scholarly and political, and stands or falls on its own merits. Whether or not such offerings are accepted, they cannot be dismissed as tribal (they do not invoke any gnostic language inaccessible to others), irrational (they do not simply appeal to the authority of blind faith), or empirically ungrounded (they rest on a similar range of evidences as other normative political arguments in IR). They may indeed be controversial—some diplomats and protagonists in conflict situations will resist Philpott's idea of reconciliation as a credible policy aspiration, and some will balk at Charles' summons to costly humanitarian interventions on behalf of "strangers." But if there is any truth to Wight's Christian critique of modern liberal societies (invoked by Thomas), stirring up controversy may actually be a sign of a return to Christian authenticity and a proper rejection of uncritical accommodation to the politics of secular modernity. And whatever else may be implied by a "Christian perspective on International Relations," it surely does not require Christians merely to supply additional ideological legitimacy for an "apostate" culture.

This may strike some as a rather judgmental and self-righteous parting shot. We append it as a reminder that at least some of the religion that scholars and practitioners in IR—including some traditions of orthodox Christianity—will need to get their heads around in the future may not look or sound pretty, may not be clamouring to appease liberal democratic publics, and will not shore up the standard secularist and relativist nostrums still tacitly assumed by many in the field of IR. In fact, Wight's critique is actually the very opposite of self-righteous: his attack is on any civilization's presumptuous claim to self-sufficiency, and it carries with it a powerful reminder of the inherent limits of any political order to deliver full human flourishing. But whatever we make of Wight's particular challenge, the task confronting mainstream IR is to develop theoretical paradigms and diplomatic strategies that can account for and respond intelligently to religion as it presents itself to us and not as we would wish it to be. And since the "religion of secularism" which has governed the field for so long has typically appeared to adherents of other faiths as itself dogmatic, judgmental, and hegemonic, that would seem like a reasonable invitation to mutual accommodation.

Notes

Introduction

Epigraph (top). Pavlos Hatzopoulos and Fabio Petito, eds., *Religion in International Relations: The Return from Exile*, Culture and Religion in International Relations (New York: Palgrave Macmillan, 2003), 1.

Epigraph (bottom). Daniel Philpott, "The Challenge of September 11 to Secularism in International Relations," *World Politics* 55 (2002): 95.

1   Such messianic visions are not, of course, the exclusive preserve of the political right, nor of Americans. See Walter Russel Mead, *Special Providence: American Foreign Policy and How It Changed the World* (New York: Knopf, 2001). Mead quotes Otto von Bismarck: "God has a special providence for fools, drunks, and the United States of America." But the theme of providence in foreign policy does not originate in the United States. Mead followed *Special Providence* with *God and Gold: Britain, America, and the Making of the Modern World* (New York: Knopf, 2007). On the use of "providence" in post-war foreign policy, see William Inboden, *Religion and American Foreign Policy, 1945–1960: The Soul of Containment* (Cambridge: Cambridge University Press, 2009). For a contemporary theological defense of the idea, see Stephen H. Webb, *American Providence: A Nation With a Mission* (London: Continuum, 2004). For a secular critique, see William Pfaff, "Manifest Destiny: A New Direction for America," *New York Review of Books* 54, no. 2 (2007), http://www.nybooks.com/articles/19879. For Christian critiques, see James W. Skillen, *With or Against the World? America's Role Among the Nations* (Lanham, Md.: Rowman & Littlefield, 2005); and Jon P. DePriest, "Custodial

Diplomacy: Obligations of International Security and the Demise of Multilateral Strategy," *Evangelical Review of Society and Politics* 2, no. 1 (2008): 1–15.

2   Skillen, *With or Against the World.*

3   E.g., "We remain a young nation, but in the words of Scripture, the time has come to set aside childish things. The time has come to reaffirm our enduring spirit; to choose our better history; to carry forward that precious gift, that noble idea, passed on from generation to generation: the God-given promise that all are equal, all are free, and all deserve a chance to pursue their full measure of happiness." Or more forthrightly, "This is the source of our confidence: the knowledge that God calls us to shape an uncertain destiny." "Barack Obama's Inaugural Address," transcription, *The New York Times*, January 20, 2009, http://www.nytimes.com/2009/01/20/us/politics/20text-obama.html.

4   The book does not assume that there is a *single* "Christian perspective" on global affairs. It makes no pretense to represent all the main theological traditions of reflection on international relations, nor the full range of geographical and cultural contexts from which such reflection has been mounted. Obviously a comprehensive treatment of the Christian tradition would have to include, e.g., pacifist, liberationist, postcolonial, indigenous, and feminist voices, especially from the majority world. Nor does the book attempt to represent religious perspectives other than Christianity.

5   When capitalized in the text of this book (though not necessarily in quotations from other sources), this term will refer to the academic discipline of that name, as distinct to actual relations between states (and other actors) studied by that discipline.

6   Edward Luttwak, "The Missing Dimension," in *Religion, the Missing Dimension of Statecraft*, ed. Douglas Johnson and Cynthia Sampson (New York: Oxford University Press, 1994), 10 (emphasis in original).

7   Thomas F. Farr, *World of Faith and Freedom: Why International Religious Liberty is Vital to American National Security* (New York: Oxford University Press, 2008), 44.

8   For an overview of the issues, see Jeff Haynes, "Religion and International Relations: What Are the Issues?" *International Politics* 41 (2004): 451–62.

9   Samuel P. Huntington, "The Clash of Civilizations," *Foreign Affairs* 72, no. 2 (1993): 22–49; Samuel P. Huntington, *The Clash of Civilizations and the Remaking of World Order* (New York: Simon & Schuster, 1996); Samuel P. Huntington, ed., *The Clash of Civilizations: The Debate* (New York: Foreign Affairs, 1996); Jonathan Fox, "The Rise of Religion and the Fall of the Civilization Paradigm As Explanations for Intra-state Conflict," *Cambridge Review of International Affairs* 20, no. 3 (2007): 361–82.

10   For a survey of critical responses, see Jonathan Fox and Shmuel Sandler, *Bringing Religion into International Relations*, Culture and Religion in International Relations (New York: Palgrave Macmillan, 2004), chap. 6. See also David A. Welch, "The 'Clash of Civilizations' Thesis as an Argument and as a Phenomenon," *Security Studies* 6, no. 4 (1997): 197–216; and Ronald Inglehart and Pippa Norris, "The True Clash of Civilizations," *Foreign Policy*, March/April 2003, 63–70. In spite of these criticisms, Huntington's thesis remains an important reference point for the serious scholarly treatment of the role of culture and religion in international relations. Acknowledging this, Fox and Sandler, however, think this particular debate has now passed its expiry date (*Bringing Religion into International Relations*, 115). Subsequent literature certainly moves well beyond the terms set by it.

11   Hatzopoulos and Petito, *Religion in International Relations.*

12   Scott M. Thomas, *The Global Resurgence of Religion and the Transformation of International Relations: The Struggle for the Soul of the Twenty-First Century*, Culture and Religion in International Relations (New York: Palgrave Macmillan, 2005).

13   John D. Carlson and Erik C. Owens, eds., *The Sacred and the Sovereign: Religion and International Politics* (Washington, D.C: Georgetown University Press, 2003).

14   Eric O. Hanson, *Religion and Politics in the International System Today* (Cambridge: Cambridge University Press, 2006).

15   Robert A. Seiple and Dennis Hoover, *Religion and Security: The New Nexus in International Relations* (New York: Rowman & Littlefield, 2004).

16   Farr, *World of Faith*, 31.

17   The importance of a proper grasp of religion in relation to possibly the most pressing U.S. security issue today is underlined in Joshua White, *Pakistan's Islamist Frontier: Islamic Politics and U.S. Policy in Pakistan's North-West Frontier*, Religion and Security Monographs, no. 1 (Arlington, Va.: Center on Faith and International Affairs, 2008).

18   Malcolm Magee, *What the World Should Be* (Waco, Tex.: Baylor University Press, 2008). Inboden, *Religion*.

19   Fox and Sandler, *Bringing Religion into International Relations*.

20   Elizabeth Shakman Hurd, *The Politics of Secularism in International Relations*, Princeton Studies in International History and Politics (Princeton: Princeton University Press, 2008).

21   If Hurd exposes the modernist roots of the discipline of International Relations, John Gray's controversial *Black Mass: Apocalyptic Religion and the Death of Utopia* (London: Allen Lane, 2007), sheds disturbing light on the worst excesses of modernist statecraft.

22   Elizabeth Shakman Hurd, "The Political Authority of Secularism in International Relations," *European Journal of International Relations* 10, no. 2 (2004): 237. Hurd's The *Politics of Secularism* is an elaboration of this article. A parallel claim is made by Daniel Philpott, who proposes that the norms of authority presupposed in the Westphalian settlement "amount to a political theology, a doctrine of religion's role in society." "Challenge of September 11," 76.

23   Madeleine Albright, *The Mighty and the Almighty: Reflections on Power, God, and World Affairs* (New York: HarperCollins, 2006).

24   Albright, *Mighty and the Almighty*, 9. She neglects to mention in this book (though Thomas Farr reminds us) that she actually spoke out against the proposed International Religious Freedom Act, which she now praises in the book (94). See Farr, *World of Faith*, 40–41.

25   Douglas Johnson and Cynthia Sampson, eds., *Religion, the Missing Dimension of Statecraft* (New York: Oxford University Press, 1993). See also Fox and Sandler, *Bringing Religion into International Relations*, chap. 3.

26   E.g., as Edward Luttwak suggested: "Concessions [during negotiations] previously regarded as intolerable evidence of a lack of fortitude, may become politically acceptable if they can be presented as acts of deference to religion" ("Missing Dimension," 16).

27   Douglas Johnson, ed., *Faith-Based Diplomacy: Trumping Realpolitik* (New York, Oxford University Press, 2003).

28   Thomas F. Farr, "Diplomacy in an Age of Faith: Religious Freedom and National Security," *Foreign Affairs* 87, no. 2 (2008): 111.

29   The relevance to foreign policymaking of what Johnson later called "faith-based diplomacy" was already gestured toward by one of the contributors to *Religion, the Missing Dimension*. See Stanton Burnett, "Implications for the Foreign Policy

Community," 285–305. Farr examines the resistance to religious awareness in the leading U.S. foreign policy schools in "The Intellectual Sources of Diplomacy's Religious Deficit," chap. 2 in *World of Faith*, 32–52.

30   Elliott Abrams, ed., *The Influence of Faith: Religious Groups and US Foreign Policy* (New York: Rowman & Littlefield, 2001). See also Kevin R. den Dulk, "Evangelical Elites and Faith-Based Foreign Affairs," *Review of Faith and International Affairs* 4, no. 1 (2006): 21–29.

31   Walter Russell Mead, "God's Country?" *Foreign Affairs* 85, no. 5 (2006), http://www.foreignaffairs.com/articles/61914/walter-russell-mead/gods-country. See also Mead, *God and Gold*, 396–400. One of numerous examples of one-sided analysis of the role of religion under President George W. Bush is Mark Beeson, "With God on Their Side: Religion and American Foreign Policy," in *Religion, Faith and Global Politics*, by Lorraine Elliott et al., Keynotes Series (Canberra: Australian National University, Department of International Relations, 2006), 4–11.

32   Jason Kindopp and Carol Lee Hamrin, eds., *God and Caesar in China: Policy Implications of Church-State Tensions* (Washington, D.C.: Brookings, 2004). See also Jason Kindopp, "Principled Engagement in China," *Review of Faith and International Affairs* 1, no. 1 (2003): 21–30; and Carol Lee Hamrin, "A New Framework for Promoting Religious Freedom in China," *Review of Faith and International Affairs* 3, no. 1 (2005): 3–10.

33   Andrew J. Bacevich and Elizabeth H. Prodromou, "God is Not Neutral: Religion and U.S. Foreign Policy after 9/11," *Orbis* 48 (2004): 43–54.

34   See also Rogers M. Smith, "Religious Rhetoric and the Ethics of Public Discourse: The Case of George W. Bush," *Political Theory* 36, no. 2 (2008): 272–98.

35   Farr, *World of Faith*.

36   E. J. Dionne, Jean Bethke Elshtain, and Kayla Drogosz, eds., *Liberty and Power: A Dialogue on Religion and U.S. Foreign Policy in an Unjust World*, Pew Forum Dialogues on Religion and Public Life (Washington, D.C.: Brookings, 2004).

37   Walzer, "Can There Be a Moral Foreign Policy?" in Dionne, Elshtain, and Drogosz, *Liberty and Power*, 34.

38   It should be added here that not every contributor to this book might fully embrace the viewpoint implied in our final question. Even so, their chapters add important material to an assessment of such questions.

39   This default "modernist" assumption is one of four factors cited by Wald and Wilcox in explaining why the *American Political Science Review* has published so few articles on religion since its inception, even since the 1980s when religion became more politically salient. The other three are: the largely nonreligious social backgrounds of political scientists; the perceived complexity of the subject matter; and the "issue attention cycle" in the discipline. Kenneth D. Wald and Clyde Wilcox, "Getting Religion: Has Political Science Rediscovered the Faith Factor?" *American Political Science Review* 100, no. 4 (2006): 523–29.

40   José Casanova, *Public Religions in the Modern World* (Chicago: University of Chicago Press, 1994); Peter L. Berger, ed., *The Desecularization of the World: Resurgent Religion and World Politics* (Grand Rapids: Eerdmans, 1999). See also Mark Juergensmeyer, *Global Rebellion: Religious Challenges to the Secular State, from Christian Militias to Al Qaeda* (Berkeley: University of California Press, 2008); and Ted Gerard Jelen and Clyde Wilcox, *Religion and Politics in Contemporary Perspective: The One, the Few and the Many* (Cambridge: Cambridge University Press, 2002).

41   As noted by Grace Davie, "Europe: The Exception that Proves the Rule?" in Berger, *Desecularization*, 65–83.

42   Hurd, "Contested Secularisms in Turkey and Iran," chap. 4 in *Politics of Secularism*; Hurd, "The United States and Iran," chap. 6 in *Politics of Secularism*.

43   In these continents "Protestant" generally means "Evangelical," of which a substantial proportion is Pentecostal. See Paul Freston, *Evangelical Politics in Asia, Africa and Latin America* (Cambridge: Cambridge University Press, 2001).

44   The four volumes in the "Evangelical Christianity in the Global South" series are Paul Freston, ed., *Evangelical Christianity and Democracy in Latin America* (New York: Oxford University Press, 2008); Terence O. Ranger, ed., *Evangelical Christianity and Democracy in Africa* (New York: Oxford University Press, 2008); David H. Lumsdaine, ed., *Evangelical Christianity and Democracy in Asia* (New York: Oxford University Press, 2008); Timothy Samuel Shah, ed., *Evangelical Christianity and Democracy in Global Perspective* (New York: Oxford University Press, forthcoming); Philip Jenkins, *The Next Christendom: The Coming of Global Christianity* (New York: Oxford University Press, 2002).

45   S. N. Eisenstadt, "Multiple Modernities," *Daedalus* 129, no. 1 (2000): 1–29. Charles Taylor suggests a similar point in *A Secular Age* (Cambridge, Mass.: Harvard University Press, 2007). He argues that the old assumption about modern civilization inevitably bringing about the death of God is "very unconvincing," and that contemporary secularization, as we find it, is specific to the historical and cultural context of Latin Christendom (21–22).

46   Thomas, *Global Resurgence*, 49.

47   Hanson also entertains this possibility; *Religion and Politics*, 71.

48   Taylor, *Secular Age*, 20.

49   Casanova, *Public Religions*.

50   Hurd, *Politics of Secularism*, 42.

51   Hurd, *Politics of Secularism*, 43. See also Daniel Philpott, "The Religious Roots of International Relations," *World Politics* 52, no. 2 (2000): 206–45.

52   Quoted in Hurd, *Politics of Secularism*, 43.

53   Quoted in Hurd, *Politics of Secularism*, 44.

54   Those chapters that address the question would be consistent with support for what Alfred Stepan calls "the twin tolerations." Alfred Stepan, "Religion, Democracy and the 'Twin Tolerations,'" in *World Religions and Democracy*, ed. Larry Diamond, Marc F. Plattner, and Philip J. Costopoulos (Baltimore: Johns Hopkins University Press, 2005), 3–26.

55   Hatzopoulos and Petito, *Religion in International Relations*, 3.

56   See, e.g., Thomas, *Global Resurgence*, 21–26; and Hurd, *Politics of Secularism*, esp. 1–45. In chapter 2 of *Bringing Religion Into International Relations* ("The Overlooked Dimension"), Fox and Sandler argue: "that international relations theory is the discipline that most profoundly ignores religion can be explained by the fact that in many ways it is the most Western of the social sciences" (32).

57   Thomas, *Global Resurgence*, chaps. 1–3.

58   Hanson, *Religion and Politics*, 19–20.

59   Max Stackhouse, *God and Globalization*, vol. 4, *Globalization and Grace* (New York: Continuum, 2007), 36. See also Wald and Wilcox, "Getting Religion," which cites the social distance from and indifference to religion in the backgrounds of most leading political scientists as a factor in the discipline's neglect of the theme.

60   For discussions of different definitions of "religion" in IR, see, e.g., Thomas, *Global Resurgence*, chap. 1; Hanson, *Religion and Politics*, 73; and Fox and Sandler, *Bringing Religion into International Relations*, chap. 1.

61   Hanson defines "religion" as "that pattern of beliefs and activities that expresses ultimate meaning in a person's life" (*Religion and Politics*, 73). Stackhouse's definition of "faith" comes closer to ours: "A confidence in a comprehensive worldview or 'metaphysical-moral vision' that is accepted as binding because it is held to

be . . . basically true and just. . . . [It] provides a framework for interpreting the realities of life in the world, it guides the basic beliefs and behaviors of persons and it empowers believers to seek to transform the world in accordance with some normative ethic of what should be." *God and Globalization*, 4:7.

62   E.g., Beier exposes the latent assumptions in Westphalian International Relations by contrasting it with the alternative cosmology of the Lakota people. From such a radically different perspective, Western international politics is no longer a mere diplomatic technique but operates on assumptions which go "all the way down." J. Marshall Beier, *International Relations in Uncommon Places: Indigeneity, Cosmology and the Limits of International Theory* (New York: Palgrave Macmillan, 2005).

63   Hatzopoulos and Petito, *Religion in International Relations*, 9; Stackhouse, *God and Globalization*, vol. 4.

64   William Connolly, e.g., locates faith, alongside forces such as emotions, passions, drives, prejudices, desires, identities, and so forth, within what he calls "the visceral register of subjectivity and inter-subjectivity." Connolly, *Why I Am Not a Secularist* (Minneapolis: University of Minnesota Press, 1999), chap. 1. This is an evocative but not a very precise phrase as it bundles together too many different cognitive or affective entities. On the rationality of faith and the faith underlying rationality, see, e.g., John Paul II, *Fides et Ratio* (London: Catholic Truth Society, 1998); Alvin Plantinga and Nicholas Wolterstorff, eds., *Faith and Rationality: Reason and Belief in God* (Notre Dame, Ind.: University of Notre Dame Press, 1983); Roy A. Clouser, *The Myth of Religious Neutrality: An Essay on the Hidden Role of Religious Belief in Theories*, rev. ed. (Notre Dame, Ind.: University of Notre Dame Press, 2005); and Ronald A. Kuipers, *Critical Faith: Toward a Renewed Understanding of Religious Life and Its Public Accountability* (New York: Rodopi, 2002).

65   Hanson, *Religion and Politics*, 6.

66   Vendulka Kubálková, "Toward an International Political Theology," in Hatzopoulos and Petito, *Religion in International Relations* (emphasis added). She proposes this be construed as analogous to the sub-field of international political economy.

67   Hurd, for instance, discloses that the operative "faith" in her own theoretical framework draws on a "weak ontology" which has parallels with Buddhist notions of an "impermanent and fluctuating nature of the self and a deeply empathetic realization of the interconnectedness of all sentient beings." *Politics of Secularism*, 17–18.

68   Hanson, *Religion and Politics*, 8.

69   For a thoughtful secularist critique of this proposal, see Terry Nardin, "Epilogue," in Hatzopoulos and Petito, *Religion in International Relations*, 277–82.

70   Setting aside the numerous recent writings by Christian authors on just-war theory, pacifism, and peacemaking, the following are efforts in this direction, even though they do not all announce themselves as specifically "Christian": James W. Skillen, ed., *Prospects and Ambiguities of Globalization: Critical Assessments at a Time of Growing Turmoil* (Lanham, Md.: Lexington, 2009); Skillen, *With or Against the World*; Webb, *American Providence*; Luis E. Lugo, ed., *Sovereignty at the Crossroads? Morality and International Politics in the Post–Cold War Era* (Lanham, Md.: Rowman & Littlefield, 1996); Max Stackhouse, *God and Globalization*, vols. 1–4 (Harrisburg, Pa.: Trinity, 2000–2007); Nigel Biggar, ed., *Burying the Past: Making Peace and Doing Justice After Conflict* (Washington, D.C.: Georgetown University Press, 2003); Hanson, *Religion and Politics*.

71   On how such a "blind spot" obscures journalistic vision, see Paul Marshall, Lela Gilbert, and Roberta Green-Ahmanson, *Blind Spot: When Journalists Don't Get*

Religion (Oxford: Oxford University Press, 2009). This book forcefully exposes journalists' myopic tendencies regarding religion and global affairs. Marshall quotes Roy Peter Clark, a senior scholar at the Poynter Institute, thus: "I attend Catholic Mass most Sundays, but in my life as a citizen I am a thorough secularist. . . . My blind spots blot out half of America. And that makes me less of a citizen, and less of a journalist." Marshall, "Introduction," in Marshall, Gilbert, and Green-Ahmanson, *Blind Spot*, 5.

72   See also Dennis Hoover and Thomas Farr, eds., "Religious Freedom and U.S. Foreign Policy," special issue, *Review of Faith and International Affairs* 6, no. 2 (2008).

73   See also Dennis Hoover, ed., "Islam and Pluralism," special issue, *Review of Faith and International Affairs* 6, no. 4 (2008); Nina Shea, *The Contest of Ideas with Radical Islam: The Centrality of the Idea of Religious Freedom and Tolerance*, Perspectives for the New Administration (Washington, D.C.: Hudson Institute, 2009).

74   See also Dennis Hoover, ed., "Evangelicals and the Israeli-Palestinian Conflict," special issue, *Review of Faith and International Affairs* 5, no. 4 (2007).

75   William Pfaff suggests a movement in that direction in "Manifest Destiny."

76   See also Daniel Philpott, ed., *The Politics of Past Evil: Religion, Reconciliation and the Dilemmas of Transitional Justice* (Notre Dame, Ind.: University of Notre Dame Press, 2006). In a similar vein, see Richard Falk, "Politicizing Religion? Toward a New Global Ethic," in Hatzopoulos and Petito, *Religion in International Relations*, 181–208; and Thomas, *Global Resurgence*, chaps. 6–9.

Chapter 1

*   This is an edited version of an article first published in *Diplomatic History* 30.5 (November 2006), under the title "Bridging the Gap between the Sacred and the Secular in the History of American Foreign Relations." © copyright 2006 Blackwell Publishing. Reproduced with permission of Blackwell Publishing Ltd. Specialist diplomatic historians may wish to consult the journal article for more comprehensive citations of literature, at least up to 2005.

1   The four quotations are from, respectively, Harry S. Truman, "Address at a Luncheon of the National Conference of Christians and Jews," November 11, 1949, *Public Papers of the Presidents: Harry S. Truman, 1949* (Washington, D.C.: Government Printing Office, 1964), 563; Truman, "Remarks in Alexandria, Va., at the Cornerstone Laying of the Westminster Presbyterian Church," November 23, 1952, *Public Papers of the Presidents: Harry S. Truman, 1952–53* (Washington, D.C.: Government Printing Office, 1966), 1063; Dwight D. Eisenhower, "Remarks to the First National Conference on the Spiritual Foundations of American Democracy" (November 9, 1954), in *Public Papers of the Presidents: Dwight D. Eisenhower, 1954* (Washington, D.C.: Government Printing Office, 1960), 1031; and John F. Kennedy, "Inaugural Address," January 20, 1961, *Public Papers of the Presidents: John F. Kennedy, 1961* (Washington, D.C.: Government Printing Office, 1962), 1.

2   See, e.g., Melvyn P. Leffler, "Bush's Foreign Policy," *Foreign Policy*, September/October 2004, 22–28; Leffler, "9/11 and American Foreign Policy," *Diplomatic History* 29 (2005): 395–413; John Lewis Gaddis, *Surprise, Security, and the American Experience* (Cambridge, Mass.: Harvard University Press, 2004); and Niall Ferguson, *Colossus: The Price of America's Empire* (New York: Penguin, 2004). For a persuasive analysis that argues the opposite, see Ivo H. Daalder and James M. Lindsay, *America Unbound: The Bush Revolution in Foreign Policy* (Washington, D.C.: Brookings, 2003).

3   At least, straightforward for historians' purposes because a definition of religion is neither an objective itself nor a means to provide a general theory to explain why people are religious. The work of anthropologists, sociologists, and religious philosophers, whose attempts to define religion revolve around both these purposes, illustrate that defining religion is not an inherently easy task. Witness the work of Pascal Boyer, a leading social anthropologist who argues that while religion as a general phenomenon is universal and innate, it is also indefinable. See especially his *The Naturalness of Religious Ideas: A Cognitive Theory of Religion* (Berkeley: University of California Press, 1994). On the interdisciplinary controversy over how to define religion, see Peter B. Clarke and Peter Byrne, *Religion Defined and Explained* (New York: St. Martin's, 1993), 3–27. On efforts to devise a general theory of religion, see Stewart Elliott Guthrie, "Religion: What Is It?" *Journal for the Scientific Study of Religion* 35 (1996): 412–19. My own definition, which can apply equally to the work of theologians (who tend to accept the general naturalness of religion) and anthropologists and sociologists (who tend to perceive religion as a particular social or cultural construct), loosely follows that of Walter Burkert, *Creation of the Sacred: Tracks of Biology in Early Religions* (Cambridge, Mass.: Harvard University Press, 1996), esp. 4–8, 80–81.

4   Gunnar Myrdal, *An American Dilemma: The Negro Problem and Modern Democracy* (New York: Harper & Bros., 1944); Will Herberg, *Protestant-Catholic-Jew: An Essay in American Religious Sociology*, rev. ed. (Garden City, N.Y.: Doubleday, 1960), 75. The literature on civil religion—which overlaps considerably with those of political culture, exceptionalism, and nationalism—is simply too vast even to summarize here. But in the American context, the pioneering work is Robert N. Bellah, "Civil Religion in America," in *Religion in America*, ed. William G. McLoughlin and Robert N. Bellah (Boston: Houghton Mifflin, 1968), 3–23.

5   "Lived religion" is a form of the social history of religion, and refers to how ordinary people, as opposed to ecclesiastical and institutional authorities, practiced their faith. For the best examples, see Robert A. Orsi, *Madonna of 115th Street: Faith and Community in Italian Harlem, 1880–1950* (New Haven: Yale University Press, 1985); Orsi, *Thank You, St. Jude: Women's Devotion to the Patron Saint of Hopeless Causes* (New Haven: Yale University Press, 1996); and Orsi, *Between Heaven and Earth: The Religious Worlds People Make and the Scholars Who Study Them* (Princeton: Princeton University Press, 2005).

6   For an excellent example of this approach, see Jeffrey F. Meyer, *Myths in Stone: Religious Dimensions of Washington, D.C.* (Berkeley: University of California Press, 2001).

7   The most notable exceptions are Ernest Lee Tuveson, *Redeemer Nation: The Idea of America's Millennial Role* (Chicago: University of Chicago Press, 1968); Anders Stephanson, *Manifest Destiny: American Expansion and the Empire of Right* (New York: Hill & Wang, 1995); Andrew J. Rotter, *Comrades at Odds: The United States and India, 1947–1964* (Ithaca: Cornell University Press, 2000); Seth Jacobs, *America's Miracle Man in Vietnam: Ngo Dinh Diem, Religion, Race, and U.S. Intervention in Southeast Asia, 1950–1957* (Durham, N.C.: Duke University Press, 2004); William Inboden, *Religion and American Foreign Policy, 1945–1960: The Soul of Containment* (Cambridge: Cambridge University Press, 2008); and, from the field of American studies, Melani McAlister, *Epic Encounters: Culture, Media, and U.S. Interests in the Middle East since 1945*, rev. ed. (Berkeley: University of California Press, 2005).

8   Leo P. Ribuffo, "Afterword: Cultural Shouting Matches and the Academic Study of American Religious History," in *Religious Advocacy and American History*, ed. Bruce Kuklick and D. G. Hart (Grand Rapids: Eerdmans, 1997), 222.

9   Stephen Tuck, "The New American Histories," *Historical Journal* 48 (2005): 828.

10   Anders Stephanson, "Rethinking Cold War History," review of *We Now Know: Rethinking Cold War History* by John Lewis Gaddis, *Review of International Studies* 24 (1998): 122. See also Anders Stephanson, "Ideology and Neorealist Mirrors," *Diplomatic History* 17 (1993): 285–95; and Odd Arne Westad, "The New International History of the Cold War: Three (Possible) Paradigms," *Diplomatic History* 24 (2000): 553–54.

11   Sacvan Bercovitch, *The Rites of Assent: Transformations in the Symbolic Construction of America* (New York: Routledge, 1993), 13.

12   These phrases are from, respectively, Sydney E. Ahlstrom, *A Religious History of the American People* (New Haven: Yale University Press, 1972), 12, 965; and Harold Bloom, *American Religion: The Emergence of the Post-Christian Nation* (New York: Simon & Schuster, 1992).

13   For a more detailed discussion, see David A. Hollinger, "The 'Secularization' Question and the United States in the Twentieth Century," *Church History* (March 2001): 132–43.

14   Nathan O. Hatch, *The Sacred Cause of Liberty: Republican Thought and the Millennium in Revolutionary New England* (New Haven: Yale University Press, 1977), 3.

15   Rotter, *Comrades at Odds*, 220.

16   On the inverse relationship between levels of religion and education in postwar America, see Robert Wuthnow, *The Restructuring of American Religion: Society and Faith Since World War II* (Princeton: Princeton University Press, 1988), 168–71.

17   For precisely such a warning—to keep the sacred and secular apart in order to guard against religious advocacy—see Murray G. Murphey, "Advocacy and Academe," in Kuklick and Hart, *Religious Advocacy*, 65–80. Some religious historians have appeared to compound the problem by explicitly calling for the injection of religious values into the university curriculum in order to overcome religion's relative neglect by usually secularist academics. See especially George M. Marsden, *The Soul of the American University: From Protestant Establishment to Established Nonbelief* (New York: Oxford University Press, 1992); and Marsden, *The Outrageous Idea of Christian Scholarship* (New York: Oxford University Press, 1997).

18   On this point, see Robert A. Orsi, "The Disciplinary Vocabulary of Modernity," *International Journal* 59 (2004): 879–85.

19   See, e.g., Christopher Tyerman, *Fighting for Christendom: Holy War and the Crusades* (Oxford: Oxford University Press, 2004); Thomas Asbridge, *The First Crusade: A New History* (Oxford: Oxford University Press, 2004); and Jonathan Phillips, *The Fourth Crusade and the Sack of Constantinople* (New York: Viking, 2004).

20   Gordon A. Craig, "Political and Diplomatic History," in *Historical Studies Today*, ed. Felix Gilbert and Stephen R. Graubard (New York: Norton, 1972), 362. See also Michael H. Hunt, "Ideology," in *Explaining the History of American Foreign Relations*, ed. Michael J. Hogan and Thomas G. Paterson (New York: Cambridge University Press, 2004), 227–28.

21   Bruce Kuklick, *Churchmen and Philosophers: From Jonathan Edwards to John Dewey* (New Haven: Yale University Press, 1985), 255.

22   Melvyn P. Leffler, "New Approaches, Old Interpretations, and Prospective Configurations," *Diplomatic History* 19 (1995): 180–85; Robert Buzzanco, "What Happened to the New Left? Toward a Radical Reading of American Foreign Relations," *Diplomatic History* 23 (1999): 585–88; Buzzanco, "Where's the Beef? Culture without Power in the Study of U.S. Foreign Relations," *Diplomatic History* 24 (2000): 623–32.

23   Paul T. McCartney, "American Nationalism and U.S. Foreign Policy from September 11 to the Iraq War," *Political Science Quarterly* 119 (2004): 401.

24   Prominent examples of these traditional but by no means obsolete schools of
      thought are, respectively, Melvyn P. Leffler, *A Preponderance of Power: National
      Security, the Truman Administration, and the Cold War* (Stanford: Stanford Uni-
      versity Press, 1992); John Lewis Gaddis, *Strategies of Containment: A Critical
      Appraisal of Postwar American National Security Policy* (New York: Oxford Uni-
      versity Press, 1982); Tony Smith, *America's Mission: The United States and the
      Worldwide Struggle for Democracy in the Twentieth Century* (Princeton: Princeton
      University Press, 1994); and Thomas J. McCormick, *America's Half-Century:
      United States Foreign Policy in the Cold War* (Baltimore: Johns Hopkins University
      Press, 1989).

25   Gerald K. Haines and J. Samuel Walker, eds., *American Foreign Relations: A His-
      toriographical Review* (Westport, Conn.: Greenwood Press, 1981), 366; Michael
      J. Hogan, ed., *America in the World: The Historiography of American Foreign Rela-
      tions Since 1941* (New York: Cambridge University Press, 1995), 614; Michael
      J. Hogan, ed., *Paths to Power: The Historiography of American Foreign Relations to
      1941* (New York: Cambridge University Press, 2000), 301; Robert D. Schulz-
      inger, ed., *A Companion to American Foreign Relations* (Oxford: Blackwell, 2003),
      558; Hogan and Paterson, *Explaining the History*, 363. However, all of these
      guides do examine, to some extent, the role of American missionaries overseas
      in the late nineteenth and early twentieth centuries.

26   See, e.g., Robert Dallek, *The American Style of Foreign Policy: Cultural Politics and
      Foreign Affairs* (New York: Knopf, 1983); Michael H. Hunt, *Ideology and U.S. For-
      eign Policy* (New Haven: Yale University Press, 1987); Warren I. Cohen, ed., *The
      Cambridge History of American Foreign Relations*, 4 vols. (Cambridge: Cambridge
      University Press, 1993); and George C. Herring, *From Colony to Superpower: U.S.
      Foreign Relations since 1776.* (New York: Oxford University Press, 2008). For an
      example of "providence," see Mead, *Special Providence*. For examples of "mis-
      sion," see Frederick Merk, *Manifest Destiny and Mission in American History: A
      Reinterpretation* (New York: Knopf, 1963); and Smith, *America's Mission*. For an
      example of "human rights," see Elizabeth Borgwardt, *A New Deal for the World:
      America's Vision for Human Rights* (Cambridge, Mass.: Harvard University Press,
      2005).

27   For broad overviews of American military history that do not include religion,
      see, e.g., Samuel P. Huntington, *The Soldier and the State: The Theory and Politics
      of Civil-Military Relations* (Cambridge, Mass.: Harvard University Press, 1957);
      James M. McPherson, *Battle Cry of Freedom: The Civil War Era* (New York: Oxford
      University Press, 1988); John Morgan Dederer, *War in America to 1775: Before
      Yankee Doodle* (New York: New York University Press, 1990); and Fred Anderson
      and Andrew Cayton, *The Dominion of War: Empire and Liberty in North America,
      1500–2000* (New York: Viking, 2005).

28   For Gaddis' emphasis on communist ideology, see his *We Now Know: Rethinking
      Cold War History* (New York: Oxford University Press, 1997), esp. 289–91. For
      Leffler's reappraisal of ideology's importance, see his article "Bringing it Together:
      The Parts and the Whole," in *Reviewing the Cold War: Approaches, Interpretations,
      Theory*, ed. Odd Arne Westad (London: Frank Cass, 2000), 44–47.

29   Similar pleas have been made on behalf of environmental history and domestic
      politics. For the former, see John G. Clark, "Making Environmental Diplomacy
      an Integral Part of Diplomatic History," *Diplomatic History* 21 (1997): 453–60;
      and Kurk Dorsey, "Dealing with the Dinosaur (and Its Swamp): Putting the
      Environment in Diplomatic History," *Diplomatic History* 29 (2005): 573–87. For
      the latter, see Jussi M. Hanhimäki, "Global Visions and Parochial Politics: The
      Persistent Dilemma of the 'American Century,'" *Diplomatic History* 27 (2003):
      423–47.

30 One important, albeit partial, exception is the linkage between American Protestantism and imperial continental expansion in Martin E. Marty, *Righteous Empire: The Protestant Experience in America* (New York: Dial Press, 1970), 5–130. Another is Warren L. Vinz, *Pulpit Politics: Faces of American Protestant Nationalism in the Twentieth Century* (Albany: State University of New York Press, 1997).

31 See, e.g., Edwin S. Gaustad, *Religion in America: History and Historiography* (Washington, D.C:. American Historical Association, 1973); and John F. Wilson, *Religion and the American Nation: Historiography and History* (Athens: University of Georgia Press, 2003). Although it includes a chapter on post-1945 foreign missionaries, another major work of religious historiography otherwise ignores U.S. foreign relations: Harry S. Stout and D. G. Hart, eds., *New Directions in American Religious History* (New York: Oxford University Press, 1997).

32 Paul Boyer, "In Search of the Fourth 'R': The Treatment of Religion in American History Textbooks and Survey Courses," *History Teacher* 29 (1996): 195–216; Jon Butler, "Jack-in-the-Box Faith: The Religion Problem in Modern American History," *Journal of American History* 90 (2004): 1357–78.

33 See, e.g., J. Bryan Hehir et al., *Liberty and Power: A Dialogue on Religion and U.S. Foreign Policy in an Unjust World*, Pew Forum Dialogues on Religion and Public Life (Washington, D.C.: Brookings, 2004).

34 This is obviously not to suggest any moral equivalence between their actions, only to take note of the widespread influence of their respective religious views.

35 The phrase was given prominence, if not exactly coined, by Fareed Zakaria, "Why Do They Hate Us? The Politics of Rage," *Newsweek*, October 15, 2001, 22–40. See especially the section under the subtitle "Enter Religion," 32–35. For a fuller treatment of Zakaria's analysis of religion and international relations, see his *The Future of Freedom: Illiberal Democracy at Home and Abroad* (New York: Norton, 2003), 30–35, 38–42, 59–60, 107–13, 117–55, 205–15, 233–37, 261–62.

36 This famous phrase comes, of course, from a book that was given new life by the 9/11 attacks: Huntington, *The Clash of Civilizations and the Remaking of World Order*. As the University of Chicago political economist Daniel W. Drezner comments on his blog, even though Huntington's thesis is flawed, Drezner's "first intellectual response to the 9/11 attacks was to take it off my bookshelf." See "Great But Wrong Books," http://www.danieldrezner.com/archives/000670. html#000670.

37 In addition to the titles cited in the introduction, see also Bruce Lincoln, *Holy Terrors: Thinking about Religion after September 11* (Chicago: University of Chicago Press, 2003); Mary Ann Tétreault and Robert A. Denemark, eds., *Gods, Guns, and Globalization: Religious Radicalism and International Political Economy* (Boulder, Colo.: Lynne Rienner, 2004); Pippa Norris and Ronald Inglehart, *Sacred and Secular: Religion and Politics Worldwide* (Cambridge: Cambridge University Press, 2004); Micheline R. Ishay, *The History of Human Rights: From Ancient Times to the Globalization Era* (Berkeley: University of California Press, 2004); and Malise Ruthven, *Fundamentalism: The Search for Meaning* (Oxford: Oxford University Press, 2004).

38 Emily S. Rosenberg, "'Foreign Affairs' after World War II: Connecting Sexual and International Politics," *Diplomatic History* 18 (1994): 59–70; Frank Costigliola, "'Unceasing Pressure for Penetration': Gender, Pathology, and Emotion in George Kennan's Formation of the Cold War," *Journal of American History* 83 (1997): 1309–39; Robert D. Dean, *Imperial Brotherhood: Gender and the Making of Cold War Foreign Policy* (Amherst: University of Massachusetts Press, 2001).

39 Butler, "Jack-in-the-Box Faith," 1359–60. Interestingly, and tellingly, while Butler lists the overlooked importance of religion to modern American politics and

elections, and to the process of economic, technological, and intellectual change, he fails to note its neglect in the study of foreign relations.

40   James Kurth, "The Protestant Deformation and American Foreign Policy," *Orbis* 42 (1998): 221, 235–39.

41   David Gelernter, "Americanism—and Its Enemies," *Commentary* 119 (2005): 41–48.

42   William Martin, "With God on Their Side: Religion and U.S. Foreign Policy," in *Religion Returns to the Public Square: Faith and Policy in America*, ed. Hugh Heclo and Wilfred M. McClay (Baltimore: Johns Hopkins University Press, 2003), 327–59.

43   McCartney, "American Nationalism," 400–407.

44   Leo P. Ribuffo, "Religion and American Foreign Policy: The Story of a Complex Relationship," *National Interest* 52 (1998): 36–51; Ribuffo, "Religion in the History of U.S. Foreign Policy," in Abrams, *Influence of Faith*, 1–27; Ribuffo, "Religion," in *Encyclopedia of American Foreign Policy*, ed. Alexander DeConde, Richard Dean Burns, and Fredrik Logevall (New York: Scribner's, 2002), 371–91.

45   See, e.g., Arthur M. Schlesinger Jr., "America: Experiment or Destiny," *American Historical Review* 82 (1977): 514–17; Seymour Martin Lipset, *American Exceptionalism: A Double-Edged Sword* (New York: Norton, 1996), 18–20, 60–67, 91–93, 154–57; Daniel T. Rodgers, "Exceptionalism," in *Imagined Histories: American Historians Interpret the Past*, ed. Anthony Molho and Gordon S. Wood (Princeton: Princeton University Press, 1998), 23–24, 27; and Anatol Lieven, *America Right or Wrong: An Anatomy of American Nationalism* (New York: Oxford University Press, 2004), 33–34.

46   For the Revolution, see Edmund S. Morgan, "The Puritan Ethic and the American Revolution," *William and Mary Quarterly*, 3rd series, 24 (1967): 3–43; and Sacvan Bercovitch, *The American Jeremiad* (Madison: University of Wisconsin Press, 1978), 120–34, 141–61, 170–73. For Vietnam, see Loren Baritz, *Backfire: A History of How American Culture Led Us Into Vietnam and Made Us Fight the Way We Did* (New York: William Morrow, 1985), 25–34. See also, more generally, David L. Larson, ed., *The Puritan Ethic in United States Foreign Policy* (Princeton, N.J.: Van Norstrand, 1966); and George McKenna, *The Puritan Origins of American Patriotism* (New Haven: Yale University Press, 2007). For a critique of anachronistically presentist concerns of works on the Puritans, see Janice Knight, *Orthodoxies in Massachusetts: Rereading American Puritanism* (Cambridge, Mass.: Harvard University Press, 1994), 1–2, 215–16 n. 3.

47   Stephanson, *Manifest Destiny*, esp. 3–15. See also Conrad Cherry, ed., *God's New Israel: Religious Interpretations of American Destiny*, rev. ed. (Chapel Hill: University of North Carolina Press, 1998); and Johan Galtung, "U.S. Foreign Policy as Manifest Theology," in *Culture and International Relations*, ed. Jongsuk Chay (New York: Praeger, 1990), 119–40.

48   Walter A. McDougall, *Promised Land, Crusader State: The American Encounter with the World since 1776* (Boston: Houghton Mifflin, 1997), 15–38. Stephanson, it should be noted, also acknowledges the exemplary, isolationist spirit of Puritanism, but argues that it was not the movement's dominant strain.

49   See, e.g., Andrew J. Bacevich, *The New American Militarism: How Americans are Seduced by War* (New York: Oxford University Press, 2005), 122. Many religious historians, however, do not agree and instead argue that the Puritans were not embarking on an expansionist mission by seeking a deliberate break with the Old World. For the most authoritative accounts, see David Cressy, *Coming Over: Migration and Communication between England and New England in the Seventeenth Century* (Cambridge: Cambridge University Press, 1987); and Theodore Dwight

Bozeman, *To Live Ancient Lives: The Primitivist Dimension in Puritanism* (Chapel Hill: University of North Carolina Press, 1988).

50   T. H. Breen, "English Origins and New World Development: The Case of the Covenanted Militia in Seventeenth-Century Massachusetts," *Past and Present* 57 (1972): 74–96.

51   Alfred A. Cave, *The Pequot War* (Amherst: University of Massachusetts Press, 1996). Arguing that it was not genocide is Steven T. Katz, "The Pequot War Reconsidered," *New England Quarterly* 64 (1991): 206–24; and Katz, "Pequots and the Question of Genocide: A Reply to Michael Freeman," *New England Quarterly* 68 (1995): 641–49. Arguing that it was is Michael Freeman, "Puritans and Pequots: The Question of Genocide," *New England Quarterly* 68 (1995): 278–93.

52   Jill Lepore, *The Name of War: King Philip's War and the Origins of American Identity* (New York: Knopf, 1998), xiv.

53   Richard I. Melvoin, *New England Outpost: War and Society in Colonial Deerfield* (New York: Norton, 1989); Mark A. Noll, *America's God: From Jonathan Edwards to Abraham Lincoln* (New York: Oxford University Press, 2002), 78–80; Evan Haefeli and Kevin Sweeney, *Captors and Captives: The 1704 French and Indian Raid on Deerfield* (Amherst: University of Massachusetts Press, 2003).

54   Fred Anderson, *Crucible of War: The Seven Years' War and the Fate of Empire in British North America, 1754–1766* (New York: Knopf, 2000), 374; Anderson, *A People's Army: Massachusetts Soldiers and Society in the Seven Years' War* (Chapel Hill: University of North Carolina Press, 1984), 155–57.

55   Alan Heimert, *Religion and the American Mind: From the Great Awakening to the Revolution* (Cambridge, Mass.: Harvard University Press, 1966), 324–39, 345–47.

56   Frank Lambert, *"Pedlar in Divinity": George Whitefield and the Transatlantic Revivals* (Princeton: Princeton University Press, 1994), 198. See also Heimert, *Religion and the American Mind*, 27–158; and Noll, *America's God*, 53–157.

57   Carl Bridenbaugh, *Mitre and Sceptre: Transatlantic Faiths, Ideas, Personalities, and Politics, 1689–1775* (New York: Oxford University Press, 1962), 171–340; Harry S. Stout, "Religion, Communication, and the Ideological Origins of the American Revolution," *William and Mary Quarterly*, 3rd series, 34 (1977): 519–41; Hatch, *Sacred Cause of Liberty*; Rhys Isaac, *The Transformation of Virginia, 1740–1790* (Chapel Hill: University of North Carolina Press, 1982), 243–85, 312–17; Ruth H. Bloch, *Visionary Republic: Millennial Themes in American Thought, 1756–1800* (Cambridge: Cambridge University Press, 1985), xii–xiv, 53–93.

58   Mark A. Noll, *One Nation Under God? Christian Faith and Political Action in America* (San Francisco: Harper & Row, 1988), 35.

59   Frank Lambert, *The Founding Fathers and the Place of Religion in America* (Princeton: Princeton University Press, 2003), 207.

60   Jon Butler, *Awash in a Sea of Faith: Christianizing the American People* (Cambridge, Mass.: Harvard University Press, 1990), 194–224.

61   On the neglect and misunderstanding of this period, see Jonathan Dull, "American Foreign Relations Before the Constitution: A Historiographical Wasteland," in Haines and Walker, *American Foreign Relations*, 3–15; Ronald L. Hatzenbuehler, "The Early National Period, 1789–1815: The Need for Redefinition," in Haines and Walker, *American Foreign Relations*, 17–32; Emily S. Rosenberg, "A Call to Revolution: A Roundtable on Early U.S. Foreign Relations," *Diplomatic History* 22 (1998): 63–64; Bradford Perkins, "Early American Foreign Relations: Opportunities and Challenges," *Diplomatic History* 22 (1998): 115–20; and William Earl Weeks, "New Directions in the Study of Early American Foreign Relations," in Hogan, *Paths to Power*, 8–10.

62   On religion and the War of 1812, see esp. William Gribbin, *The Churches Mili-tant: The War of 1812 and American Religion* (New Haven: Yale University Press, 1973). On religion and Manifest Destiny, see esp. Tuveson, *Redeemer Nation*, 122–36; and Stephanson, *Manifest Destiny*. On religion and the Mexican-American War, see James M. McCaffrey, *Army of Manifest Destiny: The American Soldier in the Mexican War, 1846–1848* (New York: New York University Press, 1992), 71–73, 147–49, 152–57.

63   On American missionaries, see esp. William R. Hutchison, *Errand to the World: American Protestant Thought and Foreign Missions* (Chicago: University of Chicago Press, 1987). On Catholic missionaries, see esp. Angelyn Dries, *The Missionary Movement in American Catholic History* (Maryknoll, N.Y.: Orbis, 1998). On the missionaries' role in Asia, especially China, during the era of formal overseas U.S. imperialism, see Paul A. Varg, *Missionaries, Chinese, and Diplomats: The American Protestant Missionary Movement in China, 1890–1952* (Princeton: Princeton University Press, 1958); John K. Fairbank, ed., *The Missionary Enterprise in China and America* (Cambridge, Mass.: Harvard University Press, 1974); Michael H. Hunt, *The Making of a Special Relationship: The United States and China to 1914* (New York: Columbia University Press, 1983), 154–68, 285–98; and James Reed, *The Missionary Mind and American East Asia Policy, 1911–1915* (Cambridge, Mass.: Council on East Asian Studies, Harvard University, 1983).

64   See, e.g., Martin E. Marty, *Modern American Religion*, vol. 3, *Under God, Indivisible, 1941–1960* (Chicago: University of Chicago Press, 1996), 15–112; and Gerald L. Sittser, *A Cautious Patriotism: The American Churches and the Second World War* (Chapel Hill: University of North Carolina Press, 1997).

65   On the religious elements of isolationism, see Alan Brinkley, *Voices of Protest: Huey Long, Father Coughlin, and the Great Depression* (New York: Knopf, 1982); Leo P. Ribuffo, *The Old Christian Right: The Protestant Far Right from the Great Depression to the Cold War* (Philadelphia: Temple University Press, 1983); and Glen Jeansonne, *Gerald K. Smith: Minister of Hate* (New Haven: Yale University Press, 1988). On reactions to the atomic bomb, see especially Paul Boyer, *When Time Shall Be No More: Prophecy Belief in Modern American Culture* (Cambridge, Mass.: Harvard University Press, 1992), 115–22; and Boyer, *By the Bomb's Early Light: American Thought and Culture at the Dawn of the Atomic Age*, 2nd ed. (Chapel Hill: University of North Carolina Press, 1994), 196–229.

66   For a multinational introduction, see Dianne Kirby, ed., *Religion and the Cold War* (New York: Palgrave, 2003). On the role of American religious groups, see Alfred A. Hero Jr., *American Religious Groups View Foreign Policy: Trends in Rank-and-File Opinion, 1937–1969* (Durham, N.C.: Duke University Press, 1973).

67   Dianne Kirby, "Divinely Sanctioned: The Anglo-American Cold War Alliance and the Defence of Western Civilization and Christianity, 1945–48," *Journal of Contemporary History* 35 (2000): 385–412.

68   On Niebuhr, see Roger L. Shinn, "Realism, Radicalism, and Eschatology in Reinhold Niebuhr: A Reassessment," *Journal of Religion* 54 (1974): 409–23; Richard Wightman Fox, *Reinhold Niebuhr: A Biography*, rev. ed. (Ithaca: Cornell University Press, 1996); Campbell Craig, *Glimmer of a New Leviathan: Total War in the Realism of Niebuhr, Morgenthau, and Waltz* (New York: Columbia University Press, 2003); Michael G. Thompson, "An Exception to Exceptionalism: A Reflection on Reinhold Niebuhr's Vision of 'Prophetic' Christianity and the Problem of Religion and U.S. Foreign Policy," *American Quarterly* 59 (2007): 833–55; and Mark Edwards, "'God Has Chosen Us': Re-Membering Christian Realism, Rescuing Christendom, and the Contest of Responsibilities during the Cold War," *Diplomatic History* 33 (2009): 67–94. On Graham, see esp. Marshall Frady, *Billy Graham: A Parable of American Righteousness* (Boston: Little, Brown, 1979).

69   Inboden, *Religion and American Foreign Policy*.

70   Rotter, *Comrades at Odds*, 220–48.

71   Edward Tivnan, *Lobby: Jewish Political Power and American Foreign Policy* (New York: Simon & Schuster, 1987); Tony Smith, *Foreign Attachments: The Power of Ethnic Groups in the Making of American Foreign Policy* (Cambridge, Mass.: Harvard University Press, 2000), 52–59, 67–68, 107–22, 153–54, 158–61; and John J. Mearsheimer and Stephen M. Walt, *The Israel Lobby and U.S. Foreign Policy* (New York: Farrar, Straus & Giroux, 2007).

72   Jacobs, *America's Miracle Man*. See also Wilson D. Miscamble, "Francis Cardinal Spellman and 'Spellman's War,'" in *The Human Tradition in the Vietnam Era*, ed. David L. Anderson (Wilmington, Del.: Scholarly Resources, 2000), 3–22.

73   Mitchell K. Hall, *Because of Their Faith: CALCAV and Religious Opposition to the Vietnam War* (New York: Columbia University Press, 1990); David W. Levy, *The Debate Over Vietnam* (Baltimore: Johns Hopkins University Press, 1995), 91–102. On King's opposition to the war, see David J. Garrow, *Bearing the Cross: Martin Luther King, Jr., and the Southern Christian Leadership Conference* (New York: William Morrow, 1986); and Simon Hall, *Peace and Freedom: The Civil Rights and Antiwar Movements of the 1960s* (Philadelphia: University of Pennsylvania Press, 2005). On Coffin's, see Warren Goldstein, *William Sloane Coffin, Jr.: A Holy Impatience* (New Haven: Yale University Press, 2004). On the Berrigans', see Murray Polner and Jim O'Grady, *Disarmed and Dangerous: The Radical Lives and Times of Daniel and Philip Berrigan* (New York: Basic, 1997).

74   John A. Thompson, *Woodrow Wilson* (London: Longman, 2002), 18–20, 249–50; Thompson, "More Tactics Than Strategy: Woodrow Wilson and World War I, 1914–1919," in *Artists of Power: Theodore Roosevelt, Woodrow Wilson, and Their Enduring Impact on U.S. Foreign Policy*, ed. William N. Tilchin and Charles E. Neu (Westport, Conn.: Praeger, 2006), 95–115. However, for the predominance of Wilson's religious influence, see Arthur S. Link, *Wilson the Diplomatist: A Look at His Major Foreign Policies* (Baltimore: Johns Hopkins University Press, 1957), 12–17; John M. Mulder, *Woodrow Wilson: The Years of Preparation* (Princeton: Princeton University Press, 1978); and Malcolm D. Magee, *What the World Should Be: Woodrow Wilson and the Crafting of a Faith-Based Foreign Policy* (Waco, Tex.: Baylor University Press, 2008).

75   Arthur M. Schlesinger Jr., *The Cycles of American History* (Boston: Houghton Mifflin, 1986), 394. For historians who concur with Schlesinger, see Jacobs, *America's Miracle Man*; and Inboden, *Religion and American Foreign Policy*. For those who do not, see Ronald W. Pruessen, *John Foster Dulles: The Road to Power* (New York: Free Press, 1982); and Richard H. Immerman, *John Foster Dulles: Piety, Pragmatism, and Power in U.S. Foreign Policy* (Wilmington, Del.: Scholarly Resources, 1999).

76   Zbigniew Brzezinski, *Power and Principle: Memoirs of the National Security Advisor, 1977–1981* (New York: Farrar, Straus & Giroux, 1983), 49.

77   Lou Cannon, *President Reagan: The Role of a Lifetime* (New York: Simon & Schuster, 1991), 287–90, 318–19, 486, 757; Boyer, *When Time Shall Be No More*, 142–46; Beth A. Fischer, *The Reagan Reversal: Foreign Policy and the End of the Cold War* (Columbia: University of Missouri Press, 1997), 103, 106–8; Frances FitzGerald, *Way Out There In the Blue: Reagan, Star Wars, and the End of the Cold War* (New York: Simon & Schuster, 2000), 25–27; Paul Lettow, *Ronald Reagan and His Quest to Abolish Nuclear Weapons* (New York: Random House, 2005).

78   See, e.g., James Carroll, *Crusade: Chronicles of an Unjust War* (New York: Metropolitan, 2004); Peter Singer, *The President of Good and Evil: The Ethics of George W. Bush* (New York: Dutton, 2004); Bob Woodward, *Plan of Attack* (New York:

Simon & Schuster, 2004), 85–86, 379, 421; Lieven, *America Right or Wrong*, 127–130; McCartney, "American Nationalism"; Bacevich, *New American Militarism*, 12–13, 122, 145; Kevin Phillips, *American Dynasty: Aristocracy, Fortune, and the Politics of Deceit in the House of Bush* (New York: Viking, 2004), 211–44; Phillips, *American Theocracy: The Peril and Politics of Radical Religion, Oil, and Borrowed Money in the 21st Century* (New York: Viking, 2006), 99–262; and John B. Judis, "The Chosen Nation: The Influence of Religion on U.S. Foreign Policy," Carnegie Endowment for International Peace, Policy Brief 37 (March 2005), http://www.carnegieendowment.org/files/PB37.judis.FINAL.pdf. For hagiographical perspectives, see Stephen Mansfield, *The Faith of George W. Bush* (New York: Tarcher, 2003); and Paul Kengor, *God and George W. Bush: A Spiritual Life* (New York: Regan, 2004).

79   Anders Stephanson, "Diplomatic History in the Expanded Field," *Diplomatic History* 22 (1998): 597.

80   Brenda Gayle Plummer, *Rising Wind: Black Americans and U.S. Foreign Affairs, 1935–1960* (Chapel Hill: University of North Carolina Press, 1996); Mary L. Dudziak, *Cold War Civil Rights: Race and the Image of American Democracy* (Princeton: Princeton University Press, 2000); Thomas Borstelman, *The Cold War and the Color Line: American Race Relations in the Global Arena* (Cambridge, Mass.: Harvard University Press, 2001).

81   Patricia R. Hill, "Religion as a Category of Diplomatic Analysis," *Diplomatic History* 24 (2000): 633–34.

82   Brenda Gayle Plummer, "Introduction," in *Window on Freedom: Race, Civil Rights, and Foreign Affairs, 1945–1988*, ed. Brenda Gayle Plummer (Chapel Hill: University of North Carolina Press, 2003), 3.

83   Costigliola, "Unceasing Pressure for Penetration," 1338. See also Kristin Hoganson, *Fighting for American Manhood: How Gender Politics Provoked the Spanish-American and Philippine-American Wars* (New Haven: Yale University Press, 1998), 9–14.

84   Emily S. Rosenberg, "Gender," *Journal of American History* 77 (1990): 121.

85   A point made by Lieven, *America Right or Wrong*; and Mark Lilla, "Godless Europe," *The New York Times*, April 2, 2006.

86   Andrew J. Rotter, "Christians, Muslims, and Hindus: Religion and U.S.–South Asian Relations, 1947–1954," *Diplomatic History* 24 (2000): 594.

87   Consider the divided historical opinion about the importance of religion to two of the most celebrated cases—Woodrow Wilson and John Foster Dulles. Of all modern U.S. policymakers, their religious motivations should be the easiest to prove, and yet historians remain deeply divided over just how much the religious views of Wilson and Dulles guided their foreign policy views. See the references in notes 74 and 75, above. There will almost certainly emerge a similar historiographical divide over the role of religion in the presidency of George W. Bush.

88   See, e.g., Melvyn P. Leffler, "The Cold War: What Do 'We Now Know'?" *American Historical Review* 104 (1999): 501–24.

89   See also the editors' response to the question of "partisanship" in the introduction.

90   Butler, "Jack-in-the-Box Faith," 1377; Edmund S. Morgan, *The Genuine Article: A Historian Looks at Early America* (New York: Norton, 2004), ix.

Chapter 2

Epigraph. James Madison, "Memorial and Remonstrance Against Religious Assessment" (1785). Robert S. Alley, "Selected Madison Papers," in Robert S. Alley, ed., *James Madison on Religious Liberty* (Buffalo, N.Y.: Prometheus Books, 1985), 52.

*   This chapter is an edited version of a chapter that first appeared in *World of Faith and Freedom: Why International Religious Liberty is Vital to American National Security* (Oxford: Oxford University Press, 2008). Used by permission of Oxford University Press.

1   Thomas, *Global Resurgence*, 216.

2   On the enduring salience of religious communities into the foreseeable future, see Todd M. Johnston and David B. Barrett, "Quantifying Alternate Futures of Religion and Religions," *Futures* 36 (2004).

3   Hatzopoulos and Petito, *Religion in International Relations*.

4   In addition to Hatzopoulos and Petito, *Religion in International Relations*, see, e.g., Thomas, *Global Resurgence*; Fox and Sandler, *Bringing Religion into International Relations*; and an earlier path-breaking work, Johnson and Sampson, *Religion, The Missing Dimension*.

5 · An instructive example of this is the reflections of Albright, *Mighty and the Almighty*.

6   A good analysis of how religion is affecting U.S. foreign policy is Walter Russell Mead, "Religion and U.S. Foreign Policy," *Foreign Affairs* 85, no. 5 (2006): 24–44. The article does not investigate religion as an object of foreign policy, but how American evangelicalism is influencing its practice.

7   Hurd, "Political Authority of Secularism," 235–62. The argument of this article is elaborated in Hurd, *Politics of Secularism*. See also Philpott, "Challenge of September 11," 66–95.

8   Liora Danan and Alice Hunt, *Mixed Blessings: U.S. Government Engagement with Religion in Conflict Prone Settings* (Washington, D.C.: Center for Strategic and International Studies, 2007), 3. See also Thomas F. Farr and Dennis R. Hoover, *The Future of International Religious Freedom Policy: A Policy Report with Recommendations for the Obama Administration* (forthcoming—will be available at http://berkleycenter.georgetown.edu/).

9   See the Henry Luce Initiative on Religion and International Affairs, http://www.hluce.org/hrlucerelintaff.aspx.

10   Kevin Seamus Hasson, *The Right to Be Wrong: Ending the Culture War Over Religion in America* (San Francisco: Encounter, 2005), 40–42.

11   Farr, *World of Faith*, 53–77. See also Fox and Sandler, *Bringing Religion into International Relations*, chaps. 2, 8; Thomas, *Global Resurgence*, 54–69; Philpott, "Challenge of September 11," 78–81.

12   See Farr, *World of Faith*, 7–10. Also see Farr, "Diplomacy," 110–24.

13   See, e.g., Paul Johnson, "The Almost Chosen People," *First Things* 164 (2006), 22; Samuel P. Huntington, *Who Are We? The Challenges to America's National Identity* (New York: Simon & Schuster, 2004), 78–79; 336.

14   See Thomas, *Global Resurgence*, 35–36.

15   See Philip Hamburger, *The Separation of Church and State* (Cambridge, Mass.: Harvard University Press, 2002).

16   Email exchange with a legal expert at an executive branch agency with foreign affairs responsibilities.

17   According to the CSIS study, "Many government officials remain skeptical or concerned about engaging religion abroad because of the domestic and legal tradition surrounding the separation of religion and state. . . . Some officials said they believe the Establishment Clause categorically limits government activities related to religion, while many others said they were not sure of the ways the clause should shape their actions and decisions." Danan and Hunt, *Mixed Blessings*, 39.

18   Quoted in John I. Jenkins and Thomas Burish, "Reason and Faith at Harvard,"

Washington Post, October 23, 2006. Ultimately Harvard considered adding religion to its core curriculum but rejected the idea.

19   See, e.g., my exchange with a retired diplomat on this subject in *First Things*, October 2006. Thomas F. Farr and John E. Eddy, "Farr Gone on Religion," correspondence, *First Things* 166 (2006): 2–3.

20   U.S. National Security Council, *The National Security Strategy of the United States of America* (Washinton, D.C., 2006), section II, http://georgewbush-whitehouse. archives.gov/nsc/nss/2006/sectionII.html.

21   U.S. National Security Council, *National Strategy for Combating Terrorism* (Washington, D.C., September 2006), 1. http://georgewbush-whitehouse.archives.gov/ nsc/nsct/2006/.

22   The State Department's *2006 Annual Report on International Religious Freedom* (hereafter, IRF Report) reported: "The Government [of Afghanistan] also responded positively to international approaches on religious freedom and worked effectively on high-profile cases such as [that of] Abdul Rahman." U.S. Department of State, *2006 Report on International Religious Freedom* (Washington, D.C., 2006), available at http://www.state.gov/g/drl/rls/irf/2006/.

23   At a March 6, 2006, State Department press conference, Under Secretary Nicholas Burns related his private remarks to visiting Afghan Foreign Minister Abdullah: "I said on behalf of our government that we hope very much the judicial case . . . would be held in a transparent way. And of course, as our government is a great supporter of freedom of religion and as the Afghan constitution affords freedom of religion to all Afghan citizens, we hope very much that . . . the right of freedom of religion will be upheld in Afghan court." Burns was incorrect about freedom of religion in the Afghan constitution. See footnote 9, this chapter. Again, on March 20, department spokesman Sean McCormack: "It's important, we believe, that the Afghan authorities conduct this trial and any proceedings that lead up to it in as transparent a manner as possible. Our view . . . is that tolerance, freedom of worship is an important element of any democracy and these are issues as Afghan democracy matures that they are going to have to deal with increasingly."

24   For a compendium of critical comments on the administration's handling of the Rahman affair by religious supporters, including Colson's, see Rob Moll, "Should Evangelicals Support Bush's Foreign Policy If He Can't Guarantee Religious Freedom?" *Christianity Today Online*, April 24, 2006, http://www.christianitytoday .com/ct/2006/117/13.0.html.

25   Statement of ambassador at large for international religious freedom to the Congressional Human Rights Caucus, April 7, 2006.

26   Constitution of Afghanistan, preamble, paragraph 8.

27   Zalmay Khalizad, "Afghanistan's Milestone," *Washington Post*, January 6, 2004, A17.

28   U.S. Department of State, *2005 Report on International Religious Freedom* (Washington, D.C., November 2005).

29   Commission on International Religious Freedom (hereafter CIRF), "Afghanistan: Freedom and Electoral Democracy," press release, September 13, 2004, available at http://www.uscirf.gov/.

30   United States Institute of Peace, "Establishing the Rule of Law in Afghanstan," Special Report 117, March 2004, 7.

31   CIRF, "Afghanistan."

32   CIRF, "Afghanistan: Draft Constitution Could Codify Repression," press release, April 17, 2003, with text of CIRF letter to the president.

33   Constitution of Afghanistan, articles 2 and 3, respectively. The latter added, "and the values of this Constitution."

34 Nina Shea, "Conclusion: American Responses to Extreme *Shari'a*," in *Radical Islam's Rules: The Worldwide Spread of Extreme Shari'a Law*, ed. Paul Marshall (Lanham, Md.: Rowman & Littlefield, 2005), 209.

35 U.S. Department of State, *2006 IRF Report*.

36 Jeremy M. Sharp, *U.S. Democracy Promotion in the Middle East: The Islamist Dilemma* (Washington, D.C.: Congressional Research Service, June 15, 2006), 10; David E. Kaplan, "Hearts, Minds and Dollars," *U.S. News and World Report*, April 25, 2005; Government Accounting Office, *U.S. Public Diplomacy: State Department Efforts to Engage Muslim Audiences Lack Certain Communication Elements and Face Significant Challenges*, GAO-06-535 (Washington, D.C.: GAO, May 3, 2006).

37 Interview with senior State Department official, July 27, 2005. Also see David E. Kaplan's update on his 2005 article in 2006: "Of Jihad, Networks and the War of Ideas," *U.S. News and World Report*, June 22, 2006, http://www.usnews.com/usnews/news/articles/060622/22natsec.htm.

38 Albright, *Mighty and the Almighty*, 8.

39 LTG Karl Eikenberry, USA, quoted in *Newsweek*, October 2, 2006, 28.

40 See the poll results at http://www.worldopinion.org/.

41 U.S. National Security Council, *The National Security Strategy of the United States of America* (Washington, D.C., September 2002), 3.

42 Farr, *World of Faith*, 203–5.

43 I am indebted for this formulation to Kevin Seamus Hasson. See his book, *Right to Be Wrong*. My understanding of the meaning and reach of religious freedom as discussed in this section and elsewhere in the book has been influenced by, inter alia, Vatican II, *Declaration on Religious Freedom*, in *Documents of Vatican II*, ed. Austin P. Flannery (Grand Rapids: Eerdmans, 1975); John Courtney Murray, *We Hold These Truths: Catholic Reflections on the American Proposition* (Kansas City, Mo.: Sheed & Ward, 1960); Russell Hittinger, *The First Grace: Recovering the Natural Law in a Post-Christian World* (Wilmington, Del.: ISI Books, 2003); Robert P. George, *Making Men Moral* (New York: Oxford University Press, 1995); Keith J. Pavlischek, "Questioning the New Natural Law Theory: The Case of Religious Liberty as Defended by Robert P. George in *Making Men Moral*," in *A Moral Enterprise: Politics, Reason and the Common Good*, ed. Kenneth L. Grasso and Robert P. Hunt (Wilmington, Del.: ISI Books, 2002), 127–42; Christopher Wolfe, *Natural Law Liberalism* (Cambridge: Cambridge University Press, 2006); George Weigel, *Freedom and Its Discontents: Catholicism Confronts Modernity* (Washington, D.C.: Ethics and Public Policy Center, 1991). None of these authors, of course, is responsible for any errors of fact or interpretation on my part. For the influence of the Vatican II's *Declaration* on my approach, see Farr, "Religious Realism in American Foreign Policy: Lessons from Vatican II," *Review of Faith and International Affairs* 3, no. 3 (2005): 25–33.

44 *Zorach v. Clauson*, 343 U.S. 306, 313 (1952).

45 For a discussion of the relative merits of theological discussions within Shiite and Sunni Islam, and in comparison with Christianity, see James A. Bill and John Alden Williams, *Roman Catholics and Shi'i Muslims: Prayer, Passion and Politics* (Chapel Hill: University of North Carolina Press, 2002), esp. 17–20.

46 Johnson, *Faith-Based Diplomacy*.

47 Michael J. Sandel, "Freedom of Conscience or Freedom of Choice," in *Articles of Faith, Articles of Peace: The Religious Liberty Clauses and the American Public Philosophy*, ed. James Davison Hunter and Os Guinness (Washington, D.C.: Brookings, 1990), 74–92.

48 Sandel, "Freedom of Conscience," 77.

49   Albright, *Mighty and the Almighty*, 104, 160–61.
50   The Regensburg speech of September 12, 2006, is widely available. See, e.g., http://www.ewtn.com/. See also the response by a variety of Muslim jurists, "Open Letter to His Holiness Pope Benedict XVI," *Islamica Magazine*, October 12, 2006.
51   Vendulka Kubálková, "International Political Theology," 88.
52   For a sampling of the rich literature on what constitutes "religion," the reader may consult the classic statement from William James, *The Varieties of Religious Experience* (New York: Mentor, 1958), esp. 39, 42. Two worthy treatments by historians are Arnold Toynbee, *An Historian's Approach to Religion* (Oxford: Oxford University Press, 1956); and Huston Smith, *The Religions of Man* (New York: Harper Colophon, 1958). An excellent study of religion as an object of philosophical study is Jude P. Dougherty, *The Logic of Religion* (Washington, D.C.: Catholic University Press, 2003). I am aware that my definition will seem simplistic to some, especially the incumbents of religious studies departments at American universities, whose professions seem to require complexification.
53   See, e.g., Richard Dawkins, *The God Delusion* (New York: Houghton Mifflin, 2006); and Christopher Hitchens, *God Is Not Great: How Religion Poisons Everything* (New York: Hachette, 2007).
54   On the freedom of all religious communities within civil society, see Robert P. George and William L. Saunders Jr. "Dignitatis Humanae: The Freedom of the Church and the Responsibility of the State," in *Catholicism and Religious Freedom: Contemporary Reflections on Vatican II's Declaration on Religious Liberty*, ed. Kenneth Grasso and Robert P. Hunt (New York: Rowman & Littlefield, 2006).
55   See, e.g., Skillen, *With or Against the World*.

Chapter 3

1   Farr, *World of Faith*, 44.
2   Farr, *World of Faith*, 31.
3   Apart from articles cited elsewhere in the notes, this chapter also draws on Paul Marshall, Lela Gilbert, and Roberta Green, *Islam at the Crossroads* (Grand Rapids: Baker, 2002); Paul Marshall, "Religion and Terrorism: Misreading Bin Laden," in Marshall, Gilbert, and Green Ahmanson, *Blind Spot*; Paul Marshall, "The Next Hotbed Of Islamic Radicalism," *Washington Post*, October 8, 2002; Paul Marshall, "Political Leaders Can No Longer Ignore Religion," *Dallas Morning News*, April 5, 2003; Paul Marshall, "World Silence over Slain Muslims," *Boston Globe*, October 13, 2003; Paul Marshall, "Radical Islam's Move on Africa," *Washington Post*, October 16, 2003; Paul Marshall, "The Southeast Asian Front," *Weekly Standard*, April 5, 2004; Paul Marshall, "Four Million: The Number to Keep in Mind This November," *National Review Online*, August 27, 2004; Paul Marshall, "The Islamists' Other Weapon," *Commentary* 119, no. 4 (2005).
4   Hurd, *Politics of Secularism*, 1.
5   Edward Luttwak, "Missing Dimension," 9.
6   Edward Luttwak, "Missing Dimension," 9–10.
7   Edward Luttwak, "Missing Dimension," 10.
8   Thomas F. Farr, "Religious Freedom and National Security," in *Religious Freedom in the World*, ed. Paul Marshall (Lanham, Md.: Rowman & Littlefield, 2008), 17–22.
9   Quoted in Tim Rutten, "Same Sex Marriage, Civil Unions, Gays and Lesbians," *Los Angeles Times*, March 6, 2004.
10   "October 21, 2001 Mubarak to 'Washington Post': US should strike balance between fighting terrorism and moving forward in ME peace process," *Egypt*

State Information Service, October 21, 2001. http://www.us.sis.gov.eg/En/Politics/ Presidency/President/Interview/000001/0401050300000000000069.htm

11 Quoted in Daniel Pipes, "God and Mammon: Does Poverty Cause Militant Islam?" *National Interest* (Winter, 2001), http://www.nationalinterest.org/ General.aspx?id=92&id2=11154

12 Osama bin Laden, "Declaration of Jihad Against the Americans Occupying the Land of the Two Sacred Mosques" (August 23, 1996), in *Jihad: Bin Laden in His Own Words*, ed. Brad K. Berner (Charleston, S.C.: Book Surge, 2006), 40, 36–37; Bin Laden, "Declaration of Jihad" (August 23, 1996), in *Messages to the World: The Statements of Osama Bin Laden*, ed. Bruce Lawrence (New York: Verso, 2005), 28, 25.

13 Bin Laden, "Declaration of Jihad," 59.

14 In his *Knights Under the Prophet's Banner*, released December 2001, bin Laden's deputy Ayman Al-Zawahiri implied that he and his confreres had been "the least active in championing the Palestinian cause." See Gilles Kepel and Jean-Pierre Milelli, *Al Qaeda in Its Own Words* (Cambridge, Mass.: Harvard University Press, 2008), 197.

15 Quoted in Peter L. Bergen, *Holy War, Inc: Inside the Secret World of Osama bin Laden* (New York: Free Press, 2001), 53.

16 "Jihad Against Jews and Crusaders," World Islamic Front Statement, *Washington Post*, February 23, 1998; "The World Islamic Front," in Lawrence, *Messages*, 58–60; "Declaration of the World Islamic Front for Jihad Against the Jews and Crusaders," Berner, *Jihad*, 80, 78.

17 Osama bin Laden, interview by Al Jazeera, September 20, 2001, translated by BBC Monitoring Service, September 22, 2001; al Qaeda, "A Muslim Bomb," in Lawrence, *Messages*, 73.

18 The late head of al Qaeda in Iraq, Abu Musab al-Zarqawi, who professed allegiance to bin Laden in October 2004, refers in a September 11, 2004, audiotape to Musa Ibn Nusayr, the conqueror of Spain.

19 See al Qaeda, "Crusader Wars," in Lawrence, *Messages*, 134–37; al Qaeda, "Speech Against the Crusaders and the U.N.," in Berner, *Jihad*, 145–48.

20 Osama bin Laden, "To the Americans," in Lawrence, *Messages*, 166–68; "Letter to the American People," in Berner, *Jihad*, 194–97. The October 6, 2002, date is given by Lawrence, while Berner lists the address under September/October 2002. In November, the message appeared in the British press; see the *Guardian*, November 24, 2002. A year later, his October 18, 2003, "Message to the American People" told Americans, "you are vulgar and without sound ethics or good manners" and referred to Vietnam, the Zionist lobby, Palestinians, oil, and the situation of Native Americans (Al Jazeera, October 18, 2003). This uncharacteristic campaign to connect American preoccupations to his jihad reemerged in the run up to the 2004 American elections. In October, he stressed that he had been deeply affected by the Israeli invasion of Lebanon—an issue he had strangely neglected in his previous hundreds of pages of grievances. For the benefit of the U.S. electorate, he also added boilerplate about the Patriot Act, electoral fraud, campaign finance, the deficit, Halliburton, and President Bush's reading of *My Pet Goat* on 9/11 (Middle East Media Research Institute [MEMRI], "The Full Version of Osama bin Laden's Speech," *Special Dispatch* 811, November 5, 2004), http://memri.org/bin/articles.cgi?Page=archives&Area=sd&ID= SP81104. Zawahiri has also castigated "usurious banks, giant companies, misleading media outlets, homosexual marriage, American support for the Copts and called for sharia law (Joseph Braude, "On Message," *New Republic Online*, February 11, 2005). Bin Laden's January 19, 2006, Al Jazeera audio address

referenced Vietnam and opinion polls; "Osama bin Laden," in *Al Qaeda 2006 Yearbook*, ed. Laura Mansfield (London: TLG Publications, 2007), 43–52. Zawahiri's May 5, 2007, interview, also subtitled in English, plays to environmental themes and the underprivileged (see MEMRI, "Al-Qaeda Deputy Leader Ayman Al-Zawahiri Interview Produced By Al-Sahab Media," *Special Dispatch* 1575, May 8, 2007, http://www.memri.org/bin/articles.cgi?Page=archives&Area=sd&ID=SP157507.

21   Fifteen minutes of this address was broadcast by Al Jazeera on January 4, 2004, and the website of the Islamic Studies and Research Center published a translation of the entire text on March 7, 2004. Bin Laden, "Resist the New Rome," in Lawrence, *Messages*, 214, 216–17; Bin Laden, "Message to the Islamic Nation," Berner, *Jihad*, 266, 268–69.

22   *JihadUnspun*, December 16, 2004, http://www.jihadunspun.com/; excerpts in MEMRI, "Osama Bin Laden to the Iraqi People: It Is Forbidden to Participate in Iraqi & PA Elections; Jihad in Palestine and Iraq is Incumbent upon Residents of All Muslim Countries, Not Just Iraqis and Palestinians; Zarqawi is the Commander of Al-Qa'ida in Iraq," *Special Dispatch* 838, December 30, 2004, http://www.memri.org/bin/articles.cgi?Page=archives&Area=sd&ID=SP8370; "Depose The Tyrants," in Lawrence, *Messages*, 250–51; "To the Muslims of Saudi Arabia in Particular and to the Muslims of Other Countries in General," in Berner, *Jihad*, 317–18.

23   MEMRI, "Osama Bin Laden: 'Today There is a Conflict between World Heresy Under the Leadership of America on the One Hand and the Islamic Nation with the Mujahideen in its Vanguard on the Other,'" *Special Dispatch* 837, December 30, 2004, http://www.memri.org/bin/articles.cgi?Page=archives&Area=sd&ID=SP83804; "To the Muslims in Iraq in Particular and the Islamic Nation in General," in Berner, *Jihad*, 331–33.

24   Apparently the rumor that Abbas is a Baha'i is widespread in the Middle East, though Baha'i organizations have repeatedly affirmed that there is no truth to it.

25   Bruce Loudon, "Terror Group's Threat Raises Dalai Lama Alert," *Australian*, April 3, 2007.

26   See MEMRI, "Arab Reformists Under Threat by Islamists: Bin Laden Urges Killing of 'Freethinkers,'" *Special Dispatch* 1153, May 3, 2006, http://www.memri.org/bin/articles.cgi?Page=archives&Area=sd&ID=SP115306; Walid Phares, "Bin Laden's 'State Of Jihad' Speech," Counterterrorism Blog, April 24, 2006, http://counterterrorismblog.org/2006/04/bin_ladens_state_of_jihad_spee.php; and Osama bin Laden, "Osama bin Laden: O, People of Islam," in Mansfield, *Al Qaeda*, 111–48.

27   "Dr. Ayman al Zawahiri: Supporting the Palestinians," in Mansfield, *Al Qaeda*, 180–81; Ayman al Zawahiri, "Supporting the Palestinians," in *His Own Words: A Translation of the Writings of Dr. Ayman al Zawahiri*, trans. and ed. Laura Mansfield (Old Tappan, N.J.: TLG Publications, 2006), 347.

28   "Dr. Ayman al Zawahiri: Elegizing the Ummah's Martyr and Commander of the Martyrdom-seekers," in Mansfield, *Al Qaeda*, 190–93.

29   Ayman al Zawahiri, "Bush, the Pope, and Darfur," in Mansfield, *Al Qaeda*, 465–80.

30   See "Crusader Wars," in Lawrence, *Messages*, 134–37.

31   "World's Most Wanted Terrorist: An Interview with Osama bin Laden." ABC-NEWS Online, January 2, 1999, http://jya.com/bin-laden-abc.htm.

32   See Bernard Lewis, *What Went Wrong? The Clash Between Islam and Modernity in the Middle East* (San Francisco: Harper, 2003).

33 Edward Wong, "Iraqi Video Shows Beheading of Man Said to be American," *The New York Times*, September 21, 2004.
34 Paul Marshall, "This War We're In," *National Review Online*, November 26, 2002; *Al Jazeera*, October 14, 2002; Nadia Abou El-Magd, "Bin Laden Statement Praises Attacks," Associated Press, October 14, 2002.
35 Pamela Constable, "Proposed Afghan Constitution Fits U.S. Model," *Washington Post*, November 4, 2003; Carlotta Gall, "Afghans' King Receives Draft of Constitution," *The New York Times*, November 4, 2003; Burt Herman, "Afghanistan Unveils Long-Delayed Draft Constitution, Key Step on Road to Recovery," Associated Press, November 3, 2003; Paul Marshall, "'Taliban Lite': Afghanistan Fast Forwards," *National Review Online*, November 7, 2003.
36 Lisa Miller and Mathew Philips, "Caliwho? Why Is President Bush Talking about an Islamic Caliphate? And What Does the Word Mean?" *Newsweek*, October 13, 2006.
37 Speech by Nicolas Sarkozy, president of the French Republic, at the opening of the Fifteenth Ambassadors' Conference, Paris, August 27, 2007.

Chapter 4

1   See, e.g., Abrams, *Influence of Faith*.
2   Thomas, *Global Resurgence*, 21–26.
3   Fox and Sandler, *Bringing Religion into International Relations*, 32.
4   Fox and Sandler, *Bringing Religion into International Relations*, 176–77.
5   Warren Hoge, "Despite U.S. Opposition, United Nations Budget Is Approved," *The New York Times*, December 23, 2007.
6   Editorial, "Annapolis Unsettled," *Financial Times*, December 17, 2007. The Bush administration subsequently failed to place any strong pressure on Israel to conform to its negotiating commitments made in Annapolis. President Bush's statements when traveling in the Middle East in early January 2008 (see Michael Abramowitz and Jonathan Finer, "Bush Alters Stand on Palestinians," *Washington Post*, January 11, 2008) sounded much more evenhanded toward Israel and the Palestinians but were not backed up by evenhanded action. At time of writing (mid-2009) it remained unclear how far President Obama would translate his more critical language toward Israel (e.g., concerning settlements in Jerusalem) into changed policy.
7   The American Puritan settlers came from England where the Puritans had already taken to themselves an Old Testament identity of "the re-embodied saints of Israel." Barbara W. Tuchman, *Bible and Sword: England and Palestine from the Bronze Age to Balfour* (New York: Ballantine, 1956), 122, 121–46. See also George McKenna, *The Puritan Origins of American Patriotism* (New Haven: Yale University Press, 2007), 1–43; and Noll, *America's God*, 19–26, 31–42.
8   The gradual development from New England Puritanism to an American civil religion that operates even among those who do not think of themselves as traditionally religious is summarized well by Geiko Muller-Fahrenholz, *America's Battle for God* (Grand Rapids: Eerdmans, 2007), 1–22. He cites some of the key studies that offer a more detailed account, including: Herberg, *Protestant-Catholic-Jew*; Robert N. Bellah, *The Broken Covenant: American Civil Religion in a Time of Trial*, 2nd ed. (Chicago: University of Chicago Press, 1992); and Richard T. Hughes, *Myths America Lives By* (Urbana: University of Illinois Press, 2004).
9   McKenna, *Puritan Origins*, 4.
10 Tuchman, *Bible and Sword*, 122. "With the [English] Puritans," writes Tuchman, "came an invasion of Hebraism transmitted through the Old Testament, but

distorted by the effort to apply to post-Renaissance England the ethics, laws, and manners native to a Middle Eastern people of more than two thousand years earlier. In their devotion to chapter and verse of the Hebrew testaments the Puritans, undaunted by the mental jump of two millennia, adapted to themselves the thoughts of tribal herdsmen groping their way out of idolatry toward monotheism in the time of Abraham, or of slaves triumphing over Pharoah in the time of the Exodus, or of warriors carving the frontiers of a new state in the time of Saul and David. . . . It did not matter that [the biblical narrative] covered a period, from Abraham to Maccabaeus, of nearly a millennium and a half; the Puritans swallowed the whole with equal zeal. . . . As early as 1573 one of their articles of faith, according to the indictment of Sandys, Bishop of London, was that 'the judicial laws of Moses are binding on Christian princes and they ought not in the slightest degree to depart from them.' They followed the letter of the Old Testament for the very reason that they saw their own faces reflected in it. They too were a group led by God in the struggle against idolators [sic] and tyrants." *Bible and Sword*, 123–24.

11   On the isolationist-internationalist dialectic, see Walter A. McDougall, *Promised Land, Crusader State: The American Encounter with the World Since 1776* (Boston: Houghton Mifflin, 1997); Andrew J. Bacevich, *American Empire* (Cambridge, Mass.: Harvard University Press, 2002); and Ferguson, *Colossus*.

12   Michael B. Oren, *Power, Faith, and Fantasy: America in the Middle East, 1776 to the Present* (New York: Norton, 2007), 88.

13   Oren, *Power, Faith*, 85.

14   Noll, *America's God*, 137.

15   Oren, *Power, Faith*, 85.

16   Oren, *Power, Faith*, 86.

17   McKenna, *Puritan Origins*, 7.

18   McKenna, *Puritan Origins*, 7. McKenna helps us understand the transfer of Puritan new-Israelite thinking to the American nation as a whole. He points to Edward Johnson's book *Wonder-Working Providence of Sion's Savior in New-England* (1654) (Delmar, New York.: Scholars Facsimiles and Reprints, 1974), "the first sustained mythicizing of the American experience. Purportedly a history of the colony from 1628–1652, it actually amounted to an effort to recast the historical facts (altering them when necessary) into a giant Old Testament epic with providential overtones. New Englanders were God's new chosen people, a prophetic army, a model to the world" (*Puritan Origins*, 36–37). Johnson's tale aimed in part to place "spiritually unfulfilled, guilt-ridden children of the second generation" within the chosen people as a whole. Here, says McKenna, "was a comforting message: do not worry too much about inner motives, for you live in a community that has collectively been sent forth by God, and you will share its grace as long as the community 'keep[s] close to Christ.' By this logic, the individual could justify himself by justifying his community in the soil of the New World" (37). This sort of logic was further extended by Solomon Stoddard, who first made room in the church for those who were not regenerate and then argued from the Old Testament by analogy that God's people were a nation. "Stoddard's idea was that of an all-embracing American church. He was suggesting that America can be a Christian nation in the same way that the Jews were a nation—not mere occupiers of a territory but a chosen people dedicated to the purpose of realizing in the wilderness a task given to them before they embarked on their perilous journey" (*Puritan Origins*, 53). Not every individual had to be a confessing member of the church in order to be part of the American Christian nation. It was a small step from Stoddard to the civil-religious nationalism of the

American founding. There could be many different kinds of churches and many citizens who were not members of churches, but everyone could be part of God's new Israel, America.

19   McKenna, *Puritan Origins*, 48.

20   Muller-Fahrenholz, *America's Battle*, 20.

21   Martin Luther King Jr., *I Have a Dream: Writings and Speeches that Changed the World*, ed. James M. Washington (San Francisco: HarperSanFrancisco, 1992), 104–6.

22   I have developed this argument more fully in Skillen, *With or Against the World.*

23   On Herzl, see Walter Laqueur, *A History of Zionism* (New York: Holt, Rinehart & Winston, 1972), 84–135; Shlomo Avineri, *The Making of Modern Zionism: The Intellectual Origins of the Jewish State* (New York: Basic, 1981), 88–100; Ronald Sanders, *The High Walls of Jerusalem: A History of the Balfour Declaration and the Birth of the British Mandate for Palestine* (New York: Holt, Rinehart & Winston, 1983), 1–38; and Tuchman, *Bible and Sword*, 281–309.

24   See Colin Chapman, *Whose Promised Land? The Continuing Crisis over Israel and Palestine* (Grand Rapids: Baker, 2002), 1–30.

25   Avineri, *Modern Zionism*, 8.

26   Avineri, *Modern Zionism*, 10.

27   Avineri, *Modern Zionism*, 11.

28   Much of the Jewish opposition to Herzl in Europe came from those who had hopes of becoming fully assimilated or solidifying their status as equal citizens in their respective countries, including the freedom to practice their religion in private insofar as they were religious. Herzl's efforts might well have revived anti-Semitism where it had disappeared or was in retreat. Lord Nathaniel Mayer Rothschild, the "lay leader of English Jewry, a peer since 1885, eldest son of that Lionel de Rothschild who had fought for years to be the first member of his faith to sit in Parliament . . . looked upon Zionism's claim that Jews were not just a religious group, but a nation, as the antithesis of everything he and his family stood for." Sanders, *High Walls*, 29.

29   Avineri, *Modern Zionism*, 13. "Herzl's vision of the future [Jewish] state [in his 1902 utopian novel *Altneuland*]," explains Laqueur, "is that of a typical liberal, permeated with optimism and enlightened ideals, a model society on a progressive pattern. *Altneuland* thus refutes any attempt to regard the breakdown of liberalism as the key to Herzl's political thought. He had despaired of Jews finding a place in European society, but his vision of the future state was in fact so tolerant and cosmopolitan that it was bound to provoke resentment among cultural Zionists like Ahad Ha'am. What was specifically Jewish in the new state, Ahad Ha'am asked. The very name Zion did not once appear, its inhabitants did not speak Hebrew, and there was little if any mention of Jewish culture. It was just another modern, secular state, and Ahad Ha'am resented what he regarded as one more manifestation of assimilation." Laqueur, *Zionism*, 133. Cf. Sanders, *High Walls*, 28–29.

30   Avineri, *Modern Zionism*, 78–79.

31   Max Nordau, "On Zionism," (1922), quoted in Avineri, *Modern Zionism*, 107.

32   Avineri, *Modern Zionism*, 154, 158.

33   On the history of early labor movements, socialism, and Marxism among the nonreligious Zionist leaders who laid the groundwork for and developed the labor movements that continued on into the politics of Israel after 1948, see Laqueur, *Zionism*, 270–337.

34   David Ben-Gurion, quoted in Avineri, *Modern Zionism*, 200.

35   A great part of the land Jews acquired before 1929 was purchased from large and

predominantly absentee landlords. Some of the richest parts of Palestine were
sold to immigrating Jews by the Sursock family. Extremely wealthy, they had
purchased land from Ottoman officials as early as 1872. "In a series of transactions from 1891 to 1920 [the Sursocks] sold it all to the Zionists, as unmoved
by high appeals to their sense of Arab history as by workaday calls on their
conscience." Chapman, *Whose Promised Land?* 58–61.

36   Leo Pinsker, *Autoemancipation* (1932) quoted in Avineri, *Modern Zionism*, 81.

37   Herzl had turned to leaders wherever he could gain access—in Germany,
France, Turkey, Russia, England—to seek help in creating a homeland for the
Jews. He always held out high hope for help from England. At one point, after
ardent lobbying in London, he was called before a Royal commission headed by
Lord Rothschild, who was no fan of Herzl. Rothschild and other British leaders
were concerned about the rapid pace of Jewish immigration to Palestine and
the problems it created for Britain's dealings with the Arabs. Herzl explained to
the commission that he wanted to found a Jewish colony in British territory and
Rothschild proposed Uganda as the place. Though Herzl had earlier been open
to that idea and others, he responded that the Zionists would accept land only
in the Sinai Peninsula, or Egyptian Palestine, or in Cyprus. Tuchman, *Bible and
Sword*, 293. See also Sanders, *High Walls*, 30–38. On the efforts that led up to the
Balfour Declaration and the consensus on a homeland in Palestine, see Tuchman,
Bible and Sword, 310–47; Jehuda Reinharz, *Chaim Weizmann: The Making of a
Statesman* (New York: Oxford University Press, 1993); Margaret Macmillan, *Paris
1919* (New York: Random House, 2001), 410–26; and Sanders, *High Walls*.

38   Avineri, *Modern Zionism*, 89.

39   We must not overlook the fact that extensive efforts at evangelism and service
through the establishment of schools and hospitals were made by Christians
throughout the Middle East. As Rashid Khalidi says, the United States was
viewed rather positively in the Middle East from the nineteenth century until
after World War II because of its opposition to colonialism and its many constructive contributions. "Where the United States was involved in the Middle
East, it was via the work of Protestant missionaries, who established churches,
schools and hospitals. This effort aroused surprisingly little local antagonism,
since the missionaries quickly learned to confine their proselytizing to local
orthodox and Catholic Christians and to Jews, rather than targeting members of
the Muslim majority, who were generally unresponsive to conversion." Rashid
Khalidi, *Resurrecting Empire: Western Footprints and America's Perilous Path in the
Middle East* (Boston: Beacon, 2004), 31. See also Oren, *Power, Faith*, 122–41,
376–97.

40   See Khalidi, *Resurrecting Empire*, 74–117; and Oren, *Power, Faith*, 407–32.

41   See Tuchman, *Bible and Sword*, 208–80; and MacMillan, *Paris 1919*, 3–106,
366–426.

42   MacMillan, *Paris 1919*, 422.

43   MacMillan, *Paris 1919*, 422–23.

44   Laqueur, *Zionism*, 585.

45   Laqueur, *Zionism*, 599.

46   Laqueur, *Zionism*, 598–99.

47   Early negative reactions to Herzl and to his *Der Judenstaat*, as well as many
subsequent reactions to Zionism, were divided, according to Laqueur. "The
majority thought it was a chimera, a revival of medieval messianism. [Moritz]
Gudenmann, Vienna's chief rabbi, who had been close to Herzl, sharply attacked
his ideas in a pamphlet in which he protested against the '*Kuckuckse* of Jewish
nationalism,' maintaining that Jews were not a nation, that they had in common

only their faith in God, and that Zionism was incompatible with the teachings of Judaism." *Zionism*, 96. According to Avineri, "Zionist ideology and the Zionist movement were generally viewed with suspicion, if not outright hostility, by the Jewish religious establishment; Zionism was modernizing, nonreligious, and secular. For all the deep differences between East European Orthodoxy and the more liberal Reform movement in the West, both showed a fundamental opposition to Zionism, albeit for different reasons. Most Zionist activists thus found themselves both in Eastern as well as Western Europe (and in America) having to confront a hostile religious leadership that viewed Zionism as another ill-fated messianism." *Modern Zionism*, 187.

48   The quotations in this paragraph are from Kook, "The Land of Israel," "Lights for Rebirth," and "The War," in Arthur Hertzberg, *The Zionist Idea*, rev. ed. (New York: n.p., 1969). All are cited in Avineri, *Modern Zionism*, 187–97.

49   Roberta Strauss Feuerlicht, *The Fate of the Jews: A People Torn Between Israeli Power and Jewish Ethics* (New York: New York Times Books, 1983), 185–87, quoted in Marc H. Ellis, *Toward a Jewish Theology of Liberation*, 3rd ed. (Waco, Tex.: Baylor University Press, 2004), 45.

50   Michael Lerner, "The Occupation: Immoral and Stupid," *Tikkun* 3 (1988), 7–9, quoted in Ellis, *Theology of Liberation*, 97–98.

51   Lerner, "The Occupation," quoted in Ellis, *Theology of Liberation*, 98.

52   Ellis, *Theology of Liberation*, 232–33. There are critics within Israel, including those who do not identify with the religious communities, who are raising similar moral concerns about the state and its conduct. See, e.g., David Remnick, "The Apostate," *New Yorker*, July 30, 2007, 32–37. Remnick's fascinating essay is about Avraham Burg, a former speaker of the Knesset and member of a family that has long given leadership in the Zionist establishment, who has become a harsh and even embarrassing critic of life and the government in Israel.

53   See Oren, *Power, Faith*, 351–502.

54   Oren, *Power, Faith*, 483–90.

55   Recently, the influence of the Jewish lobby in American politics sparked a major national debate over an essay in the *London Review of Books* 28, no. 6 (March 23, 2006) by John J. Mearsheimer and Stephen M. Walt, titled "The Israel Lobby." The essay was backed up by a more extensive paper published on the website of Harvard's Kennedy School of Government, where Walt is a professor. The essay's thesis is that American national interests are being compromised by too strong an influence from the Israel lobby. That lobby binds American policy in the Middle East too tightly to Israel's interests. Many critics, both wild and measured, attacked or disagreed with the authors, calling forth a book-length response from them titled *The Israel Lobby and U.S. Foreign Policy* (New York: Penguin, 2007). Around the same time, former president Jimmy Carter published his *Palestine: Peace Not Apartheid* (New York: Simon & Schuster, 2006), which also drew many attacks for being more critical of Israel than of the Palestinians. The charge that American foreign policy has become too narrowly defined and hemmed in by Israel's interests would appear to find confirmation in a statement by Israeli Prime Minister Ehud Olmert early in January 2008, on the eve of President Bush's visit to the Middle East. Olmert "called Bush a 'giant friend of ours, he's not doing a single thing that I don't agree to. He doesn't support anything that I oppose. He doesn't say a thing he thinks will make life harder for Israel'" (*Financial Times*, January 8, 2008). Not all Israeli prime ministers have spoken that way, of course, but the absoluteness of Olmert's comment is not shocking or surprising.

56   "At its simplest," says Stephen Sizer, "Christian Zionism is a political form of

philo-Semitism, and can be defined as 'Christian support for Zionism.' The term 'Christian Zionist' first appears to have been used by Theodor Herzl to describe Henri Dunant, the Swiss philanthropist and founder of the Red Cross. Dunant was one of only a handful of Gentiles to be invited to the First World Zionist Congress." Stephen Sizer, *Christian Zionism: Road-map to Armageddon?* (Leicester, UK: InterVarsity, 2004), 19.

57   Sizer, *Christian Zionism*, 34 (see 30–80). *Premillennialism* is the belief that Christ will return to earth to exercise a thousand-year reign of righteousness before the final judgment and the full establishment of God's kingdom. *Dispensationalism* argues that God rules and saves in different ways during different historical periods or dispensations. The dispensation of God's work through Israel, e.g., is different in operation and aim from the dispensation of God's work through the church.

58   Sizer, *Christian Zionism*, 39.

59   Sizer, *Christian Zionism*, 255. The debates over dispensationalism and premillennialism come down to different interpretations of the Bible. On those differences, see Colin Chapman, *Whose Promised Land?* 113–238, 287–305.

60   Michael D. Evans, *The American Prophecies: Ancient Scriptures Reveal Our Nation's Future* (New York: Warner Faith, 2004).

61   Evans, *American Prophecies*, 212; see also 50–61, 213–50.

62   Tuchman, *Bible and Sword*, xiv.

63   Joanna and Ebenezer Cartwright, *The Petition of the Jews for the Repealing of the Act of Parliament for Their Banishment Out of England* (London, 1649). Quoted by Tuchman from a facsimile reprinted in Don Patenkin, "Mercantilism and the Readmission of the Jews to England," *Jewish Social Studies* (July 1946), in Tuchman, *Bible and Sword*, 121.

64   Tuchman, *Bible and Sword*, 122.

65   Tuchman, *Bible and Sword*, 178. "Why must the church stand with Israel?" Evans asks, and "Why does Satan fear Israel so much?" The reason, says Evans, is that "Israel's restoration will trigger the coming of our Lord and Savior." *American Prophecies*, 249–50. Israel and modern Jewry, from this point of view, are merely instruments in the fulfillment of endtimes prophecies.

66   Sizer, *Christian Zionism*, 55–57; and Tuchman, *Bible and Sword*, 175–207.

67   Sizer, *Christian Zionism*, 61.

68   Sizer, *Christian Zionism*, 60.

69   Sizer, *Christian Zionism*, 61.

70   Sizer, *Christian Zionism*, 151.

71   Sizer, *Christian Zionism*, 160.

72   On biblical interpretations of the meaning of God's judgments that sent Israel and then Judah into exile and on the promise of return, see Chapman, *Whose Promised Land?* 127–33, 159–77. And on the extent of the territory that should belong to Israel, see Sizer, *Christian Zionism*, 162–66; Chapman, *Whose Promised Land?* 117–19; and Gary M. Burge, *Whose Land? Whose Promise?* (Cleveland: Pilgrim, 2003).

73   President Harry Truman, says Oren, could not ignore congressional calls or "the pro-Zionist telegrams that overwhelmed the White House at the end of the war with Japan" calling for Jewish statehood. The pressure kept up as the UN approached decision time on the issue; "once again, the White House was inundated with thousands of letters urging it to adopt a patently pro-partition stance" that would make room for a Jewish state. Oren, *Power, Faith*, 484, 492. Today the inundation comes more in phone calls and e-mails, and now by the hundreds of thousands at any given time.

74 See Sizer, *Christian Zionism*, 216–19.

75 Sizer, *Christian Zionism*, 215.

76 Evans, *American Prophecies*, 245.

77 For an elaboration of this summary, see Evans, *American Prophecies*, 160–63 and 188–94.

78 Sizer provides a more detailed overview of the political/lobbying agenda of Christian Zionists that includes full support for Israel's settlements on Palestinian land, promoting the Temple Mount movement to rebuild the temple, and opposing all peace efforts that would appear to weaken or limit Israel. *Christian Zionism*, 211–53.

79 Sizer, *Christian Zionism*, 254–55.

80 See, e.g., Eric Voegelin, *From Enlightenment to Revolution*, ed. John H. Hallowell (Durham, N.C.: Duke University Press, 1975); Karl Lowith, *Meaning in History* (Chicago: University of Chicago Press, 1949); Herman Dooyeweerd, *The Collected Works of Herman Dooyeweerd*, series B, vol. 3, *Roots of Western Culture: Pagan, Secular, and Christian Options* (Lewiston, N.Y.: Edwin Mellen, 2003); and John Caputo, ed., *Deconstruction in a Nutshell: A Conversation with Jacques Derrida* (New York: Fordham University Press, 1997).

81 For a good introduction to modern, mostly Western, ideologies, see David T. Koyzis, *Political Visions and Illusions: A Survey and Christian Critique of Contemporary Ideologies* (Downers Grove, Ill.: InterVarsity, 2003).

Chapter 5

* This chapter draws on material appearing in *God and the Atlantic: America, Europe, and the Religious Divide* (Oxford University Press, forthcoming). An earlier version of this essay appeared in the journal *The Hedgehog Review* (vol. 8, Spring/ Summer 2006, 116–26). Used by permission of the author.

1 Peter Schneider, "Across a Great Divide," *The New York Times*, March 12, 2004, 7.

2 Scheider, "Across a Great Divide."

3 Andrei S. Markovits, *Uncouth Nation: Why Europe Dislikes America* (Princeton: Princeton University Press, 2007), 154.

4 Jürgen Habermas and Jacques Derrida, "Unsere Erneuerung; Nach dem Krieg: Die Wiedergeburt Europas," *Frankfurter Allgemeine Zeitung*, May 31, 2003, 33.

5 Habermas and Derrida, "Unsere Erneuerung."

6 Gianni Vattimo, "L'unione affronta i nodi decisivi del suo sviluppo," *La Stampa*, May 31, 2003, 23.

7 Vattimo, "L'unione affronta."

8 As the sociologist Peter Berger writes: "Explaining European secularity, especially in contrast with America, is one of the most interesting topics for the study of contemporary religion." See Berger, "Religion in the West," *National Interest* 80 (2005): 1113.

9 Part of the problem lies in a systemic inattention to religion in the shaping of the field of International Relations. For criticisms of this inattention and efforts to retrieve religion both as an object of study and as a source of scholarly insight, see the fine collection of essays in Hatzopoulos and Petito, *Religion in International Relations*. Cf. Philpott, "Challenge of September 11," 66–95.

10 C. Vann Woodward, *The Old World's New World* (New York: Oxford University Press, 1991), 21–22, 28–29.

11 To quote Markovits again: "One would be hard pressed to arrive at any items in politics apart from . . . anti-Americanism in which there has been such a strong

and lasting concordance between the extreme Right and the extreme Left in virtually every European country." Markovits, *Uncouth Nation*, 198.

12   Marc Pachter and Frances Wein, eds., *Abroad in America: Visitors to the New Nation, 1776–1914* (Reading, Mass.: Addison-Wesley, 1976), xiii.

13   Alexis de Tocqueville, *Democracy in America*, trans. Henry Reeve (New York: Knopf, 1945), 1:319.

14   Noted in Günter Moltmann, "Deutscher Antiamerikanismus Heute und Früher," in *Vom Sinn der Geschichte*, ed. Otmar Franz (Stuttgart: Seewald, 1976), 92.

15   Johann Georg Hülsemann, *Geschichte der Democratie in den Vereinigten Staaten von Nord-America* (Göttingen, 1823), vii–viii.

16   Pope Gregory XVI, *Mirari Vos*, "On Liberalism and Religious Indifferentism," encyclical, August 15, 1832, quoted in John Noonan, *The Church that Can and Cannot Change* (Notre Dame, Ind.: University of Notre Dame Press, 2005), 148.

17   See the entry on "America" in volume 9 of *Kirchen-Lexikon: Oder, Encyklopædie der katholischen Theologie und ihrer Hilfswissenschaften*, ed. Heinrich Joseph Wetzer and Benedikt Welte (Freiburg im Breisgau: Karl Herder, 1854).

18   J. E. Jörg, *Geschichte des Protestantismus in Seiner Neuesten Entwicklung* (Freiburg im Breisgau: Herder'sche Verhandlung, 1858), 2:457.

19   Karl August von Reisach, "Il Mormonismo nelle sue attinenze col moderno protestantismo," *La Civiltà Cattolica*, 4th series, 6 (May 19, 1860): 394. I thank Mark Noll for calling my attention to this article.

20   See Pope Leo XIII, *Testem benevolentiae nostrae*, "Concerning New Opinions, Virtue, Nature and Grace, with Regard to Americanism," encyclical, January 12, 1899.

21   Abbé Henry Delassus, *L'Américanisme et la conjuration antichrétienne* (Paris: Société de Saint-Augustin, Desclée De Brouwer et Cie, 1899).

22   See Gerald P. Fogarty, *The Vatican and the American Hierarchy from 1870 to 1965* (Collegeville, Minn.: Liturgical, 1982); and Michael Davies, *The Second Vatican Council and Religious Liberty* (Long Prairie, Minn.: Neumann, 1992).

23   Frances Trollope, *Domestic Manners of the Americans* (New York: Penguin, 1997), 84.

24   Anthony Trollope, *North America*, ed. Donald Smalley and Bradford Allen Booth (New York: Knopf, 1951), 277–78.

25   Samuel Wilberforce, *A History of the Protestant Episcopal Church in America* (New York: Standford & Swords, 1849), 290–91.

26   Wilberforce, *History*, 291.

27   Charles Dickens, *American Notes* (London: Chapman & Hall, 1842), 141.

28   See the many disparaging comments about the United States, e.g., recorded in Benjamin Evans Lippincott, *Victorian Critics of Democracy: Carlyle, Ruskin, Arnold, Stephen, Maine, Lecky* (New York: Octagon, 1964).

29   Matthew Arnold, *Civilization in the United States*, 6th ed. (Boston, Mass.: DeWolfe, Friske, 1900), 140.

30   Philip Schaff, *The Principle of Protestantism*, trans. John Nevin (Chambersburg, Pa.: Publication of the German Reformed Church, 1845), 149–50.

31   Ferdinand Kürnberger, *Der Amerikamüde* (Berlin: Freitag Verlag, 1982), 220–21.

32   Kürnberger, *Amerikamüde*, 221.

33   G. W. F. Hegel, *Werke* (Frankfurt am Main: Suhrkamp, 1970), 12:114.

34   Hegel, *Werke*, 12:114.

35   Hegel, *Werke*, 12:112–13.

36   On this topic, see especially Georg Kamphausen's illuminating book, *Die Erfindung Amerikas in der Kulturkritik der Generation von 1890* (Göttingen: Velbrück Wissenschaft, 2002).

37 Werner Sombart, *Händler and Helden: Patriotische Besinnungen* (Munich, 1914); quoted in Fritz K. Ringer, *The Decline of the German Mandarins: The German Academic Community, 1890–1933* (Cambridge, Mass.: Harvard University Press, 1969), 183.

38 Friedrich Nietzsche, *The Gay Science*, trans. Walter Kaufmann (New York: Random House, 1974), 258–59.

39 Max Weber, *The Protestant Ethic and the Spirit of Capitalism*, trans. Talcott Parsons (New York: Scribner's, 1958), 181ff.

40 Max Weber, "The Protestant Sects and the Spirit of Capitalism," in *From Max Weber: Essays in Sociology*, ed. H. H. Gerth and C. Wright Mills (New York: Oxford University Press, 1946), 322.

41 See Herbert Marcuse, *One-Dimensional Man* (Boston: Beacon, 1991); and Jean Baudrillard, *America*, trans. Chris Turner (Lodon: Verso, 1988). Cf. James W. Ceasar, *Reconstructing America: The Symbol of America in Modern Thought* (New Haven: Yale University Press, 1997), 190.

42 Martin Heidegger, *Einführung in die Metaphysik*, in *Gesamtausgabe* (Frankfurt am Main: Klostermann, 1975), 40:40–41.

43 Heidegger, "Hölderlins Hymne," in *Gesamtausgabe*, 53:86.

44 Heidegger, *Holzwege* (Frankfurt: Vittoria Klostermann, 1957), 103, quoted in Ceasar, *Reconstructing America*, 9.

45 This essay, of course, just touches on the surface of the topic. For more complete renderings of the history of European anti-Americanism, see Antonello Gerbi, *The Dispute of the New World: The History of a Polemic, 1750–1900*, trans. Jeremy Moyle (Pittsburgh: University of Pittsburgh Press, 1973); and, more recently, Philippe Roger, *The American Enemy: The Story of French Anti-Americanism*, trans. Sharon Bowman (Chicago: University of Chicago Press, 2005).

46 It is helpful to remember that debates about anti-Americanism are as much an intra-European affair as one that divides the two continents. For a forceful European/French critique of European anti-Americanism, see Jean-François Revel, *Anti-Americanism*, trans. Diarmid Cammell (San Francisco: Encounter, 2000).

47 See Petito and Hatzopoulous, *Religion in International Relations*.

Chapter 6

1 For an eyewitness account of the revolutions of 1989 in Eastern Europe, see Timothy Garton Ash's *The Magic Lantern: The Revolutions of 1989 Witnessed in Warsaw, Budapest, Berlin and Prague* (New York: Random House, 1990). See also John A. Bernbaum, "Revolution '89: The Spiritual Dimension," *Christian Science Monitor*, August 15, 1990.

2 One of the best descriptions of the collapse of the Soviet Union is David Remnick's *Lenin's Tomb: The Last Days of the Soviet Empire* (New York: Random House, 1993). The first sentence of James Billington's book *Russia Transformed: Breakthrough to Hope* (New York: Free Press, 1992) reads as follows: "The events of August 1991 in Moscow may in time be recognized to have been the most important single political happening of the second half of the twentieth century" (p. 3).

3 Robert F. Byrnes, *After Brezhnev: Sources of Soviet Conduct in the 1980s* (Washington, D.C.: CSIS, 1983), xvi.

4 Hedrick Smith, *The New Russians* (New York: Random House, 1990), xvi. Smith's earlier book was *The Russians* (New York: Ballantine, 1976).

5 Robert G. Kaiser, "Gorbachev: Triumph and Failure," *Foreign Affairs* 70, no. 2 (1991): 160.

6 Many of the books written about the collapse of Communism by Western journalists stationed in Russia focus largely on the importance of American political

leadership in undermining the Soviet regime. E.g., Fred Coleman's book, *The Decline and Fall of the Soviet Empire* (New York: St. Martin's, 1996), puts it this way: "American leadership of NATO was a truly outstanding performance by presidents from both parties, from Truman to Reagan . . . The overall U.S. policy cannot be faulted. It was right, and it worked in bringing the Soviet threat to an end" (p. 210).

7   An example of this analysis would be Anders Aslund's book, *How Russia Became a Market Economy* (Washington, D.C.: Brookings, 1995). In response to the question "Why did the Soviet Union collapse?" Aslund wrote, "In the early 1980s, a basic problem was that economic growth had slowed significantly. Economic petrification raised the question of the Soviet system's long-term viability. . . . The severity of the acute financial crisis of 1991 can hardly be exaggerated. . . . When Gorbachev finally stepped down as President of the Soviet Union in December 1991, he left behind a country in a state of utter and complete collapse" (pp. 50–52).

8   Zbigniew Brzezinski, *The Grand Failure: The Birth and Death of Communism in the Twentieth Century* (New York: Scribner's, 1989).

9   Richard Pipes, "The Soviet Union Adrift," in "America and the World," special issue, *Foreign Affairs* 70, no. 1 (1990): 70–87.

10   Two significant studies have been published that address this issue. The first is *Religion: The Missing Dimension of Statecraft*, edited by Douglas Johnson and Cynthia Sampson, and the second is *Bringing Religion into International Relations*, by Jonathan Fox and Shmuel Sandler.

11   George Weigel, *Faith, Reason, and the War Against Jihadism* (New York: Doubleday, 2007), 14.

12   Mikhail Gorbachev, *Perestroika: New Thinking for Our Country and the World* (New York: Harper & Row, 1987), 18–22.

13   Gorbachev, *Perestroika*, 30, 35.

14   "East-West: Gorbachev, God and Socialism," *Time*, December 11, 1989, 37.

15   Fyodor Burlatsky, "Democracy is a Long March," in *Voices of Glasnost: Interviews with Gorbachev's Reformers*, ed. Stephen F. Cohen and Katrina Vanden Heuvel (New York: Norton, 1990), 191.

16   George Weigel, *The Final Revolution: The Resistance Church and the Collapse of Communism* (New York: Oxford University Press, 1992), 34.

17   For an overview of various religious communities during the Soviet regime, see the following: Eugene B. Shirley Jr. and Michael Rowe, eds., *Candle in the Wind: Religion in the Soviet Union* (Washington, D.C., Ethics and Public Policy Center, 1989); and Barbara Von Der Heydt, *Candles Behind the Wall: Heroes of the Peaceful Revolution That Shattered Communism* (Grand Rapids: Eerdmans, 1993).

18   Michael Novak, *The Spirit of Democratic Capitalism* (New York: Simon & Schuster, 1982), 31–48.

19   Richard Pipes, "Putin & Co.: What Is to Be Done?" *Commentary* 125, no. 5 (2008): 30–36.

20   Dmitri Trenin, "Reading Russia Right," *Carnegie Endowment Policy Brief* (Washington, D.C.: Carnegie Endowment, October 2005), 5.

21   Lawrence E. Harrison and Samuel P. Huntington, eds., *Culture Matters: How Values Shape Human Progress* (New York: Basic, 2000).

22   Lawrence E. Harrison, "The Culture Club: Exploring the Central Liberal Truth," *National Interest* 83 (2006): 97.

23   For a series of essays on Russians' "DNA," see my Reflections on Russia—"Fear of Invasion" (August 2006), "Lack of Trust" (September 2006), "Fear of Anarchy" (March 2007), "Giantism" (April 2007), "Deep-Seated Spirituality" (May 2007),

and "Unsettled Identity" (June 2007); these "reflections" can be located at http://www.racu.org/.

24 Michael Mandelbaum, "Democracy Without America: The Spontaneous Spread of Freedom," *Foreign Affairs* 86, no. 5 (2007): 121–22.

25 Mandelbaum, "Democracy Without America," 23.

26 Thomas, *Global Resurgence*, 1–12.

27 Lawrence E. Harrison, *The Central Liberal Truth* (New York: Oxford University Press, 2006), 152–53.

28 For a description of Russia's experience with "shock therapy," see Marshall I. Goldman, *Lost Opportunity: What Has Made Economic Reform in Russia So Difficult?* (New York: Norton, 1996), 94–121. The impact of these dramatic economic reforms on the Russian people is analyzed in a study by Bertram Silverman and Murray Yanowitch entitled *New Rich, New Poor, New Russia* (Armonk, N.Y.: M. E. Sharpe, 2000).

29 Vladimir Shlapentokh, "Trust in Public Institutions in Russia: The Lowest in the World," *Johnson's Russia List*, no. 9186, June 28, 2005. Shlapentokh notes that "the church, with its 43 percent trust rating, is the most trusted institution in the country aside from Putin as a personality. . . . Russians look to the church not so much as a repository of their religious feelings, but as an institution that can play a positive role in society" (p. 9).

30 James W. Skillen, *In Pursuit of Justice* (Lanham, Md.: Rowman & Littlefield, 2004), 11.

31 "20 Million Live in Poverty in Russia," *Kommersant*, May 15, 2008. Reprinted in *Johnson's Russia List* #2008-96, May 15, 2008.

32 Farr, "Diplomacy," 110–11.

33 Brian J. Grim, "Religious Freedom: Good For What Ails Us," *Review of Faith and International Affairs* 6, no. 2 (2008): 3–7.

34 Grim, "Religious Freedom," 4–5.

35 John Anderson, *Religion, State and Politics in the Soviet Union and Successor States* (New York: Cambridge University Press, 1994), 137–41.

36 William Yoder, "Cooperation is the Order of the Day," press release, Russian Union of Evangelical Christians-Baptists, June 21, 2008.

37 Grim, "Religious Freedom," 3.

38 Farr, "Diplomacy," 124.

39 Corwin Smidt, "Introduction," in Corwin Smidt, ed., *Religion as Social Capital: Producing the Common Good* (Waco, Tex.: Baylor University Press, 2003), 1–6.

40 R. D. Putnam, *Bowling Alone: The Collapse and Revival of American Community* (New York: Simon & Schuster, 2000), 66.

41 Smidt, "Religion as Social Capital," 216–21.

42 Harrison, *Central Liberal Truth*, xiv.

Chapter 7

* A modified version of this essay was given as an address at Princeton University at teh conference "Moral Conflict and the Free Society," sponsored by the James Madison Program in American Ideals and Institutions on May 12–13, 2008.

1 James Turner Johnson, "Humanitarian Intervention, Christian Ethical Reasoning, and the Just-War Idea," in Lugo, *Sovereignty at the Crossroads*, 127. The reasons for this are fairly obvious: preoccupation of the policy community and ethicists with the U.S.-Soviet rivalry, the problem of nuclear weapons, and the conception of the world as two primary spheres of influence.

2 Ludu Sein Win, veteran Burmese (and Rangoon-based) journalist, cited in *Irrawaddy*, April 2008, 5.

3   This instability may be characteristic of new states, failed states, or those states on the verge of collapse.

4   I am using the term "humanitarian" in its narrower sense, i.e., the sense in which intervention is undertaken to promote the welfare of humanity, especially through the elimination of gratuitous pain and suffering.

5   Paul Ramsey, "The Ethics of Intervention," *Review of Politics* 25, no. 3 (1965): 288–89; see also Ramsey, *The Just War: Force and Political Responsibility* (New York: Scribner's, 1968), 19–41.

6   Ramsey, *Just War*, 23.

7   Ramsey, "Ethics of Intervention," 291.

8   Significantly, the occasion for Ramsey's reflections on humanitarian intervention was an address before the Religious Leaders' Conference on Peace, held at the Church Center for the United Nations in New York on January 12–14, 1965. There Ramsey cautioned his audience against the common tendency among religious people to "spiritualize politics" and become skeptical toward judgments about political justice.

9   The classical just-war tradition offers the best framework for considering the moral arguments for and against humanitarian intervention due to its philosophical commitment—anchored in natural-law reasoning and represented in the traditional *ius ad bellum* and *ius in bello* criteria—to severely qualify both whether and how to apply force. I would argue that a third category of considerations— *ius post bellum* (justice after war)—is a natural and necessary extension of these two, although a discussion thereof carries us too far afield. See, nevertheless, J. Daryl Charles and David D. Corey, "*Jus Post Bellum*: Extending the Implications of Just-War Thinking to Post-War Reconstruction," chap. 10 in *Justice in an Age of Terror: The Just War Tradition Reconsidered*, American Ideals and Institutions (Wilmington, Del.: ISI Books, forthcoming).

10   Cf. Luke 10:25-37 and the parable of the Good Samaritan.

11   One need not rehearse here the various schools of realism that have been influential in helping dictate foreign policy in the United States over the last 50–80 years.

12   Invariably, "social justice" (at least as it is typically construed in academic and theological circles) is cast in economic terms that flow from the reigning "trinitarian" paradigm of race, class, and gender. Tragically, it is quite rare to find exponents of "social justice" applying moral-philosophical rigor or any sort of political astuteness to the question of what "justice" might require.

13   Rightly has Oliver O'Donovan noted that the church itself constitutes a *public* realm and that in recent years Christian thinkers, by largely failing to grasp the importance of this fact, encourage an unfortunate trend, namely, focusing on an individual's welfare rather than the good of the community as a whole. O' Donovan, *Principles in the Public Realm: The Dilemma of Christian Moral Witness* (Oxford: Clarendon, 1984), 6–8.

14   On the pernicious effects of the false dichotomy between political power and ethics, John Courtney Murray's remarks remain timeless: "It is the function of morality to command the use of power, to forbid it, to limit it, or, more in general, to define the ends for which power may or must be used and to judge the circumstances of its use. But moral principles cannot effectively impart this sense of direction to power until they have first, as it were, passed through the order of politics; that is, until they have first become incarnate in public policy. It is public policy in all its varied concretions that must be 'moralized' (to use an abused word in its good sense)." Murray, *We Hold These Truths*, 273.

15   Paul Marshall, "Universal Human Rights and the Role of the State," in Lugo, *Sovereignty at the Crossroads*, 153.

16 Alasdair MacIntyre, *After Virtue: A Study in Moral Theory*, 3rd ed. (Notre Dame, Ind.: University of Notre Dame Press, 2007). This work has also appeared in Danish, Polish, Spanish, Portuguese, French, German, Italian, Turkish, Chinese, and Japanese. MacIntyre, *Whose Justice? Which Rationality?* (Notre Dame, Ind.: University of Notre Dame Press, 1988).

17 MacIntyre, *After Virtue*, 70. Much of *Whose Justice* extends this line of reasoning.

18 In the now-famous concluding sentence of *After Virtue*, following MacIntyre's musings on the parallels between the Roman Empire's decline into the Dark Ages and the present cultural climate in Europe and North America, MacIntyre states that we are awaiting another St. Benedict. Herewith, of course, he is making reference to the emergence of monastic communities that in the seventh, eighth, and ninth centuries faithfully preserved what was of enduring value. And perhaps indeed it is this very choice of saints—Benedict of the monastic tradition—which explains why MacIntyre is so popular among cultural separatists. But whatever our problems with modernism, we are tempted to ask: might we not better await another *Augustine* rather than a Benedict, since it is not Benedict but Augustine who better exemplifies the reality of our two citizenships in a culture that, according to many, is (quite literally) crumbling around us? In a similar way, the concluding chapter of *Whose Justice*, with its teasing though grammatically conflicted title of "Contested Justices, Contested Rationalities," causes the reader to begin to be hopeful. Alas, nothing practical emerges here either, only the observation by MacIntyre that various "traditions of justice" can "survive very different environments." One can grant some merit in MacIntyre's argument that Aristotelian rationality, mediated through Aquinas, is as safe a place as any to begin thinking about justice, but I suspect that Aristotle and Aquinas both would have more substantively to say about justice as it expresses itself in a public and practical context than MacIntyre permits them to say.

19 For a very useful and worthy critique of this social-legal tendency, see Mary Ann Glendon, *Rights Talk: The Impoverishment of Political Discourse* (New York: Free Press, 1991).

20 Moreover, given the widespread aversion to natural-law thinking among Protestant thinkers in general, one should not be surprised at the degree of moral deficit characterizing contemporary religious thinking as it applies to responsible statecraft. Nevertheless, a discussion of human rights might be enriched from insights that stem from an understanding of "Christian social ethics" that is rooted in the natural-law tradition. While Marshall, "Universal Human Rights," 153–75, does not explicitly anchor his understanding of universal human rights in natural-law thinking, his analysis of the present deficiency in Western political thought is deft.

21 No contractual or positive legal right can account for one's basic right to life; such transcends human convention or adjudicating. At the same time, while health and life are a fundamental human "right," the degree or amount of health or life insurance is negotiable.

22 This essay is reproduced in Jerome Kohn, ed., *Hannah Arendt: Essays in Understanding, 1930–1954* (New York: Harcourt Brace, 1994), 133–35.

23 This post-WWII development has been corrected, observed, and examined by Nicholas Rengger and Renée Jeffery, "Moral Evil and International Relations," *SAIS Review* 25, no. 1 (2005): 3–4.

24 Thus, so-called political evil is none other than moral evil in the realm of IR and politics. In this regard, the suggestion by Rengger and Jeffery, "Moral Evil," 7, that "a [U.S.] president who claims to be a born-again Christian" appears to

"employ a Manichean view of evil in the world," thereby "championing heresy," simultaneously assumes too much and succumbs to the very dualism that they are criticizing. Moreover, Rengger and Jeffery curiously avoid acknowledging the fact that Ronald Reagan (who previously did the same of the Soviet Union) and John Paul II were indeed right.

25 To illustrate, what is perhaps most striking about Europe today is the degree of fear and loathing that characterizes the attitude of most nations toward their cultural and religious heritage. In this regard, see, e.g., Bruce Bawer, *While Europe Slept: How Radical Islam Is Destroying from Within* (New York: Broadway, 2007); Walter Laqueur, *The Last Days of Europe: Epitaph for an Old Continent* (New York: St. Martin's, 2007); Michael Burleigh, "Some European Perspectives on Terrorism," address to the Foreign Policy Research Institute Study Group, April 7, 2008, accessible at http://www.fpri.org/enotes/200805.burleigh.europeanperspectivesterrorism.html; Jytte Klausen, *The Islamic Challenge: Politics and Religion in Western Europe* (Oxford: Oxford University Press, 2005); and George Weigel, *The Cube and the Cathedral: Europe, America, and Politics without God* (New York: Basic, 2005).

26 Nina Shea, "Genocide Doesn't Just Happen," *National Review Online*, June 1, 2007.

27 Stanley Hoffmann, "The Politics and Ethics of Military Intervention," *Survival* 37, no. 4 (1995): 30–32, is correct to insist that it is wrong to assume that the dilemma of intervention, which is as old as international relations, has become particularly salient only (or mainly) in the post–Cold War era.

28 On the possibilities of this necessary shift, see Jennifer M. Welsh, ed., *Humanitarian Intervention and International Relations* (Oxford: Oxford University Press, 2003); and Thomas G. Weiss, *Humanitarian Intervention: Ideas in Action* (Cambridge: Polity, 2007), esp. chap. 4.

29 Michael Walzer's analogy in this regard is helpful: in foreign affairs, political and territorial sovereignty in our day function much like individual rights in the domestic sphere; that is, they take on a near-sacred cast. See Walzer, *Just and Unjust Wars: A Moral Argument with Historical Illustrations*, 2nd ed. (New York: Basic, 1992), 58–64.

30 Thomas G. Weiss, "Principles, Politics, and Humanitarian Action," *Ethics & International Affairs* 13 (1999): 1–2; and more recently, Weiss, *Humanitarian Intervention*, 73–87.

31 Weiss ("Principles," 1–5) distinguishes between four groups of humanitarians who disagree along political and strategic lines—classicists, minimalists, maximalists, and solidarists. On a scale of political involvement, classicists are committed (at least ideologically) to little or no political involvement, while solidarists confront hostile governments and commit themselves to partisan public policy strategies. See as well Peter J. Hoffman and Thomas G. Weiss, *Sword and Salve: Confronting New Wars and Humanitarian Crises* (Lanham, Md.: Rowman & Littlefield, 2006), 84–85.

32 Jean Bethke Elshtain has persuasively argued for a holistic approach to this moral-political reality in "International Justice as Equal Regard and the Use of Force," *Ethics & International Affairs* 17, no. 2 (2003): 63–70.

33 So, persuasively, Fernando R. Tesón, "Self-Defense in International Law and Rights of Persons," *Ethics & International Affairs* 18, no. 1 (2004): 87–91. Tesón's argument should be noncontroversial: when tyrants oppose a humanitarian (or military) intervention that is justified, they are not defending the state; rather, they are grasping at power and defending themselves.

34 A state that claims sovereignty, in the words of Stanley Hoffmann, "deserves

respect only as long as it protects the basic rights of its subjects. It is from their rights that it derives its own. When it violates them, what Walzer called the 'presumption of fit' between the government and the governed vanishes, and the state's claim to full sovereignty falls with it" ("Politics and Ethics," 35).

35 By "classical just-war" reasoning, I refer to the consensus regarding severely qualifying war and coercive force that extends from the period of Ambrose and Augustine through Gratian and Aquinas to Luther, Vitoria, Suárez, and Grotius and down to the present. This tradition mirrors both continuity and refinement— "refinement" in the sense that the tradition undergoes periodic reexamination and new applications based on the cultural context. In my view, there is something to be said for Joseph Boyle's argument that classical just-war theory issued out of a wider view of moral and social life and focused on the common good of a polity, whereas contemporary construals of the same tend to agonize over border crossings or violating territorial sovereignty per se rather than the demands of justice. Joseph Boyle, "Traditional Just War Theory and Humanitarian Intervention," in *Humanitarian Intervention*, Nomos 47, ed. Terry Nardin and Melissa S. Williams (New York: New York University Press, 2006), 33–34.

36 Boyle, "Traditional Just War Theory," 66.

37 Hereon see, e.g., Taylor B. Seybolt, "The Myth of Neutrality," *Peace Review* 8 (1996): 521–27; Richard Betts, "The Delusion of Impartial Intervention," *Foreign Affairs* 73, no. 6 (1994): 20–33; and Weiss, "Principles," 10–21.

38 Hadley Arkes, *First Things: An Inquiry into the First Principles of Morals and Justice* (Princeton: Princeton University Press, 1986). Here Arkes is interacting with Michael Walzer's argument on the need for humanitarian intervention, derived from chapters 6 and 16 of *Just and Unjust Wars*.

39 Walzer, *Just and Unjust Wars*, 107.

40 I readily grant that stopping ethnic cleansing, genocide, civil war, and the like constitutes the *beginnings* of HI and that much political and moral wisdom is needed, as part of a reconstructive project, to establish the authority of local political leaders and to begin rebuilding the nation's infrastructure. Nevertheless, our shared humanity and transcendent notions of justice require that we begin at the point of human need and suffering, namely, by removing the source of dehumanizing and oppressive injustice.

41 Arkes, *First Things*, 234 (emphasis in original).

42 Arkes, *First Things*, 235–36.

43 Todd Gitlin, "Do Less Harm: The Lesser Evil of Non-Intervention," *World Affairs* (Summer 2008), available at http://www.worldaffairsjournal.org/2008%20-%20 summer/full-gitlin.html.

44 Walzer, *Just and Unjust Wars*, 262.

45 Alex J. Bellamy, *Just Wars: From Cicero to Iraq* (Cambridge: Polity, 2006), 203–4.

46 So Larry Minear and Thomas G. Weiss, *Mercy Under Fire* (Boulder, Colo.: Westview, 1995), 63.

47 Few have argued this more lucidly than John Langan, "Humanitarian Intervention: From Concept to Reality," in *Close Calls: Intervention, Terrorism, Missile Defense, and "Just War" Today*, ed. Elliott Abrams (Washington, D.C.: Ethics and Public Policy Center, 1998), 109–24.

48 James Carafano and Dana Dillon, "Winning the Peace: Principles for Post-Conflict Operations," *Heritage Foundation Backgrounder* #1859, June 13, 2003, available at http://www.heritage.org/research/nationalsecurity/bg1859.cfm.

49 Similarly, the *Congressional Research Service Report for Congress* (Washington, D.C.: Congressional Research Service, 1995), appendix I, distinguishes between "peacemaking," "peacekeeping," "peace enforcement," and "peace-building."

50 Andrew Natsios, "Complex Humanitarian Emergencies and Moral Choice," in Abrams, *Close Calls*, 125–43. Barbara Harff, "No Lessons Learned from the Holocaust? Assessing Risks of Genocide and Political Mass Murder since 1955," *American Political Science Review* 97, no. 1 (2003): 57–74, estimates that of 126 instances of internal war and regime collapse that occurred between 1955 and 1997, genocide or politicide evolved from 35 of these episodes of state failure.

51 Stanley Hoffmann, "The Politics and Ethics of Military Intervention," *Survival* 37, no. 4 (1995–1996): 31. Similarly, David A. Crocker, "Reckoning with Past Wrongs: A Normative Framework," *Ethics & International Affairs* 13 (1999): 43–44, distinguishes more broadly between post-conflict societies such as Bosnia, Cambodia, and Rwanda, which aspire to democratic transition, and authoritarian or conflict-ridden societies like former Yugoslavia, Peru, and Indonesia, which were victims of civil war or internal strife.

52 Natsios, "Complex Humanitarian Emergencies," 126.

53 Natsios, "Complex Humanitarian Emergencies," 127.

54 William J. Lahneman, "Military Intervention: Lessons for the Twenty-First Century," in *Military Intervention: Cases in Context for the Twenty-First Century*, ed. William J. Lahneman, (Lanham, Md.: Rowman & Littlefield, 2004), 167–68.

55 Surely, there are multiple factors that contribute to nations' reticence in the present day to intervene. Not least among these are the perception, however accurate or inaccurate, of U.S. involvement in Afghanistan and Iraq, the psychological effect created by the media in covering international disasters, developed nations' wish to avoid casualties to national troops where national interests are not at stake, the preference to work through UN-sanctioned responses, and the politics of obstruction at the level of the UN Security Council.

56 So Jean Bethke Elshtain, "Just War and Humanitarian Intervention," *Ideas* 8, no. 2 (2001): 2.

57 This wider assumption undergirds two very different volumes by Jean Bethke Elshtain, *Augustine and the Limits of Power* (Notre Dame, Ind.: University of Notre Dame Press, 1991); and Elshtain, *Just War Against Terror: The Burden of American Power in a Violent World* (New York: Basic, 2003).

58 And as recent experiences in Afghanistan and Iraq have demonstrated, yet a third category—*ius post bellum*, i.e., justice after war—needs far greater forethought and attention in our day. The need for *post bellum* moral reflection is discussed in Charles and Corey, *Justice in an Age of Terror*.

59 Hence, Aquinas can argue that "those who are attacked should be attacked because they deserve it on account of some fault." *Summa Theologica*, trans. Fathers of the English Dominican Province (New York: Benziger Bros., 1947), 2.2 Q. 40 [hereafter *S.T.*].

60 Jean Bethke Elshtain, "What Is a Just War?" chap. 3 in *Just War Against Terror*, presses this distinction with considerable cogency.

61 Hoffmann, "Politics and Ethics," 38.

62 Although just cause is rooted in (and responds to) the violation of basic human rights, it needs reiteration that the *defense* of these rights, not merely the punishment of those who violate them, constitutes just cause. See, in this regard, Boyle, "Traditional Just War Theory," 53–54.

63 Arkes, *First Things*, 268–71, argues this point quite lucidly.

64 The distinction between the right and the duty to intervene is helpfully discussed by C. A. J. Coady in *The Ethics of Armed Humanitarian Intervention* (Washington, D.C.: United States Institute of Peace, 2002), 24–25.

65 Aquinas *S.T.* 2.2 Q. 40.

66 So, e.g., Augustine *Contra Faustum* 22.74 (accessible at http://www.newadvent.org/fathers/1406.htm); and Aquinas *S.T.* 2.2 Q. 40.

67   Aquinas, *S.T.* 2.2 Q. 40. Bellamy, *Just War*, 208–11, helpfully cites the symbiotic link between just cause and proper authority as a principal contribution of the just-war tradition to HI. Without authorized intervention, we might set the threshold too high or too low.

68   Four potential sources of "right authority" are cited by Bellamy in *Just War*: invitation of the host country, the UN Security Council, individual states, and regional organizations. Yet neither regional nor worldwide authority constitutes, in Thomistic terms, the authority of the political sovereign; the common good cannot be guarded by some version of a "superpolity." That is, a "superpolity" possesses neither the capacity for governance nor the normative representation with which the "prince" (so Aquinas) or the "magistrate" (so the New Testament) is endowed. In this regard I am indebted to the discussion of "proper authority" which is found in Boyle, "Traditional Just War Theory," 36–38.

69   While nations should work in concert through groups like the UN, NATO, and the African Organization of Unity, the reality is that these groups might *block* what is in fact morally necessary because intervention might not serve their own interests.

70   It goes without saying that in humanitarian debate the issue of proper authority is one of the most contentious. Three general positions can be identified: (1) HI must be authorized by the UN Security Council; (2) HI must be authorized by some democratic alliance of states; and (3) unauthorized HI by democratic states may be legitimate, absent formal approval by the UN or other states. For a clear-sighted discussion of the difficulties and moral inadequacies of being limited by the UN Security Council, see Fernando R. Tesón, "Ending Tyranny in Iraq," *Ethics & International Affairs* 19, no. 2 (2005): 16–19.

71   Michael Walzer, *Arguing about War* (New Haven: Yale University Press, 2004), 88.

72   Not only is this priority implied in Aquinas' treatment (*S.T.* 2.2 Q. 40), it is affirmed by present-day just-war theorists such as Michael Walzer and James Turner Johnson. Most contemporary discussions of just-war criteria, by contrast, fail to make the critical distinction between primary and secondary (i.e., prudential) criteria.

73   This term derives from Jean Bethke Elshtain. See *inter alia* her essay "Just War," 18–21.

74   Elshtain, "Just War," 18–19.

75   Elshtain, "Just War," 19.

76   John Hittinger, "Just War and Defense Policy," in *Natural Law and Contemporary Public Policy*, ed. David F. Forte (Washington, D.C.: Georgetown University Press, 1998), 342.

77   This reveals my fundamental assumption that retributive justice is not merely "retributive" as most understand the concept; rather, it has restorative and pedagogical components that are indispensable to "civil" society. Here I refer the reader to my discussion of the distinction between retribution and revenge (i.e., retributivism) in *Retrieving the Natural Law: A Return to Moral First Things*, Critical Issues in Bioethics (Grand Rapids: Eerdmans, 2008), 305–11.

78   Elshtain, "International Justice," 67.

79   United Nations General Assembly, "Universal Declaration of Human Rights," General Assembly Resolution 217A, December 10, 1948.

80   United Nations General Assembly, "Convention on the Prevention and Punishment of the Crime of Genocide," General Assembly Resolution 260A, December 9, 1948.

81   Thomas G. Weiss and Cindy Collins, *Humanitarian Challenges and Intervention*, 2nd ed. (Boulder, Colo.: Westview, 2000), 19.

82   Most estimates range between 800,000 and 1.25 million people slaughtered. For a rather sobering in-depth account of how this remarkable brutality was prepared, and subsequently ignored, by the international community, see Linda Melvern, "A Conspiracy to Murder: The Rwandan Genocide," parliamentary lecture, London, May 18, 2004, available at http://www.lindamelvern.com/parliament_lecture.htm.

83   It remains to be seen whether the 2001 report *The Responsibility to Protect*, published by the International Commission on Intervention and State Sovereignty and adopted at the United Nations World Summit in 2005, will change the tenor of international response to "humanitarian catastrophes," notwithstanding the optimism of people like Anthony Lewis in "The Challenge of Global Justice Now," *Daedalus* 132, no. 1 (2003): 8. No region of the world serves as a litmus test for "R2P," as it is called, as the continent of Africa. So writes Thelma Ekiyor, of the West Africa Civil Society Institute, in "The Responsibility to Protect (R2P): A Way Forward—Or Rather Part of the Problem?" *Foreign Voices* 1 (2008): 3: "While there is acceptance that the responsibility for safeguarding international peace and security lies with the UN Security Council, limited political will in the Security Council to readily intervene in past African crises has generated support for 'African solutions to African problems.'" Ekiyor cites Sudan as a case in point: "On the one hand, international accord exists that the inhuman victimization, rape and killings of the Darfurians in Sudan is abominable, and that the Khartoum government's unwillingness and increasing inability to protect civilians is a clear case for reaction by the international community. On the other hand, galvanizing decisive support for that reaction has been slow. The old problem of power struggles and competing agendas in the [UN] Security Council has hindered action; Russia and China with economic ties with Sudan are not in favour of a robust intervention, while the United States[,] though speaking forcefully against the Khartoum government, is weakened by the Iraq experience and is hesitant to intervene in another Islamic State" (4).

84   None has framed this matter more poignantly than Michael Walzer in "The Politics of Rescue," *Social Research* 62, no. 1 (1995): 53–66, reproduced more recently in Walzer, *Arguing about War*, 67–81.

85   Few have argued this as persuasively as Arkes, *First Things*, 288–308.

86   It is difficult to disagree with Walzer ("Politics of Rescue," 53–54) on this point. This observation, however, should not be construed as an argument against the just-war consideration of calculating the chances of success in intervention. Rather, our argument is only intended to underscore the *morality* of intervention: resisting evil cannot be reduced to utilitarian calculus.

87   Hereon see especially chapters 12 ("The Morality of Intervention") and 13 ("The Obligation to Rescue and Supererogatory Acts") in Arkes, *First Things*, whose thoughtful argument and rationale for intervention on moral grounds commends itself to the reader.

88   Arkes, *First Things*, 290.

89   Arkes, *First Things*, 291.

90   The transcript of this address appeared in the *Washington Post*, February 2, 1997, C4. Goldstone's comments highlight an important truth: justice entails retribution (over against mere revenge), and it does not disregard the past. Given the moral significance of personal accountability, the identity of violators of basic human rights, on the one hand, and of those who heroically acted to prevent those violations, on the other hand, should be brought to light and made public. See in this regard Crocker, "Reckoning with Past Wrongs," 49–55.

91 Ramsey, "Ethics of Intervention," 305.
92 Ramsey, "Ethics of Intervention," 306. Ramsey, however, was careful to distinguish between ultimate and penultimate grounds for intervention (296–308). In the end, justification for intervening was predicated upon and to be guided by classical just-war moral criteria (296–97, 307), which presume justice to be *universal and non-fluid* in nature, and hence, the regulative ideal of politics.
93 Humanitarian scholar Simon Chesterton, in assessing the international catastrophes that prompted interventions during the 1990s, writes that "there is a desperate need for more research on the prevention and amelioration of such crises." Chesterton, *Just War or Just Peace? Humanitarian Intervention and International Law* (Oxford: Oxford University Press, 2001), 224. I am inclined to disagree. The "desperate need" is that of moral backbone and political will, not the absence of research data.
94 These two forms of intervention are considered by Michael Walzer in *Arguing about War*, 76–77.
95 I am well aware of the potential reaction from the reader that my argument in this essay amounts to "imperialism"—a word that is thrown around much these days. But the perspective on HI that I am defending differs greatly from "imperialism" insofar as (a) it entails no imposition of a permanent external power structure (but rather assumes that a collapsed nation will need assistance in rebuilding structure from within), and (b) unlike past episodes of imperialism, it entails no "colonization." The very fear of public or world perception itself is sufficient to prevent a moral response to catastrophe, and thus, the question of HI in our day calls for moral honesty as well as courage. And, from the standpoint of Christian faith, it is a matter of stewardship.
96 Proverbs 24:10-12.

Chapter 8

1 The exact number of countries that have become democracies since the "third wave" began in 1974 is not clear. In his *The Third Wave: Democratization in the Late Twentieth Century* (Norman: University of Oklahoma Press, 1991), Samuel P. Huntington documents thirty transitions between 1974 and 1989. Freedom House reports that the number of "free" countries increased by thirteen from 1989 to 2004. See Freedom House, "Russia Downgraded to 'Not Free,'" press release (Washington, D.C.: Freedom House, 2004); and Freedom House, *Freedom in the World 2005: The Annual Survey of Political Rights and Civil Liberties* (Washington, D.C.: Freedom House, 2005). Democracy theorist Larry Diamond estimates that between 1974 and 1996, between thirty-six and seventy-seven states became democracies, depending on how one counts democratization exactly. See Diamond, "Is the Third Wave of Democratization Over? An Empirical Assessment" (Kellogg Institute for International Studies Working Paper Series, no. 236, March 1997).
2 On the liberal peace, see Roland Paris, "Peacebuilding and the Limits of Liberal Internationalism," *International Security* 22, no. 2 (1997); Oliver P. Richmond, "The Problem of Peace: Understanding the 'Liberal Peace,'" *Conflict, Security, & Development* 6, no. 3 (2006).
3 Timothy Garton Ash, "True Confessions," *New York Review of Books* 44 (1997): 37–38; Rajeev Bhargava, "Restoring Decency to Barbaric Societies," in *Truth v. Justice: The Morality of Truth Commissions*, ed. Robert Rotberg and Dennis Thompson (Princeton: Princeton University Press, 2000), 60–63; David A. Crocker, "Retribution and Reconciliation," *Philosophy and Public Policy* 20, no. 1 (2000): 6;

David A. Crocker, "Truth Commissions, Transitional Justice, and Civil Society," in Rotberg and Thompson, *Truth v. Justice*, 108; Amy Gutmann and Dennis Thompson, "The Moral Foundations of Truth Commissions," in Rotberg and Thompson, *Truth v. Justice*, 32–33; Michael Ignatieff, "Articles of Faith," *Index on Censorship* 25, no. 5 (1996): 111–13, 21–22.

4   Kent Greenawalt, "Amnesty's Justice," in Rotberg and Thompson, *Truth v. Justice*, 199; Gutmann and Thompson, "Moral Foundations."

5   Mohammed Abu-Nimer, *Nonviolence and Peace Building in Islam* (Gainesville: University Press of Florida, 2003); John W. De Gruchy, *Reconciliation: Restoring Justice* (Minneapolis: Fortress, 2003); Marc Gopin, *Between Eden and Armageddon: The Future of World Religions, Violence, and Peacemaking* (Oxford: Oxford University Press, 2000); Alan Torrance, "The Theological Grounds for Advocating Forgiveness and Reconciliation in the Sociopolitical Realm," in Philpott, *Politics of Past Evil*, 45–86; Miroslav Volf, *Exclusion and Embrace: A Theological Exploration of Identity, Otherness, and Reconciliation* (Nashville: Abingdon, 1996).

6   See Elizabeth Achtemeier, "Righteousness in the OT," in *The Interpreter's Dictionary of the Bible*, ed. G. A. Buttrick (Nashville: Abingdon, 1962); Christopher D. Marshall, *Beyond Retribution: A New Testament Vision for Justice, Crime and Punishment* (Grand Rapids: Eerdmans, 2001).

7   De Gruchy, *Reconciliation*, 46, 51.

8   Scriptural references are taken from the New International Version unless otherwise indicated.

9   Perry Yoder, *Shalom: The Bible's Word for Salvation, Justice, and Peace* (Newton, Kans.: Faith and Life, 1987), 10–23; Howard Zehr, *Changing Lenses* (Scottdale, Pa.: Herald, 1990), 130–32.

10   Ulrich Mauser, *The Gospel of Peace: A Scriptural Message for Today's World* (Louisville, Ky.: Westminster John Knox, 1992), 33.

11   Pope John Paul II, *Dives in Misericordia*, encyclical, November 30, 1980, §6. MacIntyre finds a similar conception of mercy in the thought of Thomas Aquinas. See Alasdair C. MacIntyre, *Dependent Rational Animals: Why Human Beings Need the Virtues* (Chicago, Ill.: Open Court, 1999), 124–25.

12   The Jewish Study Bible translates *hesed* here as goodness rather than mercy. Other translations of the bible, like the NIV, which I use here, render it as "mercy."

13   See Jon D. Levenson, *Creation and the Persistence of Evil* (Princeton: Princeton University Press, 1988); Susan Neiman, *Evil in Modern Thought: An Alternative History of Philosophy* (Princeton: Princeton University Press, 2002).

14   Matthew 12:20. See also N. T. Wright, *Evil and the Justice of God* (Downers Grove, Ill.: InterVarsity, 2006), 64. Jesus' restorative mission is also revealed in the words with which he inaugurates his ministry in the Gospel of Luke: "The Spirit of the Lord is on me, because he has anointed me to preach good news to the poor. He has sent me to proclaim freedom for the prisoners and recovery of sight for the blind, to release the oppressed, to proclaim the year of the Lord's favor" (4:18). Here, he quotes from Isaiah 61:1-2; see also Isaiah 58:6.

15   See Peter Schmiechen, *Saving Power: Theories of Atonement and Forms of the Church* (Grand Rapids: Eerdmans, 2005), 37–45.

16   De Gruchy, *Reconciliation*, 44–76.

17   See, among his many other writings, Gustavo Gutiérrez, *A Theology of Liberation*, trans. Sister Caridad Inda and John Eagleson (Maryknoll, N.Y.: Orbis, 1988).

18   See Gutiérrez, *Theology of Liberation*; Jürgen Moltmann, *The Crucified God: The Cross of Christ as the Foundation and Criticism of Christian Theology* (Minneapolis: Fortress, 1993).

19   Abu-Nimer, *Nonviolence and Peace Building*, 60; Majid Khadduri, *The Islamic*

Conception of Justice (Baltimore: Johns Hopkins University Press, 1984), 3–12; Carol Schersten LaHurd, "'So That the Sinner Will Repent': Forgiveness in Islam and Christianity," *Dialog* 35, no. 4 (1996): 28; A. Rashied Omar, "Between Compassion and Justice: Locating an Islamic Definition of Peace," *Peace Colloquy* 7 (2005), 9.

20   Abdulaziz Abdulhussein Sachedina, *The Islamic Roots of Democratic Pluralism* (New York: Oxford University Press, 2001), 106.

21   Nawal H. Ammar, "Restorative Justice in Islam: Theory and Practice," in *The Spiritual Roots of Restorative Justice*, ed. Michael L. Hadley (Albany: State University of New York Press, 2001), 169–73.

22   Abu-Nimer, *Nonviolence and Peace Building*, 102–8; George E. Irani and Nathan C. Funk, "Rituals of Reconciliation: Arab-Islamic Perspectives," *Arab Studies Quarterly* 20, no. 4 (1998).

23   On the importance of practices in ethics, see Alasdair MacIntyre, *After Virtue: A Study in Moral Theory*, 2nd ed. (Notre Dame, Ind.: University of Notre Dame Press, 1984), 187.

24   Susan Sachs, "Iraqis Seek Justice, or Vengeance, for Victims of the Killing Fields," *The New York Times*, November 4, 2003.

25   On religion and nationalism in Iraq, see Juan R. I. Cole, "The Rise of Religious and Ethnic Mass Politics in Iraq," in *Religion and Nationalism in Iraq*, ed. David Little and Donald Swearer (Cambridge, Mass.: Harvard University Press, 2006).

26   Nouri Al-Maliki, "Iraq PM Unveils National Reconciliation Plan," *Telegraph*, June 26, 2006, http://www.telegraph.co.uk/. News reports differ about exactly how many points the reconciliation plan contains. On the South African influence, see Mohamed Hasni, "Iraq Reconciliation Plan Inspired by South Africa," *Mail & Guardian Online*, June 25, 2006, http://www.mg.co.za/.

27   In October 2006, fifty *ulema* (religious scholars) from both the Sunni and Shiite communities convened under the auspices of the fifty-seven-state Organization of the Islamic Conference to develop and issue the Makkah Document, a call for reconciliation and an end to violence among Muslims that elicited the approval and endorsement of Prime Minister Maliki and top religious leaders Ali Al-Sistani and Moqtada Sadr. Then, in December 2006, a "National Reconciliation Conference" brought together major Iraqi government and religious leaders, including Prime Minster Maliki, to attempt to settle differences. In October 2007, the United States Institute of Peace, in partnership with the U.S. military, the State Department, and the United States Agency for International Development, convened in Baghdad a reconciliation conference of thirty-one tribal sheikhs from Mahmoudiya. On the latter, see United States Institute of Peace, "USIP-Facilitated Iraq Reconciliation Agreement a Key Breakthrough for Stability Effort in South Baghdad's 'Triangle of Death,'" news release, October 19, 2007, http://www.usip.org/newsroom/news/usip-facilitated-iraq-reconciliation-agreement-key-breakthrough-stability-effort-south.

28   U.S. Deputy Secretary of State John D. Negroponte said in December 2007 that "the security surge had delivered significant results . . . Now progress on political reconciliation, including key national legislation as well as economic advances, is needed to consolidate the gains. If progress is not made on these fronts we risk falling back toward the more violent habits of the past." Quoted in Peter Graff and Waleed Ibrahim, "U.S. Seeks Political Gains; Sunnis End Boycott," *Boston Globe*, December 2, 2007.

29   The most thorough description of an official political approach to reconciliation that I have found is that of the Iraq Study Group, *Iraq Study Group Report: The Way Forward—A New Approach* (New York: Vintage). See pp. 64–70 in particular.

30 See, e.g., M. Cherif Bassiouni, *Iraq Post-Conflict Justice: A Proposed Comprehensive Plan* (Chicago: DePaul University International Human Rights Law Institute, 2004), http://www.law.depaul.edu/centers_institutes/ihrli/downloads/Iraq_Proposal_04.pdf.

31 By the end of 2007, the death rate in Iraq had fallen to one-fifth of what it was a year earlier and ethno-sectarian violence was mostly limited to areas west of Baghdad and Rusafa. See U.S. Department of Defense, *Measuring Stability and Security in Iraq: Report to Congress in Accordance with the Department of Defense Appropriations Act 2007* (Washington, D.C., 2007), 18.

32 International Center for Transitional Justice and Human Rights Center, University of California, Berkeley, *Iraqi Voices: Attitudes Towards Transitional Justice and Social Reconstruction*, Occasional Paper (New York: International Center for Transitional Justice, May 2004), 38, see 37–40.

33 *Iraqi Voices*, 40; Robert F. Worth, "The Struggle for Iraq: The Past; Planning a Museum to Tell Iraq's Story," *The New York Times*, September 9, 2003.

34 *Iraqi Voices*, 40.

35 Stuart E. Eizenstat, "Reconciliation, Not Just Reconstruction," *The New York Times*, July 4, 2003.

36 C. Marshall, *Beyond Retribution*, 97–144.

37 For an excellent analysis of the justice in Saddam's trial and execution, see John D. Carlson, "Discerning Justice in the Trial and Execution of Saddam Hussein," in *Enemy Combatants, Terrorism, and Armed Conflict Law: A Guide to the Issues*, ed. David K. Linnan (Westport, Conn.: Praeger Security International, 2008).

38 U.S. Department of Defense, *Measuring Stability*.

39 James Phillips, "Proposed Timetables for U.S. Withdrawal Would Sabotage Reconciliation in Iraq," Heritage Foundation WebMemo #1632, September 31, 2007, http://www.heritage.org/Research/MiddleEast/wm1632.cfm.

40 Iraq Study Group, *Iraq Study Group Report*, 68.

41 On the other gatherings, see note 26. On the work of Canon White, see Robert McFarlane, "The Iraqi 'Nation,'" *Wall Street Journal*, June 27 2007; Foundation for Relief and Reconciliation in the Middle East, "Peace Progress in Cairo," Foundation for Relief and Reconciliation in the Middle East, *News and Prayer Letter*, no. 7 (London: Naaman Trust, November 2007).

Chapter 9

Epigraph (top). Dorothy L. Sayers, *Begin Here: A War-Time Essay* (London: Victor Gollancz, 1940), 80.

Epigraph (bottom). William J. Lederer and Eugene Burdick, *The Ugly American* (New York: Fawcett Crest, 1958), 226.

1 Gilles Kepel, *The Revenge of God* (University Park: Penn State University Press, 1994); Godfrey Hodgson, "God Fights Back," in *People's Century* (London: BBC Books, 1996), 251; Mark Juergensmeyer, *Terror in the Mind of God* (Berkeley: University of California Press, 2000). McTernan's view is different, and by speaking instead of "violence in God's name" he indicates that it is *our* violence projected onto a deity, rather than the deity's inherent violence, that is at issue. This suggests a critical, reflexive recognition that *we* are very much a part of what is being studied in IR and not objectively set apart from it. Oliver McTernan, *Violence in God's Name: Religion in an Age of Global Conflict* (London: Darton, Longman, Todd, 2003).

2 See, e.g., the American Social Science Research Council (SSRC) working group on Religion and International Affairs, and SSRC's academic blog *The Immanent*

Frame; the Program on Religion, Diplomacy, and International Affairs at the Liechtenstein Institute on Self-Determination, initiated by Princeton University; the Henry R. Luce Foundation's Initiative on Religion and International Affairs, and the British International Studies Association (BISA) working group on International Relations, Security, and Religion.

3   What the religious turn may be saying about internal developments within religious communities in the United States and how they are responding to the global resurgence of religion would require a separate study.

4   Daniel Philpott sets out the amount of work still to be done in this regard in "Has the Study of Global Politics Found Religion?" *Annual Review of Political Science* 12 (2009): 183–202.

5   Seiple and Hoover, *Religion and Security*.

6   Thomas, *Global Resurgence*, chap. 6 (entitled "'Creating a Just and Durable Peace': Religion and International Cooperation"), 149–72; Heather Warren, *Theologians of a New World Order: Reinhold Niebuhr and the Christian Realists, 1920–1948* (Oxford: Oxford University Press, 1997), John Nurser, *For All Peoples and All Nations: Christian Churches and Human Rights* (Geneva: World Council of Churches, 2005).

7   Support for the theory of secularization has been declining over the past twenty years due to the revisionist work of Peter Berger, Robert Wuthnow, Grace Davie, Mary Douglas, and others. Steve Bruce, Ronald Inglehart, and Pippa Norris remain significant exceptions.

8   It was the great *Western* European sociologists who created this "grand narrative" of secularization and modernization. The intellectual traditions of *central* Europe, including their views of religious toleration, are only now being reintegrated into IR in the West. At the time of the "wars of religion" in France, the new Polish-Lithuanian Commonwealth passed laws to support religious toleration in response to the St. Bartholomew's Day massacre in 1572. Unexpectedly, the commonwealth's multinational and multireligious history turns out to be increasingly relevant to Europe today.

9   Peter Berger, Grace Davie, and Effie Fokas, *Religious America, Secular Europe? A Theme and Variations* (London: Ashgate, 2008).

10   Charles Reynolds, *Theory and Explanation in International Politics* (Oxford: Martin Robertson, 1973); Martin Hollis and Steve Smith, *Explaining and Understanding International Relations* (Oxford: Clarendon, 1991); Malja Kurki, "Causes of a Divided Discipline: Rethinking the Concept of Cause in International Relations Theory," *Review of International Studies* 32, no. 2 (2006): 189–216.

11   Scott M. Thomas, "Faith, History, and Martin Wight: The Role of Religion in the Historical Sociology of the English School of International Relations," *International Affairs* 77, no. 4 (2001): 905–29; Adda B. Bozeman, *Politics & Culture in International History* (New Brunswick, N.J.: Transaction, 1994).

12   Thomas, *Global Resurgence*.

13   David Aikman, "The Great Revival: Understanding Religious Fundamentalism," *Foreign Affairs* 82, no. 4 (2003): 188–93.

14   Hurd, *Politics of Secularism*.

15   Hurd, e.g., raises the question of how the rise of the AKP, the main Islamic party in Turkey, should be interpreted: As "political Islam"—a theocratic threat to Turkey's secular democracy (something for the EU to avoid)? Or as a newly emerging Islamic model of religious differentiation and accommodation (something for the EU to embrace)?

16   W. B. Gallie, "Essentially Contested Concepts," in *Philosophy and the Historical Understanding* (London: Chatto & Windus, 1964), 157–91.

17   Philpott, "Religious Roots," 206–45.

18   Witness the way Ikenberry, e.g., characterizes the global resurgence of religion as
     "*wreaking havoc* on old traditions of diplomacy, development, and Western hege-
     mony, and transforming international affairs in the process" (emphasis added).
     See G. John Inkenberry's review of Thomas, *Global Resurgence*, *Foreign Affairs* 84,
     no. 3 (2005), 132–33.
19   For some of the growing literature, see Daniel Philpott, "Westphalia and Sov-
     ereignty in International Society," *Political Studies* 47, no. 3 (1999): 566–89;
     Daniel Philpott, *Revolutions in Sovereignty: How Ideas Shaped Modern International
     Relations* (Princeton: Princeton University Press, 2001); Stephen Krasner, "Com-
     promising Westphalia," *International Security* 20, no. 3 (1995): 115–51; Andreas
     Osiander, "Sovereignty, International Relations, and the Westphalian Myth,"
     International Organization 55, no. 2 (2001): 251–87; Benno Teschke, "Theoriz-
     ing the Westphalian System of States: International Relations from Absolutism
     to Capitalism," *European Journal of International Relations* 8, no. 1 (2002): 5–48;
     and Benno Teschke, *The Myth of 1648: Class, Geopolitics and the Making of Modern
     International Relations* (London: Verso, 2003).
20   Christian Reus-Smit, *The Moral Purpose of the State* (Princeton: Princeton Univer-
     sity Press, 1999); Friedrich Kratochwil, "Sovereignty as Dominium: Is There a
     Right to Humanitarian Intervention?" in *Beyond Westphalia: State Sovereignty and
     International Intervention*, ed. Gene M. Lyons and Michael Mastanduno (Balti-
     more: Johns Hopkins University Press, 1995), 21–42.
21   Bruce Kuklick, *Blind Oracles: Intellectuals and War from Kennan to Kissinger* (Princ-
     eton: Princeton University Press, 2006).
22   Contrary to popular opinion, the "ugly American" is the hero in this book, and
     he represents the opposite of U.S. imperialism or ethnocentrism. The term refers
     to a rather "ugly" guy, Homer Atkins, a U.S. foreign aid worker who learned the
     local language (unlike the U.S. embassy personnel, including the ambassador),
     lived happily in a hut among the ordinary people of Sarkhan (read: Vietnam),
     and saw that they needed what we now call "appropriate technology"—water
     pumps run by bicycles to help irrigate their rice fields—rather than the big
     dams, prestige projects, and military roads the U.S. government wanted to
     build for them (with congressional support, since the funding would help the
     industries back home in their districts), and which were being preached to them
     by arrogant, ethnocentric, top bureaucrats in Washington and in the local U.S.
     embassy. Lederer and Burdick, *The Ugly American*, 226. (See also Adam Roberts,
     "Buddhism and Politics in South Vietnam," *World Today* 21 [1965]: 240–50.)
     While the U.S. ambassabor knew little about Sarkhan, the Soviet ambassador
     studied at the Moscow School for Asian Areas where he learned to read and write
     Sarkhanese. He read Sarkhanese drama and literature and regularly attended
     lectures in Buddhist religion and practices. He arrived exactly one week after the
     new U.S. ambassador but the very next day traveled to the great monastery on
     the outskirts of the capital city to pay his respects to the Chief Abbot, the leader
     of all Buddhists in the area (*The Ugly American*, 30–37). What happened in real
     life? When Andrei Gromyko was appointed Soviet ambassador to the United
     States Stalin urged him to attend an American church each Sunday since this
     would provide him with unique insights into the American mindset and value
     system (Inboden, *Religion and American Foreign Policy*, 1). On China, Thomas F.
     Farr writes: "A few years ago the new American ambassador to Beijing was asked
     for his thoughts about China's persecution of underground Protestant house
     churches. 'What,' he asked, 'is a house church?' The State Department's briefings
     for the envoy had evidently omitted the subject. And he probably saw questions
     of religion as largely irrelevant to his mission." ("Cold War Religion," *First Things*
     194 [2009], 47.)

23   Reuel Marc Gerecht, "The Counterterrorist Myth," *Atlantic Monthly*, July/August 2001.

24   So after Bush's militant unilateralism the United States is relearning the virtue of diplomacy, not as an alternative to power but as a complement to power— something the early English School argued a half century ago. Jakub Grygiel, "The Diplomacy Fallacy," *American Interest* 3, no. 5 (2008): 26–35.

25   My analysis of the challenges still facing the study of religion in IR complements that proposed by Daniel Philpott, "Study of Global Politics," 198–99. Philpott lists the following: a better understanding of religion's relationship to modernity, more studies that take religious actors themselves as the unit of analysis, more explanation of the character of relationships between religion and state, better accounts of religion's influence in large-scale shifts and innovations in the inter-national system, and more theorizing about religion's political influence.

26   William Cavanaugh, "Killing for the Telephone Company: Why the Nation-State is Not the Keeper of the Common Good," *Modern Theology* 20, no. 2 (2004): 263.

27   William Cavanaugh, "'The Violence of Religion': Examining a Prevalent Myth" (Kellogg Institute for International Studies Working Paper Series, no. 310, 2004).

28   Mead, *Special Providence*.

29   John Mueller, "Terrorphobia: Our False Sense of Insecurity," *American Interest* 3, no. 5 (2008): 6–13.

30   Barry Buzan, Ole Waever, and J. de Wilde, *Security: A New Framework for Analy-sis* (Boulder, Colo.: Lynne Rienner, 1998); Carsten B. Lausten and Ole Waever, "In Defense of Religion: Sacred Referent Objects for Securitization," *Millennium* 29, no. 3 (2000): 705–39; Holger Stritzel, "Towards a Theory of Securitization: Copenhagen and Beyond," *European Journal of International Relations* 13, no. 3 (2007): 357–83.

31   Daniel Philpott, "Explaining the Political Ambivalence of Religion," *American Political Science Review* 101, no. 3 (2007): 505–25.

32   Friedrich Kratochwil, "Constructing a New Orthodoxy? Wendt's 'Social Theory of International Politics' and the Constructivist Challenge," *Millennium* 29, no. 1 (2000): 73–101.

33   Joseph Ratzinger (Pope Benedict XVI) and Marecello Pera, *Without Roots: The West, Relativism, Christianity, Islam*, trans. Michael F. Moore (New York: Basic Books, 2006).

34   See Rowan Williams, "Saint for Europe and Our Age," *Tablet*, June 13, 2008.

35   Letter from Martin Wight to J. H. Oldham, September 27, 1946, LSE Archives. Oldham was one of the main architects of the World Council of Churches. See Keith Clements, *Faith on the Fronier: A Life of J. H. Oldham* (Edinburgh: T&T Clark, 1999).

36   Martin Wight, "The Crux for an Historian Brought up in the Christian Tradition," in *A Study of History*, vol. 7, ed. Arnold Toynbee (Oxford: Oxford University Press, 1954), Annex VII A (III) (a) Annex III, 737–48.

37   For background on Wight's Christianity and his role in the English School of International Relations see, Thomas, "Faith, History, and Martin Wight"; Brian Porter, "The International Political Thought of Martin Wight," *International Affairs* 83, no. 4 (2007): 783–89; Robert Jackson, "From Colonialism to Theol-ogy: Encounters with Martin Wight's International Thought," *International Affairs* 84, no. 2 (2008): 351–64; Ian Hall, *The International Political Thought of Martin Wight* (New York: Palgrave, 2006).

38   Martin Wight, "Why Is There No International Theory?" in *Diplomatic Inves-tigations: Essays in the Theory of International Politics*, ed. Herbert Butterfield

and Martin Wight (London: Allen & Unwin, 1966), 17–34. Recently, William Inboden has argued that for Truman, Eisenhower, Dulles, and other American leaders, the Cold War *was* a religious war. Inboden, *Religion and American Foreign Policy.*

39   Herbert Butterfield, the other early English School scholar, and a devout Methodist, argued that diplomacy as a systematic activity, as a dialogue between states, was in some sense the work of "angels" maintaining the functioning of international society, sometimes in spite of what its members did. Paul Sharp has argued that, for Butterfield, diplomacy, when well executed, was based on charity and sympathy toward others and humility about one's own sense of righteousness, and came close to the teachings of Jesus. See Karl W. Schweizer and Paul Sharp, eds., *The International Thought of Herbert Butterfield* (New York: Palgrave, 2007); Paul Sharp, "Herbert Butterfield, the English School and the Civilizing Virtues of Diplomacy," *International Affairs* 79, no. 4 (2003): 855–78; Julia Stapleton, "Modernism, the English Past, and Christianity: Herbert Butterfield and the Study of History," *Historical Journal* 51 (2008): 547–57.

40   Martin Wight, *International Theory: The Three Traditions* (Leicester, UK: Leicester University Press, 1991). This was not a counsel of despair, a call to do nothing. Like Niebuhr, Wight was fully aware of the irony and ambiguity of power. At the beginning of *International Theory*, he recalled T. S. Eliot's admonition in *East Coker*, the poem named after the village from which his Puritan ancestors left for America: "For us, there is only the trying. The rest is not our business."

41   Martin Wight, "The Church, Russia, and the West," *Ecumenical Review* 1, no. 1 (1948): 25–45.

42   Wight, "The Church, Russia," 25. In a similar way, the Episcopal Church in the United States argued right after September 11 that "the underlying issue is one of reconciliation, and the church is called to 'wage reconciliation' as the answer to globalization and terrorism." James Solheim and Jan Nunley, "Bishops Call Waging Reconciliation the Answer to Globalization, Terrorism," Episcopal News Service, September 28, 2001.

43   Wight, "The Church, Russia," 25 (emphasis added).

44   Wight, "The Church, Russia," 25 (emphasis added).

45   Wight, "The Church, Russia," 25.

46   Wight, "The Church, Russia," 26 (emphasis added).

47   Wight, "The Church, Russia," 26–27.

48   Wight, "The Church, Russia," 27.

49   Wight, "The Church, Russia," 27.

50   Wight, "The Church, Russia," 27.

51   The fact that some Christians, whom the *Spectator*, Britain's leading conservative magazine, dubbed "loopy American born-again Christians," have misused biblical eschatology, does not detract from its role in Christian theology (Damian Thompson, "Fundamentally Wrong," *Spectator*, September 29, 2001, 15–16). The recovery of biblical apocalyptic as a type of religious literature, which revived interest in the eschatological dimension of the New Testament, is regarded as one of the most important discoveries in the study of the New Testament in the twentieth century. See George Elton Ladd and Donald A. Hagner, *A Theology of the New Testament* (Grand Rapids: Eerdmans, 1974).

52   Wight considered the unhealthy preoccupation some Christians have with the details of biblical prophecy to be contrary to the teaching of the New Testament. They use the apocalyptic or eschatological sections of the Bible as a mawkish Bible game akin to that great British pastime called "train-spotting," as if the main purpose of the apocalyptic literature is to enable us to spot the events

that contribute to the end times. The apocalyptic literature primarily called for a moral or spiritual recognition of the insecurity and uncertainty in which we are *always* living, and of the false idols in which we *always* place our hope and security. It is in this light that we should always be *ready*. Wight recognized this was the characteristic perspective of the Old Testament prophets. See also, Richard Bauckham & Trevor Hart, *Hope Against Hope: Christian Eschatology in Contemporary Context* (London: Darton, Longman & Todd, 1999).

53   Andrew Linklater, "The Achievements of Critical Theory," in Steve Smith, Ken Booth, Marysia Zalewski, eds., *International Theory: Positivism and Beyond* (Cambridge: Cambridge University Press, 1996), chap. 13, pp. 279–98; Richard Devetak, "Critical Theory," in *Theories of International Relations*, 4th ed. by Scott Burchill et al (London: Palgrave, 2009), 155–80.

54   Oliver O'Donovan, *The Desire of the Nations: Rediscovering the Roots of Political Theology* (Cambridge: Cambridge University Press, 1996), 273–74.

55   Olivier Roy, *Globalized Islam* (London: Hurst, 2002).

56   Roger Scruton, *The West and the Rest* (London: Continuum, 2002).

Conclusion

1   MacIntyre, *After Virtue*, 2nd ed., 213.

2   MacIntyre, *Whose Justice*, chap. 17.

3   Charles Taylor's *A Secular Age* will likely remain the principal reference point for such discussions for years to come. For another philosophical analysis of the issue, see David Walsh, *The Growth of the Liberal Soul* (Columbia: University of Missouri Press, 1997). For a theological analysis, see Robert Song, *Christianity and Liberal Society* (Oxford: Clarendon, 1997). For a historical analysis, see Joshua Mitchell, *Not By Reason Alone: Religion, History, and Identity in Early Modern Political Thought* (Chicago: University of Chicago Press, 1993).

4   Hatzopoulos and Petito, *Religion in International Relations*, 9.

5   Wald and Wilcox, "Getting Religion," 526.

6   Philpott, "Study of Global Politics," argues that while rational choice analysis (which is not to be identified with what Scott Thomas summarizes as "rationalism") is not necessarily reductive, it has a tendency to operate with too narrow a conception of religion. Commenting on the work of Anthony Gill, he writes: "Gill takes religion seriously. Rational choice analysis does not always posit preferences for wealth and power but sometimes assumes ideational ends. . . . Still, Gill's description of religious preferences is a thin one, containing little analysis of distinct doctrines or practices. The question then becomes whether the ends in play are adequate for explanation or whether a thicker description of religious actors and their motivation is required" (193).

7   For an illuminating and compelling statement of what an explicitly Christian approach to IR and peace studies might mean for university teaching, see Daniel Philpott, "One Professor's Guide to Studying International Relations and Peace Studies from a Catholic Perspective," *University of Notre Dame Magazine*, Summer 2009, http://magazine.nd.edu/news/11933.

Bibliography

Abrams, Elliott, ed. *Close Calls: Intervention, Terrorism, Missile Defense, and "Just War" Today*. Washington, D.C.: Ethics and Public Policy Center, 1998.

———, ed. *The Influence of Faith: Religious Groups and US Foreign Policy*. New York: Rowman & Littlefield, 2001.

Abu-Nimer, Mohammed. *Nonviolence and Peace Building in Islam*. Gainesville: University Press of Florida, 2003.

Achtemeier, Elizabeth. "Righteousness in the OT." In *The Interpreter's Dictionary of the Bible*, vol. 4, edited by G. A. Buttrick, 80–85. Nashville: Abingdon, 1962.

Ahlstrom, Sydney E. *A Religious History of the American People*. New Haven: Yale University Press, 1972.

Aikman, David. "The Great Revival: Understanding Religious Fundamentalism." *Foreign Affairs* 82, no. 4 (2003): 188–93.

Albright, Madeleine. *The Mighty and the Almighty: Reflections on Power, God, and World Affairs*. New York: HarperCollins, 2006.

Alley, Robert S. "Selected Madison Papers," in *James Madison on Religious Liberty*, edited by Robert S. Alley. Buffalo, New York: Prometheus Books, 1985, 35–94.

Al-Maliki, Nouri. "Iraq PM Unveils National Reconciliation Plan." *Telegraph*, June 26, 2006, http://www.telegraph.co.uk/.

"America." In *Kirchen-Lexikon: Oder, Encyklopædie der Katholischen Theologie und Ihrer Hilfswissenschaften*, edited by Heinrich Joseph Wetzer and Benedikt Welte. vol. 9. Freiburg im Breisgau: Karl Herder, 1854.

Ammar, Nawal H. "Restorative Justice in Islam: Theory and Practice." In *The Spiritual*

Roots of Restorative Justice, edited by Michael L. Hadley, 161–80. Albany: State University of New York Press, 2001.

Anderson, Fred. *Crucible of War: The Seven Years' War and the Fate of Empire in British North America, 1754–1766*. New York: Knopf, 2000.

———. *A People's Army: Massachusetts Soldiers and Society in the Seven Years' War*. Chapel Hill: University of North Carolina Press, 1984.

Anderson, Fred, and Andrew Cayton. *The Dominion of War: Empire and Liberty in North America, 1500–2000*. New York: Viking, 2005.

Anderson, John. *Religion, State and Politics in the Soviet Union and Successor States*. New York: Cambridge University Press, 1994.

Aquinas, Thomas. *Summa Theologica*. Translated by the Fathers of the English Dominican Province. New York: Benziger Bros., 1947.

Arkes, Hedley. *First Things: An Inquiry into the First Principles of Morals and Justice*. Princeton: Princeton University Press, 1986.

Arnold, Matthew. *Civilization in the United States*. 6th ed. Boston: DeWolfe, Friske, 1900.

Asbridge, Thomas. *The First Crusade: A New History*. Oxford: Oxford University Press, 2004.

Aslund, Anders. *How Russia Became a Market Economy*. Washington, D.C.: Brookings, 1995.

Avineri, Shlomo. *The Making of Modern Zionism: The Intellectual Origins of the Jewish State*. New York: Basic, 1981.

Bacevich, Andrew J., and Elizabeth H. Prodromou. "God is Not Neutral: Religion and U.S. Foreign Policy after 9/11." *Orbis* 48 (2004): 43–54.

Bacevich, Andrew J. *American Empire*. Cambridge, Mass.: Harvard University Press, 2002.

———. *The New American Militarism: How Americans are Seduced by War*. New York: Oxford University Press, 2005.

Baritz, Loren. *Backfire: A History of How American Culture Led Us Into Vietnam and Made Us Fight the Way We Did*. New York: William Morrow, 1985.

Bassiouni, M. Cherif. *Iraq Post-Conflict Justice: A Proposed Comprehensive Plan*. Chicago: DePaul University International Human Rights Law Institute, 2004. http://www.law.depaul.edu/centers_institutes/ihrli/downloads/Iraq_Proposal_04.pdf.

Bauckham, Richard, and Trevor Hart. *Hope Against Hope: Christian Eschatology in Contemporary Context*. London: Darton, Longman & Todd, 1999.

Baudrillard, Jean. *America*. Translated by Chris Turner. London: Verso, 1988.

Bawer, Bruce. *While Europe Slept: How Radical Islam Is Destroying from Within*. New York: Broadway, 2007.

Beeson, Mark. "With God on Their Side: Religion and American Foreign Policy." In Elliott et al., *Religion, Faith*, 4–11.

Beier, J. Marshall. *International Relations in Uncommon Places: Indigeneity, Cosmology and the Limits of International Theory*. New York: Palgrave Macmillan, 2005.

Bellah, Robert N. *The Broken Covenant: American Civil Religion in a Time of Trial*. 2nd ed. Chicago: University of Chicago Press, 1992.

———. "Civil Religion in America." In *Religion in America*, edited by William G. McLoughlin and Robert N. Bellah, 3–23. Boston: Houghton Mifflin, 1968.

Bellamy, Alex J. *Just Wars: From Cicero to Iraq*. Cambridge: Polity, 2006.

Benedict XVI. "Faith, Reason, and the University: Memories and Reflections." Lecture, University of Regensburg, Regensburg, Germany, September 12, 2006. http://www.vatican.va/holy_father/benedict_xvi/speeches/2006/september/documents/hf_ben-xvi_spe_20060912_university-regensburg_en.html.

Bercovitch, Sacvan. *The American Jeremiad*. Madison: University of Wisconsin Press, 1978.

———. *The Rites of Assent: Transformations in the Symbolic Construction of America.* New York: Routledge, 1993.

Bergen, Peter. *Holy War, Inc.: Inside the Secret World of Osama bin Laden.* New York: Free Press, 2001.

Berger, Peter L., ed. *The Desecularization of the World: Resurgent Religion and World Politics.* Grand Rapids: Eerdmans, 1999.

———. "Religion in the West." *National Interest* 80 (2005): 1112–19.

Berger, Peter, Grace Davie, and Effie Fokas. *Religious America, Secular Europe? A Theme and Variations.* London: Ashgate, 2008.

Bernbaum, John A. Reflections on Russia. Monthly blog. Russian-American Institute. http://www.racu.org/.

———. "Revolution '89: The Spiritual Dimension." *Christian Science Monitor*, August 15, 1990.

Betts, Richard. "The Delusion of Impartial Intervention." *Foreign Affairs* 73, no. 6 (1994): 20–33.

Bhargava, Rajeev. "Restoring Decency to Barbaric Societies." In Rotberg and Thompson, *Truth v. Justice*, 45–67.

Biggar, Nigel, ed. *Burying the Past: Making Peace and Doing Justice after Conflict.* Washington, D.C.: Georgetown University Press, 2003.

Bill, James A., and John Alden Williams. *Roman Catholics and Shi'i Muslims: Prayer, Passion and Politics.* Chapel Hill: University of North Carolina Press, 2002.

Billington, James. *Russia Transformed: Breakthrough to Hope.* New York: Free Press, 1992.

Bin Laden, Osama. "Declaration of Jihad Against the Americans Occupying the Land of the Two Sacred Mosques" (August 23, 1996). In *Jihad: Bin Laden in His Own Words*, edited by Brad K. Berner, 35–72. Charleston, S.C.: Book Surge, 2006.

———. Interview by Al Jazeera. September 20, 2001. Translated by BBC Monitoring Service, September 22, 2001.

———. "To the Americans." In Lawrence, *Messages*, 16–18.

Bloch, Ruth H. *Visionary Republic: Millennial Themes in American Thought, 1756–1800.* Cambridge: Cambridge University Press, 1985.

Bloom, Harold. *American Religion: The Emergence of the Post-Christian Nation.* New York: Simon & Schuster, 1992.

Borgwardt, Elizabeth. *A New Deal for the World: America's Vision for Human Rights.* Cambridge, Mass.: Harvard University Press, 2005.

Borstelman, Thomas. *The Cold War and the Color Line: American Race Relations in the Global Arena* (Cambridge, Mass.: Harvard University Press, 2001).

Boyer, Pascal. *The Naturalness of Religious Ideas: A Cognitive Theory of Religion.* Berkeley: University of California Press, 1994.

Boyer, Paul. *By the Bomb's Early Light: American Thought and Culture at the Dawn of the Atomic Age.* 2nd ed. Chapel Hill: University of North Carolina Press, 1994.

———. "In Search of the Fourth 'R': The Treatment of Religion in American History Textbooks and Survey Courses." *History Teacher* 29 (1996): 195–216.

———. *When Time Shall Be No More: Prophecy Belief in Modern American Culture.* Cambridge, Mass.: Harvard University Press, 1992.

Boyle, Joseph. "Traditional Just War Theory and Humanitarian Intervention." In *Humanitarian Intervention, Nomos* 47, edited by Terry Nardin and Melissa S. Williams, 31–57. New York: New York University Press, 2006.

Bozeman, Adda B. *Politics & Culture in International History.* New Brunswick, N.J.: Transaction, 1994.

Bozeman, Theodore Dwight. *To Live Ancient Lives: The Primitivist Dimension in Puritanism.* Chapel Hill: University of North Carolina Press, 1988.

Braude, Joseph. "On Message." *New Republic Online*, February 11, 2005. http://www
.tnr.com/.

Breen, T. H. "English Origins and New World Development: The Case of the Covenanted Militia in Seventeenth-Century Massachusetts." *Past and Present* 57
(1972): 74–96.

Bridenbaugh, Carl. *Mitre and Sceptre: Transatlantic Faiths, Ideas, Personalities, and Politics, 1689–1775*. New York: Oxford University Press, 1962.

Brinkley, Alan. *Voices of Protest: Huey Long, Father Coughlin, and the Great Depression*.
New York: Knopf, 1982.

Brzezinski, Zbigniew. *The Grand Failure: The Birth and Death of Communism in the
Twentieth Century*. New York: Scribner's, 1989.

——. *Power and Principle: Memoirs of the National Security Advisor, 1977–1981*. New
York: Farrar, Straus & Giroux, 1983.

Burge, Gary M. *Whose Land? Whose Promise?* Cleveland: Pilgrim, 2003.

Burkert, Walter. *Creation of the Sacred: Tracks of Biology in Early Religions*. Cambridge,
Mass.: Harvard University Press, 1996.

Burleigh, Michael. "Some European Perspectives on Terrorism." Address to the Foreign Policy Research Institute Study Group, April 7, 2008. http://www.fpri
.org/enotes/200805.burleigh.europeanperspectivesterrorism.html.

Burnett, Stanton. "Implications for the Foreign Policy Community." In Johnson and
Sampson, *Religion*, 285–305.

Butler, Jon. *Awash in a Sea of Faith: Christianizing the American People*. Cambridge,
Mass.: Harvard University Press, 1990.

——. "Jack-in-the-Box Faith: The Religion Problem in Modern American History."
Journal of American History 90 (2004): 1357–78.

Buzan, Barry, Ole Waever, and J. de Wilde. *Security: A New Framework for Analysis*.
Boulder, Colo.: Lynne Rienner, 1998.

Buzzanco, Robert. "What Happened to the New Left? Toward a Radical Reading of
American Foreign Relations." *Diplomatic History* 23 (1999): 575–607.

——. "Where's the Beef? Culture without Power in the Study of U.S. Foreign Relations." *Diplomatic History* 24 (2000): 623–32.

Byrnes, Robert F. *After Brezhnev: Sources of Soviet Conduct in the 1980s*. Washington,
D.C.: CSIS, 1983.

Cannon, Lou. *President Reagan: The Role of a Lifetime*. New York: Simon & Schuster,
1991.

Caputo, John, ed. *Deconstruction in a Nutshell: A Conversation with Jacques Derrida*.
New York: Fordham University Press, 1997.

Carafano, James Jay, and Dana R. Dillon. "Winning the Peace: Principles for Post-
Conflict Operations." *Heritage Foundation Backgrounder* 1859, June 13, 2005.
www.heritage.org/research/nationalsecurity/bg1859.cfm.

Carlson, John D. "Discerning Justice in the Trial and Execution of Saddam Hussein."
In *Enemy Combatants, Terrorism, and Armed Conflict Law: A Guide to the Issues*,
edited by David K. Linnan, 307–26. Westport, Conn.: Praeger Security International, 2008.

Carlson, John D., and Erik C. Owens, eds. *The Sacred and the Sovereign: Religion and
International Politics*. Washington, D.C.: Georgetown University Press, 2003.

Carroll, James. *Crusade: Chronicles of an Unjust War*. New York: Metropolitan, 2004.

Carter, Jimmy. *Palestine: Peace Not Apartheid*. New York: Simon & Schuster, 2006.

Casanova, José. *Public Religions in the Modern World*. Chicago: University of Chicago
Press, 1994.

Cavanaugh, William. "Killing for the Telephone Company: Why the Nation-State
is Not the Keeper of the Common Good." *Modern Theology* 20, no. 2 (2004):
243–74.

———. "'The Violence of Religion': Examining a Prevalent Myth." Kellogg Institute for International Studies Working Paper Series, no. 310, 2004.

Cave, Alfred A. *The Pequot War*. Amherst: University of Massachusetts Press, 1996.

Ceasar, James W. *Reconstructing America: The Symbol of America in Modern Thought*. New Haven: Yale University Press, 1997.

Chapman, Colin. *Whose Promised Land? The Continuing Crisis over Israel and Palestine*. Grand Rapids: Baker, 2002.

Charles, J. Daryl. *Retrieving the Natural Law: A Return to Moral First Things*. Critical Issues in Bioethics. Grand Rapids: Eerdmans, 2008.

Charles, J. Daryl, and David D. Corey. *Justice in an Age of Terror: The Just War Tradition Reconsidered*. American Ideals and Institutions. Wilmington, Del.: ISI Books, forthcoming.

Cherry, Conrad, ed. *God's New Israel: Religious Interpretations of American Destiny*. Rev. ed. Chapel Hill: University of North Carolina Press, 1998.

Chesterton, Simon. *Just War or Just Peace? Humanitarian Intervention and International Law*. Oxford: Oxford University Press, 2001.

Clark, John G. "Making Environmental Diplomacy an Integral Part of Diplomatic History." *Diplomatic History* 21 (1997): 453–60.

Clarke, Peter B. and Peter Byrne. *Religion Defined and Explained*. New York: St. Martin's, 1993.

Clements, Keith. *Faith on the Frontier: A Life of J. H. Oldham*. Edinburgh: T&T Clark, 1999.

Clouser, Roy A. *The Myth of Religious Neutrality: An Essay on the Hidden Role of Religious Belief in Theories*. Rev. ed. Notre Dame, Ind.: University of Notre Dame Press, 2005.

Coady, C. A. J. *The Ethics of Armed Humanitarian Intervention*. Washington, D.C.: United States Institute of Peace, 2002.

Cohen, Stephen F., and Katrina Van den Heuvel, eds. *Voices of Glasnost: Interviews with Gorbachev's Reformers*. New York: Norton, 1990.

Cohen, Warren I., ed. *The Cambridge History of American Foreign Relations*. 4 vols. Cambridge: Cambridge University Press, 1993.

Cole, Juan R. I. "The Rise of Religious and Ethnic Mass Politics in Iraq." In *Religion and Nationalism in Iraq: A Comparative Perspective*, edited by David Little and Donald Swearer, 43–72. Cambridge, Mass.: Harvard University Press, 2006.

Coleman, Fred. *The Decline and Fall of the Soviet Empire*. New York: St. Martin's, 1996.

Commission on International Religious Freedom. "Afghanistan: Freedom and Electoral Democracy." Press release. September 13, 2004. http://www.uscirf.gov/.

Congressional Research Service Report for Congress. Washington, D.C.: Congressional Research Service, 1995.

Connolly, William. *Why I Am Not a Secularist*. Minneapolis: University of Minnesota Press, 1999.

Constable, Pamela. "Proposed Afghan Constitution Fits U.S. Model." *Washington Post*, November 4, 2003.

Costigliola, Frank. "'Unceasing Pressure for Penetration': Gender, Pathology, and Emotion in George Kennan's Formation of the Cold War." *Journal of American History* 83 (1997): 1309–39.

Craig, Campbell. *Glimmer of a New Leviathan: Total War in the Realism of Niebuhr, Morgenthau, and Waltz*. New York: Columbia University Press, 2003.

Craig, Gordon A. "Political and Diplomatic History." In *Historical Studies Today*, edited by Felix Gilbert and Stephen R. Graubard, 356–71. New York: Norton, 1972.

Cressy, David. *Coming Over: Migration and Communication between England and New England in the Seventeenth Century*. Cambridge: Cambridge University Press, 1987.

Crocker, David A. "Reckoning with Past Wrongs: A Normative Framework." *Ethics & International Affairs* 13 (1999): 43–64.

———. "Retribution and Reconciliation." *Philosophy and Public Policy* 20, no. 1 (2000): 1–6.

———. "Truth Commissions, Transitional Justice, and Civil Society." In Rotberg and Thompson, *Truth v. Justice*, 99–121.

Daalder, Ivo H., and James M. Lindsay. *America Unbound: The Bush Revolution in Foreign Policy*. Washington, D.C.: Brookings, 2003.

Dallek, Robert. *The American Style of Foreign Policy: Cultural Politics and Foreign Affairs*. New York: Knopf, 1983.

Danan, Liora, and Alice Hunt. *Mixed Blessings: U.S. Government Engagement with Religion in Conflict Prone Settings*. Washington, D.C.: Center for Strategic and International Studies, 2007.

Davie, Grace. "Europe: The Exception that Proves the Rule?" In Berger, *Desecularization*, 65–83.

Davies, Michael. *The Second Vatican Council and Religious Liberty*. Long Prairie, Minn.: Neumann, 1992.

Dawkins, Richard. *The God Delusion*. New York: Houghton Mifflin, 2006.

De Gruchy, John W. *Reconciliation: Restoring Justice*. Minneapolis: Fortress, 2003.

Dean, Robert D. *Imperial Brotherhood: Gender and the Making of Cold War Foreign Policy*. Amherst: University of Massachusetts Press, 2001.

Dederer, John Morgan. *War in America to 1775: Before Yankee Doodle*. New York: New York University Press, 1990.

Delassus, Abbé Henry. *L'Américanisme et la conjuration antichrétienne*. Paris: Société de Saint-Augustin, Desclée De Brouwer et Cie, 1899.

den Dulk, Kevin R. "Evangelical Elites and Faith-Based Foreign Affairs." *Review of Faith and International Affairs* 4, no. 1 (2006): 21–29.

DePriest, Jon P. "Custodial Diplomacy: Obligations of International Security and the Demise of Multilateral Strategy." *Evangelical Review of Society and Politics* 2, no. 1 (2008): 1–15.

Devetak, Richard. "Critical Theory." In *Theories of International Relations*, 4th ed., by Scott Burchill et al., 155–80. London: Palgrave, 2009.

Diamond, Larry. "Is the Third Wave of Democratization Over? An Empirical Assessment." Kellogg Institute for International Studies Working Paper Series, no. 236, March 1997.

Dickens, Charles. *American Notes*. London: Chapman & Hall, 1842.

Dionne, E. J., Jean Bethke Elshtain, and Kayla Drogosz, eds. *Liberty and Power: A Dialogue on Religion and U.S. Foreign Policy in an Unjust World*. Pew Forum Dialogues on Religion and Public Life. Washington, D.C.: Brookings, 2004.

Dooyeweerd, Herman. *The Collected Works of Herman Dooyeweerd*. Series B, vol. 3, *Roots of Western Culture: Pagan, Secular, and Christian Options*. Lewiston, N.Y.: Edwin Mellen, 2003.

Dorsey, Kurk. "Dealing with the Dinosaur (and Its Swamp): Putting the Environment in Diplomatic History." *Diplomatic History* 29 (2005): 573–87.

Dougherty, Jude P. *The Logic of Religion*. Washington, D.C.: Catholic University Press, 2003.

Dries, Angelyn. *The Missionary Movement in American Catholic History*. Maryknoll, N.Y.: Orbis, 1998.

Dudziak, Mary L. *Cold War Civil Rights: Race and the Image of American Democracy*. Princeton: Princeton University Press, 2000.

Dull, Jonathan. "American Foreign Relations Before the Constitution: A Historiographical Wasteland." In Haines and Walker, *American Foreign Relations*, 3–15.

"East-West: Gorbachev, God and Socialism." *Time*, December 11, 1989, 37.

Edwards, Mark. "'God Has Chosen Us': Re-Membering Christian Realism, Rescuing Christendom, and the Contest of Responsibilities during the Cold War." *Diplomatic History* 33 (2009): 67–94.

Egypt State Information Service. "October 21, 2001 Mubarak to 'Washington Post': US should strike balance between fighting terrorism and moving forward in ME peace process." *Egypt State Information Service*, October 21, 2001. http://www.us.sis.gov.eg/En/Politics/Presidency/President/Interview/000001/0401050300000000000069.htm

Eisenhower, Dwight D. "Remarks to the First National Conference on the Spiritual Foundations of American Democracy" (November 9, 1954). In *Public Papers of the Presidents: Dwight D. Eisenhower, 1954*. Washington, D.C.: Government Printing Office, 1960.

Eisenstadt, S. N. "Multiple Modernities." *Daedalus* 129, no. 1 (2000): 1–29.

Eizenstat, Stuart E. "Reconciliation, Not Just Reconstruction." *The New York Times*, July 4, 2003.

Ekiyor, Thelma. "The Responsibility to Protect (R2P): A Way Forward—Or Rather Part of the Problem?" *Foreign Voices* 1 (2008): 1–8.

Elliott, Lorraine, Mark Beeson, Shahram Akbarzadeh, Greg Fealy, Stuart Harris. *Religion, Faith and Global Politics*. Keynotes Series. Canberra: Australian National University, Department of International Relations, 2006.

Ellis, Marc H. *Toward a Jewish Theology of Liberation*. 3rd ed. Waco, Tex.: Baylor University Press, 2004.

Elshtain, Jean Bethke. *Augustine and the Limits of Power*. Notre Dame, Ind.: University of Notre Dame Press, 1991.

———. "International Justice as Equal Regard and the Use of Force." *Ethics & International Affairs* 17, no. 2 (2003): 63–70.

———. *Just War Against Terror: The Burden of American Power in a Violent World*. New York: Basic, 2003.

———. "Just War and Humanitarian Intervention." *Ideas* 8, no. 2 (2001): 2–21.

Evans, Michael D. *The American Prophecies: Ancient Scriptures Reveal Our Nation's Future*. New York: Warner Faith, 2004.

Fairbank, John K., ed. *The Missionary Enterprise in China and America*. Cambridge, Mass.: Harvard University Press, 1974.

Falk, Richard. "Politicizing Religion? Toward a New Global Ethic." In Hatzopoulos and Petito, *Religion in International Relations*, 181–208.

Farr, Thomas F. "Cold War Religion," *First Things* 194 (2009): 47–49.

———. "Diplomacy in an Age of Faith: Religious Freedom and National Security." *Foreign Affairs* 87, no. 2 (2008): 110–24.

———. "Religious Freedom and National Security." In *Religious Freedom in the World*, edited by Paul Marshall, 17–22. Lanham, Md.: Rowman & Littlefield, 2007.

———. "Religious Realism in American Foreign Policy: Lessons from Vatican II." *Review of Faith and International Affairs* 3, no. 3 (2005): 25–33.

———. *World of Faith and Freedom: Why International Religious Liberty is Vital to American National Security*. New York: Oxford University Press, 2008.

Farr, Thomas F., and John J. Eddy. "Farr Gone on Religion." Correspondence. *First Things* 166 (2006): 2–3.

Farr, Thomas F., and Dennis R. Hoover. *The Future of International Religious Freedom Policy: A Policy Report with Recommendations for the Obama Administration*. Forthcoming. http://www.berkleycenter.georgetown.edu/.

Ferguson, Niall. *Colossus: The Price of American Empire*. New York: Penguin, 2004.

Fischer, Beth A. *The Reagan Reversal: Foreign Policy and the End of the Cold War*. Columbia: University of Missouri Press, 1997.

FitzGerald, Frances. *Way Out There in the Blue: Reagan, Star Wars, and the End of the Cold War*. New York: Simon & Schuster, 2000.

Fogarty, Gerald P. *The Vatican and the American Hierarchy from 1870 to 1965*. Collegeville, Minn.: Liturgical, 1982.

Foundation for Relief and Reconciliation in the Middle East. "Peace Progress in Cairo." *News and Prayer Letter*, no. 7. London: The Naaman Trust, November 2007.

Fox, Jonathan. "The Rise of Religion and the Fall of the Civilization Paradigm as Explanations for Intra-State Conflict." *Cambridge Review of International Affairs* 20, no. 3 (2007): 361–82.

Fox, Jonathan, and Shmuel Sandler. *Bringing Religion into International Relations*. Culture and Religion in International Relations. New York: Palgrave Macmillan, 2004.

Fox, Richard Wightman. *Reinhold Niebuhr: A Biography*. Rev. ed. Ithaca: Cornell University Press, 1996.

Frady, Marshall. *Billy Graham: A Parable of American Righteousness*. Boston: Little, Brown, 1979.

Freedom House. *Freedom in the World 2005: The Annual Survey of Political Rights and Civil Liberties*. Washington, D.C.: Freedom House, 2005.

———. "Russia Downgraded to 'Not Free.'" Press release. Washington, D.C.: Freedom House, 2004.

Freeman, Michael. "Puritans and Pequots: The Question of Genocide." *New England Quarterly* 68 (1995): 278–93.

Freston, Paul, ed. *Evangelical Christianity and Democracy in Latin America*. New York: Oxford University Press, 2008.

———. *Evangelical Politics in Asia, Africa and Latin America*. Cambridge: Cambridge University Press, 2001.

Gaddis, John Lewis. *Strategies of Containment: A Critical Appraisal of Postwar American National Security Policy*. New York: Oxford University Press, 1982.

———. *Surprise, Security, and the American Experience*. Cambridge, Mass.: Harvard University Press, 2004.

———. *We Now Know: Rethinking Cold War History*. New York: Oxford University Press, 1997.

Gall, Carlotta. "Afghans' King Receives Draft of Constitution," *The New York Times*, November 4, 2003.

Gallie, W. B. "Essentially Contested Concepts." In *Philosophy and the Historical Understanding*, 157–191. London: Chatto & Windus, 1964.

Galtung, Johan. "U.S. Foreign Policy as Manifest Theology." In *Culture and International Relations*, edited by Jongsuk Chay, 119–40. New York: Praeger, 1990.

Garrow, David J. *Bearing the Cross: Martin Luther King, Jr., and the Southern Christian Leadership Conference*. New York: William Morrow, 1986.

Garton Ash, Timothy. *The Magic Lantern: The Revolutions of 1989 Witnessed in Warsaw, Budapest, Berlin and Prague*. New York: Random House, 1990.

———. "True Confessions." *New York Review of Books* 44 (1997): 37–38.

Gaustad, Edwin S. *Religion in America: History and Historiography*. Washington, D.C.: American Historical Association, 1973.

Gelernter, David. "Americanism—and Its Enemies." *Commentary* 119 (2005): 41–48.

George, Robert P. *Making Men Moral*. New York: Oxford University Press, 1995.

George, Robert P., and William L. Saunders Jr. "Dignitatis Humanae: The Freedom of the Church and the Responsibility of the State." In *Catholicism and Religious Freedom: Contemporary Reflections on Vatican II's Declaration on Religious Liberty*, edited by Kenneth L. Grasso and Robert P. Hunt, 1–18. New York: Rowman & Littlefield, 2006.

Gerbi, Antonello. *The Dispute of the New World: The History of a Polemic, 1750–1900*. Translated by Jeremy Moyle. Pittsburgh: University of Pittsburgh Press, 1973.

Gerecht, Reuel Marc. "The Counterterrorist Myth." *Atlantic Monthly*, July/August 2001.

Gerth, H. H., and C. Wright Mills, eds. *From Max Weber: Essays in Sociology*. New York: Oxford University Press, 1946.

Gitlin, Todd. "Do Less Harm: The Lesser Evil of Non-Intervention." *World Affairs* (Summer 2008). http://www.worldaffairsjournal.org/2008%20-%20summer/full-gitlin.html.

Glendon, Mary Ann. *Rights Talk: The Impoverishment of Political Discourse*. New York: Free Press, 1991.

Goldman, Marshall I. *Lost Opportunity: What Has Made Economic Reform in Russia So Difficult?* New York: Norton, 1996.

Goldstein, Warren. *William Sloane Coffin, Jr.: A Holy Impatience*. New Haven: Yale University Press, 2004.

Goldstone, Richard J. "War Crimes: When Amnesia Causes Cancer." *Washington Post*, February 2, 1997.

Gopin, Marc. *Between Eden and Armageddon: The Future of World Religions, Violence, and Peacemaking*. Oxford: Oxford University Press, 2000.

Gorbachev, Mikhail. *Perestroika: New Thinking for Our Country and the World*. New York: Harper & Row, 1987.

Government Accounting Office. *U.S. Public Diplomacy: State Department Efforts to Engage Muslim Audiences Lack Certain Communication Elements and Face Significant Challenges*. GAO-06-535. Washington, D.C.: GAO, 2006.

Graff, Peter, and Waleed Ibrahim. "U.S. Seeks Political Gains; Sunnis End Boycott." *Boston Globe*, December 2, 2007.

Gray, John. *Black Mass: Apocalyptic Religion and the Death of Utopia*. London: Allen Lane, 2007.

Greenawalt, Kent. "Amnesty's Justice." In Rotberg and Thompson, *Truth v. Justice*, 189–210.

Gribbin, William. *The Churches Militant: The War of 1812 and American Religion*. New Haven: Yale University Press, 1973.

Grim, Brian J. "Religious Freedom: Good For What Ails Us." *Review of Faith and International Affairs* 6, no. 2 (2008): 3–7.

Grygiel, Jakub. "The Diplomacy Fallacy." *American Interest* 3, no. 5 (2008): 26–35.

Guthrie, Stewart Elliott. "Religion: What Is It?" *Journal for the Scientific Study of Religion* 35 (1996): 412–19.

Gutiérrez, Gustavo. *A Theology of Liberation*. Translated by Sister Caridad Inda and John Eagleson. Maryknoll, N.Y.: Orbis, 1988.

Gutmann, Amy, and Dennis Thompson. "The Moral Foundations of Truth Commissions." In Rotberg and Thompson, *Truth v. Justice*, 22–45.

Habermas, Jürgen, and Jacques Derrida. "Unsere Erneuerung; Nach dem Krieg: Die Wiedergeburt Europas." *Frankfurter Allgemeine Zeitung*, May 31, 2003.

Haefeli, Evan, and Kevin Sweeney. *Captors and Captives: The 1704 French and Indian Raid on Deerfield*. Amherst: University of Massachusetts Press, 2003.

Haines, Gerald K., and J. Samuel Walker, eds. *American Foreign Relations: A Historiographical Review*. Westport, Conn.: Greenwood Press, 1981.

Hall, Ian. *The International Political Thought of Martin Wight*. New York: Palgrave, 2006.

Hall, Mitchell K. *Because of Their Faith: CALCAV and Religious Opposition to the Vietnam War*. New York: Columbia University Press, 1990.

Hall, Simon. *Peace and Freedom: The Civil Rights and Antiwar Movements of the 1960s*. Philadelphia: University of Pennsylvania Press, 2005.

Hamburger, Philip. *The Separation of Church and State*. Cambridge, Mass.: Harvard University Press, 2002.

Hamrin, Carol Lee. "A New Framework for Promoting Religious Freedom in China." *Review of Faith and International Affairs* 3, no. 1 (2005): 3–10.

Hanhimäki, Jussi M. "Global Visions and Parochial Politics: The Persistent Dilemma of the 'American Century.'" *Diplomatic History* 27 (2003): 423–47.

Hanson, Eric O. *Religion and Politics in the International System Today*. Cambridge: Cambridge University Press, 2006.

Harff, Barbara. "No Lessons Learned from the Holocaust? Assessing Risks of Genocide and Political Mass Murder since 1955." *American Political Science Review* 97, no. 1 (2003): 57–74.

Harrison, Lawrence E. *The Central Liberal Truth*. New York: Oxford University Press, 2006.

———. "The Culture Club: Exploring the Central Liberal Truth." *National Interest* 83 (2006): 94–100.

Harrison, Lawrence E., and Samuel P. Huntington, eds. *Culture Matters: How Values Shape Human Progress*. New York: Basic, 2000.

Hasni, Mohamed. "Iraq Reconciliation Plan Inspired by South Africa." *Mail & Guardian Online*, June 25, 2006. http://www.mg.co.za/.

Hasson, Kevin Seamus. *The Right to Be Wrong: Ending the Culture War Over Religion in America*. San Francisco: Encounter, 2005.

Hatch, Nathan O. *The Sacred Cause of Liberty: Republican Thought and the Millennium in Revolutionary New England*. New Haven: Yale University Press, 1977.

Hatzenbuehler, Ronald L. "The Early National Period, 1789–1815: The Need for Redefinition." In Haines and Walker, *American Foreign Relations*, 17–32.

Hatzopoulos, Pavlos, and Fabio Petito, eds. *Religion in International Relations: The Return from Exile*. Culture and Religion in International Relations. New York: Palgrave Macmillan, 2003.

Haynes, Jeff. "Religion and International Relations: What Are the Issues?" *International Politics* 41 (2004): 451–462.

Hegel, G. W. F. *Werke*. Vol. 12. Frankfurt am Main: Suhrkamp, 1970.

Hehir, J. Bryan, Michael Walzer, Louise Richardson, Shibley Telhami, Charles Krauthammer, and James Lindsay. *Liberty and Power: A Dialogue on Religion and U.S. Foreign Policy in an Unjust World*. Pew Forum Dialogues on Religion and Public Life. Washington, D.C.: Brookings, 2004.

Heidegger, Martin. *Einführung in die Metaphysik*. In *Gesamtausgabe*, vol. 40. Frankfurt am Main: Klostermann, 1975.

———. "Hölderlins Hymne." In *Gesamtausgabe*, vol. 53. Frankfurt am Main: Klostermann, 1975.

Heimert, Alan. *Religion and the American Mind: From the Great Awakening to the Revolution*. Cambridge, Mass.: Harvard University Press, 1966.

Herberg, Will. *Protestant-Catholic-Jew: An Essay in American Religious Sociology*. Rev. ed. Garden City, N.Y.: Doubleday, 1960.

Herman, Burt. "Afghanistan Unveils Long-Delayed Draft Constitution, Key Step on Road to Recovery." *Associated Press*, November 3, 2003.

Hero, Alfred A., Jr. *American Religious Groups View Foreign Policy: Trends in Rank-and-File Opinion, 1937–1969*. Durham, N.C.: Duke University Press, 1973.

Herring, George C. *From Colony to Superpower: U.S. Foreign Relations since 1776*. New York: Oxford University Press, 2008.

Hill, Patricia R. "Religion as a Category of Diplomatic Analysis." *Diplomatic History* 24 (2000): 633–40.

Hitchens, Christopher. *God Is Not Great: How Religion Poisons Everything*. New York: Hachette Book Group, 2007.

Hittinger, John. "Just War and Defense Policy." In *Natural Law and Contemporary Public Policy*, edited by David F. Forte, 333–60. Washington, D.C.: Georgetown University Press, 1998.

Hittinger, Russell. *The First Grace: Recovering the Natural Law in a Post-Christian World*. Wilmington, Del.: ISI Books, 2003.

Hodgson, Godfrey. "God Fights Back." In *People's Century*, 251–74. London: BBC Books, 1996.

Hoffman, Peter J., and Thomas G. Weiss. *Sword and Salve: Confronting New Wars and Humanitarian Crises*. Lanham, Md.: Rowman & Littlefield, 2006.

Hoffmann, Stanley. "The Politics and Ethics of Military Intervention." *Survival* 37, no. 4 (1995): 29–51.

Hogan, Michael J., ed. *America in the World: The Historiography of American Foreign Relations Since 1941*. New York: Cambridge University Press, 1995.

———, ed. *Paths to Power: The Historiography of American Foreign Relations to 1941*. New York: Cambridge University Press, 2000.

Hoganson, Kristin. *Fighting for American Manhood: How Gender Politics Provoked the Spanish-American and Philippine-American Wars*. New Haven: Yale University Press, 1998.

Hollinger, David A. "The 'Secularization' Question and the United States in the Twentieth Century." *Church History* (March 2001): 132–43.

Hollis, Martin, and Steve Smith. *Explaining and Understanding International Relations*. Oxford: Clarendon, 1991.

Hoover, Dennis, ed. "Evangelicals and the Israeli-Palestinian Conflict." Special issue, *Review of Faith and International Affairs* 5, no. 4 (2007).

———, ed. "Islam and Pluralism." Special issue, *Review of Faith and International Affairs* 6, no. 4 (2008).

Hoover, Dennis, and Thomas Farr, eds. "Religious Freedom and U.S. Foreign Policy." Special issue, *Review of Faith and International Affairs* 6, no. 2 (2008).

Hughes, Richard T. *Myths America Lives By*. Urbana: University of Illinois Press, 2004.

Hülsemann, Johann Georg. *Geschichte der Democratie in den Vereinigten Staaten von Nord-America*. Göttingen, 1823.

Hunt, Michael H. "Ideology." In *Explaining the History of American Foreign Relations*, 2nd ed., edited by Michael J. Hogan and Thomas G. Paterson, 221–40. New York: Cambridge University Press, 2004.

———. *Ideology and U.S. Foreign Policy*. New Haven: Yale University Press, 1987.

———. *The Making of a Special Relationship: The United States and China to 1914*. New York: Columbia University Press, 1983.

Huntington, Samuel P. "The Clash of Civilizations." *Foreign Affairs* 72, no. 2 (1993): 22–49.

———, ed. *The Clash of Civilizations: The Debate*. New York: Foreign Affairs, 1996.

———. *The Clash of Civilizations and the Remaking of World Order*. New York: Simon & Schuster, 1996.

———. *The Soldier and the State: The Theory and Politics of Civil-Military Relations*. Cambridge, Mass.: Harvard University Press, 1957.

———. *The Third Wave: Democratization in the Late Twentieth Century*. Norman: University of Oklahoma Press, 1991.

————. *Who Are We? The Challenges to America's National Identity* (New York: Simon & Schuster, 2004).

Hurd, Elizabeth Shakman. "The Political Authority of Secularism in International Relations." *European Journal of International Relations* 10, no. 2 (2004): 235–62.

————. *The Politics of Secularism in International Relations.* Princeton Studies in International History and Politics. Princeton: Princeton University Press, 2008.

Hutchison, William R. *Errand to the World: American Protestant Thought and Foreign Missions.* Chicago: University of Chicago Press, 1987.

Ignatieff, Michael. "Articles of Faith." *Index on Censorship* 25, no. 5 (1996): 110–22.

Ikenberry, G. John. Review of *The Global Resurgence of Religion and the Transformation of International Relations,* by Scott M. Thomas. *Foreign Affairs* 84, no. 3 (2005): 132–33.

Immerman, Richard H. *John Foster Dulles: Piety, Pragmatism, and Power in U.S. Foreign Policy.* Wilmington, Del.: Scholarly Resources, 1999.

Inboden, William. *Religion and American Foreign Policy, 1945–1960: The Soul of Containment.* Cambridge: Cambridge University Press, 2009.

Inglehart, Ronald, and Pippa Norris. "The True Clash of Civilizations." *Foreign Policy,* March/April 2003, 63–70.

International Center for Transitional Justice and Human Rights Center, University of California, Berkeley. *Iraqi Voices: Attitudes Towards Transitional Justice and Social Reconstruction.* Occasional Paper. New York: International Center for Transitional Justice, May 2004.

International Commission on Intervention and State Sovereignty. *The Responsibility to Protect: Report of the International Commission on Intervention and State Sovereignty.* Ottawa: International Development Research Centre, 2001.

Irani, George E., and Nathan C. Funk. "Rituals of Reconciliation: Arab-Islamic Perspectives." *Arab Studies Quarterly* 20, no. 4 (1998): 53–74.

Iraq Study Group. *The Iraq Study Group Report: The Way Forward—A New Approach.* New York: Vintage, 2006.

Isaac, Rhys. *The Transformation of Virginia, 1740–1790.* Chapel Hill: University of North Carolina Press, 1982.

Ishay, Micheline R. *The History of Human Rights: From Ancient Times to the Globalization Era.* Berkeley: University of California Press, 2004.

Jackson, Robert. "From Colonialism to Theology: Encounters with Martin Wight's International Thought." *International Affairs* 84, no. 2 (2008): 351–64.

Jacobs, Seth. *America's Miracle Man in Vietnam: Ngo Dinh Diem, Religion, Race, and U.S. Intervention in Southeast Asia, 1950–1957.* Durham, N.C.: Duke University Press, 2004.

James, William. *The Varieties of Religious Experience.* New York: Mentor, 1958.

Jeansonne, Glen. *Gerald K. Smith: Minister of Hate.* New Haven: Yale University Press, 1988.

Jelen, Ted Gerard, and Clyde Wilcox. *Religion and Politics in Contemporary Perspective: The One, the Few and the Many.* Cambridge: Cambridge University Press, 2002.

Jenkins, John I., and Thomas Burish. "Reason and Faith at Harvard." *Washington Post,* October 23, 2006.

Jenkins, Philip. *The Next Christendom: The Coming of Global Christianity.* New York: Oxford University Press, 2002.

John Paul II. *Dives in misericordia.* Encyclical, November 30, 1980.

————. *Fides et ratio.* London: Catholic Truth Society, 1998.

Johnson, Douglas, ed. *Faith-Based Diplomacy: Trumping Realpolitik.* New York: Oxford University Press, 2003.

Johnson, Douglas, and Cynthia Sampson, eds. *Religion, the Missing Dimension of State-craft*. New York: Oxford University Press, 1994.

Johnson, James Turner. "Humanitarian Intervention, Christian Ethical Reasoning, and the Just-War Idea." In Lugo, *Sovereignty at the Crossroads*, 127–44.

Johnson, Paul. "The Almost Chosen People." *First Things* 164 (2006): 17–22.

Johnston, Todd M., and David B. Barrett. "Quantifying Alternate Futures of Religion and Religions." *Futures* 36 (2004): 947–60.

Jörg, J.E. *Geschichte des Protestantismus in seiner neuesten Entwicklung*. Vol. 2. Freiburg im Breisgau: Herder'sche Verhandlung, 1858.

Judis, John B. "The Chosen Nation: The Influence of Religion on U.S. Foreign Policy." Carnegie Endowment for International Peace. Policy Brief 37, March 2005. http://www.carnegieendowment.org/files/PB37.judis.FINAL.pdf.

Juergensmeyer, Mark. *Global Rebellion: Religious Challenges to the Secular State, from Christian Militias to Al Qaeda*. Berkeley: University of California Press, 2008.

———. *Terror in the Mind of God*. Berkeley: University of California Press, 2000.

Kaiser, Robert G. "Gorbachev: Triumph and Failure." *Foreign Affairs* 70, no. 2 (1991): 160–74.

Kamphausen, Georg. *Die Erfindung Amerikas in der Kulturkritik der Generation von 1890*. Göttingen: Velbrück Wissenschaft, 2002.

Kaplan, David E. "Hearts, Minds and Dollars." *U.S. News and World Report*, April 25, 2005.

———. "Of Jihad, Networks and the War of Ideas." *U.S. News and World Report*, June 22, 2006. http://www.usnews.com/usnews/news/articles/060622/22natsec.htm.

Katz, Steven T. "Pequots and the Question of Genocide: A Reply to Michael Freeman." *New England Quarterly* 68 (1995): 641–49.

———. "The Pequot War Reconsidered." *New England Quarterly* 64 (1991): 206–24.

Kengor, Paul. *God and George W. Bush: A Spiritual Life*. New York: Regan, 2004.

Kennedy, John F. "Inaugural Address." January 20, 1961. *Public Papers of the Presidents: John F. Kennedy, 1961*. Washington, D.C.: Government Printing Office, 1962.

Kepel, Gilles. *The Revenge of God*. University Park: Penn State University Press, 1994.

Kepel, Gilles and Jean-Pierre Milelli, *Al Qaeda in Its Own Words*. Cambridge, Mass.: Harvard University Press, 2008.

Khadduri, Majid. *The Islamic Conception of Justice*. Baltimore: Johns Hopkins University Press, 1984.

Khalidi, Rashid. *Resurrecting Empire: Western Footprints and America's Perilous Path in the Middle East*. Boston: Beacon, 2004.

Khalizad, Zalmay. "Afghanistan's Milestone." *Washington Post*, January 6, 2004.

Kindopp, Jason. "Principled Engagement in China." *Review of Faith and International Affairs* 1, no. 1 (2003): 21–30.

Kindopp, Jason, and Carol Lee Hamrin, eds. *God and Caesar in China: Policy Implications of Church-State Tensions*. Washington, D.C.: Brookings, 2004.

King, Martin Luther, Jr. *I Have a Dream: Writings and Speeches that Changed the World*. Edited by James M. Washington. San Francisco: HarperSanFrancisco, 1992.

Kirby, Dianne. "Divinely Sanctioned: The Anglo-American Cold War Alliance and the Defence of Western Civilization and Christianity, 1945–48." *Journal of Contemporary History* 35 (2000): 385–412.

———, ed. *Religion and the Cold War* (New York: Palgrave, 2003).

Klausen, Jytte. *The Islamic Challenge: Politics and Religion in Western Europe*. Oxford: Oxford University Press, 2005.

Knight, Janice. *Orthodoxies in Massachusetts: Rereading American Puritanism*. Cambridge, Mass.: Harvard University Press, 1994.

Kohn, Jerome, ed. *Hannah Arendt: Essays in Understanding, 1930–1954*. New York: Harcourt Brace, 1994.

Koyzis, David T. *Political Visions and Illusions: A Survey and Christian Critique of Contemporary Ideologies*. Downers Grove, Ill.: InterVarsity, 2003.

Krasner, Stephen. "Compromising Westphalia." *International Security* 20, no. 3 (1995): 115–51.

Kratochwil, Friedrich. "Constructing a New Orthodoxy? Wendt's 'Social Theory of International Politics' and the Constructivist Challenge." *Millennium* 29, no. 1 (2000): 73–101.

———. "Sovereignty as Dominium: Is There a Right to Humanitarian Intervention?" In *Beyond Westphalia: State Sovereignty and International Intervention*, edited by Gene M. Lyons and Michael Mastanduno, 21–42. Baltimore: John Hopkins University Press, 1995.

Kubálková, Vendulka. "Toward an International Political Theology." In Hatzopoulos and Petito, *Religion in International Relations*, 79–105.

Kuipers, Ronald A. *Critical Faith: Toward a Renewed Understanding of Religious Life and its Public Accountability*. New York: Rodopi, 2002.

Kuklick, Bruce. *Blind Oracles: Intellectuals and War from Kennan to Kissinger*. Princeton: Princeton University Press, 2006.

———. *Churchmen and Philosophers: From Jonathan Edwards to John Dewey*. New Haven: Yale University Press, 1985.

Kuklick, Bruce, and D. G. Hart, eds. *Religious Advocacy and American History*. Grand Rapids: Eerdmans, 1997.

Kurki, Malja. "Causes of a Divided Discipline: Rethinking the Concept of Cause in International Relations Theory." *Review of International Studies* 32, no. 2 (2006): 189–216.

Kürnberger, Ferdinand. *Der Amerikamüde*. Berlin: Freitag Verlag, 1982.

Kurth, James. "The Protestant Deformation and American Foreign Policy." *Orbis* 42 (1998): 221–38.

Ladd, George Elton, and Donald A. Hagner. *A Theology of the New Testament*. Rev. ed. Grand Rapids: Eerdmans, 1993.

Lahneman, William J. "Military Intervention: Lessons for the Twenty-First Century." In *Military Intervention: Cases in Context for the Twenty-First Century*, edited by William J. Lahneman, 165–99. Lanham, Md.: Rowman & Littlefield, 2004.

LaHurd, Carol Schersten. "'So That the Sinner Will Repent': Forgiveness in Islam and Christianity." *Dialog* 35, no. 4 (1996): 287–92.

Lambert, Frank. *The Founding Fathers and the Place of Religion in America*. Princeton: Princeton University Press, 2003.

———. *"Pedlar in Divinity": George Whitefield and the Transatlantic Revivals*. Princeton: Princeton University Press, 1994.

Langan, John. "Humanitarian Intervention: From Concept to Reality." In Abrams, *Close Calls*, 109–24.

Laqueur, Walter. *A History of Zionism*. New York: Holt, Rinehart & Winston, 1972.

———. *The Last Days of Europe: Epitaph for an Old Continent*. New York: St. Martin's, 2007.

Larson, David L., ed. *The Puritan Ethic in United States Foreign Policy*. Princeton: Van Norstrand, 1966.

Lausten, Carsten B., and Ole Waever. "In Defense of Religion: Sacred Referent Objects for Securitization." *Millennium* 29, no. 3 (2000): 705–39.

Lawrence, Bruce, ed. *Messages to the World: The Statements of Osama Bin Laden*. New York: Verso, 2005.

Lederer, William J., and Eugene Burdick. *The Ugly American*. New York: Fawcett Crest, 1958.

Leffler, Melvyn P. "9/11 and American Foreign Policy." *Diplomatic History* 29 (2005): 395–413.

———. "Bringing it Together: The Parts and the Whole." In *Reviewing the Cold War: Approaches, Interpretations, Theory,* edited by Odd Arne Westad, 43–63. London: Frank Cass, 2000.

———. "Bush's Foreign Policy." *Foreign Policy,* September/October 2004, 22–28.

———. "The Cold War: What Do 'We Now Know'?" *American Historical Review* 104 (1999): 501–24.

———. "New Approaches, Old Interpretations, and Prospective Configurations." *Diplomatic History* 19 (1995): 172–96.

———. *A Preponderance of Power: National Security, the Truman Administration, and the Cold War.* Stanford: Stanford University Press, 1992.

Leo XIII. *Testem benevolentiae nostrae.* "Concerning New Opinions, Virtue, Nature and Grace, with Regard to Americanism." Encyclical, January 12, 1899.

Lepore, Jill. *The Name of War: King Philip's War and the Origins of American Identity.* New York: Knopf, 1998.

Lettow, Paul. *Ronald Reagan and His Quest to Abolish Nuclear Weapons.* New York: Random House, 2005.

Levenson, Jon D. *Creation and the Persistence of Evil.* Princeton: Princeton University Press, 1988.

Levy, David W. *The Debate Over Vietnam.* Baltimore: Johns Hopkins University Press, 1995.

Lewis, Anthony. "The Challenge of Global Justice Now." *Daedalus* 132, no. 1 (2003): 5–9.

Lewis, Bernard. *What Went Wrong? The Clash Between Islam and Modernity in the Middle East.* San Francisco: Harper, 2003.

Lieven, Anatol. *America Right or Wrong: An Anatomy of American Nationalism.* New York: Oxford University Press, 2004.

Lilla, Mark. "Godless Europe." *The New York Times,* April 2, 2006.

Lincoln, Bruce. *Holy Terrors: Thinking about Religion after September 11.* Chicago: University of Chicago Press, 2003.

Link, Arthur S. *Wilson the Diplomatist: A Look at His Major Foreign Policies.* Baltimore: Johns Hopkins University Press, 1957.

Linklater, Andrew. "The Achievements of Critical Theory," in *International Theory: Positivism and Beyond,* edited by Steve Smith, Ken Booth, and Marysia Zalewski. Cambridge: Cambridge University Press, 1996: 279–98.

Lippincott, Benjamin Evans. *Victorian Critics of Democracy: Carlyle, Ruskin, Arnold, Stephen, Maine, Lecky.* New York: Octagon, 1964.

Lipset, Seymour Martin. *American Exceptionalism: A Double-Edged Sword.* New York: Norton, 1996.

Loudon, Bruce. "Terror Group's Threat Raises Dalai Lama Alert." *Australian,* April 3, 2007.

Löwith, Karl. *Meaning in History.* Chicago: University of Chicago Press, 1949.

Lugo, Luis E., ed. *Sovereignty at the Crossroads? Morality and International Politics in the Post–Cold War Era.* Lanham, Md.: Rowman & Littlefield, 1996.

Lumsdaine, David H., ed. *Evangelical Christianity and Democracy in Asia.* New York: Oxford University Press, 2008.

Luttwak, Edward. "The Missing Dimension." In Johnson and Sampson, *Religion,* 8–19.

MacIntyre, Alasdair. *After Virtue: A Study in Moral Theory.* 2nd ed. Notre Dame, Ind.: University of Notre Dame Press, 1984.

———. *Dependent Rational Animals: Why Human Beings Need the Virtues.* Chicago: Open Court, 1999.

———. *Whose Justice? Which Rationality?* Notre Dame, Ind.: University of Notre Dame Press, 1988.

Macmillan, Margaret. *Paris 1919.* New York: Random House, 2001.

Magee, Malcolm D. *What the World Should Be: Woodrow Wilson and the Crafting of a Faith-Based Foreign Policy.* Waco, Tex.: Baylor University Press, 2008.

Mandelbaum, Michael. "Democracy Without America: The Spontaneous Spread of Freedom." *Foreign Affairs* 86, no. 5 (2007): 119–30.

Mansfield, Laura, ed. *Al Qaeda 2006 Yearbook* (London: TLG Publications, 2007).

———, trans. and ed. *His Own Words: A Translation of the Writings of Dr. Ayman al Zawahiri.* Old Tappan, N.J.: TLG Publications, 2006.

Mansfield, Stephen. *The Faith of George W. Bush.* New York: Tarcher, 2003.

Marcuse, Herbert. *One-Dimensional Man.* Boston: Beacon, 1991.

Markovits, Andrei S. *Uncouth Nation: Why Europe Dislikes America.* Princeton: Princeton University Press, 2007.

Marsden, George M. *The Outrageous Idea of Christian Scholarship.* New York: Oxford University Press, 1997.

———. *The Soul of the American University: From Protestant Establishment to Established Nonbelief.* New York: Oxford University Press, 1992.

Marshall, Christopher D. *Beyond Retribution: A New Testament Vision for Justice, Crime and Punishment.* Grand Rapids: Eerdmans, 2001.

Marshall, Paul. "Four Million: The Number to Keep in Mind This November." *National Review Online,* August 27, 2004. http://search.nationalreview.com/.

———. "The Islamists' Other Weapon." *Commentary* 119, no. 4 (2005): 60–63.

———. "The Next Hotbed of Islamic Radicalism." *Washington Post,* October 8, 2002.

———. "Political Leaders Can No Longer Ignore Religion." *Dallas Morning News,* April 5, 2003.

———. "Radical Islam's Move on Africa." *Washington Post,* October 16, 2003.

———, ed. *Radical Islam's Rules: The Worldwide Spread of Extreme Shari'a Law.* Lanham, Md.: Rowman & Littlefield, 2005.

———. "Religion and Terrorism: Misreading Bin Laden." In Marshall, Gilbert, and Green-Ahmanson, *Blind Spot,* 31–46.

———. "The Southeast Asian Front." *Weekly Standard,* April 5, 2004.

———. "'Taliban Lite': Afghanistan Fast Forwards." *National Review Online,* November 7, 2003. http://search.nationalreview.com/.

———. "This War We're In," *National Review Online,* November 26, 2002. http://search.nationalreview.com/.

———. "Universal Human Rights and the Role of the State." In Lugo, *Sovereignty at the Crossroads,* 153–76.

———. "World Silence over Slain Muslims." *Boston Globe,* October 13, 2003.

Marshall, Paul, Lela Gilbert, and Roberta Green. *Islam at the Crossroads.* Grand Rapids: Baker, 2002.

Marshall, Paul, Lela Gilbert, and Roberta Green Ahmanson, *Blind Spot: When Journalists Don't Get Religion.* Oxford: Oxford University Press, 2009.

Martin, William. "With God on Their Side: Religion and U.S. Foreign Policy." In *Religion Returns to the Public Square: Faith and Policy in America,* edited by Hugh Heclo and Wilfred M. McClay, 327–59. Baltimore: Johns Hopkins University Press, 2003.

Marty, Martin E. *Modern American Religion.* Vol. 3, *Under God, Indivisible, 1941–1960.* Chicago: University of Chicago Press, 1996.

———. *Righteous Empire: The Protestant Experience in America.* New York: Dial Press, 1970.

Mauser, Ulrich. *The Gospel of Peace: A Scriptural Message for Today's World*. Louisville, Ky.: Westminster John Knox, 1992.

McAlister, Melanie. *Epic Encounters: Culture, Media, and U.S. Interests in the Middle East since 1945*. Rev. ed. Berkeley: University of California Press, 2005.

McCaffrey, James M. *Army of Manifest Destiny: The American Soldier in the Mexican War, 1846–1848*. New York: New York University Press, 1992.

McCartney, Paul T. "American Nationalism and U.S. Foreign Policy from September 11 to the Iraq War." *Political Science Quarterly* 119 (2004): 399–423.

McCormick, Thomas J. *America's Half-Century: United States Foreign Policy in the Cold War*. Baltimore: Johns Hopkins University Press, 1989.

McDougall, Walter A. *Promised Land, Crusader State: The American Encounter with the World Since 1776*. Boston: Houghton Mifflin, 1997.

McFarlane, Robert. "The Iraqi Nation." *Wall Street Journal*, June 27, 2007.

McKenna, George. *The Puritan Origins of American Patriotism*. New Haven: Yale University Press, 2007.

McPherson, James M. *Battle Cry of Freedom: The Civil War Era*. New York: Oxford University Press, 1988.

McTernan, Oliver. *Violence in God's Name: Religion in an Age of Global Conflict*. London: Darton, Longman, Todd, 2003.

Mead, Walter Russell, *God and Gold: Britain, America, and the Making of the Modern World* (New York: Knopf, 2007).

———. "God's Country?" *Foreign Affairs* 85, no. 5 (2006): 24–43. http://www.foreignaffairs.com/articles/61914/walter-russell-mead/gods-country.

———. *Special Providence: American Foreign Policy and How It Changed the World*. New York: Knopf, 2001.

Mearsheimer, John J., and Stephen M. Walt. "The Israel Lobby." *London Review of Books* 28, no. 6 (March 23, 2006), 3–12.

———. *The Israel Lobby and U.S. Foreign Policy*. New York: Penguin, 2007.

Melvern, Linda. "A Conspiracy to Murder: The Rwandan Genocide." Parliamentary lecture, London, May 18, 2004. http://www.lindamelvern.com/parliament_lecture.htm.

Melvoin, Richard I. *New England Outpost: War and Society in Colonial Deerfield*. New York: Norton, 1989.

Merk, Frederick. *Manifest Destiny and Mission in American History: A Reinterpretation*. New York: Knopf, 1963.

Meyer, Jeffrey F. *Myths in Stone: Religious Dimensions of Washington, D.C.* Berkeley: University of California Press, 2001.

Middle East Media Research Institute (MEMRI). "Al-Qaeda Deputy Leader Ayman Al-Zawahiri Interview Produced By Al-Sahab Media." *Special Dispatch* 1575 (May 8, 2007). http://www.memri.org/bin/articles.cgi?Page=archives&Area=sd&ID=SP157507.

———. "Arab Reformists Under Threat by Islamists: Bin Laden Urges Killing of 'Freethinkers.'" *Special Dispatch* 1153 (May 3, 2006). http://www.memri.org/bin/articles.cgi?Page=archives&Area=sd&ID=SP115306.

———. "The Full Version of Osama bin Laden's Speech," *Special Dispatch* 811 (November 5, 2004). http://memri.org/bin/articles.cgi?Page=archives&Area=sd&ID=SP81104.

———. "Osama Bin Laden: 'Today There is a Conflict between World Heresy Under the Leadership of America on the One Hand and the Islamic Nation with the Mujahideen in its Vanguard on the Other.'" *Special Dispatch* 837 (December 30, 2004). http://www.memri.org/bin/articles.cgi?Page=archives&Area=sd&ID=SP83804.

———. "Osama Bin Laden to the Iraqi People: It Is Forbidden to Participate in Iraqi & PA Elections; Jihad in Palestine and Iraq is Incumbent upon Residents of All Muslim Countries, Not Just Iraqis and Palestinians; Zarqawi is the Commander of Al-Qa'ida in Iraq." *Special Dispatch* 838 (December 30, 2004). http://www.memri.org/bin/articles.cgi?Page=archives&Area=sd&ID=SP83704.

Miller, Lisa, and Mathew Philips. "Caliwho? Why is President Bush Talking about an Islamic Caliphate? And What Does the Word Mean?" *Newsweek*, October 13, 2006.

Minear, Larry, and Thomas Weiss. *Mercy under Fire*. Boulder, Colo.: Westview, 1995.

Miscamble, Wilson D. "Francis Cardinal Spellman and 'Spellman's War.'" In *The Human Tradition in the Vietnam Era*, edited by David L. Anderson, 3–22. Wilmington, Del.: Scholarly Resources, 2000.

Mitchell, Joshua. *Not By Reason Alone: Religion, History, and Identity in Early Modern Political Thought*. Chicago: University of Chicago Press, 1993.

Moll, Rob. "Should Evangelicals Support Bush's Foreign Policy If He Can't Guarantee Religious Freedom?" *Christianity Today Online*, April 24, 2006. http://www.christianitytoday.com/ct/2006/117/13.0.html.

Moltmann, Günter. "Deutscher Antiamerikanismus Heute und Früher." In *Vom Sinn der Geschichte*, edited by Otmar Franz, 85–105. Stuttgart: Seewald, 1976.

Moltmann, Jürgen. *The Crucified God: The Cross of Christ as the Foundation and Criticism of Christian Theology*. Minneapolis: Fortress, 1993.

Morgan, Edmund S. *The Genuine Article: A Historian Looks at Early America*. New York: Norton, 2004.

———. "The Puritan Ethic and the American Revolution." *William and Mary Quarterly*, 3rd series, 24 (1967): 3–43.

Mueller, John. "Terrorphobia: Our False Sense of Insecurity." *American Interest* 3, no. 5 (2008): 6–13.

Mulder, John M. *Woodrow Wilson: The Years of Preparation*. Princeton: Princeton University Press, 1978.

Muller-Fahrenholz, Geiko. *America's Battle for God*. Grand Rapids: Eerdmans, 2007.

Murphey, Murray G. "Advocacy and Academe." In Kuklick and Hart, *Religious Advocacy*, 65–80.

Murray, John Courtney. *We Hold These Truths: Catholic Reflections on the American Proposition*. Kansas City, Mo.: Sheed & Ward, 1960.

Myrdal, Gunnar. *An American Dilemma: The Negro Problem and Modern Democracy*. New York: Harper & Bros., 1944.

Nardin, Terry. "Epilogue." In Hatzopoulos and Petito, *Religion in International Relations*, 277–82.

Natsios, Andrew. "Complex Humanitarian Emergencies and Moral Choice." In Elliott, *Close Calls*, 125–43.

Neiman, Susan. *Evil in Modern Thought: An Alternative History of Philosophy*. Princeton: Princeton University Press, 2002.

Nietzsche, Friedrich. *The Gay Science*. Translated by Walter Kaufmann. New York: Random House, 1974.

Noll, Mark A. *America's God: From Jonathan Edwards to Abraham Lincoln*. New York: Oxford University Press, 2002.

———. *One Nation Under God? Christian Faith and Political Action in America*. San Francisco: Harper & Row, 1988.

Noonan, John. *The Church that Can and Cannot Change*. Notre Dame, Ind.: University of Notre Dame Press, 2005.

Norris, Pippa, and Ronald Inglehart. *Sacred and Secular: Religion and Politics Worldwide*. Cambridge: Cambridge University Press, 2004.

Novak, Michael. *The Spirit of Democratic Capitalism*. New York: Simon & Schuster, 1982.

Nurser, John. *For All Peoples and All Nations: Christian Churches and Human Rights*. Geneva: World Council of Churches, 2005.

Obama, Barack. "Barack Obama's Inaugural Address," transcription, *The New York Times*, January 20, 2009. http://www.nytimes.com/2009/01/20/us/politics/20text-obama.html.

O'Donovan, Oliver. *The Desire of the Nations: Rediscovering the Roots of Political Theology*. Cambridge: Cambridge University Press, 1996.

———. *Principles in the Public Realm: The Dilemma of Christian Moral Witness*. Oxford: Clarendon, 1984.

Omar, A. Rashied. "Between Compassion and Justice: Locating an Islamic Definition of Peace." *Peace Colloquy* 7 (2005).

"Open Letter to His Holiness Pope Benedict XVI." *Islamica Magazine*, October 12, 2006.

Oren, Michael B. *Power, Faith, and Fantasy: America in the Middle East, 1776 to the Present*. New York: Norton, 2007.

Orsi, Robert A. *Between Heaven and Earth: The Religious Worlds People Make and the Scholars Who Study Them*. Princeton: Princeton University Press, 2005.

———. "The Disciplinary Vocabulary of Modernity." *International Journal* 59 (2004): 879–85.

———. *Madonna of 115th Street: Faith and Community in Italian Harlem, 1880–1950*. New Haven: Yale University Press, 1985.

———. *Thank You, St. Jude: Women's Devotion to the Patron Saint of Hopeless Causes*. New Haven: Yale University Press, 1996.

Osiander, Andreas. "Sovereignty, International Relations, and the Westphalian Myth." *International Organization* 55, no. 2 (2001): 251–87.

Pachter, Marc, and Frances Wein, eds. *Abroad in America: Visitors to the New Nation, 1776–1914*. Reading, Mass.: Addison-Wesley, 1976.

Paris, Roland. "Peacebuilding and the Limits of Liberal Internationalism." *International Security* 22, no. 2 (1997): 54–89.

Pavlischek, Keith J. "Questioning the New Natural Law Theory: The Case of Religious Liberty as Defended by Robert P. George in *Making Men Moral*." In *A Moral Enterprise: Politics, Reason and the Common Good*, edited by Kenneth L. Grasso and Robert P. Hunt, 127–42. Wilmington, Del.: ISI Books, 2002.

Perkins, Bradford. "Early American Foreign Relations: Opportunities and Challenges." *Diplomatic History* 22 (1998), 115–20.

Pfaff, William. "Manifest Destiny: A New Direction for America." *New York Review of Books* 54, no. 2 (2007). http://www.nybooks.com/articles/19879.

Phares, Walid. "Bin Laden's 'State Of Jihad' Speech." Counterterrorism Blog, April 24, 2006. http://counterterrorismblog.org/2006/04/bin_ladens_state_of_jihad_spee.php.

Phillips, James. "Proposed Timetables for U.S. Withdrawal Would Sabotage Reconciliation in Iraq." Heritage Foundation WebMemo #1632, September 31, 2007. http://www.heritage.org/Research/MiddleEast/wm1632.cfm.

Phillips, Jonathan. *The Fourth Crusade and the Sack of Constantinople*. New York: Viking, 2004.

Phillips, Kevin. *American Dynasty: Aristocracy, Fortune, and the Politics of Deceit in the House of Bush*. New York: Viking, 2004.

———. *American Theocracy: The Peril and Politics of Radical Religion, Oil, and Borrowed Money in the 21st Century*. New York: Viking, 2006.

Philpott, Daniel, "The Challenge of September 11 to Secularism in International Relations." *World Politics* 55 (2002): 66–95.

———. "Explaining the Political Ambivalence of Religion." *American Political Science Review* 101, no. 3 (2007): 505–25.

———. "Has the Study of Global Politics Found Religion?" *Annual Review of Political Science* 12 (2009): 183–202.

———. "One Professor's Guide to Studying International Relations and Peace Studies from a Catholic Perspective." *University of Notre Dame Magazine*, Summer 2009. http://magazine.nd.edu/news/11933.

———, ed. *The Politics of Past Evil: Religion, Reconciliation and the Dilemmas of Transitional Justice*. Notre Dame, Ind.: University of Notre Dame Press, 2006.

———. "The Religious Roots of Modern International Relations." *World Politics* 52, no. 2 (2000): 206–45.

———. *Revolutions in Sovereignty: How Ideas Shaped Modern International Relations*. Princeton: Princeton University Press, 2001.

———. "Westphalia and Sovereignty in International Society." *Political Studies* 47, no. 3 (1999): 566–89.

Pipes, Daniel. "God and Mammon: Does Poverty Cause Militant Islam?" *National Interest* Winter, 2001. http://www.nationalinterest.org/General.aspx?id=92&id2=11154.

Pipes, Richard, "Putin & Co.: What Is to Be Done?" *Commentary* 125, no. 5 (2008): 30–36.

———. "The Soviet Union Adrift." In "America and the World," special issue, *Foreign Affairs* 70, no. 1 (1990): 70–87.

Plantinga, Alvin, and Nicholas Wolterstorff, eds. *Faith and Rationality: Reason and Belief in God*. Notre Dame, Ind.: University of Notre Dame Press, 1983.

Plummer, Brenda Gayle. "Introduction." In *Window on Freedom: Race, Civil Rights, and Foreign Affairs, 1945–1988*, edited by Brenda Gayle Plummer, 1–20. Chapel Hill: University of North Carolina Press, 2003.

———. *Rising Wind: Black Americans and U.S. Foreign Affairs, 1935–1960*. Chapel Hill: University of North Carolina Press, 1996.

Polner, Murray, and Jim O'Grady. *Disarmed and Dangerous: The Radical Lives and Times of Daniel and Philip Berrigan*. New York: Basic, 1997.

Porter, Brian. "The International Political Thought of Martin Wight." *International Affairs* 83, no. 4 (2007): 783–89.

Pruessen, Ronald W. *John Foster Dulles: The Road to Power*. New York: Free Press, 1982.

Putnam, Robert D. *Bowling Alone: The Collapse and Revival of American Community*. New York: Simon & Schuster, 2000.

Ramsey, Paul. "The Ethics of Intervention." *Review of Politics* 25, no. 3 (1965): 287–310.

———. *The Just War: Force and Political Responsibility*. New York: Scribner's, 1968.

Ranger, Terence O., ed. *Evangelical Christianity and Democracy in Africa*. New York: Oxford University Press, 2008.

Ratzinger, Joseph and Maracello Pera, *Without Roots: The West, Relativism, Christianity, Islam*. Trans. Michael F. Moore. New York: Basic Books, 2006.

Reed, James. *The Missionary Mind and American East Asia Policy, 1911–1915*. Cambridge, Mass.: Council on East Asian Studies, Harvard University, 1983.

Reinharz, Jehuda. *Chaim Weizmann: The Making of a Statesman*. New York: Oxford University Press, 1993.

Reisach, Karl August von. "Il Mormonismo nelle sue attinenze col moderno protestantismo." *La Civiltà Cattolica*, 4th series, 6 (May 19, 1860): 391–413.

Remnick, David. "The Apostate." *New Yorker*, July 30, 2007, 32–37.

———. *Lenin's Tomb: The Last Days of the Soviet Empire*. New York: Random House, 1993.

Rengger, Nicholas, and Renée Jeffery. "Moral Evil and International Relations." *SAIS Review* 25, no. 1 (2005): 3–16.

Reus-Smit, Christian. *The Moral Purpose of the State*. Princeton: Princeton University Press, 1999.

Revel, Jean-François. *Anti-Americanism*. Translated by Diarmid Cammell. San Francisco: Encounter, 2000.

Reynolds, Charles. *Theory and Explanation in International Politics*. Oxford: Martin Robertson, 1973.

Ribuffo, Leo P. "Afterword: Cultural Shouting Matches and the Academic Study of American Religious History." In Kuklick and Hart, *Religious Advocacy*, 221–33.

———. "Religion." In *Encyclopedia of American Foreign Policy*, edited by Alexander DeConde, Richard Dean Burns, and Fredrik Logevall, 371–91. New York: Scribner's, 2002.

———. "Religion and American Foreign Policy: The Story of a Complex Relationship." *National Interest* 52 (1998): 36–51.

———. "Religion in the History of U.S. Foreign Policy." In Abrams, *Influence of Faith*, 1–27.

———. *The Old Christian Right: The Protestant Far Right from the Great Depression to the Cold War*. Philadelphia: Temple University Press, 1983.

Richmond, Oliver P. "The Problem of Peace: Understanding the 'Liberal Peace.'" *Conflict, Security, & Development* 6, no. 3 (2006), 291–314.

Ringer, Fritz K. *The Decline of the German Mandarins: The German Academic Community, 1890–1933*. Cambridge, Mass.: Harvard University Press, 1969.

Roberts, Adam. "Buddhism and Politics in South Vietnam." *World Today* 21 (1965): 240–50.

Rodgers, Daniel T. "Exceptionalism." In *Imagined Histories: American Historians Interpret the Past*, edited by Anthony Molho and Gordon S. Wood, 21–40. Princeton: Princeton University Press, 1998.

Roger, Philippe. *The American Enemy: The Story of French Anti-Americanism*. Translated by Sharon Bowman. Chicago: University of Chicago Press, 2005.

Rosenberg, Emily S. "A Call to Revolution: A Roundtable on Early U.S. Foreign Relations." *Diplomatic History* 22 (1998): 63–70.

———. "'Foreign Affairs' after World War II: Connecting Sexual and International Politics." *Diplomatic History* 18 (1994): 59–70.

———. "Gender." *Journal of American History* 77 (1990), 116–24.

Rotberg, Robert I., and Dennis Thompson, eds. *Truth v. Justice: The Morality of Truth Commissions*. Princeton: Princeton University Press, 2000.

Rotter, Andrew J. "Christians, Muslims, and Hindus: Religion and U.S.–South Asian Relations, 1947–1954." *Diplomatic History* 24 (2000): 593–612.

———. *Comrades at Odds: The United States and India, 1947–1964*. Ithaca: Cornell University Press, 2000.

Roy, Olivier. *Globalized Islam*. London: Hurst, 2002.

Ruthven, Malise. *Fundamentalism: The Search for Meaning*. Oxford: Oxford University Press, 2004.

Rutten, Tim. "Same Sex Marriage, Civil Unions, Gays and Lesbians." *Los Angeles Times*, March 6, 2004.

Sachedina, Abdulaziz Abdulhussein. *The Islamic Roots of Democratic Pluralism*. New York: Oxford University Press, 2001.

Sachs, Susan. "Iraqis Seek Justice, or Vengeance, for Victims of the Killing Fields." *The New York Times*, November 4, 2003.

Sandel, Michael J. "Freedom of Conscience or Freedom of Choice." In *Articles of Faith, Articles of Peace: The Religious Liberty Clauses and the American Public Philosophy*, edited by James Davison Hunter and Os Guinness, 74–92. Washington, D.C.: Brookings, 1990.

Sanders, Ronald. *The High Walls of Jerusalem: A History of the Balfour Declaration and the Birth of the British Mandate for Palestine*. New York: Holt, Rinehart & Winston, 1983.

Sarkozy, Nicolas. Speech of president of the French Republic at the opening of the Fifteenth Ambassadors' Conference, Paris, August 27, 2007.

Sayers, Dorothy L. *Begin Here: A War-Time Essay*. London: Victor Gollancz, 1940.

Schaff, Philip. *The Principle of Protestantism*. Translated by John Nevin. Chambersburg: Publication of the German Reformed Church, 1845.

Schlesinger, Arthur M., Jr. "America: Experiment or Destiny?" *American Historical Review* 82 (1977), 505–30.

———. *The Cycles of American History*. Boston: Houghton Mifflin, 1986.

Schmiechen, Peter. *Saving Power: Theories of Atonement and Forms of the Church*. Grand Rapids: Eerdmans, 2005.

Schneider, Peter. "Across a Great Divide." *The New York Times*, March 12, 2004.

Schulzinger, Robert D., ed. *A Companion to American Foreign Relations*. Oxford: Blackwell, 2003.

Schweizer, Karl W. and Paul Sharp, eds. *The International Thought of Herbert Butterfield*. New York: Palgrave, 2007.

Scruton, Roger. *The West and the Rest*. London: Continuum, 2002.

Seiple, Robert A., and Dennis R. Hoover. *Religion & Security: The New Nexus in International Relations*. Lanham, Md.: Rowman & Littlefield, 2004.

Seybolt, Taylor B. "The Myth of Neutrality." *Peace Review* 8 (1996): 521–27.

Shah, Timothy Samuel, ed. *Evangelical Christianity and Democracy in Global Perspective*. New York: Oxford University Press, forthcoming.

Sharp, Jeremy M. *U.S. Democracy Promotion in the Middle East: The Islamist Dilemma*. Washington, D.C.: Congressional Research Service, June 15, 2006.

Sharp, Paul. "Herbert Butterfield, the English School and the Civilizing Virtues of Diplomacy." *International Affairs* 79, no. 4 (2003): 855–878.

Shea, Nina. "Conclusion: American Responses to Extreme *Shari'a*." In *Radical Islam's Rules: The Worldwide Spread of Extreme Shari'a Law*, edited by Paul Marshall (Lanham, Md.: Rowman & Littlefield, 2005), 195–212.

———. *The Contest of Ideas with Radical Islam: The Centrality of the Idea of Religious Freedom and Tolerance*. Perspectives for the New Administration. Washington, D.C.: Hudson Institute, 2009.

———. "Genocide Doesn't Just Happen." *National Review Online*, June 1, 2007. http://www.nationalreview.com/.

Shinn, Roger L. "Realism, Radicalism, and Eschatology in Reinhold Niebuhr: A Reassessment." *Journal of Religion* 54 (1974): 409–23.

Shirley, Eugene B., Jr., and Michael Rowe, eds. *Candle in the Wind: Religion in the Soviet Union*. Washington, D.C.: Ethics and Public Policy Center, 1989.

Shlapentokh, Vladimir. "Trust in Public Institutions in Russia: The Lowest in the World." *Johnson's Russia List*, no. 9186, June 27, 2005.

Silverman, Bertram, and Murray Yanowitch. *New Rich, New Poor, New Russia*. Armonk, N.Y.: M. E. Sharpe, 2000.

Singer, Peter. *The President of Good and Evil: The Ethics of George W. Bush*. New York: Dutton, 2004.

Sittser, Gerald L. *A Cautious Patriotism: The American Churches and the Second World War*. Chapel Hill: University of North Carolina Press, 1997.

Sizer, Stephen. *Christian Zionism: Road-map to Armageddon?* Leicester, UK: InterVarsity, 2004.

Skillen, James W. *In Pursuit of Justice*. Lanham, Md.: Rowman & Littlefield, 2004.

———, ed. *Prospects and Ambiguities of Globalization: Critical Assessments at a Time of Growing Turmoil*. Lanham, Md.: Lexington, 2009.

———. *With or Against the World? America's Role Among the Nations*. Lanham, Md.: Rowman & Littlefield, 2005.

Smidt, Corwin, ed. *Religion as Social Capital: Producing the Common Good*. Waco, Tex.: Baylor University Press, 2003.

Smith, Hedrick. *The New Russians*. New York: Random House, 1990.

———. *The Russians*. New York: Ballantine, 1976.

Smith, Huston. *The Religions of Man*. New York: Harper Colophon, 1958.

Smith, Rogers M. "Religious Rhetoric and the Ethics of Public Discourse: The Case of George W. Bush." *Political Theory* 36, no. 2 (2008): 272–98.

Smith, Tony. *America's Mission: The United States and the Worldwide Struggle for Democracy in the Twentieth Century*. Princeton: Princeton University Press, 1994.

———. *Foreign Attachments: The Power of Ethnic Groups in the Making of American Foreign Policy*. Cambridge, Mass.: Harvard University Press, 2000.

Solheim, James, and Jan Nunley. "Bishops Call Waging Reconciliation the Answer to Globalization, Terrorism." Episcopal News Service, September 28, 2001.

Song, Robert. *Christianity and Liberal Society*. Oxford: Clarendon, 1997.

Stackhouse, Max. *God and Globalization*. 4 vols. Harrisburg, Pa.: Trinity, 2000–2007.

Stapleton, Julia. "Modernism, the English Past, and Christianity: Herbert Butterfield and the Study of History." *Historical Journal* 51 (2008): 547–57.

Stepan, Alfred. "Religion, Democracy and the 'Twin Tolerations.'" In *World Religions and Democracy*, edited by Larry Diamond, Marc F. Plattner, and Philip J. Costopoulos, 3–26. Baltimore: Johns Hopkins University Press, 2005.

Stephanson, Anders. "Diplomatic History in the Expanded Field." *Diplomatic History* 22 (1998): 595–603.

———. "Ideology and Neorealist Mirrors." *Diplomatic History* 17 (1993): 285–95.

———. *Manifest Destiny: American Expansion and the Empire of Right*. New York: Hill & Wang, 1995.

———. "Rethinking Cold War History." Review of *We Now Know: Rethinking Cold War History* by John Lewis Gaddis. *Review of International Studies* 24 (1998): 119–24.

Stout, Harry S. "Religion, Communication, and the Ideological Origins of the American Revolution." *William and Mary Quarterly*, 3rd series, 34 (1977): 519–41.

Stout, Harry S., and D. G. Hart, eds. *New Directions in American Religious History*. New York: Oxford University Press, 1997.

Stritzel, Holger. "Towards a Theory of Securitization: Copenhagen and Beyond." *European Journal of International Relations* 13, no. 3 (2007): 357–83.

Taylor, Charles. *A Secular Age*. Cambridge, Mass.: Harvard University Press, 2007.

Teschke, Benno. *The Myth of 1648: Class, Geopolitics and the Making of Modern International Relations*. London: Verso, 2003.

———. "Theorizing the Westphalian System of States: International Relations from Absolutism to Capitalism." *European Journal of International Relations* 8, no. 1 (2002): 5–48.

Tesón, Fernando R. "Ending Tyranny in Iraq." *Ethics & International Affairs* 19, no. 2 (2005): 1–19.

———. "Self-Defense in International Law and Rights of Persons." *Ethics & International Affairs* 18, no. 1 (2004): 87–92.

Tétreault, Mary Ann, and Robert A. Denemark, eds. *Gods, Guns, and Globalization: Religious Radicalism and International Political Economy*. Boulder, Colo.: Lynne Rienner, 2004.

Thomas, Scott M. "Faith, History, and Martin Wight: The Role of Religion in the Historical Sociology of the English School of International Relations." *International Affairs* 77, no. 4 (2001): 905–29.

———. *The Global Resurgence of Religion and the Transformation of International Relations: The Struggle for the Soul of the Twenty-First Century*. Culture and Religion in International Relations. New York: Palgrave Macmillan, 2005.

Thompson, Damian. "Fundamentally Wrong." *Spectator*, September 29, 2001, 15–16.

Thompson, John A. "More Tactics than Strategy: Woodrow Wilson and World War I, 1914–1919." In *Artists of Power: Theodore Roosevelt, Woodrow Wilson, and Their Enduring Impact on U.S. Foreign Policy*, edited by William N. Tilchin and Charles E. Neu, 95–115. Westport, Conn.: Praeger, 2006.

———. *Woodrow Wilson*. London: Longman, 2002.

Thompson, Michael G. "An Exception to Exceptionalism: A Reflection on Reinhold Niebuhr's Vision of 'Prophetic' Christianity and the Problem of Religion and U.S. Foreign Policy." *American Quarterly* 59 (2007): 833–55.

Tivnan, Edward. *Lobby: Jewish Political Power and American Foreign Policy*. New York: Simon & Schuster, 1987.

Tocqueville, Alexis de. *Democracy in America*. Translated by Henry Reeve. Vol. 1. New York: Alfred A. Knopf, 1945.

Torrance, Alan. "The Theological Grounds for Advocating Forgiveness and Reconciliation in the Sociopolitical Realm." In Philpott, *Politics of Past Evil*, 45–86.

Toynbee, Arnold. *An Historian's Approach to Religion*. Oxford: Oxford University Press, 1956.

Trenin, Dmitri. "Reading Russia Right." *Carnegie Endowment Policy Brief*. Washington, D.C.: Carnegie Endowment, October 2005, 1–12.

Trollope, Anthony. *North America*. Edited by Donald Smalley and Bradford Allen Booth. New York: Knopf, 1951.

Trollope, Frances. *Domestic Manners of the Americans*. New York: Penguin, 1997.

Truman, Harry S. "Address at a Luncheon of the National Conference of Christians and Jews." In *Public Papers of the Presidents: Harry S. Truman, 1949*. Washington, D.C.: Government Printing Office, 1964.

———. "Remarks in Alexandria, Va., at the Cornerstone Laying of the Westminster Presbyterian Church." In *Public Papers of the Presidents: Harry S. Truman, 1952–53*. Washington, D.C.: Government Printing Office, 1966.

Tuchman, Barbara W. *Bible and Sword: England and Palestine from the Bronze Age to Balfour*. New York: Ballantine Books, 1956.

Tuck, Stephen. "The New American Histories." *Historical Journal* 48 (2005): 811–32.

Tuveson, Ernest Lee. *Redeemer Nation: The Idea of America's Millennial Role*. Chicago: University of Chicago Press, 1968.

Tyerman, Christopher. *Fighting for Christendom: Holy War and the Crusades*. Oxford: Oxford University Press, 2004.

U.S. Department of Defense. *Measuring Stability and Security in Iraq: Report to Congress in Accordance with the Department of Defense Appropriations Act 2007*. Washington, D.C., 2007.

U.S. Department of State. *2005 Report on International Religious Freedom*. Washington, D.C.: Government Printing Office, 2005.

———. *2006 Report on International Religious Freedom*. Washington, D.C.: Government Printing Office, 2006.

U.S. National Security Council. *The National Security Strategy of the United States of America*. Washington, D.C., September 2002. http://georgewbush-whitehouse.archives.gov/nsc/nss/2002/.

———. *The National Security Strategy of the United States of America*. Washington, D.C., 2006. http://georgewbush-whitehouse.archives.gov/nsc/nss/2006/.

———. *National Strategy for Combating Terrorism.* Washington, D.C., September 2006. http://georgewbush-whitehouse.archives.gov/nsc/nsct/2006/.

United States Institute of Peace. "Establishing the Rule of Law in Afghanistan." Special Report 117, March 2004.

———. "USIP-Facilitated Iraq Reconciliation Agreement a Key Breakthrough for Stability Effort in South Baghdad's 'Triangle of Death.'" News release, October 19, 2007. http://www.usip.org/newsroom/news/usip-facilitated-iraq-reconciliation-agreement-key-breakthrough-stability-effort-south.

Varg, Paul A. *Missionaries, Chinese, and Diplomats: The American Protestant Missionary Movement in China, 1890–1952.* Princeton: Princeton University Press, 1958.

Vatican II. "Declaration of Religious Freedom." In *Documents of Vatican II,* edited by Austin P. Flannery, 719–812. Grand Rapids, MI.: Eerdmans, 1975.

Vattimo, Gianni. "L'unione affronta i nodi decisivi del suo sviluppo." *La Stampa,* May 31, 2003.

Vinz, Warren L. *Pulpit Politics: Faces of American Protestant Nationalism in the Twentieth Century.* Albany: State University of New York Press, 1997.

Voegelin, Eric. *From Enlightenment to Revolution.* Edited by John H. Hallowell. Durham, N.C.: Duke University Press, 1975.

Volf, Miroslav. *Exclusion and Embrace: A Theological Exploration of Identity, Otherness, and Reconciliation.* Nashville, Tenn.: Abingdon, 1996.

Von Der Heydt, Barbara. *Candles Behind the Wall: Heroes of the Peaceful Revolution That Shattered Communism.* Grand Rapids: Eerdmans, 1993.

Wald, Kenneth D., and Clyde Wilcox. "Getting Religion: Has Political Science Rediscovered the Faith Factor?" *American Political Science Review* 100, no. 4 (2006): 523–29.

Walsh, David. *The Growth of the Liberal Soul.* Columbia: University of Missouri Press, 1997.

Walzer, Michael. *Arguing about War.* New Haven: Yale University Press, 2004.

———. "Can There Be a Moral Foreign Policy?" In Dionne, Elshtain, and Drogosz, *Liberty and Power,* 34–53.

———. *Just and Unjust Wars: A Moral Argument with Historical Illustrations.* 2nd ed. New York: Basic, 1992.

———. "The Politics of Rescue." *Social Research* 62, no. 1 (1995): 53–66.

Warren, Heather. *Theologians of a New World Order: Reinhold Niebuhr and the Christian Realists, 1920–1948.* Oxford: Oxford University Press, 1997.

Webb, Stephen H. *American Providence: A Nation With a Mission.* London: Continuum, 2004.

Weber, Max. *The Protestant Ethic and the Spirit of Capitalism.* Translated by Talcott Parsons. New York: Scribner's, 1958.

Weeks, William Earl. "New Directions in the Study of Early American Foreign Relations." In Hogan, *Paths to Power,* 8–43.

Weigel, George. *The Cube and the Cathedral: Europe, America, and Politics without God.* New York: Basic, 2005.

———. *Faith, Reason, and the War Against Jihadism.* New York: Doubleday, 2007.

———. *The Final Revolution: The Resistance Church and the Collapse of Communism.* New York: Oxford University Press, 1992.

———. *Freedom and Its Discontents: Catholicism Confronts Modernity.* Washington, D.C.: Ethics and Public Policy Center, 1991.

Weiss, Thomas G. *Humanitarian Intervention: Ideas in Action.* Cambridge: Polity, 2007.

———. "Principles, Politics, and Humanitarian Action." *Ethics & International Affairs* 13 (1999): 1–22.

Weiss, Thomas G., and Cindy Collins. *Humanitarian Challenges and Intervention*. 2nd ed. Boulder, Colo.: Westview, 2000.

Welch, David A. "The 'Clash of Civilizations' Thesis as an Argument and as a Phenomenon." *Security Studies* 6, no. 4 (1997): 197–216.

Welsh, Jennifer M., ed. *Humanitarian Intervention and International Relations*. Oxford: Oxford University Press, 2003.

Westad, Odd Arne. "The New International History of the Cold War: Three (Possible) Paradigms." *Diplomatic History* 24 (2000): 551–65.

White, Joshua. *Pakistan's Islamist Frontier: Islamic Politics and U.S. Policy in Pakistan's North–West Frontier*. Religion and Security Monographs No. 1. Arlington, Va.: Center on Faith and International Affairs, 2008.

Wight, Martin. "The Church, Russia, and the West." *Ecumenical Review* 1, no. 1 (1948): 25–45.

———. "The Crux for an Historian Brought up in the Christian Tradition." In *A Study of History*, vol. 7, edited by Arnold Toynbee, Annex VII A (III) (a) *Annex III*, 737–48. Oxford: Oxford University Press, 1954.

———. *International Theory: The Three Traditions*. Leicester, UK: Leicester University Press, 1991.

———. "Why Is There No International Theory?" In *Diplomatic Investigations: Essays in the Theory of International Politics*, edited by Herbert Butterfield and Martin Wight, 17–34. London: Allen & Unwin, 1966.

Wilberforce, Samuel. *A History of the Protestant Episcopal Church in America*. New York: Standford & Swords, 1849.

Williams, Rowan. "Saint for Europe and Our Age." *Tablet*, June 13, 2008.

Wilson, John F. *Religion and the American Nation: Historiography and History*. Athens: University of Georgia Press, 2003.

Wolfe, Christopher. *Natural Law Liberalism*. Cambridge: Cambridge University Press, 2006.

Wong, Edward. "Iraqi Video Shows Beheading of Man Said to be American." *The New York Times*, September 21, 2004.

Woodward, Bob. *Plan of Attack*. New York: Simon & Schuster, 2004.

Woodward, C. Vann. *The Old World's New World*. New York: Oxford University Press, 1991.

Worth, Robert F. "The Struggle for Iraq: The Past; Planning a Museum to Tell Iraq's Story." *The New York Times*, September 9, 2003.

Wright, N. T. *Evil and the Justice of God*. Downers Grove, Ill.: InterVarsity, 2006.

Wuthnow, Robert. *The Restructuring of American Religion: Society and Faith Since World War II*. Princeton: Princeton University Press, 1988.

Yoder, Perry. *Shalom: The Bible's Word for Salvation, Justice, and Peace*. Newton, Kans.: Faith & Life, 1987.

Yoder, William. "Cooperation is the Order of the Day." Press release, Russian Union of Evangelical Christians-Baptists, June 21, 2008.

Zakaria, Fareed. *The Future of Freedom: Illiberal Democracy at Home and Abroad*. New York: Norton, 2003.

———. "Why Do They Hate Us? The Politics of Rage." *Newsweek*, October 15, 2001, 22–40.

Zehr, Howard. *Changing Lenses*. Scottdale, Pa.: Herald, 1990.

About the Contributors

JOHN A. BERNBAUM is founder of the Russian-American Christian University (recently renamed the Russian-American Institute) in Moscow and currently serves as the university's president. He has worked for the U.S. State Department and the Council for Christian Colleges & Universities. He has authored many articles and two books, *Why Work? Careers and Employment in Biblical Perspective* (Baker, 1986) and *Perspectives on Peacemaking: Biblical Options in the Nuclear Age* (Regal, 1984). He holds a Ph.D. in European and Russian history from the University of Maryland.

JONATHAN CHAPLIN is director of the Kirby Laing Institute for Christian Ethics, Tyndale House, Cambridge, and a member of the divinity faculty of Cambridge University. From 1999 to 2006 he was associate professor of political theory at the Institute for Christian Studies, where he also held the Dooyeweerd Chair in Social and Political Philosophy from 2004 to 2006. He has edited or co-edited five books, including *Political Theory and Christian Vision* (University Press of America, 1994) and a volume on British political theology entitled *God and Government* (SPCK, 2009). He is author of *Talking God: The Legitimacy of Religious Public Reasoning* (Theos, 2009) and numerous articles on Christian political thought. A monograph on the Dutch Christian political philosopher Herman Dooyeweerd is forthcoming with University of Notre Dame Press in 2011. He holds a Ph.D. in political theory from the London School of Economics and Political Science.

J. DARYL CHARLES is director and senior fellow of the Bryan Institute for Critical Thought and Practice, Bryan College, and served as the 2007/2008 William E. Simon Visiting Fellow in Religion and Public Life, James Madison Program in American Ideals and Institutions, Department of Politics, Princeton University. Author or editor of ten books, including most recently (with David D. Corey) *Justice in an Age of Terror* (ISI Books, forthcoming), (with David B. Capes) *Thriving in Babylon* (Wipf & Stock, forthcoming), and *Retrieving the Natural Law: A Return to Moral First Things* (Eerdmans, 2008), Charles also serves on the editorial advisory board of the journals *Pro Ecclesia* and *Cultural Encounters* and is a contributing editor to *Touchstone*. His work has been published in a wide array of scholarly journals, including *Journal of Church and State*, *National Catholic Bioethics Quarterly*, *Journal of Religious Ethics*, *Academic Questions*, *First Things*, *Pro Ecclesia*, *Philosophia Christi*, *Books & Culture*, and *Christian Scholars Review*.

THOMAS F. FARR is a visiting associate professor of religion and international affairs at Georgetown University's Edmund A. Walsh School of Foreign Service. He is also a senior fellow at the Berkley Center for Religion, Peace, and World Affairs, where he directs the center's program on Religion and U.S. Foreign Policy. He has written widely on religion and international affairs, including "Diplomacy in an Age of Faith," *Foreign Affairs* (March/April 2008), and a recent book, *World of Faith and Freedom: Why International Religious Liberty is Vital to American National Security* (Oxford University Press, 2008). Farr was the first director of the State Department's Office of International Religious Freedom.

THOMAS ALBERT HOWARD is associate professor of history at Gordon College (Mass.), where he is founding director of the Jerusalem & Athens Forum. His articles, essays, and reviews have appeared in numerous journals, and he is the author of *Religion and the Rise of Historicism* (Cambridge University Press, 2000) and *The Making of the Modern German University* (Oxford University Press, 2006). He holds a Ph.D. in history from the University of Virginia. His chapter draws from a larger work, *God and the Atlantic: America, Europe, and the Religious Divide* (Oxford University Press, forthcoming).

ROBERT JOUSTRA is on the staff of the Canadian think tank Cardus, where he was lead researcher on the project "Stained Glass Urbanism." He is a Ph.D. candidate in International Relations at the University of Bath working under the supervision of Scott Thomas and a part-time lecturer in International Relations at Redeemer University College, Ancaster, Ontario. He holds an M.A. in globalization studies from McMaster University, Hamilton, Ontario. He is author of "Globalization and Religious Fundamentalism," in Michael W. Goheen and Erin Glanville, eds., *Globalization and the Gospel: Probing the Religious Foundations of Globalization* (Regent and Geneva Society, 2009), and writes regularly for the Cardus journal *Comment*.

PAUL MARSHALL is a senior fellow in the Center for Religious Freedom at the Hudson Institute. He is the author or editor of over twenty books on religion and politics, especially religious freedom, including *Blind Spot: When Journalists Don't Get Religion* (Oxford University Press, 2009), *Religious Freedom in the World* (Rowman & Littlefield, 2008), *Radical Islam's Rules: The Worldwide Spread of Extreme Sharia Law* (Rowman & Littlefield, 2005), *The Rise of Hindu Extremism* (Center for Religious Freedom, 2003), and *Islam at the Crossroads* (Baker, 2002). He holds a Ph.D. from York University and an M.Phil. from the Institute for Christian Studies in Toronto, where he taught political theory for sixteen years.

DANIEL PHILPOTT is an associate professor in the Department of Political Science and the Joan B. Kroc Institute for International Peace Studies at the University of Notre Dame. He is a senior associate at the International Center for Religion and Democracy and a board member of the Catholic Peacebuilding Network. He is author of *Revolutions in Sovereignty: How Ideas Shaped Modern International Relations* (Princeton University Press, 2001) and editor of *The Politics of Past Evil: Religion, Reconciliation, and the Dilemmas of Transitional Justice* (University of Notre Dame Press, 2006). He is completing a book entitled *Just and Unjust Peace: An Ethic of Political Reconciliation*. He holds a Ph.D. from Harvard University.

ANDREW PRESTON is a senior lecturer in history and a fellow of Clare College at Cambridge University. He is the author of *The War Council: McGeorge Bundy, the NSC, and Vietnam* (Harvard University Press, 2006) and co-editor, with Fredrik Logevall, of *Nixon in the World: American Foreign Relations, 1969–1977* (Oxford University Press, 2008). He is currently writing a book on the religious influence on American war and diplomacy from the colonial era to the present, to be published by Knopf.

JAMES W. SKILLEN was president of the Center for Public Justice from 1981 until 2009 and is now senior fellow. He has authored, edited, or co-edited more than twenty books, most recently *Prospects and Ambiguities of Globalization: Critical Assessment at a Time of Growing Turmoil* (Lexington, 2009), *With or Against the World? America's Role Among the Nations* (Rowman & Littlefield, 2005), and *In Pursuit of Justice* (Rowman & Littlefield, 2004). He holds a Ph.D. in political science from Duke University and a B.D. from Westminster Theological Seminary.

SCOTT M. THOMAS teaches international relations and the politics of developing countries in the Department of Economics & International Development at the University of Bath. He is a graduate of the School of International Service at American University, Washington, D.C., and holds a Ph.D. in international relations from the London School of Economics and Political Science. He is the author of *The Diplomacy of Liberation: the Foreign Relations of the ANC of South Africa since 1960* (I. B. Tauris, 1995), and most recently, *The Global Resurgence of Religion and the Transformation of International Relations: The Struggle for the Soul of the Twenty-First Century* (Palgrave Macmillan, 2005). He has also published chapters in over ten books and articles on religion and international relations in various journals, including *Millennium*, *International Affairs*, the *SAIS Review*, and the *Journal of International Affairs*, and is a contributing editor of the *Review of Faith & International Affairs*.

Index

295